**Royal Commission on
Electoral Reform and
Party Financing**

**Commission royale sur
la réforme électorale et
le financement des partis**

CANADA

FINAL REPORT

VOLUME 2

This is Volume 2 of the *Final Report* of the Royal Commission on Electoral Reform and Party Financing. The Report is published in four volumes:

Volumes 1 and 2	*Reforming Electoral Democracy*
Volume 3	*Proposed Legislation*
Volume 4	*What Canadians Told Us*

Royal Commission on
Electoral Reform and
Party Financing

Commission royale sur
la réforme électorale et
le financement des partis

CANADA

Reforming
Electoral
Democracy

Volume 2

~

The Report is available in both official languages as a set or as
individual volumes.

Available in Canada through
Associated Bookstores
and other booksellers

or by mail from
Canada Communication Group – Publishing
Ottawa, Canada K1A 0S9

Catalogue No. Z1-1989/2-2-1991E
ISBN 0-660-14246-5 (vol. 2)
    0-660-14244-9 (set)

Canadian Cataloguing in Publication Data

Canada. Royal Commission on Electoral Reform and Party Financing

  Reforming electoral democracy : final report

  Chairman: Pierre Lortie
  Partial contents: vol. 3: Proposed legislation; –
  v. 4: What Canadians told us.
  ISBN 0-660-14244-9 (set);
  0-660-14245-7 (vol. 1); 0-660-14246-5 (v. 2);
  0-660-14247-3 (v. 3); 0-660-14248-1 (v. 4)
  DSS cat. nos. Z1-1989/2-1991E (set);
  Z1-1989/2-1-1991E (vol. 1); Z1-1989/2-2-1991E (v. 2);
  Z1-1989/2-3-1991E (v. 3); Z1-1989/2-4-1991E (v. 4)

  1. Elections – Canada. 2. Election law – Canada. 3. Advertising,
  Political – Canada. 4. Campaign funds – Canada. 5. Voter
  registration – Canada. I. Title.

JL193.C35 1991   324.6'0971   C91-098741-6

TO HIS EXCELLENCY
THE GOVERNOR GENERAL IN COUNCIL

MAY IT PLEASE YOUR EXCELLENCY

We, the Commissioners, appointed by Order in Council dated 15th November 1989, as revised and amended on 3rd October 1990, to inquire into and report on the appropriate principles and process that should govern the election of members of the House of Commons and the financing of political parties and of candidates' campaigns

BEG TO SUBMIT TO YOUR EXCELLENCY THIS REPORT.

Pierre Lortie, Chairman

Pierre Wilfrid Fortier

William Knight

Robert Thomas Gabor

Lucie Pépin

November 1991

CONTENTS

~

Following is the complete Table of Contents for volumes 1 and 2 of the *Final Report* of the Royal Commission on Electoral Reform and Party Financing.

VOLUME 1

VOLUME 2

1

THE REGISTRATION OF VOTERS

INTRODUCTION

T HE REGISTRATION OF VOTERS serves two essential purposes that maintain the integrity of the vote. First, it determines the eligibility of voters to vote. Second, it prevents voters from voting more than once. The registration of voters is thus an essential quality control mechanism of the electoral process. The voters list also assists candidates and political parties in canvassing voters and getting their supporters to vote. In these indirect ways, the voters list helps mobilize voters, promoting political participation and voting itself.

The current Canadian approach to the registration of voters contains three principal elements:

(1) Enumeration or census of voters, administered by returning officers in each constituency using specially appointed enumerators for each polling division.
(2) Revision of the preliminary lists produced by the enumeration. This is an appeal process; those not enumerated may apply to be registered or deleted, corrections may be made, and objections to those on the preliminary lists may be made.
(3) In rural polling divisions, those not on the voters list can register and hence vote on election day at their polling station if another registered voter from the same polling division vouches for them.

The enumeration phase is a massive logistical undertaking conducted in a very short period of time after the election writs are issued. In the 1988 election, for instance, returning officers in 295 constituencies had to appoint, train and supervise some 90 000 enumerators to register approximately 17 million voters in seven days.

In urban areas the *Canada Elections Act* requires two enumerators for each polling division. They visit all residences in the division, taking the names of all qualified voters at each address. If no one answers the door, they leave a written notice giving the date and time for a return call. Enumerators must make their calls at times prescribed in the *Canada Elections Act*: the first is to take place between 9 a.m. and 6 p.m., the second between 7 p.m. and 10 p.m. If no one answers the second call, they leave a notice of final visit, informing any voters at the residence of the last date for revising the preliminary lists and the telephone number of the constituency returning officer.

In rural areas, only one enumerator is required. Rural enumerators post public announcements of the enumeration and the subsequent revision. Then they compile a list of voters in the polling division using information from any available source.

At the end of the enumeration period, enumerators transfer each voter's name to a typed or handwritten list from a carbon copy of the enumeration slips, the original of which has been left with voters enumerated at their residence. If an enumerator supplies a handwritten list, it must be typed at the office of the returning officer. In urban polling divisions, lists are compiled geographically by street and consecutive address; in rural polling divisions, lists are assembled in alphabetical order by voters' names.

Once the preliminary lists have been compiled, voters missed by enumeration can be added to the list through the revision process. Because the original objective of revision was to determine eligibility to vote, the Act places this process under the authority of judges acting as ex officio revising officers for all urban polling divisions. In practice, however, they appoint substitute revising officers. In rural polling divisions, the enumerator is also a revising officer. In addition, recognizing that the primary purpose of revision is now to add the names of voters missed by enumeration, returning officers in urban constituencies must divide their constituencies into 'revisal districts' and appoint two revising agents for each district who, as far as possible, should represent two different political parties.

Revision begins the day the preliminary lists are submitted by enumerators. Until the seventeenth day before election day, in urban areas, revising agents may complete applications submitted by voters who have not been enumerated or by certain relatives on their behalf. Applications are then submitted to revising officers, who decide on them and any others made by voters to returning officers or to revising officers directly during a formal three-day revision period. On the thirteenth day before election day, the revising officers decide on any objections to names on the preliminary lists. In rural polling divisions, the enumerators, acting as revising officers, perform similar functions, but they are required to sit formally for only one day, the nineteenth day before election day, to consider applications for additions, deletions or corrections.

Finally, voters in rural polling divisions, but not in urban polling divisions, can register on election day at their polling station and then vote. This distinction between voters in urban and rural polling divisions was predicated on the assumption that in rural polling divisions voters will likely be known by election officials and the representatives of candidates. This constitutes a sufficient safeguard to protect the integrity of the vote.

In addition to these procedures, the *Canada Elections Act* provides Special Voting Rules for voters who are members of the Canadian forces in Canada and abroad, certain civilian employees of the Department of National Defence stationed abroad, the spouses and dependants of these Canadian forces personnel and employees if living abroad with them, certain veterans residing in institutions, and federal public servants posted abroad including their spouses and dependants living abroad with them. For those who qualify under these rules, registration and voting procedures are special because they are not governed by the same procedures that apply to all other voters.

Except for this last category of voters, the Canadian approach to registration has two major characteristics. First, it is initiated by the state through a national enumeration carried out under the direction of Elections Canada. Second, enumeration is conducted only after the election writ is issued. In both respects, Canada's approach is unique among western democracies.

This approach assumes that a state enumeration is the most effective and efficient method of ensuring that qualified voters are registered. When the state carries out an enumeration, it is assumed, those who may not fully understand their rights as voters will be enumerated and, hence, eligible to vote. Conducting an enumeration after an election is called, it is assumed, makes voters more aware that they must be registered to vote. The enumeration thus alerts voters to the election.

The current enumeration process also assumes that citizens, as well as non-citizens living in Canada, are to be trusted when they provide information to enumerators. In conducting the door-to-door enumeration, enumerators are neither required nor permitted to challenge householders' statements about the names of persons in each residence who are citizens, 18 years of age and over, and residents of the polling division. Although a few ineligible people may be enumerated, this is considered a minimal price to pay for a process that is relatively efficient and exists without excessive regulations and controls. Those enumerated have their addresses included on the voters lists, and objections may be made to any name on the preliminary lists. These voters vote in person and may be challenged when they vote. This procedure constitutes an additional check and justifies the approach to enumeration.

To ensure that the election lists are as complete, accurate and current as possible, it is essential that the state maintain its responsibility for registering voters. This does not mean that voters should not be required to initiate their own registration in certain circumstances; rather, it means that as a general rule, the state should continue to ensure that citizens do not have to assume sole responsibility for their own registration or that responsibility for voter registration be thrust on candidates or political parties.

To ensure that voters are neither statutorily nor administratively disfranchised by the registration process, it is also essential that enumeration, revision and election-day registration constitute consecutive phases, or integrated components, of a registration process. This is not the case with the current *Canada Elections Act*. Although the three major elements are present, revision was not designed to complement enumeration, and election-day registration is limited to those residing in rural polling divisions. As a result, the current approach has not accommodated or responded to major social, demographic, technological and political changes that have occurred since it was put in place more than half a century ago. Moreover, the detailed prescriptions in the Act have hampered adaptation to these changes; the process is frozen in time and, hence, has restricted the gradual introduction of new techniques.

HISTORY, COMPARATIVE PERSPECTIVES AND ASSESSMENT

Historical Evolution

As with the election law for the franchise and candidacy, rules governing registration of voters were initially left to the provinces. From 1867 to 1885, the election lists were those used by the provinces for their provincial and municipal elections. These were based primarily on municipal assessment rolls, with some provision for revision by local officials.

Early attempts by Conservative governments to bring registration under federal control were opposed by the opposition Liberals who had greater electoral success in the provinces. The opposing views on the issue of federal versus provincial control over the compilation and revision of lists, not surprisingly, were mainly partisan: the two national parties and their candidates blatantly manipulated voter registration to their political advantage through officials appointed by the parties in power at each level. (Ward 1963, 189–204)

In 1885, the federal Conservative government finally established federal control over the compilation and revision of the voters list. In each electoral district, this responsibility was assigned to a federally appointed 'revising officer' who was to revise the voters list annually, with an appeal to a judge if the revising officer was not a judge. Appeals, however, were 'legalistic' and expensive. (Ward 1963, 196–97) Annual revisions, however, were not the norm.

In 1898, the federal Liberal government returned the entire process of voter registration to the provinces, notwithstanding the fact that this meant that there could be no appeals to lists in the maritime provinces where registration did not provide for such appeals. Provincial control remained until the 1917 *War-time Elections Act*. Before 1917 there were deficiencies in provincial lists in Manitoba and British Columbia, and these resulted in a requirement that federal lists in the two provinces be compiled by an enumeration of voters. This approach to compiling a voters list was extended to the entire country by the 1917 Act, with the reassertion of federal control, although enumerators based their lists largely on existing provincial lists.

In 1922, and in a reversal of their previous position, the federal Conservative government returned to using provincial lists, with some conditions. If a province's lists were more than two years old, they were to be revised. For voters living in towns of more than 1000 population, self-registration in person at a registrar's office was required, and following a period for judicial revision the lists were 'closed'. For voters in rural areas, on the other hand, any voter not on the list after an enumeration could register if vouched for by another qualified voter in the same polling division; the list was therefore 'open'. In rural areas there was thus no need for judicial revision.

From 1922 to 1930, the use of enumeration was progressively extended in urban areas; self-registration as well as the use of provincial lists was abandoned by the Liberal government in 1929. By 1930, there was a door-to-door enumeration in urban areas by two enumerators representing the two major parties, with election-day registration based on vouching. The lists compiled for this election were reported by the chief electoral officer to be the most satisfactory since the creation of the office of the CEO in 1920. (Ward 1963, 201)

In 1934, however, the Conservative government reverted to an annual revision of the lists by registrars in each electoral district. Registrars were appointed by a Dominion Franchise Commissioner who was appointed by resolution of the House of Commons, with the support of both the Conservative and Liberal parties in the House. The revised lists, however, were 'closed' following the annual revision; registration on election day by vouching was eliminated, even in rural areas.

This system was used only once – for the 1935 general election. The CEO considered it inferior to the system in place for the 1930 general election, and a Special Committee on Elections and Franchise Acts agreed. (Canada, House of Commons 1937) It recommended a return to the system used for the 1930 election, and the 1938 *Dominion Elections Act* reinstated that system. Thus enumeration was to be the basis for compiling preliminary voters lists and undertaken after the election writs were issued. Enumeration was conducted by two enumerators in urban polling divisions and one in rural polling divisions working under the supervision of each constituency's returning officer. Urban enumerators were required by law to conduct a door-to-door enumeration, after which they could also use any other means to place qualified voters' names on the lists; rural enumerators were to use any means, including door-to-door visits, to compile their lists. One urban enumerator was nominated by the political party whose candidate came first in the previous election, the other by the party whose candidate came second. After judicial revision of the preliminary lists in urban polling divisions, the lists were closed. After enumerators compiled and revised preliminary lists in rural polling divisions, the lists remained open because qualified voters not on the list could be vouched for by another qualified voter from the same polling division and could thus vote.

The system put in place in 1938 remains the basic approach to federal voter registration. Returning officers in each constituency, appointed by the Governor in Council, are responsible for managing the enumeration and appointing the enumerators who compile the preliminary list in each polling division of a constituency. The enumeration of voters is thus a state responsibility. In urban polling divisions, two enumerators are used, one nominated by each of the candidates who finished first and second in the previous election. Enumeration therefore has a partisan control mechanism built in. The enumeration in urban polling divisions must be done door-to-door to make it as complete as possible. The revision process augments and corrects the preliminary lists. In rural polling divisions, enumeration is done by only one person, who is not required to visit door-to-door to complete the lists; election-day registration completes the process. Finally, the enumeration is conducted after the writs are issued to make the lists as current as possible.

Provincial Approaches

The federal approach to voter registration varies from that found in the provinces and territories in several ways. Three provinces – Newfoundland, Alberta and British Columbia – do not have an enumeration following the issuance of writs. Newfoundland and Alberta compile their lists based on an enumeration, but they conduct the enumeration outside the election period: Newfoundland at the discretion of the provincial government but usually within a year of an election; and Alberta in the second calendar year following a provincial election and each succeeding year if no election is held in the interim, and not in the year when a constituency boundaries commission is established or for the 12 months following the establishment of a commission. British Columbia uses a continually updated voters list based on self-registration by voters, although an enumeration is conducted every three years to update the list. The other seven provinces and the two territories compile their preliminary lists based on enumerations conducted after the writs are issued.

In Newfoundland, Manitoba, Saskatchewan and the Northwest Territories there is one enumerator per polling division, and one or two may be used at the discretion of the returning officer in British Columbia and the Yukon. All provinces have a residency requirement of six months for a person to be qualified as a voter in their province, and in the two territories a person must be resident for 12 months. The voting age is 18 years except in British Columbia where it is 19.

Six provinces allow revision of the preliminary list closer to election day than is the case federally when revision closes on the seventh day before election day. In Ontario revision can occur up to and including the day before election day. Ontario, however, does not provide election-day registration for those residing in urban polling divisions.

Seven provinces and the Northwest Territories have election-day registration for all qualified voters; Ontario allows this in rural polling divisions. Only Quebec, British Columbia and the Yukon have no provision for election-day registration.

Costs of Registration

The registration of voters in Canada is not only a huge administrative exercise, it is also expensive. By far the most expensive portion is the enumeration. The cost of the 1988 federal enumeration was about $24 655 000. This included the fees, training pay and travel expenses of enumerators. The cost of revision was about $3 145 000. This included the fees for those acting as revising officers, the fees for revising agents, travel expenses and office rental for revision sittings. The total cost of enumeration and revision was about $27 800 000. In addition, the cost of printing 'vote-at cards' was $2 525 600 and the postage for these cards was $5 822 000. Hence, the total cost of voter registration for the 1988 federal election was just over $36 000 000. Detailed comparative costs for voter registration in all provinces are not available. However, the provincial data available indicate that a comparable amount was spent to register voters for recent provincial and territorial elections.

Assessment

From the perspective of the individual voter, the two most important things about any registration system are the extent to which the individual voter has to take initiatives to register and the opportunities he or she has to register up to and including election day. The former is minimized to the extent that the state assumes responsibility for initiating the registration of voters; the latter is enhanced to the degree that voters lists are open rather than closed up to and including election day.

On the basis of the Canadian experience at all levels, Canadians clearly favour state-initiated registration. In some large part this is obviously due to the long history of enumeration-based registration in Canada at the federal level and, with only a few exceptions, at the provincial-territorial level. As John Courtney and David Smith note:

> Among Western democracies the Canadian government alone assumes responsibility for sending voter registration officials (enumerators) to the home of every potential elector in the country. As a consequence eligible electors who are omitted from the voters' list believe that they have grounds for harbouring a grievance against the election administration, a belief not shared by citizens elsewhere. Since in countries where the onus for becoming listed rests on the citizen, it would be perverse for him or her to blame others for the failure to register. (1991 RC)*

The critical issue that was raised time and again at our public hearings and that has been acknowledged by election administrators, federally and provincially, as an increasingly serious problem over the past two decades, is the number of voters who are missed by enumeration. This concern is twofold. First, there are the complaints at every election that certain areas are left unenumerated in major urban centres. Second, there are the complaints that large numbers of certain categories of voters are left unenumerated – the homeless, the hearing handicapped, new Canadians and voters whose occupations require frequent absence from their residences. Although the reasons for the shortcomings of enumeration vary, the outcomes

---

* In references to Royal Commission research studies, the date is followed by the initials RC.

are the same – some voters are not enumerated. These outcomes are to be expected. Any census-type count of a large population cannot be other than incomplete and inaccurate to some degree. Statistics Canada, for example, estimates that it undercounts the Canadian population at the decennial census by approximately 3 per cent. Applied to the total electorate in the 1988 election, this would mean that the enumeration undercounted by at least 500 000 voters. In addition, the recent experience with enumerations conducted at elections indicates clearly that the level of coverage has declined. This means that enumeration must be considered but one phase of a registration process.

For those missed by enumeration, the second major part of the registration process is the extent to which there are sufficient opportunities to register during the election period. Here the differences between registration systems within Canada, and even within a single system, are striking in terms of their responsiveness. The most important difference between the responsiveness of the federal system and most provincial-territorial systems lies in the fact that several provinces allow for the revision of voters lists much later in the election period and, most critical of all, allow for election-day registration. Provincial election officials in provinces with this latter provision point to it as the single most crucial factor in minimizing citizen complaints about voter registration. The reason is obvious – those who really do wish to vote may be registered on election day. At the federal level, the absence in federal electoral law of this provision for voters in urban polling divisions fuels many of the complaints about the shortcomings of the registration system, especially as the same federal law allows those in rural polling divisions to register and vote on election day. Although complaints about this differential treatment in federal law are not new – the report of the chief electoral officer of Canada in 1922 discussed the subject in response to complaints – they now take on a new hue with the guarantees of equal treatment found in the Charter. (Courtney and Smith 1991 RC) This is especially the case since many 'rural' polling divisions in fact contain areas that are suburban in character and thus are indistinguishable from similar areas in urban polling divisions. Many voters consider it unfair to have different standards for voters in urban and rural polling divisions. Moreover, this different treatment could be successfully challenged in the courts. If this occurred during an election, it would cause a major disruption in the administration of the vote on election day.

The question of the extent to which voters lists are open up to and including election day is obviously the easiest issue to address by comparative assessment. The provincial-territorial experience in all but three provinces and one territory, as well as the federal and Ontario experience in rural polling divisions, indicates that election-day registration can be effectively managed with minimum disruption to the voting process while securing the integrity of the vote.

Improving the revision of voters lists is likewise relatively straightforward through comparative assessment. The closer that the revision process is open to election day and the degree to which it is under the authority of returning officers, and thus considered a consecutive phase of registration, the greater the opportunity of voters to have their names on the voters lists.

The comparative perspective on the enumeration phase of voter registration is more complicated. Election officials at all levels of government in which enumerations are conducted during the election period, as well as the Alberta officials responsible for their non-election period enumeration, report that enumeration in major urban centres has become increasingly difficult to conduct successfully in terms of coverage and accuracy. Although the major causes of this are interrelated in some ways, two sets of issues stand out.

First, both election officials and interveners at our hearings drew attention to the fact that over the past two decades access to voters at their residences has become increasingly problematic. The increased percentage of women in the labour force, as well as changing lifestyles, makes it less likely that enumerators will find someone to answer their calls. An increasing number of voters are away from home for lengthy periods for work-related reasons and cannot be contacted even with two visits. In urban areas in particular, increasing concerns with personal safety make some voters, especially the elderly and those who live alone, unwilling to respond to unannounced callers. An increasing number of multiple-residence buildings, especially condominiums, have policies not to allow persons into their buildings to conduct door-to-door calls. Although none of these factors constitutes a new phenomenon, the incidence of each has increased as a factor militating against access; taken together, they make a census-type count of voters more difficult than in the past.

In addition, election officials are now more cognizant of the fact that hearing-impaired persons may not be aware that someone may be calling at their door, that illiterate persons may be hesitant to respond to official callers for fear of revealing their handicaps, that persons without a command of English or French may be hesitant to reveal their difficulty with either official language and that new Canadians may be hesitant to respond to callers representing the state given their experiences in their country of origin. Again, none of these factors is entirely new to enumeration, but citizens in the last three categories have increased substantially in both absolute and relative numbers over the past two decades.

The more important challenges facing enumeration, however, stem from the widely acknowledged problem of finding enough capable enumerators in many urban centres. The pool of potential enumerators in these centres has been reduced considerably over recent decades for at least two reasons. First, the increased numbers of women in the paid workforce has diminished the number who are able to take on this short-term assignment. Second, fears of personal safety in major urban areas have also taken their toll. At the federal and provincial levels, the shortfall of enumerators has required election officials to take extraordinary steps to find enumerators and to extend the time period of enumeration. It is also the experience of Newfoundland and British Columbia, with enumerations outside the election period, that these problems are more easily overcome because of the greater time available to seek out enumerators. However, officials in Alberta, where the enumeration is also conducted outside the election period, report problems in finding enumerators in certain urban areas. This indicates that conducting enumeration outside the election period does not, in itself, overcome the problem of finding enumerators.

Complicating matters further, moreover, are the various requirements found in federal and provincial election laws concerning the number of enumerators used as well as the appointment process and qualifications for enumerators. The federal law and that of several provinces requires that returning officers in urban constituencies appoint two enumerators; before enumerators are appointed, however, they must await nominations from the political parties in their constituencies whose candidates placed first and second in the previous election, or nominations from the candidates themselves. This requirement was originally adopted as a check against partisan manipulation in the compilation of voters lists. Given that candidates and their parties could use these government-paid positions as recognition for the party faithful, they were usually able to supply the returning officer with enough names in very short order. In many urban areas today, however, the political parties are unable to nominate the required number of enumerators. In a survey of constituency party associations conducted for our research program, 32 per cent of local party officials from the major parties reported they "barely managed to name [the] required number of" enumerators. As well, 19 per cent of the respondents stated that their local party association was unable to "find enough enumerators". (Carty 1991a RC) The potential pool, as we have noted, has diminished and candidates and parties in many urban areas regard this obligation as an unwarranted burden and a distraction to their preparations for the campaign. They are unwilling to sidetrack their own volunteer workers from campaign activities by offering them as enumerators. This contrasts with smaller urban and rural constituencies where volunteers for enumeration are still found in sufficient numbers.

Election laws in several jurisdictions, including the *Canada Elections Act*, require that each enumerator be a qualified voter from the electoral district in which he or she is appointed. The result of these requirements is that the pool of enumerators is statutorily restricted, particularly with respect to age and residence.

Not surprisingly, the above requirements have meant in several instances that chief electoral officers or returning officers have had to use their discretionary or extraordinary powers to overcome shortfalls in the numbers of enumerators. The most common responses have been to use one enumerator instead of the required two, to use enumerators from outside the constituency in question, to appoint 16- and 17-year-olds and to go beyond the political parties to community organizations to find enumerators. The latter has been especially necessary in urban areas where proficiency in languages other than English or French and where experience with certain categories of voters, such as the homeless and transient, are deemed necessary. Again, it is not surprising that many election officials, as well as many citizens, consider the current restrictions on who may be an enumerator to be unjustified and inefficient.

The combination of the above factors has increasingly meant that too many returning officers, especially in major urban centres where the problems are most acute, cannot appoint enumerators until several days into the election period; thus, enumerators must be appointed immediately before they are sent into the field. Returning officers themselves in many instances must find enumerators when parties are unable to nominate sufficient numbers. The time for training is thus compressed. Moreover, returning officers have few support staff to conduct training and, equally critical, to provide supervision of enumerators when they are performing their task.

In addition, provisions for quality control to ensure coverage and accuracy are virtually non-existent. Returning officers and their assistants have little time and few measures with which to assess the performance of their enumerators during or immediately following the enumeration. In many areas, as election officials have pointed out with increasing concern, enumeration must be conducted by crisis management. For the 1988 federal general election, this sense of crisis management was exacerbated by the fact that "253 of the 295 returning officers ... had no previous experience of managing an election". (Canada, Chief Electoral Officer 1989, 46)

Finally, at the federal level, the shortcomings of the enumeration process are compounded because revision is a cumbersome and complex quasi-judicial procedure, is not under the authority of returning officers and is not extended late into the election period. Unlike the approach taken in many provinces, it is not structured and managed as a consecutive phase of registration. Furthermore, election-day registration is not available to voters in urban polling divisions, where the vast majority of voters reside.

REFORMING REGISTRATION

Enumeration

In Volume 2, Chapter 4, we discuss whether the Canada Elections Commission should be authorized to acquire the preliminary lists for a province from sources other than a federal enumeration. The Commission would thus not be required to conduct an enumeration in provinces where this might be done. The fact remains, however, that time and the scope of the undertaking will not allow for such alternatives to completely replace enumeration in all provinces in the immediate future, let alone in the next federal election. Consequently, it is necessary to modify the *Canada Elections Act* to ensure that the whole process of enumeration is modernized and made much more efficient.

Planning the Enumeration

Elections Canada has for many years encouraged returning officers to plan between elections; indeed, the responsibilities of returning officers require them to be prepared for an election. But with one exception, the *Canada Elections Act* does not empower the chief electoral officer (CEO) to remunerate returning officers for planning and preparations undertaken before the writs are issued. The exception is the authority to engage the services of returning officers, as necessary, to adjust the boundaries of polling divisions within their constituencies. In addition, under the tariff of fees established pursuant to the Act the CEO is authorized to engage returning officers for special assignments. The scope of this, however, is too narrow and should be expanded.

Much more needs to be done before an election, however. The normal administrative responsibilities of returning officers should include several functions on which the best returning officers already spend a good deal of time and effort, but for which they receive no additional remuneration. They include identifying polling stations for advance and regular polls, especially stations that are or could be accessible to persons with disabilities; developing strategies to reach areas and voters that are difficult to enumerate; and maintaining up-to-date lists of potential enumerators in consultation with constituency associations and community organizations.

To promote effective planning and preparation before the issue of the writ, the CEO must have the capacity to engage the services of returning officers in any or all districts where the CEO deems this to be required. The CEO should therefore recognize the extra time and effort spent by returning officers and remunerate those whose situations require extra attention in the pre-writ period. In Volume 2, Chapter 3, we recommend that the CEO be authorized by the *Canada Elections Act* to engage the services of returning officers outside an election period, as necessary, for planning and preparatory work for the registration and voting processes.

Enumerators: Recruitment, Appointment, Qualifications and Numbers

The *Canada Elections Act* requires the candidates who finished first and second in the preceding election to each nominate one enumerator in urban polling divisions. Returning officers must await these nominations, which must arrive by the forty-fifth day before election day, before appointing enumerators. Only when candidates or their constituency associations fail to nominate enough enumerators may returning officers appoint without nomination.

Rural polling divisions require only one enumerator. Although returning officers generally consult with the candidates of the parties that finished first and second in the previous election, there is no statutory requirement that returning officers await nominations.

The procedure specified for urban polling divisions increasingly impairs the efficient conduct of enumeration and serves little useful purpose.

Candidates and party associations in many electoral constituencies, especially in urban areas, have had great difficulty finding enough nominees and
in many cases have been unable to provide complete lists of nominations.
In the constituency of North York in 1988, for example, the two candidates
concerned provided the names of only 30 of the 780 enumerators required.
Many candidates and parties do not want to be required to supply names as
this interferes with the conduct of their campaigns, especially when it means
that they lose capable volunteers to the enumeration. Not surprisingly, many
names show up on the lists submitted by both parties, as individuals who do
wish to enumerate approach both parties or are referred to the parties by
returning officers. The result, in too many instances, is that the names submitted to the returning officers arrive at the last minute. In addition, many
returning officers indicated that they had problems with enumerators who
could not write or were not physically able to perform the work.

   To overcome the present shortcomings in the training of enumerators,
returning officers should have the authority to appoint enumerators as soon
as possible after the writ is issued. This is particularly important because
our recommendations require that enumerators understand the right of
voters to use the special ballot, the right of Aboriginal voters to register and
be placed on a voters list in provinces where Aboriginal constituencies are
created, and their responsibility to inform voters with special needs of the
availability of access to polling stations. This does not rule out co-operation
with candidates or local party associations; indeed, returning officers have
an incentive to co-operate with party officials, for in most cases they remain
the best source for potential enumerators. However, returning officers
should consult all registered constituency associations, giving due regard
to the standings of their respective candidates at the previous election, and
these consultations should be made early, preferably before the writ
is issued.

   Although returning officers should consult with constituency associations, they should not have to wait several days for their nominations after
the writs are issued. Once an election is called, they should be able to
appoint enumerators almost immediately. This is, in effect, the procedure
used in rural polling divisions, and we see no reason why it should not apply
to the appointment of all enumerators.

   Specific attention also should be given to voters who are members of
ethno-cultural minorities, and who may require specialized information
on the voter registration process. Several affirmative measures have been
suggested by Michael and Shelley Pinto-Duschinsky (1987) to increase registration among ethno-cultural groups in Great Britain. For example, based
on a comprehensive review of the registration process, they recommend
that the Home Office, which has responsibility for voter registration in
Great Britain, communicate regularly with Community Relations Officers,
community organizations, and the ethno-cultural press as well as local
radio stations to assist ethno-cultural voters. They note that, where possible,

individuals who can translate in the relevant ethnic minority languages should be available to assist canvassers and election registration officials. The Pinto-Duschinskys also suggest that posters, leaflets and press adver-tisements with voter registration information in the languages of these communities should be widely distributed in appropriate areas. (1987, 22)

Returning officers should also consult widely with community organi-zations to ensure that the total complement of enumerators includes persons from all the major minority groups in a constituency. It cannot be presumed that the constituency associations whose candidates finished first and second in the previous election, or even all registered constituency associations combined, have networks that extend to these minorities or to the marginal segments of a constituency such as the homeless. Yet it is persons from these communi-ties or segments of society who require the most complete coverage possible.

Recommendation 2.1.1

We recommend that

(a) **returning officers be required to**
(1) request names of enumerators from all registered constituency associations;
(2) appoint enumerators as soon as possible after the writ is issued with due regard to the standings in the previous elec-tion of the candidates of registered constituency associations that have submitted names;
(3) consult with community organizations and shelters to recruit potential enumerators; and
(b) **measures be taken to provide voters from ethno-cultural communities with information and assistance on the enumeration and voter registration process.**

The *Canada Elections Act* requires that enumerators be qualified voters in the constituency for which they are appointed. In the 1988 election, the chief electoral officer had to exercise his special powers to authorize return-ing officers to appoint persons under the age of 18 years in 10 polling divi-sions, involving six constituencies, and to appoint persons who did not reside in the constituency in 177 polling divisions, involving 18 con-stituencies. The problems that required the chief electoral officer to use these special powers were not 'unusual' or 'unforeseen'; they were pre-dictable problems that any administrator overseeing an operation of this magnitude and complexity would expect.

Although there are sound reasons for enumerators to be qualified voters living in the constituency for which they are appointed, this should not be required by the *Canada Elections Act*. In major urban areas, where the shortage of enumerators is most severe, this regulation has caused serious logistical problems. However, the small size of high-density constituencies in urban areas means that enumerators appointed from outside a constituency are likely to be neighbours of voters in the constituency in which they enumerate. In large rural constituencies, it is virtually assured that enumerators will be from the constituency. Moreover, if the pool of enumerators is increased by recruiting enumerators from all registered constituency associations in a constituency and from community organizations, the number of potential enumerators from the constituency would be expanded. Finally, if Canadian citizens aged 16 and 17 years were allowed to enumerate, as they were in the 1988 general election with the authorization of the CEO, the pool would be expanded even further.

Recommendation 2.1.2

We recommend that every person appointed enumerator be a Canadian citizen and at least 16 years of age.

The requirement that enumerators work in pairs in urban polling divisions to check against partisan interference is no longer necessary. As noted above, political parties are now willing to nominate persons who are referred to them by returning officers or who apply to them to be enumerators but are not known to them. This demonstrates that party officials are not overly concerned that the integrity of enumeration will be undermined if they do not have their own nominees acting as enumerators. Notwithstanding the shortcomings of the system in providing adequate enumeration, there is no reliable evidence to suggest that disfranchisement occurs because of partisan interference. Moreover, our recommendations on revision and election-day registration provide assurance that, if problems were to occur, they could be corrected.

The requirement for two enumerators per polling division is also an inefficient use of personnel. There is no evidence that using just one enumerator in rural areas for federal enumerations, or the use of one enumerator in Newfoundland, Manitoba and Saskatchewan for both urban and rural polling divisions, has affected the eligibility of voters or the quality of the preliminary lists. At the same time, it would be advisable for enumerators to work in pairs in some areas to ensure personal safety.

Recommendation 2.1.3

We recommend that one enumerator be appointed for each polling division, except where it is deemed prudent or advisable to appoint two.

Managing the Enumeration for Quality Control
Enumeration is carried out under the direction of a returning officer, assisted by an assistant returning officer. The scope of the returning officer's

management responsibilities – which include recruiting, training and supervising enumerators – is too great in too many instances. The present structure does not provide for another layer of management in constituencies where extra effort is required to recruit and train enumerators and where there is a need for close supervision for quality control.

The *Canada Elections Act* assumes that all constituencies, and therefore their management requirements, are identical in every respect. This is not the case, and the CEO should be able to authorize returning officers to appoint 'supervisory enumerators' to assist them in recruiting, training and supervising enumerators where necessary. The CEO, in consultation with individual returning officers, should have the authority to determine which constituencies require supervisory enumerators and how many should be appointed.

Recommendation 2.1.4

We recommend that returning officers be authorized by the chief electoral officer to appoint supervisory enumerators to assist in managing the enumeration process.

At the same time, there is a need to introduce improved methods of quality control if errors are to be identified in sufficient time for corrective action to be taken before the end of the enumeration period.

Several changes would improve the current approach. For instance, enumerators should not have to complete the enumeration before submitting voters' names. At present, unless they submit the lists well before the end of the enumeration period, there is insufficient time for the returning officer to check on the completeness of the enumeration. If time is available, returning officers should base their check primarily on their own knowledge of the areas enumerated.

If returning officers and their supervisory enumerators are to provide a thorough check on the completeness of enumeration, they require a system for processing information that begins well before the end of the enumeration period. The obvious solution is to have enumerators submit completed enumeration forms daily or every other day. They should also provide addresses where there were no voters or no one at home. In this manner, the completeness of coverage could be assessed throughout the enumeration period. To be managed effectively, this information should be entered on a computerized voters list at the returning officer's office. This would eliminate the need for enumerators to prepare their own lists at the end of the enumeration, which then have to be typed at the returning officer's office with the numerous errors that such a process necessarily entails. There would also no longer be any need to supply 10 copies of each list to every candidate; one printed copy or a copy on diskette is sufficient.

Recommendation 2.1.5

We recommend that

(a) enumerators submit completed enumeration forms with the names and addresses of voters to the office of the returning officer as directed by the supervisory enumerator or returning officer for entry on the voters lists; and

(b) one copy of the preliminary list for each polling division in each constituency be made available in machine-readable form or printed format to the candidates in each constituency two days after the enumeration ends.

On a separate matter, provision should be made to protect the privacy of the addresses of those who, especially for reasons of personal security, do not wish their address to be included on any lists made available to candidates. Australia uses a practice of 'silent lists' in which the addresses of voters on voters lists need not be publicly available. Such a provision would meet the legitimate requests of several interveners at our hearings, especially as this applies to women who live alone or at community shelters.

Recommendation 2.1.6

We recommend that, on request, the address of the office of the returning officer be given as a voter's address for all lists made available to candidates.

Enumeration Procedures

In urban polling divisions, enumerators must visit every residence at least twice and at different hours (though not different days) for each visit. They may also use other sources of information, such as names supplied by neighbours. In rural polling divisions, enumerators post a notice of enumeration and assemble voters lists using any information available. A rural enumerator may visit residences, but this is not required. Given that many rural polling divisions contain suburban areas, it is no longer appropriate that enumerators not visit residences. Elections Canada has therefore decided to require such visits at the next election except in remote rural areas.

Three issues must be addressed. First, the current distinction between urban and rural polling divisions no longer makes sense from the perspective of coverage or integrity. Second, returning officers should have some discretion to decide whether enumerators may use methods other than visits to residences. For example, many enumerators whose polling divisions include multiple residency buildings find that the most effective method of enumeration is to post an announcement in the lobby of a building and enumerate residents there. This method is not only more productive, but also often more efficient. Third, enumerators' visits must occur at different times but not on different days. This allows enumerators to conduct the second visit on the same day; indeed, the visits could be less than three hours apart. In some circumstances it makes sense to return the same day; voters not at home during the day may well be home in the evening. In other cases, however, this may not be appropriate. Judgement based on knowledge of the area being enumerated is required. The matter should be decided by returning officers, in consultation with supervisory enumerators if applicable. It is not a matter that can be addressed effectively in law or regulation.

Recommendation 2.1.7

We recommend that returning officers determine the methods and hours of enumeration to be used by enumerators in their constituencies.

Increasingly, enumerators in many areas find that they are unable to gain access to multiple residency buildings to conduct a door-to-door canvass. As is the case in seven provinces and the two territories, the *Canada Elections Act* should state clearly that enumerators have a right of access upon presentation of identification as an enumerator.

Recommendation 2.1.8

We recommend that every enumerator, upon producing proper identification and during reasonable hours, be given free access to the entrance door to each dwelling unit in any multiple residence building in order to conduct an enumeration of voters.

As we have noted, a special problem of enumeration is created by the Act's rules on the 'residence' of voters as they apply to the homeless. The Act requires anyone living in a hostel to have resided there for 10 consecutive days immediately preceding the enumeration date but many hostels limit the number of consecutive days which a person can stay to give the greatest access to as many people as possible. In its municipal elections Toronto has allowed homeless voters to be registered by using shelters as their address, and in the 1990 Laurier–Sainte-Marie federal by-election Elections Canada permitted voters to be enumerated at soup kitchens if they used them frequently. The Committee for Aboriginal Electoral Reform recommended that homeless Aboriginal voters be able to identify a local Aboriginal community office, such as a band office or Métis friendship centre, as their place of residence. These approaches help ensure that voters are not disfranchised simply because they are homeless. This requires that enumerators (and revising agents) visit shelters or soup kitchens frequented by the homeless during times when the greatest number are likely to be present. This process would be simplified if a community worker were appointed as enumerator for these locations.

Recommendation 2.1.9

We recommend that homeless voters be permitted to give the address of a shelter, soup kitchen, Indian band office or Métis friendship centre as their place of residence.

Mail-in Enumeration

If enumerators in urban polling divisions do not receive an answer on the second visit to a residence, they leave a notice of final visit that includes the telephone number of the returning officer and the last date of revision. Not surprisingly, many voters who call to be enumerated shortly after the end of enumeration are unhappy to find that they cannot be enumerated by telephone and that enumerators cannot make another visit. In these cases a revising agent visits the voter to complete a revision application or the voter applies in person at the returning officer's office (or sub-office).

Improved revision will help to address this issue, but a more effective extension of enumeration would be to institute mail-in enumeration. When enumerators do not receive an answer on their second visit, they would leave a mail-in enumeration card in place of the notice of final visit. To assist those with reading disabilities and those who have difficulty reading English or French, this card should contain the phone number of the returning officer as well as the Canada Elections Commission's logo. Addressed to the returning officer and postage-paid, the card would be numbered so that enumerators could note an identifying number on their record of addresses where cards were left. The voter would write in the name and address of all voters at that residence, certify that all information is correct by signing the card, and return the card by mail or in person to the office or sub-office of the returning officer. The deadline for receipt of this card at the office of the returning officer would be 6 p.m. on the fifth day before election day when the revised voters lists are finalized. This approach has worked well in the United States and the integrity of the system has not been questioned. (Citizens' Commission on Civil Rights 1988)

In provinces with Aboriginal constituencies, the mail-in enumeration card should inform Aboriginal voters of their right to register to vote in an Aboriginal constituency. The card should also contain a box where an Aboriginal voter could indicate that he or she, along with any other Aboriginal voters at the same residence listed on the card, wished to be registered to vote in the Aboriginal constituency. These cards, once received by the returning officer whose address would be shown on the front of the card, would then be forwarded to the returning officer for the appropriate

Aboriginal constituency so that the voters listed on the card could be added to the voters list for the Aboriginal constituency. The converse would also hold for Aboriginal people in areas predominantly populated by Aboriginal people who wanted to be registered in the general constituency.

Recommendation 2.1.10

We recommend that

(a) voters not contacted by enumerators be left a numbered mail-in enumeration card, containing the phone number of the returning officer and the Canada Elections Commission's logo, with which they can register by listing the name and address of all qualified voters at their residence, certifying that the information on the card is correct, and returning the card by mail or in person to the returning officer's office or sub-office, provided that the card is received by 6 p.m. on the fifth day before election day; and

(b) in provinces with Aboriginal constituencies, mail-in enumeration cards

(1) contain information pertaining to the right of Aboriginal voters to register to vote in an Aboriginal constituency or a general constituency;

(2) provide a place for voters to mark that it be forwarded to the returning officer for the Aboriginal constituency, if applicable, when dropped off in an area predominantly populated by non-Aboriginal people; and

(3) provide a place for voters to mark that it be forwarded to the returning officer for the general constituency, if applicable, when dropped off in an area predominantly populated by Aboriginal people.

Payment of Enumerators

Enumerators' remuneration is based on the number of names on the lists they submit at the close of the enumeration. The assumption is that all polling divisions have similar numbers of eligible voters and non-eligible persons, and that enumerators have an equal incentive to make extra visits to residences to secure additional names.

For enumerators working in polling divisions with a high percentage of ineligible persons, this payment structure is both discouraging and a disincentive to thoroughness. These enumerators are not compensated for visiting residences with no voters, and there is no recognition of the time and effort spent attempting to communicate with persons whose knowledge of English or French is limited or who are uneasy with visitors from a government agency.

A more appropriate payment structure would be to compensate enumerators for each address called at, with a differential payment for the number of voters enumerated, the number of recorded visits to residences without voters, and the number of residences where no one answered. This system would reimburse enumerators for actual work performed and thus encourage them to be thorough in their enumeration.

Recommendation 2.1.11

We recommend that enumerators be paid according to a fee structure based on the number of visits made, as indicated by the number of names of voters collected, addresses without voters, and addresses at which mail-in enumeration cards were left.

Length of Enumeration Period
The enumeration period is now set at seven days, from the thirty-eighth to the thirty-second day before election day. Not all constituencies need the full period to prepare preliminary lists, but some do. Those that do often experience difficulties in recruiting enough competent enumerators with the industry and incentive to complete their assignment in less than seven days. Enumerations at the provincial level vary in the time required by law from four to 10 days, although in Ontario it can be less than four days at the discretion of the chief election officer.

With the procedural changes we recommend, the period required to compile the preliminary voters lists may well be reduced. The length of the enumeration period should thus become a matter of administrative judgement to be exercised by the Canada Elections Commission. The Commission would assess the circumstances known or anticipated at the time the election writ is issued; it would also have the benefit of experience with procedures tried in previous elections. Except under unusual circumstances, the enumeration period should be the same for all constituencies in each province or territory. In some cases, it might become necessary to extend the enumeration period in certain constituencies or parts thereof. Whenever this occurs, the chief electoral officer should both inform the candidates in the constituency and publicize the extension.

Recommendation 2.1.12

We recommend that

(a) **the length of the enumeration period for each province and territory be designated by the Canada Elections Commission immediately following the issue of writs;**
(b) **the length of the enumeration period be designated the same for all constituencies in a province or territory;**

(c) the chief electoral officer be authorized to extend the enumeration period for one or more constituencies or one or more polling divisions as deemed necessary; and

(d) where the chief electoral officer deems it necessary to extend the period of enumeration in one or more constituencies or one or more polling divisions, the candidates and voters in these constituencies be informed.

Revision

The current revision process for urban polling divisions is cumbersome, unnecessarily complicated and not conducted under the authority of returning officers. Revision for urban polling divisions should be simplified, made more accessible, and organized as the second stage of registration for those not on the preliminary list.

Revising Officers

To better manage the revision process, revision should be placed under the authority and responsibility of returning officers who would appoint revising officers, as well as revising agents. Most returning officers at our returning officers' symposiums favoured assuming this responsibility. Revising officers should be familiar with the process and capable of directing the work of revising agents. Whenever possible, it is preferable that revising agents be appointed from those who have served as supervisory enumerators or as regular enumerators but, contrary to the current Act, they should be appointed to work anywhere in the constituency as required and directed by revising officers or the returning officer. This would increase flexibility in the administration of the revision process. They should continue to work in pairs and not represent the same political interest. Constituencies would be subdivided into revision divisions with a revising officer responsible for each. In addition, the returning officer and the assistant returning officer should be able to perform the functions of revising officers when necessary.

Revising officers would be responsible for:

- processing mail-in enumeration cards, and entering the names of voters on the appropriate voters list;
- responding to telephone or written requests for revision by visiting households that have not been enumerated or did not receive mail-in enumeration cards, and entering the names of voters on the voters list;
- upon the direct instruction of the returning officer, conducting an enumeration in lieu of a revision, in any area or areas where the returning officer deems a new enumeration to be necessary and more efficient than revision;
- processing requests for registration made in person by voters, or on behalf of a voter by a relative, at the returning officer's office (or sub-office);

- sending revising agents to any residence they know enumerators have not visited and taking the names of voters there; and
- processing any requests for corrections or deletions from the list, the latter being restricted to the deleting of a name by the voter in person, and the deleting of the name of a deceased voter on the advice of a member of the immediate family.

Recommendation 2.1.13

We recommend that

(a) **returning officers appoint revising officers in revision divisions approved by the chief electoral officer and revising agents for the constituency;**

(b) **revising officers (or returning officers and assistant returning officers) enter the names of voters on the voters lists as requested by voters at the office(s) of the returning officer or revising officer, at the residence of voters, or after receiving mail-in enumeration cards;**

(c) **revising officers direct revising agents, who shall work in pairs and not represent the same political interest, to visit residences that were not visited by the enumerators;**

(d) **revising officers, when so directed by the returning officer, conduct an enumeration, in lieu of revision, in any area where the returning officer deems this to be necessary; and**

(e) **revising officers make corrections to the voters list when requested by a voter to revise the names or addresses of a voter or voters; and delete the name of a voter when requested to do so by the voter in question or by a member of the immediate family in the case of a deceased voter.**

Registration at the Office(s) of the Returning Officer
Finally, as an extension of revision, voters should be able to register in person at the office (or sub-office) of the returning officer, upon presentation of prescribed identification, up to 6 p.m., the fifth day before election day. These voters could also register on election day, but the administration of the vote and the convenience of the voter would be enhanced to the degree that the lists for each polling division were complete and accurate before election day.

Voters should also be able to register qualified voters of their immediate family or those living at the same residence provided that they present the prescribed identification of these voters.

Recommendation 2.1.14

We recommend that voters be able to register, with identification, or to register voters of their immediate family or those living at the same residence provided that they present identification for these voters, at their returning officer's office (or sub-office) up to 6 p.m., the fifth day before election day.

Verification of Voters Lists

Voters who register for the special ballot, by revision, at a returning officer's office or on election day, with only a few exceptions, must register in person and provide prescribed identification. An election official is thus able to ascertain that the voter is a qualified voter and is a resident of the polling division for which he or she is registered. In the case of voters registered by enumeration, including mail-in enumeration (or who are listed on a voters list supplied by a province, as discussed in Chapter 4 of this volume), no identification is required, and the voter need not be contacted by an election official in person. In addition to the check that is provided by the right of a candidate or candidate's representative to challenge the eligibility of a voter at a polling station at an advance poll or on election day, a process is required to verify the eligibility of those names on the preliminary voters lists as well as the names of voters who are added to the lists by mail-in enumerations up to the close of registration on the fifth day before election day.

In the case of the preliminary voters list, the returning officer would make a copy of the certified preliminary list for the constituency available to every candidate who requests it no later than the second day after the close of the enumeration period. Any voter would then have the right to object to the inclusion of a person on the list on the ground that the person does not have the right to vote in the polling division for which he or she is registered. Such an objection would have to be made in writing, stating the grounds for the objection, and it would have to be received by the returning officer no later than the seventeenth day before the election. The returning officer then would inform the person being objected to and inform each candidate of the receipt of the objection and of the time and place where any such objections would be decided on by revising officers. On the twelfth day before election day, each revising officer would conduct a hearing and decide on the objections in her or his revision district. The persons being objected to and candidates or their representatives would have the right to attend these hearings and make presentations. The person making the objection would have the burden of proving that the person being objected to should be removed from the voters list.

Recommendation 2.1.15

We recommend that

(a) any voter be permitted to object to the inclusion of a person on a preliminary voters list on the ground that the person does not have the right to vote in the polling division for which he or she is registered;

(b) a voter who objects to a person on a preliminary voters list be required to send a written objection to the returning officer no later than the seventeenth day before election day;

(c) the written objection state the name, address and phone number of the person making the objection, the name of the person being objected to, and the grounds for the objection, and be dated and signed by the person making the objection;

(d) any person objecting to the inclusion of a person on a preliminary voters list have the burden of proving that the person should be removed from the list;

(e) the returning officer, on receipt of an objection, be required to inform the person being objected to and each candidate in the constituency of the receipt of the objection, their right to attend a hearing and make presentations, and the place and time of the hearing; and

(f) each revising officer conduct a hearing on the twelfth day before election day to hear presentations, and decide on any objections.

When registration closes at 6 p.m. constituency time on the fifth day before election day, the returning officer would prepare a list of all voters who were added to the voters list since the certified preliminary list was prepared at the conclusion of the enumeration period. On the fourth day before election day, the list of the names added would be made available to each candidate who requests it, and revising officers would meet with any candidates or their representatives before noon on this day to review the list and to enable candidates or their representatives to make objections. Where issues cannot be resolved, the revising officer would make a reasonable effort to inform the person or persons being objected to that they may be challenged at the polls when they go to vote. These persons would not, however, be deleted from the voters list since they must be given an opportunity to respond; this would be accomplished at the polling station.

Recommendation 2.1.16

We recommend that

(a) following the close of registration on the fifth day before election day, the returning officer prepare a list of all voters added to the certified preliminary voters list and, on the fourth day before election day, make this list available to any candidate who requests it; and

(b) each revising officer, before noon constituency time on the fourth day before election day, meet with candidates or candidates' representatives to review this list of voters and, where an objection cannot be resolved, make a reasonable effort to inform those objected to that they may be challenged at their polling station when they appear to vote.

Election-Day Registration

The *Canada Elections Act* allows only voters in rural polling divisions to register on election day. Seven Canadian provinces and the Northwest Territories allow any voter to register on voting day. Ontario allows voters in rural polling divisions to register on election day and urban voters to register up to the day before election day. Only Quebec, British Columbia and the Yukon do not provide election-day registration. Internationally, France and a small number of U.S. states provide election-day registration.

No Canadian jurisdiction except Manitoba collects statistics on election-day registration. In the 1990 provincial election, approximately 5 per cent of Manitobans who voted did so after registering on election day. In the 1986 British Columbia provincial election, the last election before this provision was removed, the figure was 11.8 per cent of those who voted. In the U.S. states that provide this opportunity, turnout in the last four presidential elections averaged almost 14 per cent higher than in states without this provision.

Our survey of constituency association presidents indicated that 71 per cent of respondents were in favour of election-day registration. (Carty 1991a RC) At our public hearings, support ran seven to one in favour of this provision.

Election-day registration is essential if every reasonable effort is to be made to secure the right to vote. It builds on the existing federal practice in rural polling divisions, and it is the norm in the provinces. Moreover, it need not interfere with the administration of the vote. Central polling places combining several polling stations are now common in urban areas; at these locations, election-day registration could be administered separately from and prior to voting. The function could be assigned to registration officers appointed from among those who have been revising officers and whose other duties have been completed. At locations where there is only one polling station, including temporary mobile polling stations, the returning officer could make arrangements, as necessary, to ensure that registered voters are not inconvenienced unduly by those who must register before they vote.

Nor should election-day registration interfere with the distribution of nearly complete voters lists to candidates and parties. Would the procedure discourage many voters from being enumerated or registered by revision? The evidence from rural polling divisions and the provinces suggests not. In some cases voters registering on election day could have been registered through regular enumeration or revision; but voters moving from one constituency to another during the election period also account for a percentage of those registering on election day.

For a voter who wishes to register, appropriate identification, including confirmation of the voter's address, should be sufficient to safeguard the integrity of the vote. The practice of vouching should be eliminated because it can lead to election fraud.

Recommendation 2.1.17

We recommend that

(a) voters be permitted to register on election day provided they present prescribed identification, including confirmation of their address, and swear an oath or make an affirmation that they are a qualified voter and reside in the polling division;

(b) the provision whereby a voter may be vouched for by another registered voter from the same polling division be removed from the *Canada Elections Act*; and

(c) returning officers appoint revising officers at central polling locations to provide for an efficient election-day registration that does not hamper the conduct of the vote.

Information to Voters

The system for informing voters that they have been registered and providing information on voting times and places could be more efficient and cost-effective. The enumeration slip now left at each residence does not include polling information because poll locations may not have been confirmed by this time. A Notice of Enumeration card is thus mailed to each enumerated voter with the required polling information. This card also serves to verify that a voter on the list actually resides at the address to which the card is mailed. When cards are returned to the office of the returning officer by Canada Post, a check can then be made. This final check has never been used systematically, however, given the short time available. With the shorter election period we recommend, this procedure could not be effectively utilized.

Our recommendation that the Canada Elections Commission engage returning officers well before the election is called should enable returning

officers to confirm most, if not all, polling locations by the time of enumeration and the locations and phone numbers of their offices. Thus a card
left with enumerated voters and a mail-in enumeration card could provide
polling information in most cases. In addition, voters added to election
lists by revision or registration at the office(s) of the returning officer could
be given cards with the required polling information when they register. This
card would provide information on the following: the location of the voter's
regular polling station and whether barrier-free access is available; the location of the voter's advance polling station; the hours of the voter's mobile
polling station where appropriate; and the phone number and location of
the office and sub-office(s) of the constituency returning officer.

The Notice of Enumeration, or the 'vote-at card' as it is commonly
called, would no longer be mailed to voters who are enumerated because
returning officers would have prepared the required information in advance.
Thus Voter Information cards could be left with voters when they are enumerated. They could also be given to voters who register at an office of the
returning officer or who are registered by revising agents. The cost of mailing
Notice of Enumeration cards in 1988 was almost $6 million. Even though
there would be a need to mail Voter Information cards to a few voters who
would not have been contacted at their residences, major savings would
be achieved by having enumerators distribute them.

Recommendation 2.1.18

We recommend that

(a) **Voter Information cards be given to those enumerated, given
to those registered by revising officers or at the office(s) of
the returning officer and mailed to voters registered by
means other than visits to residences; and**
(b) **Voter Information cards provide information on the location of the voter's regular polling station and the availability
of barrier-free access (using the international symbol for such
access), the location of the voter's advance polling station, the
hours of the voter's mobile polling station where appropriate,
and the phone number and location of the office and sub-
office(s), if any, of the constituency returning officer.**

Special Registration for Specified Groups

In addition to those who vote at advance or election day polling stations
using the ordinary procedures of voting, voters may vote by *special ballot*.
For some voters, the special ballot will be obtained in person from the
office(s) of their local returning officer after they are enumerated or when
they register. For those who are away from their home constituency,
however, this approach is not feasible. Special registration procedures are

therefore necessary. There are essentially two categories of voters to whom these special registration procedures apply: (1) voters living abroad and (2) voters away from their home constituency.

In each case, it is necessary that there be a definition of 'home constituency' for these voters. Under the current *Canada Elections Act*, the provisions for Special Voting Rules define an 'ordinary residence' for Canadian forces electors and public service electors and their dependants, and for veteran electors. An 'ordinary residence' is either (1) that place of residence (with or without a street address) immediately before enrolment or transfer, commencement of full-time training or service, being placed on active service, the time of joining the public service, being posted or appointed to serve outside Canada, admission to hospital or institution, or (2) the residence of a person who is her or his spouse, dependant, relative or next of kin. For those who now would be entitled to register and to vote in their home constituency while living abroad or being away from their home constituency, we propose that a general definition of home constituency be simply the constituency that includes the voter's ordinary residence if he or she is temporarily away from home (as in the case of persons travelling, in hospital or at a temporary workstation), the voter's last place of residence before he or she took up residence elsewhere (including persons living abroad or away studying full-time) or the residence of a voter's spouse, dependant or next of kin.

Recommendation 2.1.19

We recommend that a voter's home constituency be one of the following as selected by the voter: the constituency that includes the voter's ordinary place of residence, the voter's last place of residence before assuming a residence elsewhere, or the residence of a voter's spouse, dependant or next of kin.

Voters Living Abroad
Voters living abroad are now registered and able to vote only if they qualify under the Special Voting Rules of the *Canada Elections Act*. Our recommendation that Canadian voters living abroad be qualified to vote requires new procedures so that they may register and be issued a special ballot. The most effective and efficient method to accomplish these two tasks, while preserving the integrity of the vote, is to have the Canada Elections Commission maintain a register of voters living abroad. Voters living abroad would have their names and their home constituency entered on this register in one of two ways.

All voters living abroad, except for personnel of the Canadian forces and their spouses and dependants living abroad with them, would register with the Commission by mail. Applications would be obtained from the Commission or from any Canadian government office abroad. We expect that most voters moving abroad would obtain the required forms before leaving Canada. The Commission, therefore, should establish a program to provide information and application forms to businesses and organizations, as well as federal government departments and agencies, that regularly assign their personnel to work abroad. This registration would require: the name and signature of the voter; her or his last place of residence in Canada or the address of her or his spouse, dependant or next of kin; and her or his current address and identification as prescribed by the Commission (passport, citizenship card or any other identification acceptable to the Commission).

Voters would be assigned a personal voter registration number to be placed on the certificate envelope that is part of the return of the special ballot. Sections 46(2) and 50(1) (Special Voting Rules) of the *Canada Elections Act* authorize the use of the Social Insurance Number (SIN) in the preparation of voters lists for the Canadian forces. Similarly, all voters living abroad could be identified through their SIN. The use of the SIN for such purposes, to be consistent with Treasury Board guidelines, would require a specific amendment to the *Canada Elections Act*. Current federal policy requires that any authorized use of the SIN must be achieved through legislative amendments. As well, the use of the SIN as a means of identifying voters living abroad would have to meet specific conditions in the federal *Privacy Act*. Current federal policy requires that individuals must be notified when their SIN is used, for what purposes and whether there are specific sanctions involved if the SIN is not disclosed to the government department or agency requesting it. If the SIN is used in a personal information bank, the operating government agency "must so indicate and must cite the authority under which the number is collected and describe the purposes for which it is used in the *Index of Personal Information*". (Canada, Treasury Board of Canada 1989, 3) Under the *Privacy Act*, the Privacy Commissioner of Canada has the authority to examine the collection, use, disclosure and management of personal information acquired by government agencies. The registration of a voter living abroad would be valid for three years, subject to renewal providing that he or she continued to qualify as a voter.

Canadian forces personnel and their spouses and dependants who are qualified voters and living abroad would also have their names and home constituencies entered on the Commission's register. However, as there may be security reasons for not identifying the addresses abroad and given that the Department of National Defence (DND) maintains lists of its personnel and employees abroad, the most efficient method of registering these voters would be to have DND maintain the register for those voters on behalf of the Commission and provide it with a master list of all such voters abroad at the time an election writ is issued, in the format determined by the Commission.

The names and addresses of all voters on this Commission register for each constituency would be made available to candidates in each constituency, although the current addresses of Canadian forces voters could be only a post office address.

Recommendation 2.1.20

We recommend that

(a) the Canada Elections Commission maintain a voter register of Canadian voters living abroad;

(b) voters living abroad register by mail by sending a completed registration form to the Commission;

(c) Canadian forces voters abroad be on the list of voters abroad maintained by the Department of National Defence on behalf of the Commission and be provided to the Commission at the time the writ is issued;

(d) applications contain a signature, Social Insurance Number, identification as prescribed by the Commission, the last address in Canada or the Canadian address of the spouse, dependant or next of kin, and the voter's current address;

(e) each registered voter be assigned a unique voter registration number;

(f) the *Canada Elections Act* authorize the use of Social Insurance Numbers to provide voter registration numbers;

(g) this registration be for three years and renewable, provided that the voter remains qualified by not voting in a foreign national election since taking up residence abroad; and

(h) following the issue of the writ, the Commission make available to candidates the list of voters (name and address only) from their constituency on the register.

Voters Away from Their Home Constituency

All other voters away from their home constituency, including those living abroad but not on the Commission's register at the time a writ is issued, must apply in person to register for their home constituency and to receive a special ballot to vote. This process of registering and applying for a special ballot would constitute one step, using a single application form. This application would be available from the office of any returning officer in Canada and at Canadian government offices abroad.

These voters must apply in person and present identification with a signature, as prescribed by the Commission. The application must include the address of her or his home constituency, the current address (if different from the former) and a declaration that he or she will vote only by special ballot. The election official at the office of the returning officer or designated Commission agent at a Canadian government office abroad must certify on the application that the prescribed identification with signature was presented and that a special ballot was received by the voter, as well as note the number on the certificate envelope. The election official or designated agent would then send by facsimile the completed registration-special ballot application to the returning officer in the home constituency. The name and address of the voter would then be added to the voters list for the polling division in question with an indication that the voter has received a special ballot and the number of the certificate envelope.

For designated Canadian offices abroad or in Canada, such as RCMP offices in remote areas, the Commission should consider the use of their internal telecommunication facilities to help relay these registration applications to returning officers.

Voters who register in this manner must ensure that they register in time for their completed registration application to be received by the returning officer in their home constituency by 6 p.m. eastern time on the fifth day before election day.

Recommendation 2.1.21

We recommend that

(a) voters away from their home constituency be permitted to register and apply for a special ballot at any office, including any temporary office, of any returning officer in Canada, at designated Canadian government offices in Canada or abroad;

(b) all such voters apply in person, provide a signature, present identification as prescribed by the Commission, provide their address in their home constituency and sign a declaration that they will vote only once in the election;

(c) the election official or agent who registers every such voter certify on the application form for registration and the special ballot that the prescribed identification was presented and that a special ballot was given to the voter, and record the number of the certificate envelope;

(d) the completed application be forwarded forthwith by mail or facsimile by the official or agent who registers the voter to the returning officer in the home constituency of the voter;

(e) on receipt of a completed and certified application, the returning officer enter the name of the voter on the voters list for the appropriate polling division, note that the voter has received a special ballot and the number of the certificate envelope; and

(f) registration be accepted only if received by the office of the returning officer in the home constituency of the voter by 6 p.m. eastern time on the fifth day before election day.

With the exception of inmates in federal institutions, as discussed below, and of certain voters in hospitals, the above procedures and requirements for registration apply to all voters away from their home constituency. However, certain groups of such voters are found in clusters in many locations, and the Canada Elections Commission should take measures to facilitate their registration and application for a special ballot. These clusters of voters away from their home constituency include full-time students at post-secondary educational institutions, inmates in provincial and local institutions, workers at temporary worksites and Canadian forces personnel on training in Canada at other than their normal posting.

In the case of the first three clusters of voters, the Commission should instruct the local returning officer in whose constituency such educational institutions, prisons or worksites are located to establish a temporary office one week or so before election day so that these voters can register and apply for a special ballot. For Canadian forces personnel on training, the returning officer should designate an officer as election agent at such bases to accept applications for registration and for the special ballot. These election agents would assist these clusters of voters to register and apply for a special ballot and, as at any election office accepting applications, transmit the completed application form by facsimile to the office of the returning officer in the voter's home constituency.

The provision of this service would facilitate access to registration and the special ballot for these voters. In the case of post-secondary students studying away from home, for example, this service would facilitate access to the ballot for up to half a million students. Groups representing students at our hearings were critical of the restrictive and cumbersome rules for proxy voting, which is the only way students far away from home may now vote in their home constituency, as well as the fact that for many students their first vote must be cast by a proxy. The special ballot would make voting more accessible to students away from home because they would be able to register, apply for and obtain a special ballot at their place of study.

In the case of inmates in provincial and local prisons who obviously cannot leave their institution to register with a local returning officer, a temporary office would enable the local returning officer to register all those who would be qualified to vote in their home constituency by special ballot during a one-day period.

In the case of Canadian forces personnel on training in Canada but away from home, the local returning officer could simply designate a Canadian forces personnel officer as an election registration agent who would then register any voter on training away from home and provide special ballots at any time up to the deadline on the fifth day before election day.

For major temporary worksites where the local returning officer has reason to believe that voters away from their home constituency are present, the local returning officer would have an election official set up a temporary election office to provide registration and special ballots.

Voters at any of these locations who were unable to avail themselves of this service would still be able to register and apply for a special ballot by applying in person at any office of the local returning officer or to an election agent designated by the local returning officer (for instance, at Canadian forces bases or in provincial and local prisons) as long as their completed application was received by the returning officer in their home constituency by 6 p.m. eastern time on the fifth day before election day. Whenever election officials assist in returning a ballot to the office of the returning officer in a voter's home constituency, responsibility for delivery of the ballot by the deadline remains that of the voter.

Recommendation 2.1.22

We recommend that returning officers in whose constituency are located major clusters of voters who must vote by special ballot, including inmates in provincial and local prisons, full-time students at post-secondary institutions, workers at temporary worksites and Canadian forces personnel on training, make provisions, as the chief electoral officer deems appropriate, for registration and the provision of special ballots.

In the case of voters who are inmates in federal institutions, it would be administratively most efficient if Correctional Service Canada provided the Canada Elections Commission with a certified list of the names and home constituencies of all qualified voters in federal institutions at the time of the issue of the writs. This procedure would also be most effective for prison security. The Commission would then send each voter on this list a special ballot. Any qualified voter who becomes an inmate in a federal institution after the list has been sent to the Commission may apply up to the regular deadline to an election agent designated by the Commission in each institution and receive a special ballot.

Recommendation 2.1.23

We recommend that

(a) Correctional Service Canada provide the Canada Elections Commission with a list of all qualified voters who are inmates in federal institutions at the time of the issue of the writs;

(b) this list contain the names of the home constituencies of each such voter; and

(c) the Canada Elections Commission designate an election agent in each federal institution to register and accept applications for special ballots for any inmates in these institutions who are qualified voters and who were not on the list provided to the Canada Elections Commission.

Finally, we must consider voters in hospital on election day who have not voted at an advance poll or who have not applied for and received a special ballot. We propose that these voters be allowed to register and vote by special ballot on election day in their hospital. The process for this is discussed in Chapter 2 of this volume. We consider this particular provision necessary given that a large number of persons in this circumstance cannot be expected to have been able either to anticipate their admission or to have taken the necessary steps to be registered for the special ballot.

Recommendation 2.1.24

We recommend that voters in hospital on election day be permitted to register and vote by special ballot in their hospital.

VOTERS LISTS

Voters lists are required to ensure that only eligible voters are permitted to vote and that each voter votes only once. In addition to the requirement that voters and candidates or their representatives be able to object to the inclusion of names on preliminary voters lists as well as those names added by way of mail-in enumeration, voters lists are required for election administration for advance voting and election day.

Under our proposals, the revision period will end on the fifth day before election day. This means that voters lists must be prepared for the first day of advance voting on the eighth day before election day and also for the second day of advance voting and election-day voting. The first lists we call the advance poll voters lists; the second, the voters lists.

The advance poll voters lists will be used for advance voting on the eighth day before election day. These lists will include all voters who are on the preliminary voters lists, as corrected, and those added up to and including the twelfth day before election day. These lists will also indicate those voters who have received a special ballot. Voters who come to vote at this first day of advance voting may be challenged at their polling station. This opportunity to challenge the eligibility of voters is especially important in the case of those who have registered by mail-in enumeration.

The voters lists used for the second day of advance voting on the second day before election day will include all voters on the advance poll voters lists as well as those added up to and including the fifth day before election day. These lists will also indicate all those voters who voted at the first day of advance voting and all those who received special ballots. For election day these lists will be modified to indicate all those voters who voted on the second day of advance voting. Voters may be challenged at either the advance poll on the second day before election day or on election day.

With computerized entry of names and addresses to voters lists, particularly those added after the establishment of the preliminary voters lists, successive generations of voters lists can be provided both to election officials and to candidates and their representatives.

The final voters lists for each constituency will include the voters list used for election day, all voters added to it through election-day registration and those lists managed centrally by the Canada Elections Commission. These lists will constitute the voters list in each constituency and will be used to determine the electoral quotients in each province and territory and for election finance purposes.

APPENDICES: CANADA ELECTIONS COMMISSION CALENDARS

Figure 1.1
47 day election campaign, based on federal enumeration

Sunday	Monday	Tuesday	Wednesday	Thursday	Friday	Saturday
			47 Election campaign begins	46 Applications for special ballots begin when election offices open	45	44
43	42	41	40	39 Enumeration period begins[1]	38	37
36 Election advertising begins	35	34 Enumeration period ends	33	32 • Preliminary lists available • Revision period begins	31	30
29	28	27	26	25	24	23
22	21 Close of nominations (2 p.m.)	20	19	18	17 Objections in writing to names on preliminary voters list	16 Voters notified of objections
15	14	13	12 • Decisions made on objections • Advance poll voters list closed	11 • Advance poll voters list to CEO, DROs and candidates	10	9
8 First day of advance poll	7	6	5 • Revision period ends • Last day for registration at office of ROs and mail-in enumeration • Last day to apply for special ballot	4 • Review of names added to advance poll voters list • Voters lists to DROs	3	2 • Second day of advance poll • Election advertising ends (midnight)
1 Inform DROs of names of voters who voted at advance poll on Day 2	0 **Election day** • Registration at polling stations	Determination of number of names on final voters lists				

Source: Royal Commission Research Branch.

[1] The length of the enumeration period is based on the period set for the 1988 federal election.

Figure 1.2
40 day election campaign, based on federal enumeration

Sunday	Monday	Tuesday	Wednesday	Thursday	Friday	Saturday
			47	46	45	44
43	42	41	40 *Election campaign begins*	39 Applications for special ballots begin when election offices open	38	37
36	35	34	33	32 *Enumeration period begins[1]*	31	30
29 *Election advertising begins*	28 *Enumeration period ends*	27	26 • *Preliminary lists available* • *Revision period begins*	25	24	23
22	21 *Close of nominations (2 p.m.)*	20	19	18	17 Objections in writing to names on preliminary voters list	16 Voters notified of objections
15	14	13	12 • Decisions made on objections • Advance poll voters list closed	11 • Advance poll voters list to CEO, DROs and candidates	10	9
8 First day of advance poll	7	6	5 • *Revision period ends* • Last day for registration at office of ROs and mail-in enumeration • Last day to apply for special ballot	4 • Review of names added to advance poll voters list • Voters lists to DROs	3	2 • *Second day of advance poll* • *Election advertising ends (midnight)*
1 Inform DROs of names of voters who voted at advance poll on Day 2	0 **Election day** • Registration at polling stations	Determination of number of names on final voters lists				

Source: Royal Commission Research Branch.

Figure 1.3
47 day election campaign, based on federal enumeration in some provinces

Sunday	Monday	Tuesday	Wednesday	Thursday	Friday	Saturday
			47	46	45	44
43	42	41	40 *Election campaign begins*	39 Applications for special ballots begin when election offices open	38 Preliminary voters lists received from provinces and territories	37
36	35	34	33	32	31 *'Vote-at cards' mailed to voters on these lists*	30
Revision period begins for provincial and territorial preliminary voters lists — *Federal enumeration as necessary*						
29 • *Enumeration period ends* • *Election advertising begins*	28	27 • *Preliminary lists from enumeration available* • *Revision of these lists begins*	26	25	24	23
22	21 *Close of nominations (2 p.m.)*	20	19	18	17 Objections in writing to names on preliminary voters list	16 Voters notified of objections
15	14	13	12 • Decisions made on objections • Advance poll voters list closed	11 • Advance poll voters list to CEO, DROs and candidates	10	9
8 First day of advance poll	7	6	5 • *Revision period ends* • Last day for registration at office of ROs and mail-in enumeration • Last day to apply for special ballot	4 • Review of names added to advance poll voters list • Voters lists to DROs	3	2 • *Second day of advance poll* • *Election advertising ends (midnight)*
1 Inform DROs of names of voters who voted at advance poll on Day 2	0 **Election day** • Registration at polling stations	Determination of number of names on final voters lists				

Source: Royal Commission Research Branch.

Figure 1.4
40 day election campaign, based on federal enumeration in some provinces

Sunday	Monday	Tuesday	Wednesday	Thursday	Friday	Saturday
			47 *Election campaign begins*	46 Applications for special ballots begin when election offices open	45 Preliminary voters lists received from provinces and territories	44
43	42	41 *Revision period begins for provincial and territorial preliminary voters lists / 'Vote-at cards' mailed to voters on these lists*	40 *Federal enumeration as necessary*	39	38	37
36 • *Enumeration period ends* • *Election advertising begins*	35	34 • *Preliminary lists from enumeration available* • *Revision of these lists begins*	33	32	31	30
29	28	27	26	25	24	23
22	21 *Close of nominations (2 p.m.)*	20	19	18	17 Objections in writing to names on preliminary voters list	16 Voters notified of objections
15	14	13	12 • Decisions made on objections • Advance poll voters list closed	11 • Advance poll voters list to CEO, DROs and candidates	10	9
8 First day of advance poll	7	6	5 • *Revision period ends* • Last day for registration at office of ROs and mail-in enumeration • Last day to apply for special ballot	4 • Review of names added to advance poll voters list • Voters lists to DROs	3	2 • *Second day of advance poll* • *Election advertising ends (midnight)*
1 Inform DROs of names of voters who voted at advance poll on Day 2	0 **Election day** • Registration at polling stations	Determination of number of names on final voters lists				

2

THE VOTING PROCESS

INTRODUCTION

Reforms to the voting process must aim to increase the level of voter participation. The voting process should be made as voter-friendly and accessible as possible while preserving the integrity of the vote. Canadians should not be complacent about this aspect of the democratic system: roughly one-quarter of eligible voters did not exercise their franchise at the last federal election. Of these, many did not have a choice; they were disfranchised because of statutory constraints or for administrative reasons. It is our objective to ensure that no Canadian voter is deprived of the right to vote because of the administrative aspect of voting procedures. Our comparative research on international experience demonstrates that electoral systems that make it easier for voters to exercise their franchise enjoy higher voter turnout. (Black 1991 RC)

Our major recommendation regarding the voting process is to extend the current procedures known as Special Voting Rules (SVR) to all Canadians by introducing the 'special ballot'. The SVR are now restricted to members and certain employees of the Canadian forces and public servants posted abroad and their spouses and dependants, veterans in certain hospitals, and members of the Canadian forces in Canada.

The rationale for the special ballot is best understood against the backdrop of the ordinary voting procedure. The *Canada Elections Act* relies almost totally on ordinary voting, either on election day or at an advance poll. The ordinary vote is cast at a specific time and at a fixed polling station; voters mark a ballot in secret that is then placed in the ballot box under the scrutiny of the voter, election officials, and representatives of the candidates.

The ordinary voting procedure is effective and economical and permits most Canadians to vote a short distance from home. Lengthy delays at the polls are uncommon. Above all, the process is familiar, well understood and widely accepted, because its basic procedures are common to elections at all three levels of government.

The Act also provides for circumstances not covered by the ordinary vote. Students, certain categories of workers, such as fishers and mariners, and voters with an illness or physical incapacity can cast their ballot by proxy; in large hospitals where polling stations are set up, the ballot box can be removed from the polling station to allow bedside voting; voters who have reason to believe they will be unable to vote at a regular or advance poll can vote at the returning officer's office at pre-determined times; and certain categories of Canadians vote under the SVR.

In some cases, however, these procedures are unduly restrictive; in others, they are contrary to the fundamental objectives of providing a secret ballot under a system that is user-friendly and accessible to all Canadian voters. For example, patients in smaller institutions may not be able to vote if no poll is set up there, while voting by proxy compromises the secrecy of the ballot. Rather than working to improve this patchwork of procedures to encompass the needs of a greater number of voters and cover a broader set of circumstances, our proposal is to extend the scope and nature of the Special Voting Rules.

The special ballot would serve the needs of people unable to vote at their regular poll on election day or at an advance poll. For example it responds to the concerns of persons with disabilities, who recommended in the report of the Special Committee on the Disabled and the Handicapped "that the Federal Government proceed in developing legislation, together with the appropriate machinery and programs, to establish a postal vote system similar to the one that is successfully in effect in Manitoba". (Canada, House of Commons 1982, 15) The names of the candidates are not printed on the special ballot. Rather, the voter fills in the name of the candidate or party she or he wishes to vote for; thus, the special ballot is also referred to as a write-in ballot.

The special ballot would serve a variety of voters with special needs and provide an alternative for voters unable to get to an ordinary or advance poll. Similar systems are already used successfully in other Canadian jurisdictions, including British Columbia, Manitoba, Quebec, New Brunswick, Saskatchewan and the Yukon. The 'absentee ballot' is widely used in the United States and similar procedures also exist in Australia, Germany and Sweden. In Great Britain, the absentee voting provisions allow several groups of voters, including those who cannot reasonably expect to vote in person the day of the election, to vote by mail. We use the term 'special' ballot to avoid the impression that the ballot could be sent only by mail.

Unlike an ordinary ballot, a special ballot would not have to be cast at a specific time or place, so long as it was returned in time to be counted on election day. The integrity and secrecy of the vote would be protected through application procedures for the special ballot, through a system of sealed envelopes and through the process for receiving and counting special ballots. The system has proved reliable elsewhere and should give the voting process the necessary flexibility, accessibility and secrecy to enhance Canadians' access to the vote significantly.

Table 2.1 summarizes current voting procedures and the changes we propose.

Table 2.1
Voting procedures, present and proposed

Present system	Commission proposals
I. Ordinary vote	

a. Election day
  • at permanent polling station
  • by proxy
  • at mobile polls (restricted use)
	a. Election day
	  • at permanent polling station
	  • at mobile polls (expanded use)

b. Advance voting
  • at advance polling station
    (subject to statutory limitations)
	b. Advance voting
	  • at advance polling station
	  • at mobile polls

II. Special vote	
a. RO's office	a. By transmittal

b. Special Voting Rules (SVR)
  (Schedule II)
	b. By tendering ballot in RO's office or a
	  sub-office in voter's home constituency

SVR can be used by   • Members and certain
    employees of Canadian forces
  • Public servants living abroad
  • Their spouses and dependants
    if living abroad
  • Veterans in certain hospitals
	Can be used by: any voter

THE ORDINARY VOTE

Election-Day Voting

Voting Procedure

At the 1988 election, 95 per cent of Canadians who voted did so by casting a ballot at a local polling station on election day. A typical polling station serves 300 to 350 voters in urban areas and a somewhat smaller number in rural areas. Ordinary voting on election day would remain relatively unchanged under our proposals. Canadians registered on the voters list would go to a polling station in their neighbourhood. Two election officials – a deputy returning officer and a poll clerk – would be at the poll to take their vote, and scrutineers representing the candidates would be present to further ensure the integrity of the process.

We propose changes to the ballot and in the polling station to facilitate voting by people with special needs, but these changes would not affect the basic process of marking and casting a ballot. Voting may also be somewhat quicker as a result of our proposals to streamline election procedures and to computerize voters lists.

No major changes are needed in ordinary voting; the present election-day procedures work effectively and are widely accepted by Canadians.

Their use in provincial and municipal elections reinforces their familiarity among voters, election officials and party workers. There were almost no comments at our hearings regarding the basic process of election-day voting, except with regard to the need to serve people with disabilities or language difficulties. The need to facilitate voting by persons with physical disabilities was raised in both the 1986 *White Paper on Election Law Reform* (Canada, Privy Council Office 1986) and the chief electoral officer's 1989 report (Canada, Chief Electoral Officer 1989). The changes recommended were designed to improve the present process rather than to change it radically; this is our approach as well.

Recommendation 2.2.1

We recommend that

(a) the basic process of ordinary voting on election day be retained, with the improvements recommended in this report; and
(b) voting on election day continue to take place at polling stations serving a defined group of voters in a limited geographic area.

Depositing the Ballot
Under current procedures each ballot is initialled by the deputy returning officer and has a serial number on the counterfoil for identification. After the voter marks the ballot, the deputy returning officer (DRO) checks the counterfoil and initials to ensure that it is the same ballot paper that was delivered to the voter. The DRO then removes the counterfoil and puts the ballot in the ballot box. Allowing voters to deposit the ballot themselves is contrary to the procedures in the Act.

The practice of having the deputy returning officer deposit the ballot is followed in most provinces, but Quebec and New Brunswick allow voters to deposit their own ballots. This is also the practice in France, Great Britain and Australia. There is no threat to the integrity of the process in allowing voters to place the ballot in the ballot box instead of giving it to an official. After marking the ballot, the voter should give it to the deputy returning officer to allow verification of the counterfoil and initials; after the DRO tears off the counterfoil, the voter should be allowed to deposit the ballot in the ballot box if desired.

Recommendation 2.2.2

We recommend that each voter be allowed to deposit his or her own ballot in the ballot box after the deputy returning officer has checked the initials and serial number.

The Mobile Polling Station

The Act requires that voting take place at a polling station that is open for either the full 11-hour voting period on election day or for three 8-hour periods for an advance poll; in both cases, the polling station stays at a fixed location. There are two exceptions. In chronic care hospitals or similar institutions, election-day polling stations can be closed temporarily while the ballot box is being taken from room to room to allow bedside voting. Under the Special Voting Rules, mobile voting places may be established during the second week prior to election day where Canadian forces voters, their spouses and dependants or public service voters, their spouses and dependants cannot conveniently reach the voting place established at their unit or post.

In our hearings and other consultations we encountered strong arguments in favour of making procedures more flexible and voting more accessible for people in nursing homes and other small institutions. Many people living in institutions are confined to bed or have difficulty getting out to vote or arranging for a proxy vote. At the same time, the numbers in each institution are too small to justify a permanent polling station. The consequence is that people who should be able to vote are denied that right or have great difficulty arranging to vote.

This need can be met with temporary polling stations or mobile polls similar to those now used in Manitoba, New Brunswick, Quebec, and the Northwest Territories, as well as in Australia and Germany. The majority of returning officers at our two symposiums on election administration supported the idea, which also received unanimous support from interveners at our hearings. It was also supported by more than two-thirds of the constituency association presidents we surveyed. (Carty 1991a RC)

Voting at a mobile poll is similar to voting at an ordinary poll, except that voters vote during a specified period rather than any time during election day. Voters are registered on a voters list for the mobile poll, are served by the same election officials, and deposit their ballots in a regular ballot box. Candidates have the same right to appoint scrutineers, and the count at the end of the day is carried out just as in a regular polling station. Each mobile poll can cover a number of locations on election day, stopping for as little as 15 minutes or as much as several hours, depending on the number of voters at each location. This is more efficient and considerably less costly than placing a polling station at each location for the entire day.

We propose that institutions or areas to be served by a mobile poll be designated before the election begins. Voting at mobile polls should be organized in co-operation with authorities at the institutions concerned. Well before voting day the returning officer should set the schedule for each mobile polling station and ensure that voters in each mobile poll are informed where and when they can vote. The same information should also be given to candidates.

As in hospital polling stations, election officers for mobile polls should be permitted to take the ballot box to the bedside of voters who cannot come to the area where the vote is being taken. Normally a mobile poll should not move on until everyone who wishes to vote at each stopping point has done so.

Mobile polls could also be useful in other circumstances, such as small isolated communities where a polling station would not need to stay open all day or where a mobile poll could serve several communities in a day. Australia's Aboriginal and Northern Settler vote program, for example, makes voting accessible to people living in small isolated communities using mobile polls. In Canada, perhaps the best example was the mobile poll that travelled by train on election day along the string of small communities on the railway line between Thompson and Churchill. This service contravened the *Canada Elections Act*, however, and was withdrawn in the 1988 federal election. We see no purpose in such limitations, which result in administrative disfranchisement of many voters.

Another use for mobile polls would be to permit homeless people to vote at shelters, soup kitchens, Aboriginal community centres or other locations where they congregate. This follows from our recommendation in Chapter 1 of this volume, that returning officers should consult with those responsible for such community centres to recruit potential enumerators from among their staff. This would help to overcome the reluctance of some homeless people to use ordinary polling stations. Homeless people may face obstacles to voting if they are unfamiliar with the electoral system, lack knowledge of where or how to vote, or fear being embarrassed by going to an ordinary polling station.

Recommendation 2.2.3

We recommend that

(a) **mobile polls be established where they will make voting more accessible for groups of voters who would have difficulty going to an ordinary polling station;**

(b) **with the exception of the hours of voting, voting procedures and the right of candidates to be represented at mobile polls be the same as at ordinary polls;**

(c) **mobile polls not be required to remain open for the same period as ordinary polling stations on election day, provided that voting at any mobile poll end no later than voting at ordinary polling stations in the constituency;**

(d) **mobile polls be permitted to move to several locations on election day, provided that the schedule of opening hours and locations be made available in advance to candidates and voters in that mobile poll;**

(e) voting in mobile polls be organized in co-operation with the appropriate authorities of any institution, such as hospitals, shelters, soup kitchens or Aboriginal community centres, where a mobile poll is located;

(f) when a residence or institution has been designated to be served by a mobile poll, the people living there be registered for the mobile poll and not for the ordinary polling division where the institution is located;

(g) ballots from mobile polls be counted at the same time as the ordinary polls are counted; and

(h) the count take place at the returning officer's office or at another location approved by the returning officer, with prior notification to candidates.

The Advance Poll

Voting Procedure

Advance voting is well established in Canadian elections. It is also used widely in other countries, including Australia, New Zealand and the Scandinavian countries. Advance voting is a useful extension of the ordinary voting process, is simple for the voter to use, and gives voters an accessible alternative to voting on election day. These are all reasons to retain this procedure.

Voting data indicate that Canadians accept the concept of advance voting, but most still prefer to cast their vote on election day, when the campaign has ended. At the 1988 election, just over 500 000 Canadians went to the advance poll, or 3.8 per cent of the total number who voted; in 1984, the figure was 4.6 per cent.

Under the Act, voters can vote at the advance poll because they expect to be absent from their polling division and unable to vote on election day; because of "advanced age, infirmity or the probable termination of pregnancy"; or because of religious beliefs. Advance polls are held on the Saturday, Monday and Tuesday that fall nine, seven and six days before election day; advance voting hours are from noon to 8 p.m.

For the 1988 election there were 2463 advance polling stations across Canada, a ratio of about one advance poll for every 23 ordinary polls. Each ordinary polling division is assigned to an advance poll, so that voters wishing to vote report to the advance polling station for their polling division. Voters lists for all the polling divisions covered by the advance polling station are available at the advance poll.

The voting card sent to every registered voter provides advance poll locations and voting times. Casting an advance ballot follows the same process as casting an ordinary ballot on election day. The voter gives his or her name and address, receives a regular ballot, and marks it; the ballot is then deposited in an ordinary ballot box. Representatives of the candidates are present as scrutineers, and the poll is staffed by a deputy returning officer and a poll clerk. The voter does not have to produce identification unless challenged as to his or her right to vote.

Voters' names are crossed off the voters lists and recorded; this information is transferred to the voters list prepared for election day to prevent double voting. After the advance poll, the ballot boxes are kept sealed until one hour after the close of voting on election day. The ballots are counted at the place indicated in a notice published by the returning officer, usually where the advance poll was located, and the results are transmitted to the returning officer as for any other polling station.

We propose to maintain most of these procedures. However, the timing of advance polls should be changed; votes from advance polls should begin to be counted at the same time as those from ordinary polls, and greater flexibility is needed in locating advance polls. Voters in non-urban areas should also have greater choice in where they can cast an advance vote. We also propose to broaden the Act's conditions for advance voting. These conditions are adhered to in some constituencies, but in others, election officials allow any voter to vote at the advance poll. We propose that any registered voter who finds it more convenient to vote at an advance poll be eligible to do so. This effectively leaves the decision up to the voter.

Over the three days of advance polling for the 1988 election, the average number of votes cast at an advance poll was 266 in urban areas and 129 in rural areas during the 24 hours the polls were open. This compares with 254 votes in an average urban poll and 202 votes in a rural poll over the 11-hour period on election day. Using Elections Canada data, we estimate the cost of a vote at an advance poll averages about $3.42, compared with $1.38 on election day.

One of the reasons for the higher cost of advance voting is lower voter turnout. Turnout appears to be influenced by the days on which advance voting takes place. If a voter has difficulty going to vote because the election is held on a Monday, that voter may also have difficulty going to an advance poll on a Monday. In addition, there is no provision for voters to vote at an advance poll if they realize during the final week of the campaign that they will be unable to vote on election day.

Our research indicated that the largest number of advance votes are cast in the first few hours of the first day of advance polling – the Saturday nine days before election day. Some voters may be casting an advance vote before leaving on a trip; others may choose the Saturday because this is more convenient than a day during the work week. The returning officers we consulted generally agreed that advance voting turnout tends to be much lower on the second and third allotted days; more than two-thirds supported changing the advance polling period. It appears the greatest need for advance voting is on a day during the second weekend prior to election day and on the weekend just prior to election day.

We propose that the advance polling days should be changed to the Sunday of the second weekend before election day and the Saturday immediately prior to election day. These two days would give voters sufficient access to advance voting while leaving enough time to mark off the names of advance voters on the voters lists used at regular polling stations on election day.

Advance polls are open between noon and 8 p.m. The intention was to accommodate people in the work force but the result is that people cannot vote at an advance poll on a Saturday morning, one of the most convenient times in the week for many voters. We therefore recommend that the hours for advance polls held on a Saturday be 9 a.m. to 6 p.m.

For Sunday, we recommend maintaining the current hours of noon to 8 p.m. Earlier opening of advance polls on a Sunday does not appear warranted, but voters may find it convenient to cast an advance ballot in the evening, for example, if they are returning from a weekend away. These changes in hours should not cause confusion if they are well publicized; on balance, they should make advance voting much more accessible than at present.

As is now the case, the deputy returning officer would secure the ballot box and advance poll records for the period between the advance polling days. In urban areas, this could be done by depositing the ballot box with the returning officer; elsewhere it would have to be placed in safekeeping, for example, at the local bank or police station.

Advance Mobile Polls

The Act requires three days of advance polling in every city, town, or village with a population of 1000 or more. This can lead to duplication if several small municipalities are located close to each other and to underutilization because of the small number of voters served.

Given our proposal for the special ballot, which would give voters a convenient alternative to voting on election day, we do not believe that advance voting will need to be available in small communities for the same length of time as at present. Returning officers should therefore have greater discretion to determine the location and timing of advance polls, particularly in sparsely populated areas.

Two days of advance polling are justified in urban areas and should be required in every municipality or area with a population of 5000 voters or more. For communities with fewer than 5000 voters, the RO should have the discretion to determine whether a day of advance voting is warranted. In instances where the decision is made not to provide an advance poll, a mobile advance poll, which would visit such communities during the nine days before election day, should be provided and its schedule publicized well in advance.

The Act permits returning officers to create advance polling districts in rural areas and to determine which ordinary polling divisions should be placed in each advance district. We believe ROs should have the same flexibility to arrange advance polling districts in urban areas as well. Plans should be made available to registered parties or candidates that request it, and the plan should be subject to review by the chief electoral officer on the request of any candidate or registered party.

Recommendation 2.2.4

We recommend that

(a) **every voter who would find it more convenient to vote at an advance poll than at an ordinary polling station be eligible to do so;**
(b) **there be two days of advance polling in areas of more than 5000 voters; in areas with fewer than 5000 voters, the returning officer have the flexibility to determine whether an advance poll is warranted;**
(c) **a mobile advance poll be provided during the nine days preceding election day to serve any community of fewer than 5000 voters where they would not otherwise have reasonable access to an advance poll;**
(d) **the days set aside for advance polling be the Sunday of the second weekend before election day and the Saturday immediately before election day;**
(e) **the hours for advance polling be noon to 8 p.m. on Sunday and 9 a.m. to 6 p.m. on Saturday; and**
(f) **the plan for advance polling in each constituency be made available to the candidates and registered parties and subject to review by the chief electoral officer on the request of any candidate or registered party.**

VOTING BY SPECIAL BALLOT

Overview

The special ballot we propose differs from the ordinary ballot in that it does not have to be cast at a specific time or place. Once voters have received and marked a special ballot they would be responsible for transmitting it to an election office. Voters who request a special ballot in their home constituency would have the option of marking the ballot and handing it back to the election official immediately. This practice, called 'tendering', would replace the current procedure for voting in the returning officer's office.

The special ballot borrows heavily from existing procedures under the Special Voting Rules. These rules were established during the First World War for two reasons: first, the hundreds of thousands of Canadian soldiers in Europe would not have been able to vote; second, the number of voters on large military bases in Canada would have unduly affected election results in the constituencies where these bases were located if military personnel had been required to vote in those constituencies. During the 1988 election, some 53 000 votes were cast under the Special Voting Rules, but at least three-quarters were cast by members of the forces at military bases within Canada.

People who qualify under the current Special Voting Rules would be able to vote in much the same way as at present. In addition, they would be able to vote by special ballot in by-elections and postponed elections, which they cannot do now under the SVR. Thus, the special ballot elimi-nates the requirement for the Special Voting Rules.

Further, because it would apply to a broader group of voters, the spe-cial ballot would provide a flexible option for voters who cannot go to an ordinary poll. These include voters away from their home constituency, Canadians living abroad, persons with physical disabilities, voters living in remote areas, and those with chronic illnesses. The special ballot would also be more efficient and effective than the proxy vote, which is restricted to (1) certain categories of workers whose employment requires them to be away from home on a regular basis, such as fishers, prospectors and trappers; (2) people who are ill or physically incapacitated; and (3) full-time students away from home. The limited availability and use of the proxy vote provoked a large number of complaints at our hearings. With the intro-duction of the special ballot, proxy voting would no longer be required. Our survey of constituency association presidents revealed that close to 60 per cent were in favour of replacing proxy votes with a system similar to the special ballot we propose. (Carty 1991a RC) More than three-quarters of returning officers also supported the special ballot.

Our recommendation that any voter who finds it more convenient be allowed to vote at an advance poll is intended to ensure that a voter who wishes to use the advance poll cannot be prevented from doing so by an election official. For the same reason, we recommend that the special bal-lot be available to any voter who prefers it to voting by ordinary ballot on election day or at an advance poll.

The special ballot system would involve a series of envelopes to protect the secrecy of the ballot, verify the voter's identity, and provide for delivery to the election office. Under our proposal, *three envelopes would be used.*

The first envelope would be unmarked and known as the *secrecy enve-lope*. The second one, the *certificate envelope*, would allow election officials to verify the identity of the voter to ensure the integrity of the vote and avoid fraud. It would require the voter's name, address, signature and con-stituency and an attestation by the voter that he or she will not cast vote more than one ballot. For Canadians living abroad whose names are on the non-resident voters register, it would also require their unique identification num-ber and an attestation that they have not voted in a foreign national election since leaving Canada. The certificate envelope should be numbered to allow the Canada Elections Commission to administer the distribution of the spe-cial ballot more efficiently, to allow a better record of its use throughout the election system, and to allow more efficient tracing in the event of theft or fraud. The third envelope, the *return envelope*, would be used to transmit the special ballot to the appropriate election office for checking and counting. This procedure has proved workable; Manitoba uses a similar three-envelope system for its mail-in ballot.

Voters voting by special ballot would place the marked ballot in the secrecy envelope and seal it, fill in the certificate on the second envelope and seal the secrecy envelope inside it, then put the certificate envelope in the return envelope for delivery to the returning officer in their home constituency or, in certain cases, the Canada Elections Commission.

Special ballots would not list the candidates but would simply provide a blank space for the voter to fill in with the name of a candidate or party. This would reduce the possibility of fraud and the administrative load involved in special voting and would allow people to vote in the first weeks of the campaign before the regular ballots are printed. Those who wish to vote by special ballot before the closing date for nominations, which we recommend be the twenty-first day before election day, could simply mark a special ballot for either a candidate or a party. The vote would be counted unless the candidate was not nominated or the party specified by the voter did not put forward a candidate in the constituency.

Recommendation 2.2.5

We recommend that

(a) **every voter who would find it more convenient to vote by special ballot be eligible to do so;**
(b) **three separate envelopes be issued with each special ballot: the first to preserve the secrecy of the ballot, the second to allow election officials to identify the voter and verify the voter's eligibility, and the third to allow delivery of the special ballot;**
(c) **special ballots take the form of blank ballots on which voters mark the name of a candidate or party;**
(d) **the Special Voting Rules be deleted from the Act; and**
(e) **the proxy vote be abolished.**

Obtaining a Special Ballot

Canadian voters do not have to sign an application when registering to vote. As a result, our voting system has not developed the procedures found in many other jurisdictions that rely on the use of the voter's signature on a permanent register to verify identity and safeguard the integrity of the vote. Our challenge is to develop voting procedures that achieve these purposes in the context of a different approach to voter registration.

U.S. voters are commonly allowed to apply for absentee ballots by mail, without having to appear in person before an election official. The integrity of the vote is protected, however, by checking the signature on the voter's application form against the voter's original registration card, either when the ballot is applied for or when the ballot is cast. This procedure has generally proved reliable, even in elections where a very high percentage of votes are cast by mail.

We have concluded that in Canada the best way to maintain the integrity of voting by special ballot is to require people to apply for the ballot in person and to provide satisfactory identification and a sample signature at that time. It would be up to the Canada Elections Commission to determine what constitutes satisfactory proof of identity. When voters transmit the special ballot back to the Commission or the returning officer, they would sign the certificate envelope; this signature could then be verified against the signature on file with the voter's application. If a voter applied for a special ballot at a returning office or designated government office outside his or her home constituency, the application would be sent by mail or facsimile to the home constituency to permit verification of the special ballot before the count.

An exception should be made for voters confined to home because of illness or disability. The returning officer should send a representative to the voter's home at least five days before election day. Alternatively, a spouse or close relative should be permitted to deliver a signed application, with the required identification, to an election office.

The special ballot would be available as soon as a constituency returning officer's office has opened officially after a writ has been issued. To assist in meeting the demand for special ballots, returning officers should delegate authority to certain members of their staff to receive applications and to issue special ballots. Special ballots should also be available at a returning officer's sub-offices, as well as at designated government offices in remote areas. The deadline for receiving a special ballot at an office of the returning officer in one's own constituency would be 6 p.m. local time on the fifth day before election day. As noted in Chapter 1 of this volume, special ballots would also be available at any returning officer's office in Canada and at embassies and other Canadian government offices abroad for voters away from their home constituency.

Voters should be able to register to vote and apply for the special ballot at the same time. This would accommodate voters who wish to vote by special ballot before enumeration has been completed or who apply to an election office other than their own. It corresponds to our proposal to allow voters who have not been enumerated to register at their ordinary polling station on election day.

In some U.S. states, political parties and candidates have become involved in encouraging voters to apply for special ballots, distributing application forms, and even delivering completed applications to election officials. This practice could lead to abuse and would not be workable in Canada because we do not have a permanent register with each voter's signature. To protect the security of the vote and limit the opportunities to

exert undue influence on voters, the role of parties and candidates should
be limited to giving voters information about voting by special ballot.

Recommendation 2.2.6

We recommend that

(a) voters be required to apply in person for a special ballot at
any returning officer's office or at other designated government offices in Canada or abroad;

(b) if a voter is unable to go to an election office because of illness or disability, the returning officer be allowed to accept
a signed application from the voter with suitable identification delivered by a member of the immediate family or
to send an election official to the voter's home to allow the
voter to apply for and tender a special ballot;

(c) where a voter is unable to provide a signature and indicate
his or her voting choice on the special ballot, a witnessed
mark constitute an acceptable signature, the witness be
allowed to complete the special ballot on the voter's instruction and the witness be sworn to secrecy;

(d) to qualify for a special ballot, voters be required to provide
satisfactory identification, as determined by the Canada
Elections Commission, and a signature, and attest that they
will not vote more than once; in addition, Canadians abroad
be required to certify that they have not voted in a foreign
national election since taking residence abroad;

(e) any election official or agent designated by the returning
officer or the Canada Elections Commission be authorized
to receive and process applications for special ballots and
thereafter issue special ballots;

(f) special ballots be available as soon as the returning officer's offices open at the beginning of an election campaign;

(g) voters be allowed to apply for a special ballot at any office
of the returning officer in their own constituency or designated government offices in remote areas up to 6 p.m. on the
fifth day before election day;

(h) voters away from their home constituency be allowed to
apply for a special ballot at an office of any returning officer or at embassies or other Canadian government offices
abroad provided that their application is received at the
office of the returning officer in their home constituency
by 6 p.m. eastern time on the fifth day before election day;

(i) the role of parties and candidates be limited to providing information about the special ballot; and

(j) the exercise of undue influence or violation of the secrecy of the vote be an offence under the *Canada Elections Act.*

Voting Procedures

Election day is the final day when voters can cast ballots using ordinary voting procedures. The deadline for the receipt of special ballots should be this day, when all votes must be counted by election officials with candidates' representatives present. Special ballots sent directly to constituencies shall be accepted until the close of polling stations in the constituency. In the case of special ballots returned to the Canada Elections Commission, the results must be forwarded to returning officers across the country and added to the count in each constituency. Receipt of special ballots by 6 p.m., eastern time, on election day would allow these procedures to be completed.

We propose this late date and time deliberately to give voters using the special ballot the greatest opportunity to exercise their franchise and have their vote counted. We recognize that some ballots may be received after this deadline and would thus be invalidated; but there is a trade-off between giving voters the opportunity to return their special ballots up to the times proposed on election day and the risk that their vote will be invalidated if not received by this deadline. This election day deadline is justified because votes must be counted and the results made available on election night. This is to ensure that Parliament can be convened as soon as necessary, especially in a time of political crisis.

We are aware that some U.S. states allow absentee ballots to be accepted after the polls close if they are postmarked on or before election day. Canada's system of government differs from that of the United States, however. Candidates elected in U.S. elections do not take office formally until a fixed date, usually about two months after the election. Therefore any changes to election outcomes a week or so after election day would not affect the legitimacy or conduct of the executive or legislative branches of government. This is not the case in Canada, where the election determines which party will be called upon to form a government.

If the deadline we recommend was challenged successfully by a voter whose special ballot envelope was postmarked on or before election day but arrived after the deadline, the only alternative would be to push back the deadline to a point where it would be reasonably certain that all ballots could be received in time for election day. But this would merely restrict the opportunity for voters to cast a vote using the special ballot. This is contrary to our objective of giving voters maximum opportunity to vote using the special ballot.

Recommendation 2.2.7

We recommend that

(a) voters who receive special ballots be responsible for ensuring that the ballot is delivered to the appropriate election office by the closing of the polls on election day for a special ballot sent directly to the voter's constituency and 6 p.m. eastern time for a special ballot sent to the Canada Elections Commission;

(b) voters who apply for a special ballot in their home constituency be able to tender a special ballot at any office of the returning officer in that constituency by delivering it in person; and

(c) any special ballot received after the deadline on election day not be opened, counted or considered valid, regardless of why it was not received on time.

Ensuring Integrity and Secrecy

Although the circumstances of voters using the special ballot will vary, there should be common procedures to protect the integrity and secrecy of the vote.

We cannot predict how many special ballots might be cast in each constituency; presumably voters would deliver their ballots over the course of a campaign, not all at once. Verification could thus be spread out as well. As special ballots were received, they would be checked against the voter's application to verify that the voter's signature and other particulars match the information on the certificate envelope. The sealed envelope should be set aside if no record of an application from the person named on the certificate envelope is on file, if the signatures do not match, or if the person was not registered to vote. On election day, the ballot should be ruled invalid if it does not pass any one of these tests. A special ballot that has been sent to the wrong constituency should be redirected if time permits.

Valid ballots should be kept in the sealed certificate envelope until 30 minutes after the close of polls on election day, again to ensure against double voting. The voters list for each polling station would identify voters who have applied for a special ballot. If a person who has received a special ballot seeks to vote on election day, he or she should be allowed to do so upon presentation of appropriate identification and signing a declaration promising not to vote more than once. In the absence of proper identification the voter could take an oath or make an affirmation as to her or his identity. This is the same procedure that applies to voters who seek to vote on election day but find that their name has already been crossed off the list for one reason or another.

The incidence of double voting in recent Canadian elections has been virtually non-existent; hence we expect that the process of checking special ballots against the poll book on election day would not be onerous. Once checking was completed, the secrecy envelopes would be removed from the certificate envelopes. The secrecy envelopes would have to be mixed together before opening so that no individual ballot could be identified.

When someone who has received a special ballot votes at an ordinary polling station, the DRO would advise the returning officer's office within 30 minutes of the close of the polls. The special ballot issued to that voter would then be invalidated. Because all special ballot applications would be made no later than the fifth day before election day (except for voters in hospitals outside their home constituency on election day), this system to protect against double voting would be highly effective.

We have designed the special ballot system to respond to concerns that the use of such ballots could lead to electoral fraud or double voting. The three envelopes are an essential part of that control. The envelope system also ensures the secrecy of the vote, because secrecy envelopes containing marked ballots would be separated from certificate envelopes bearing voters' names, addresses and signatures before the secrecy envelopes are opened. Ballots would not be counted until this procedure had been completed for all special ballots, whether at the Commission, for ballots counted centrally, or at the returning officer's office, for ballots counted in the constituency. The wide use of absentee voting in other jurisdictions shows that voters are satisfied that an envelope system does protect secrecy. In the provinces that use the postal ballot, no incidents of voting fraud have been reported.

The process could be abused if partisans or relatives pressure voters to use the special ballot to vote a particular way. We do not see this as a major problem; the number of cases where this could occur would likely be small, and, with only a very few exceptions, voters using a special ballot would be required to apply for it in person. The Act should make it clear, however, that it is an offence to exert undue influence over someone casting a special ballot or to violate the secrecy of their vote.

Votes cast at advance polls are reported separately from those cast on election day. We recommend that votes cast by special ballot also be reported separately. There is a legitimate interest in knowing how heavily this new form of voting is used.

Recommendation 2.2.8

We recommend that

(a) **a special ballot be invalid if the voter does not register by the deadline for the special ballot in the constituency in which the vote is cast, if the signature on the certificate envelope does not match the signature on the voter's application, or if the special ballot is not received by the deadline;**

(b) a person who seeks to vote on election day and whose name is on the list as having applied for a special ballot be allowed to vote upon production of satisfactory identification as prescribed by the Canada Elections Commission and upon signing a declaration promising not to vote more than once; in the absence of satisfactory identification, the voter be required to swear an oath or make an affirmation as to his or her identity and sign a declaration promising not to vote more than once; the DRO be required to notify the RO of that voter's name and the special ballot issued in that name be invalidated;

(c) certificate envelopes containing special ballots not be opened until 30 minutes after the close of polls on election day, so that any special ballots that duplicate votes cast in person on election day can be invalidated;

(d) if more than one special ballot is cast in the name of a voter, all these special ballots be ruled invalid;

(e) candidates be permitted to have scrutineers present on election day to validate special ballot envelopes and ensure that the count of special ballots is carried out fairly and accurately;

(f) votes by special ballot be recorded separately from ordinary votes in the returns for each constituency; and

(g) it be an offence to exercise undue pressure on someone casting a vote by special ballot or to violate the secrecy of a vote by special ballot.

Voting in the Returning Officer's Office

The special ballot would allow voters to tender a vote at the returning officer's office in their home constituency. This would simplify the process of voting at the returning officer's office, reduce the administrative burden, and extend the period when this form of voting can take place.

Under the Act, votes can be cast at the returning officer's office over a 21-day period prior to election day, except for Sundays and advance polling days. A double envelope procedure is used, requiring the returning officer or a deputy to fill out certificates and witness the voter's signature. Voters must give their reason for voting at the returning officer's office, and their names must be marked off the voters list before they can vote.

The returning officer's office must be open from noon to 6 p.m. and from 7 p.m. to 9 p.m. on each day that voting is permitted, regardless of whether there is a significant demand. Voting is not permitted at a returning officer's sub-office, even if it was established to serve a part of a constituency distant from the main office.

We heard many complaints about these rules during our hearings and in our symposiums on election organization for returning officers and party officials. At the same time, however, there was substantial support for the concept: in a questionnaire distributed at the symposiums, 95 per cent of participants agreed that voting at the returning officer's office should be permitted. Returning officers were concerned about the time and resources required, however, and many recommended that a deputy returning officer and poll clerk be hired specifically to receive such votes.

Voting at returning officers' offices has been increasing in urban areas where people can reach the office easily, but there is much less use of this vote in rural constituencies. Elections Canada data show that just over 100 000 votes were cast in this way at the 1988 election, or 0.7 per cent of total voter turnout. This figure had risen from 0.2 per cent at the 1979 election, when voting at the returning officer's office was permitted for the first time.

Applying for a special ballot would not depend on a voters list, thus permitting voters to apply for a ballot at the returning officer's office as soon as a writ was issued. Because applications would be accepted until the fifth day before election day, the number of days when a ballot was available from the returning officer's office would increase significantly.

The special ballot would also be easier to administer because any authorized person on the returning officer's staff would be entitled to process applications and check a voter's identification. Moreover, applications would take less time to process because the voters list would not have to be checked before a special ballot was issued; this would be done later.

The current restrictions on how and when people can vote at a returning officer's office could also be eliminated with the special ballot. Voters would be able to apply for a special ballot at any time the returning officer's office is open, but the returning officer would not be required to keep the office open just so people can vote. The prohibition on applying for a ballot at a returning officer's sub-office would also be eliminated.

Recommendation 2.2.9

We recommend that the use of special ballots replace the present procedures for voting in the returning officer's office.

SPECIAL BALLOT VOTING PROCEDURES
FOR SPECIFIED GROUPS

For two categories of voters, the special ballot would be the only way to vote: eligible voters living abroad, and voters away from their home constituency.

Voters Living Abroad

Most Canadians living abroad are now disfranchised. We propose that these voters be entitled to vote using the special ballot. When an election is called, the Canada Elections Commission would mail a special ballot to everyone enrolled on its register of non-resident voters. The voter would mark the ballot and return it to the Canada Elections Commission by 6 p.m. eastern time, on election day. In the case of voters with the Canadian forces, special arrangements could be made at each base or unit abroad to distribute ballots to eligible voters and to ensure that completed ballots are delivered back to the Canada Elections Commission. While some government offices abroad may offer to transmit ballots back to the Commission, responsibility for ensuring that their ballot is received in time to be counted would remain with voters.

The experience of the United States and other countries is that about 30 days are required to send ballots to voters outside the country and receive them back by mail. This means that a vote would be received by the deadline, even if the length of the election period were shortened from its current minimum of 50 days, as long as the register of voters was closed the day a writ was issued.

Names on the Commission's register of non-resident voters would be identified by home constituency. Special ballots would be verified and counted centrally and the results transmitted to the home constituency returning officer by the Commission. The counting would begin on a date to be fixed by the chief electoral officer, at the earliest on the fifth day before election day, and continue as special ballots were received. Signatures should not have to be checked in most cases, however, because Canadians voting from abroad would enter a unique voter number on the certificate envelope. This number, obtained upon registering on the register of non-resident voters, would not appear on any item in the ballot package sent by the Commission; a vote could therefore be deemed valid if the voter mailed it back with the correct voter registration number. In cases where the certificate envelope did not bear the voter's signature or the envelope was received after 6 p.m. on election day, the certificate envelope would be put aside unopened.

To expedite delivery to distant countries, the Canada Elections Commission could store ballot packages at Canadian embassies and other government offices. This is feasible because the special ballot procedure relies on blank ballots. We recommend, however, that the Canada Elections Commission attempt to send a list of candidates for each constituency to offices where special ballots would be available.

Recommendation 2.2.10

We recommend that

(a) **voters living abroad vote in their home constituency using the special ballot;**
(b) **special ballots be mailed to voters on the Commission's register of non-resident voters shortly after the writ is issued;**
(c) **ballots be returned to the Commission, verified and counted centrally and the results transmitted to home constituency returning officers;**
(d) **the chief electoral officer invite each registered party to appoint scrutineers for the count of special ballots;**

(e) counting of special ballots begin on a date to be fixed by the chief electoral officer, at the earliest on the fifth day before election day; and

(f) special ballot envelopes sent from abroad be verified by comparing the unique voter number on the certificate envelope against the number on the voter's registration; and that, in cases where the voter's signature is missing or the envelope is received after 6 p.m. on election day, the certificate envelope be put aside unopened.

Voters Away from Their Home Constituency

Canadian voters away from their home constituency, whether in Canada or abroad, would follow the same voting procedures. The differences for voters in Canada would be twofold: first, they would not be listed on a central register (with the exception of prisoners in federal institutions); unlike registered non-resident voters, the onus would be on them to register in person during the election period and apply to receive a special ballot.

Second, these voters away from their home constituency would have to return the special ballot to the office of the returning officer in their home constituency by the close of polls on election day. These voters would not be permitted to tender their ballot to the election official or designated agent from whom they receive the ballot since they are outside their home constituency. In some cases, especially for voters outside Canada, a designated agent might offer to assist the voter by returning the ballot by diplomatic bag or government courier. They would not be required to do so, however, and if they did so, responsibility for ensuring that the ballot was received by the deadline would remain with the voter.

We recognize that the deadlines are tight for those who apply at the last moment. We recommend that the deadline be close to election day to allow voters the greatest possible chance of registering and voting. The voter may have to make a special effort to return the ballot on time, such as sending it by courier rather than by mail. Given that voters would have at least 40 days to vote, if they left it too close to the deadline, they would do so at their own risk.

For voters incarcerated in federal institutions, Correctional Service Canada would give the Canada Elections Commission a certified list of qualified voters and their home constituencies at the time an election writ is issued. The Commission would send each voter on this list a special ballot which the voter would return directly to the Commission. These ballots would be counted centrally by the Commission and the result included with the count of the votes from voters on the register for non-resident voters and transmitted to returning officers in the appropriate constituencies.

Recommendation 2.2.11

We recommend that

(a) votes cast by Canadians who are away from their home constituency, whether in Canada or abroad, be returned to the
returning officer's office in their home constituency and be
counted along with the other special ballots cast in that constituency, except for votes cast by inmates registered on the
list provided to the Canada Elections Commission by
Correctional Service Canada;

(b) voters away from their home constituency be responsible for
delivering the ballot back to the home constituency by the
close of the polls on election day; and

(c) ballots cast by inmates in federal prisons who are registered on the central list provided to the Commission by
Correctional Service Canada be returned to the Canada Elections Commission by 6 p.m. on election day and be counted
centrally by the Commission and the results reported to
each constituency along with the votes of Canadians registered with the Commission as non-resident voters.

VOTERS WITH SPECIAL NEEDS

Many interveners at our hearings described how to improve access to the
vote for persons with disabilities or special needs. Several groups of voters
were identified, including persons with physical disabilities, people with
reading deficiencies or with a limited knowledge of English or French, and
people needing assistance to vote. We recommend a range of provisions to
meet their needs, consistent with our desire to ensure optimal access to the
electoral process for all Canadians.

Not every need can be anticipated, however. For this reason, we believe
that the Canada Elections Commission should be on the lookout for opportunities and take all reasonable steps to serve people with special needs. For
instance, returning officers should work with community groups before and
during the election period to identify means and develop ways to facilitate
access to the electoral process. Training for returning officers and election-day
officials should include information on serving voters with special needs. In
addition, to ensure that voters with special needs have every opportunity to
vote, enumerators should be instructed to report whether there are voters
with special needs who have asked to use specific voting provisions.

Voters who cannot go to a polling station, or who are reluctant to go
because of a disability, are now excluded from voting unless they meet the
stringent conditions for using a proxy vote. This would no longer be the case
under our proposals for a special ballot. Thus, in addition to the specific steps
we propose, people with special needs would be able to apply for a special
ballot as an alternative to voting on election day or at an advance poll.

Recommendation 2.2.12

We recommend that

(a) the training of returning officers and election officials include training on how to serve voters with special needs; and

(b) enumerators be instructed to report whether there are voters with special needs who have asked to use specific voting provisions.

Voters with Physical Disabilities

Elections Canada has a policy of providing barrier-free access to all its offices and polling places except where no means exist to provide such access to an ordinary polling station and no alternative location is available. There is no legal requirement, however, to provide barrier-free access to the returning officer's office or to ordinary polling stations. The Act does specify that level access be provided at one polling station in each urban constituency.

In the 1988 election, Elections Canada instructed returning officers that all advance polling stations, central polling places (places where two or more polling stations are located), and returning officers' offices and sub-offices must provide level access. Elections Canada required that ordinary polling stations provide such access whenever possible and instructed returning officers to provide reasons to any voter who asked why a poll was not accessible to people with physical disabilities.

As a result, polling stations were moved from traditional locations to accessible buildings, and temporary ramps were built to provide access at many polling stations. Elections Canada estimates that in 1988, 92 per cent of its 55 000 polling stations provided barrier-free access. However, in certain cases, returning officers in some remote communities reported polling stations as accessible without having inspected them personally. Testimony at our public hearings revealed cases where there was barrier-free access to the building but not to the rooms where the polls were located. These cases notwithstanding, Elections Canada has made substantial progress in providing barrier-free access; this improvement was acknowledged by interveners representing groups serving persons with disabilities. But the situation can and should be improved further.

One difficulty in ensuring barrier-free access for people with physical disabilities is that, as noted by the chief electoral officer in his 1991 report, Elections Canada has received an independent legal opinion that returning officers are neither agents nor employees of Elections Canada, although they are "public officers employed by the Crown". (Canada, Chief Electoral Officer 1991) As a consequence, the chief electoral officer's authority with respect to returning officers is not clearly established; although the chief electoral officer has powers to direct returning officers, the chief electoral officer lacks the necessary sanctions if the directives are not followed. To resolve this situation, the chief electoral officer's authority over returning officers must be clearly established. This matter is considered in detail in Chapter 3 of this volume.

Our overall goal is to ensure to the greatest extent possible that voters with disabilities and elderly people can vote on election day without making special arrangements. Several people who appeared before the Commission emphasized that it is unfair to oblige these voters to cast a ballot before election day, possibly missing important developments at the end of the campaign. It is also cumbersome to make voters go out of their way to vote at a special polling place by obtaining a transfer certificate from the returning officer of their constituency, rather than voting at their local polling station.

The United States enacted a federal law in 1984 (*Voting Access for the Elderly and Handicapped Act*) to promote barrier-free access for elderly people and persons with disabilities to registration facilities and polling places for federal elections. As a result, there was a marked increase in the number of polling places evaluated that were accessible – from 73 per cent in 1986 to close to 84 per cent in 1990. The major problem among those that remain inaccessible is the lack of a ramp at the front entrance or leading to the polling place.

Providing barrier-free access should be a matter of law rather than policy, and the Canada Elections Commission should be responsible along with its returning officers for implementing this provision. Barrier-free access should be mandatory for returning officers' offices and sub-offices, for advance polling stations, for central polling places containing five or more polling stations, and their polling booths. In addition, efforts should be made to ensure that central polling places and other polling stations are equipped with appropriate tables to allow persons with physical disabilities to vote conveniently and comfortably.

At ordinary polling stations, it may not be possible to provide barrier-free access at every location. In some areas, such as remote communities and older urban areas, suitable premises may not be available, even with the use of temporary ramps. In apartment buildings large enough to have their own polling station, it may make more sense to have residents vote inside the building than to move the polling station to a building with barrier-free access from the outside but located several blocks away.

Limited exceptions to the barrier-free access rule should therefore be permitted for ordinary polling stations; but in these cases the returning officer must be prepared to justify the location of the polling station.

Special attention should be paid to notifying voters with disabilities about where they can vote. The voter information card that we recommend be given to voters when they are enumerated or registered in other ways should indicate whether the voter's polling station has barrier-free access. Where it does not, voters should be able to transfer their names to alternative polling stations with such access, either by a request to the enumerator or revising officer, or by telephoning the returning officer's office.

This procedure would be simpler than the transfer certificates now provided for under the Act, which would no longer be needed.

During our hearings it was suggested that in addition to informing individual voters, returning officers should also be required to publish lists of polling stations without barrier-free access. In view of our other recommendations, we believe that this proposal is not needed and would result in unnecessary costs.

The special ballot would give voters with disabilities an alternative means of voting. In exceptional cases, a voter confined to home should be able to ask that an election official come to the house to enable the voter to apply for and tender a special ballot. The request in this case would have to be made no later than the fifth day before election day, and the returning officer should not have to comply if the request appears frivolous or if it would be unreasonably difficult to fulfil.

A final assurance of access would be to permit election officials to take the ballot box outside the polling station to enable anyone who cannot enter to vote. This practice, known as 'curbside voting', takes place now, even though it is technically illegal. It should be seen as a last resort for cases where a voter inadvertently goes to a polling station without barrier-free access, where a polling station designated accessible proves not to be accessible, or where there is no accessible alternative place to vote. This is already the practice in several jurisdictions, including Ontario, Manitoba and the Yukon.

Recommendation 2.2.13

We recommend that

(a) the Canada Elections Commission be responsible, along with local returning officers, for ensuring access to the vote for voters with physical disabilities;

(b) barrier-free access be available at all ordinary polling stations and their polling booths except where no suitable premises exist and ramps cannot be built; and that barrier-free access be available to the returning officer's office and sub-offices and all advance polling stations and their polling booths;

(c) if barrier-free access is not provided at a polling station, the returning officer be required to justify his or her decision to locate the poll at that place;

(d) the voter information card given to voters indicate whether their ordinary polling station has barrier-free access and provide the telephone number of the returning officer, in both cases using international symbols;

(e) if barrier-free access is not provided at a polling station, voters be able to transfer their names to the voters list for a polling station that is accessible, through a simple request to the enumerator or to the returning officer;

(f) the system of transfer certificates be abolished; and

(g) election officials be permitted to take the ballot box to a voter outside the polling station if barrier-free access is not available.

Voters with Reading Deficiencies

An estimated 4.5 million Canadians, or one quarter of the adult population, are functionally illiterate. Voters who cannot read or whose reading comprehension is poor will obviously have difficulties finding out about the electoral process and casting a vote.

People who discussed literacy problems at our hearings focused on the need to provide non-written forms of communication about the election before the campaign begins, during the election period, and on election day. The use of the telephone, international symbols, photographs, videos, and material written in plain English or French were all suggested as means of helping people with reading deficiencies to participate in the electoral process.

Most people with reading difficulties can use the telephone and can understand telephone numbers on written material if the numbers are prominent and accompanied by a telephone symbol. Written material about the electoral process is widely available during elections; voters who have difficulty with written material should have access to a free telephone service that provides the same information.

Finding the returning officer's office or a polling station can be difficult for someone who cannot read. The Canada Elections Commission should publicize its logo and use it prominently during elections to assist people in identifying election offices and polling stations.

The ballot contains the name of each candidate along with the candidate's party affiliation in English and French. Apart from the space to mark a vote, the rest of the ballot is black. To help people who cannot read, the ballot should show the party's initials or logo next to the name of each candidate representing a party. This proposal was strongly supported at our hearings and was approved by almost 80 per cent of the local party officials we surveyed.

Parties' initials or logos used on ballots should be in a standard form for each party and should be subject to approval by the Canada Elections Commission at the time the party is registered or allowed to be identified on the ballot. Any changes in a party's initials or logo would also have to be submitted to the Commission, which could request changes if they were similar to ones already registered for another party. To avoid disputes over the use of unofficial logos, we recommend that independent candidates not be permitted to use a logo on the ballot.

Several interveners suggested photographs of candidates on the ballot or on a poster at each polling station. We prefer the use of posters, as is the current practice in the Northwest Territories. Posters are less expensive and easier to produce than ballots with photographs and offer better quality reproduction; photos would also be much larger than they could be on a ballot. Posters should show the name and photograph of each candidate in the constituency and the name and logo of the party if applicable. Posters should also be in the form of a ballot and displayed at every polling station and advance polling station, as well as in the office of the returning officer.

To be fair to all candidates, there must be clear rules about when and how candidates' photos are to be submitted. Some interveners suggested that candidates might feel that the use of photographs could harm them electorally; this might be the case in certain circumstances. We recommend that candidates be free to choose whether to submit a photograph for the poster. Those who wish to do so should be required to submit a photograph upon filing their nomination papers.

Recommendation 2.2.14

We recommend that

(a) the Canada Elections Commission publicize its logo and use it prominently during election periods to assist people in identifying election offices and polling stations;

(b) the ballot include a party's initials or logo next to the name of each candidate representing a party that is registered or allowed to be identified on the ballot;

(c) parties' initials or logos used on ballots be in a standard form for each party and subject to approval by the Commission;

(d) logos not appear beside the names of independent candidates;

(e) a poster in the form of a ballot be displayed at every polling station, advance poll, and returning officer's office showing the name and photograph of candidates in the constituency and the name and logo (or initials) of their parties (if authorized to be identified on the ballot); and

(f) candidates who wish their photograph to be used on the poster be required to submit it upon filing their nomination documents.

Voters with Language Difficulties

Voters who have difficulty understanding English or French may face problems similar to those people who cannot read. Elections Canada publishes material about the electoral process in many languages, but the signs and forms used at polling stations contain only the two official languages. Interpreters are seldom used, and the manual for returning officers makes no mention of the needs of voters that speak neither English nor French.

It was suggested at the hearings that election material and ballots be available in different languages in multilingual areas. We have decided not to recommend a multilingual ballot, given the potential for confusion and the fact that French and English are Canada's official languages. The use of party logos or initials on ballots and posters should assist voters of all languages.

Nonetheless, the need for better communication with voters who speak neither English nor French should be recognized. For instance, more effective registration of Aboriginal people and better access to the vote could be achieved by appointing more Aboriginal election officials. Appointing multilingual election officials and providing election information in other languages in areas where members of ethno-cultural communities are concentrated could also help to meet this objective. Our proposals would give returning officers greater latitude in appointing election-day officials, particularly poll clerks. The best means of assisting people with difficulties communicating in English or French is to have a deputy returning officer or poll clerk who speaks their language. Returning officers in several urban areas already follow this practice, and it is one that should be encouraged. Where polling stations are located in central polling places, it should be possible to provide service in several languages by choosing election-day officials who speak the languages used in the area or by making greater use of interpreters if needed.

Recommendation 2.2.15

We recommend that where polling divisions have a concentration of voters from a language group other than English or French, the returning officer assign to the polling stations election-day officials able to speak that language, or when that is not possible, interpreters be used.

Persons Needing Assistance to Vote

The Act allows voters to have assistance to vote if they cannot read or are unable to vote without help because of a physical disability. The voter must take an oath of incapacity to vote, and the friend or relative assisting the voter to mark the ballot must also take an oath. Alternatively, the voter may have the deputy returning officer mark the ballot, but this must take place in the presence of the poll clerk and any candidates' agents who are present. Apart from election officials, no one may assist more than one voter at any election.

These rules and the need to take an oath to obtain assistance may deter some people from voting. The rule allowing a relative to help only one person can also be restrictive. People seeking assistance to vote should not be required to swear an oath. The procedure does not affect the integrity of the vote and is potentially embarrassing to those who must request it.

Friends or relatives who wish to assist a voter should be required to sign a declaration, undertaking to preserve the secrecy of the vote and not to coerce the voter. The name of a person who assists a voter should be recorded in the poll book as is the current practice. A person should be able to assist only one voter per election, except in the case of members of the immediate family.

The law allows a deputy returning officer to assist a voter, but specifies that this be done in the presence of the poll clerk and candidates' representatives. These people are sworn to secrecy, but in fact the vote is not truly secret if it is witnessed by as many as half a dozen people.

This procedure fills a need for people who do not have the assistance of a friend or relative to help them vote and should therefore be continued. However, we do not see the need for additional witnesses; it is sufficient to have the deputy returning officer and poll clerk assist the voter. This would also ensure better protection for the secrecy of the vote.

Recommendation 2.2.16

We recommend that

(a) **voters not be required to swear an oath to obtain assistance to vote;**
(b) **a friend or relative who assists a voter be required to sign a declaration, in the form established by the Commission, to keep the ballot secret and not to coerce the voter and have her or his name recorded in the poll book;**
(c) **no person assist more than one voter at an election, except for an election official or a person assisting members of his or her immediate family; and**
(d) **a voter be entitled to have the assistance of a deputy returning officer in the presence of the poll clerk only.**

Voting in Hospitals

The Act takes very little account of the special needs of voters temporarily or permanently in hospitals or other chronic care institutions. Polling stations can be established, but are not required by law, in chronic care institutions and homes for the aged but not in active treatment hospitals except in wings reserved for chronic care patients; the rules of ordinary residence, requiring a person enumerated in a hospital to have been there at least 10 days, exclude anyone who has recently entered hospital. Voters in active treatment hospitals can vote only via proxy.

Our proposals would provide people in all hospitals and chronic care institutions with the opportunity to vote. Polling stations should be set up in any hospital or institution where people may have difficulty getting out to vote, and should be designated as mobile polls so that the hours of voting can be set by the returning officer in consultation with the institution. Election officials could then close the poll after everyone who wishes to vote has done so. Returning officers should determine the type of poll or other arrangements needed for each institution. They should work out these plans with the institution's administration well in advance of the election. This point was emphasized at our hearings by a number of interveners. The Act should continue to allow bedside voting for people who find it difficult to leave their room. Voters in a hospital in their constituency who did not get on the voters list in their constituency before entering hospital should be able to register and vote at the mobile polling station, as at any other poll.

Voters admitted to hospital can be excluded from voting if the hospital is not in their own constituency, they are in the hospital on election day, and they were admitted after the deadline for obtaining the special ballot. Even if they are registered to vote, they cannot obtain a special ballot after the deadline. This is a common situation for persons admitted to acute treatment or obstetrics hospitals because these institutions are regional rather than local facilities. Manitoba has overcome this problem: in that province, patients in these institutions are able to vote because a group of election officials, along with representatives of parties, establish polling facilities in each hospital and enable voters to register and vote with the equivalent of our proposed special ballot.

We propose a similar approach. Voters in such hospitals would be able to register and vote by special ballot on election day and to tender their vote to the deputy returning officer responsible for the hospital polling station. These polling stations would be created by returning officers for constituencies where such hospitals were located. Although this would be an exception to our deadline for registration and application for the special ballot, it is justified by the circumstance in which these voters find themselves. This exception also does not threaten the integrity of the vote. In these cases, the verification procedures for the special ballot would simply require that the application form be transmitted through facsimile or verified by telephone with the returning officer concerned on election day. Moreover, registration and special ballot applications would be forwarded to each returning officer so that the documents would be retained in the case of a contested election result. Voters who are in a hospital that is in their polling division and are not already registered could register on election day, in the same way as all voters, and vote via regular ballot.

At the close of the polls, the deputy returning officer and poll clerk, in the presence of the party representatives, would count the vote from the special ballots and transmit the count to the Canada Elections Commission, which would transmit the results of the special ballot, along with those of other centrally counted ballots, to each returning officer. This procedure is required to protect the secrecy of the vote.

Recommendation 2.2.17

We recommend that

(a) returning officers ensure that voting procedures are accessible in any hospital or institution where people may have difficulty getting out to vote at an ordinary polling station;
(b) mobile polling stations be used in hospitals and similar institutions and be open long enough that everyone in the institution who wishes to vote can do so;
(c) bedside voting continue to be permitted in any institution served by a regular or mobile poll;
(d) arrangements for voting in hospitals and institutions be worked out in advance between the returning officer for the area and the institution's administration;
(e) voters in a hospital not in their constituency on election day be permitted to register and vote by special ballot on election day;
(f) returning officers establish adequate polling facilities for each hospital in their constituency for registering and providing special ballots to voters;
(g) persons voting in this manner tender their ballots to the deputy returning officer in charge of the polling station; and
(h) the vote be counted at this polling station at the close of the poll and the results be transmitted to the Canada Elections Commission, which will communicate them to the constituency.

Voters with Visual Impairments

A template that fits over the ballot, developed by Elections Canada in co-operation with the Canadian National Institute for the Blind, permits people with visual impairments to cast a secret ballot without assistance. Such a template is available at every polling station, but its use is not provided for in the Act. In Quebec, Manitoba, Saskatchewan and Alberta, the provincial election law provides for such a template.

Recommendation 2.2.18

We recommend that the Act provide for the use of a template at every polling station for voting by persons with visual impairments.

Voters with Hearing Impairments

Hearing-impaired and deaf voters face several obstacles to participating in the electoral process. They may not hear the doorbell when enumerators call, and they may have difficulty communicating with the office of the local returning officer. Moreover, about 60 per cent of deaf Canadians are functionally illiterate. (Canadian Association of the Deaf, Brief 1990)*

During our hearings several groups asked that Elections Canada make sign-language interpreters available to assist people with hearing impairments in voting. We do not believe there is enough demand for this service to justify its general availability; returning officers should be encouraged to work with groups representing deaf and hearing-impaired people, however, and to provide interpretation at locations where there are concentrations of deaf or hearing-impaired voters. People with impaired hearing would of course have the same rights as other voters to assistance in voting, to use advance voting and to use the special ballot.

Recommendation 2.2.19

We recommend that returning officers work with groups representing deaf and hearing-impaired persons in their constituency to establish whether and how sign-language interpreters should be provided to help with voting or to provide other assistance that may be required by voters with hearing impairments where warranted.

Voters in Remote and Isolated Areas

The *Canada Elections Act* makes almost no special provisions for voters in remote and isolated areas, despite conditions that can have a dramatic effect on access to the vote. One witness told us that her party had rushed voters from the airport to the returning officer's office in Yellowknife while they were between planes because there was no other way for them to vote before election day. In Newfoundland, a returning officer from the riding of Burin–St. George's estimated that it would take a voter 48 hours to travel from the far end of her constituency and back in order to vote at the returning officer's office before election day. The Act does not permit voting at a returning officer's sub-office, even in a large constituency.

Several constituencies in different parts of the country have long distances, transportation and communication difficulties, and isolated communities in common; the difficulties are compounded when election procedures are inflexible and not suited to their needs. Our proposals are designed to make election procedures more flexible; further refinements are needed for constituencies designated as remote and isolated. The aim is to make access to the vote in remote areas correspond as much as possible to conditions in more populated areas, while making it easier for returning officers to conduct an election within the shorter campaign period we recommend.

---

* Briefs submitted to the Royal Commission are identified in the text only. They are not listed in the list of references at the end of this volume.

At our hearings, party and election officials from remote constituencies pointed to the difficulty of conducting an election if the campaign period were less than its current length of 50 days. We recognize their concern, but we believe it should be met by making election procedures in remote constituencies more flexible rather than by retaining an election period that most Canadians consider too long. In addition, we propose that returning officers be permitted to start organizing for an election before a writ is issued. This should be of significant help in preparing for an election in remote constituencies.

Definition of Remote Constituencies

Schedule III of the *Canada Elections Act* lists 25 constituencies that receive special treatment for proxy voting because of their size or inaccessibility: five in Newfoundland, two in Quebec, four in Ontario, six in the Prairies, five in British Columbia, one in the Yukon, and two in the Northwest Territories. Voters in these constituencies can apply for a proxy vote through the deputy returning officer for their poll as well as through the returning officer's office. This procedure can also be extended to remote parts of other constituencies designated by the chief electoral officer.

With the elimination of proxy voting, the special provisions for Schedule III constituencies would no longer apply. There would still be a need, however, to define remote and isolated constituencies for purposes of election administration. The list of remote constituencies established in the new Act should be subject to change by regulation. A proposed list is shown in Table 2.2, corresponding to the constituencies listed in Schedule III. The new Act should contain an initial list, but changes in the list of remote constituencies would be determined by the Canada Elections Commission and subject to review by the House of Commons.

Recommendation 2.2.20

We recommend that remote constituencies where special provisions for voting apply be designated in an appendix to the *Canada Elections Act* but be subject to change by regulation.

Voting Procedures in Remote Constituencies

Most people in remote constituencies live in towns or villages where the process of ordinary voting would be similar to that in more populated areas. The necessary changes affect mainly smaller communities and voters living in hamlets.

Our proposals for advance voting would allow returning officers in remote constituencies to provide advance polls in communities now too small to be served and to organize mobile advance polls to serve people in very isolated areas. People would be able to apply for a special ballot at any advance polling station; this was requested by a number of interveners from northern constituencies. In smaller communities voters would also be entitled to apply for a special ballot through the deputy returning officer for their polling division. This would be an alternative to voting at an advance poll and would avoid the cost of travelling to the returning officer's office.

Table 2.2
Proposed list of remote constituencies

Ontario	**Alberta**
Cochrane–Superior	Athabasca
Kenora–Rainy River	Peace River
Thunder Bay–Nipigon	Yellowhead
Timiskaming	
	Newfoundland
Quebec	Bonavista–Trinity–Conception
Abitibi	Burin–St. George's
Manicouagan	Gander–Grand Falls
	Humber–St. Barbe–Baie Verte
British Columbia	Labrador
Cariboo–Chilcotin	
North Island–Powell River	**Yukon**
Prince George–Bulkley Valley	Yukon
Prince George–Peace River	
Skeena	**Northwest Territories**
	Nunatsiaq
Manitoba	Western Arctic
Churchill	
Saskatchewan	
The Battlefords–Meadow Lake	
Prince Albert–Churchill River	

People living far from the returning officer's office may have difficulty applying for a special ballot. We therefore recommend that returning officers in remote constituencies designate additional places where people can apply for a special ballot, such as government offices or RCMP detachments. Special ballots would also be available from any sub-office of the returning officer.

In urban areas, voters can count on a special ballot being delivered to the returning officer by mail within two or three days. In remote constituencies, however, the rule requiring voters to return special ballots to the returning officer's office by election day may not always be workable. If delivery to that office within the allotted time is problematic, voters in remote ridings should be permitted to tender a ballot to the deputy returning officer or poll clerk for their polling division. These special ballots should be verified, then counted along with the ordinary votes on election day.

For the Yukon territorial elections, no polling station is required in remote communities where there are fewer than 25 registered voters. These voters use a postal ballot. This practice should be followed in federal elections as well. In polling divisions with fewer than 25 registered voters, everyone should vote by special ballot; the enumerator for the poll should act as an election official, issuing and receiving special ballots up to 6 p.m. the fifth day before election day. On election day these ballots should be verified and counted in the presence of the candidates' representatives or, if they are unavailable, at least two voters called in to act as witnesses.

There may be exceptional circumstances where it is not possible to communicate with a voter except by telephone, radio or facsimile. In these cases a returning officer should be able to take the voter's vote or authorize the deputy returning officer to do so by one of these means and register it as a special ballot. The procedure should be recorded in the poll book. We see this as a provision of last resort, since the vote would be known to the returning officer; it would remain a secret ballot, however, since the returning officer is bound by oath to keep it confidential. This procedure is similar to the situation when a deputy returning officer and a poll clerk give assistance to a voter. For such a vote to be accepted, the Act should require that the returning officer be satisfied as to the voter's identity.

Recommendation 2.2.21

We recommend that

(a) voters in remote constituencies and in other remote areas designated by the Canada Elections Commission be able to obtain a special ballot through local election officials or through a designated government office in their area;

(b) if it would be difficult to deliver a special ballot to the election office by election day, voters in remote constituencies be permitted to tender ballots to the deputy returning officer so that they can be counted with the votes for that poll on election day; and

(c) a returning officer be able to take a voter's vote or authorize the deputy returning officer to do so by telephone, radio or facsimile and to register it as a special ballot if there are no other means of taking the vote and if the returning officer is satisfied as to the voter's identity; and that a record of such a vote be entered in the poll book.

Administrative Issues
The widespread use of telephones and facsimile machines has made it easier to organize election campaigns in remote areas, and any obstacles to their use should be removed from the Act. For isolated polling divisions, even the distribution of ballots should be permitted by facsimile; the potential for election fraud is limited in small villages where every voter is known to election officials.

The Act establishes uniform hours of operation for all polling stations. This requirement may be too rigid for some polling divisions in remote constituencies with very few voters. In these cases, the returning officer should be able to close the polling station before the official end of polling, provided that voters could still tender a special ballot to the deputy returning officer up until the normal poll closing time.

Recommendation 2.2.22

We recommend that

(a) returning officers in remote areas be allowed to distribute election documents by facsimile where this is required to serve polling stations in isolated areas; and
(b) returning officers be allowed to designate polling stations in isolated areas as mobile polls and to vary the hours of voting at these polls, provided that voters and candidates are told in advance.

Changing Communication Technologies

Communication technologies have been changing rapidly, and the pace of change has been accelerating. The widespread introduction and use of facsimile machines is a good example. The *Canada Elections Act* must not impede the appropriate use of new technologies in the electoral process as they become available; this will help to ensure that the voting process remain user-friendly and cost-effective. Specific developments in communication technologies may be difficult to anticipate, however. The Act should not freeze voting and other election procedures at the level allowed by current technologies; but at the same time the integrity of the electoral system must be maintained. The *Canada Elections Act* should therefore authorize the Canada Elections Commission to introduce new means of communicating election documents, including ballots, by regulation under the procedures we recommended in Volume 1, Chapter 7.

Recommendation 2.2.23

We recommend that the *Canada Elections Act* authorize the Canada Elections Commission to introduce new means of communicating election documents as these means become available and that such changes be introduced through regulation.

3

ADMINISTERING THE VOTE

THE ELECTION PERIOD

O<small>NE OF THE STRONGEST</small> messages we received at our hearings was that Canadian election campaigns are too long. By a margin of six to one, interveners favoured shortening the election period. Shorter campaigns were also identified as a major benefit of adopting a central register of voters.

Interveners also proposed that elections be held at fixed intervals – for example, on a set date every four years. Some suggested this would be fairer because it would remove the governing party's potential advantage in choosing an election date. Other interveners suggested that holding elections on fixed dates would allow more time to train enumerators and to carry out enumeration and other election preparations.

The constitution provides for a fixed maximum term for the House of Commons. The *Canadian Charter of Rights and Freedoms* stipulates that "no House of Commons ... shall continue for longer than five years from the date fixed for the return of the writs at a general election of its members".[1] Once five years have elapsed Parliament is dissolved and a date must be set for an election (although neither the constitution nor the *Canada Elections Act* stipulates the maximum duration of the campaign). An election may be called earlier, however, on the recommendation of the prime minister. In addition, based on constitutional convention, a defeat in the House of Commons on a motion of non-confidence usually results in an election being called. These provisions are shared by other parliamentary democracies, although in some cases the maximum term is shorter. For example, in both Australia and New Zealand, the House of Representatives must be dissolved after three years have elapsed (although, as in Canada, an earlier dissolution is possible). A study of 83 parliaments showed that 47 lower (or only) chambers had a maximum term of five years and 26 had a maximum term of four years. (Inter-Parliamentary Union 1986)

In contrast, the legislatures in a number of non-parliamentary systems have fixed terms: elections are held at fixed intervals and cannot be called earlier or later than a set date. As a rule, these systems are characterized by the separation of powers; the executive is not chosen by the legislature and cannot (with rare exceptions, such as impeachment) be removed by a vote of its members. The United States has the oldest – and to Canadians, the best-known – form of government based on these principles.

A fixed term for the House of Commons would diminish the potential advantage to the governing party of choosing the most opportune moment to call an election and would be fairer to all political parties. A government would not be able to call an election well before its term was up – for example, because of its favourable standing in the polls or the weak condition of opposition parties. Such snap elections have not been common at the federal level (where the average term of a government since 1945 has been 3.1 years), but they have occurred on occasion in the provinces during recent decades. In some cases, this has led to a different result from the one expected!

This being said, the proposal for fixed terms presents several major problems. First, the issue raises constitutional considerations. It might be possible to adopt fixed dates for federal elections and retain the constitutional principle that defeat on a motion of non-confidence leads to a government's resignation, but the result could well be an unsatisfactory hybrid. If a government fell, an election would have to be held earlier than the fixed date. (And this would be a more likely event in the case of minority governments.) In addition, a government could take steps to engineer its own defeat in the House of Commons if it judged that the timing of an election would serve its interests. To implement a system of fixed terms with no exceptions, a constitutional restructuring of our federal legislative and executive institutions would be required. Even if agreement on the necessary amendments could be achieved, it is not at all certain that this would lead to more responsive government. In fact, the opposite might occur. At present, the possibility that a government might be overturned by a vote in the House of Commons helps secure accountability. This is particularly the case during periods of political turbulence and minority governments – as during the period between 1962 and 1968, when four general elections were held. With a fixed term, governments could seek to deflect political pressures and wait for the verdict of voters.

A further difficulty is that fixed-date elections would change significantly the length and nature of election campaigns. At present, candidates may be selected and parties begin preparations before an election is called. But the campaign does not start in earnest until the writs are issued. During this relatively short period, the election expenses of parties and candidates are subject to limits that affirm the principle of fairness in electoral competition.

In practice, at least in part because the date of the next election is always known, campaigns last much longer in the United States. Presidential campaigns are often launched 18 months or more before election day, and commentators agree that many members of the House of Representatives, who have a two-year term, never really stop campaigning. In the absence of spending limits, except for presidential campaigns, candidates' expenses are forced upward, and the time devoted to fund raising also rises. Such developments might well follow the adoption of fixed-date elections in Canada. If they did, the objective of our election spending limits would be thwarted if those with more resources spent freely during the weeks or months when campaigning was under way but an election had not actually been called. Paradoxically, adopting fixed terms could lead to longer, not shorter campaigns. Given their support for election spending limits (see Volume 1, Chapter 6), Canadians would not likely welcome this result. Rather, the evidence indicates clearly that they favour shorter election campaigns.

The major reason offered for shorter campaigns was that Canadians are over-exposed to politics and lose interest as a result. Shorter campaigns would also reduce the cost of election administration and campaigning and would make it easier to mobilize volunteers. Several interveners noted that provincial campaigns are much shorter (see Table 3.1).

Opposition to shortening the campaign came mainly from people in very large constituencies where the logistics of organizing an election would make a shorter campaign difficult. Canada's unpredictable climate and the time needed for party leaders to campaign across the country were also offered as reasons for longer campaigns. Representatives of some smaller parties said that they did not have enough campaign workers to accomplish everything that needs to be done for an election within the limits of a shorter campaign period.

Table 3.1
Federal, provincial and territorial campaign periods
(days)

Jurisdiction	Minimum campaign period	Maximum campaign period	Three most recent campaigns[a]
Newfoundland	21	None	22, 22 and 22
Prince Edward Island[b]	26	32	28, 28 and 28
Saskatchewan[b]	29	34	30, 31 and 31
Alberta	29	29	29, 29 and 29
British Columbia	29	29	38, 29 and 29
Yukon[b]	31	None	31 and 31
Manitoba[b]	35	50	36, 36 and 48
New Brunswick[b]	35	45	39, 41 and 45
Nova Scotia[b]	36	None	40, 40 and 39
Ontario[b]	37	74	39, 41 and 37
Quebec[c]	47	53	33, 41 and 48
Northwest Territories[b]	45	53	63, 61 and 50
Canada	50	None	66, 57 and 52

Source: Royal Commission Research Branch.

[a]In chronological order (last entry refers to most recent election). For example, the campaign period for the last federal election (in 1988) was 52 days; in 1984 the campaign period was 57 days and in 1980 it was 66 days.

[b]Provinces that conduct enumeration after the writs for an election have been issued.

[c]Quebec may conduct revisions annually. If the writs are issued before June 30 following the preparation of the voters list, the minimum and maximum periods are 36 and 42 days respectively.

The *Canada Elections Act* provides for a minimum of 50 days between the day the writs are issued and election day; there is no maximum. Before 1982 there was no minimum, and campaigns averaged about 60 days.

Provincial and territorial election procedures are similar to those used federally, and seven provinces have comparable enumeration systems. Yet the average duration of 35 recent provincial and territorial campaigns was 36 days, compared to an average of 58 days for the last three federal elections. Provincial and territorial elections are no doubt easier to administer because constituencies are smaller in size and number. But even in Ontario, where conditions closely parallel those in federal elections, the election period is about 10 days shorter than the federal minimum period.

A shorter campaign would help to maintain voters' interest and improve voter turnout. The experience of the provinces has convinced us that the election period can be shortened substantially, even without a central voters register. Changes in technology and communication have accelerated campaign processes; but the media and the parties are forced to follow the pace of the election administration apparatus, with no evident benefit to the voter. Means exist even in remote ridings to speed up the conduct of elections, particularly with the growing availability of facsimile machines.

The length of the election period is determined largely by procedures and deadlines in the *Canada Elections Act*, particularly with respect to enumeration and revision of voters lists. The changes we recommend would shorten the enumeration process and make it more effective. Elections Canada has determined that the election period could be shortened to as little as 39 days with the present enumeration system, but warns that this goal may not be attainable the first time new procedures are introduced.

We conclude that the campaign period can be shortened to a minimum of 40 days, if enumeration is streamlined along the lines we recommend and if the revision process is linked more closely to enumeration (see Table 3.2). The key to achieving this goal is ensuring that returning officers are in place and do most of their preparation well before an election is called. We have therefore recommended that the appointment process for returning officers be changed and that these officials be charged with and compensated for performing certain tasks between elections as well as during the election period.

No radical change in procedures is needed to shorten the campaign to 40 days. The deadline for the official nomination of candidates would have to be changed, however. This deadline is now 28 days before voting day; it should be set at 21 days before election day to give constituency associations time to nominate a candidate if they have not done so before an election is called.

A 40-day campaign using enumeration is close to the minimum that could be achieved with a more flexible system of voter registration. The Canada Elections Commission would have to mail special ballots to voters living abroad a minimum of 30 days before election day if they were to be received and returned on time. And it would be difficult to run an election in urban Canada in less than 35 days using a central voters register without sacrificing the time needed for revising the list, or to run an election in large or remote constituencies in less than 35 days.

Table 3.2
Comparative timetable of present and recommended systems
(days prior to voting day)

	Issue of the writs	Appointment of enumerators	Enumeration begins	Enumeration ends	Preliminary voters lists ready	Close of nominations	Election day
Present schedule	Day 50	Day 45–39[a]	Day 38	Day 32	Day 25	Day 28	Day 0
Recommendation (40 days)	Day 40	Day 40–33[b]	Day 34[c]	Day 28	Day 26	Day 21	Day 0

Source: Royal Commission Research Branch.

Note: Election campaign schedules are counted backward from the election, with the day of the vote as day 0. Thus, for example, setting the issue of the writs at day 50 means the writs must be issued 50 days before voting day.

[a]Candidates have up to day 45 to nominate enumerators; appointments cannot be made until this deadline has passed, even if candidates do not nominate sufficient enumerators.

[b]Parties would be consulted and asked to nominate enumerators before the writs are issued; the returning officer could recruit enumerators before the writs are issued as well as accepting these nominations; appointment of enumerators could be made or confirmed as soon as the writs are issued.

[c]This suggested enumeration period is included here only for illustration and is not part of our recommendations; the Canada Elections Commission would determine this period.

There is no maximum period for a federal election. This gives a government some flexibility in choosing an election date, but it could frustrate the objective of shortening the campaign. A longer election period also affects candidates and political parties because their spending limits remain the same no matter how long the campaign is. Some flexibility in setting an election date is reasonable, for example, if an election is unexpected or occurs in winter, but a maximum period is still required to achieve the goal of shorter campaigns.

Recommendation 2.3.1

We recommend that

(a) **the minimum election period be 40 days and the maximum 47 days; and**
(b) **the deadline for official nominations be 21 days before election day.**

ELECTION DAY

Three provinces and the territories hold elections on Mondays; no province uses Sunday or Saturday. Federal elections are held on Mondays, except for federal or provincial holidays, in which case the election is held on the Tuesday.

We gave serious consideration to changing election day to Sunday. Some 50 interveners discussed the issue at our hearings, with those in favour outnumbering those against by a margin of three to two.

Supporters of Sunday voting argued that the change would increase turnout, because most Canadians do not work on Sunday, and would eliminate line-ups and delays at the polls that occur when people vote after finishing work. It would also be easier to use public buildings for polling stations and to recruit election-day officials and party workers. In addition, it could be argued that the change would be in line with changes in attitudes among many Canadians, as reflected in the increased acceptance of shopping and other non-traditional activities on Sunday.

Opponents maintained that Sunday voting would reduce turnout and that most Canadians would oppose such a change. They voiced strong concerns about respect for religious beliefs and argued that Sunday is a day of rest, a day set aside for people to spend with their families; it should not be used for elections.

Turnout tends to be higher in countries that hold elections on Sunday, such as France and Germany. Other variables are also at work, but the European experience does suggest that holding elections on a Sunday would likely increase participation in Canadian elections as well.

Our research showed clearly, however, that Canadians are not ready to accept a move to Sunday voting. Our survey of constituency association presidents revealed that 65 per cent opposed holding elections on Sunday. (Carty 1991a RC) In a national polling study conducted in the summer of 1990, more than 70 per cent of respondents expressing an opinion thought that Sunday voting was a bad idea. Asked for an opinion, 52 per cent of the overall sample disapproved of holding federal elections on Sunday, while 39 per cent approved. In Quebec, where municipal elections are held on Sunday, 50 per cent approved of Sunday elections and 40 per cent disapproved; in other provinces the rate of disapproval was as high as 68 per cent (in Saskatchewan). (Environics 1990)

We therefore decided not to recommend a change in the practice of holding federal elections on a Monday. However, the current requirement to hold an election on a Tuesday, if the Monday of the week in which the prime minister wishes to hold an election falls on a provincial or federal holiday, should be eliminated. The prime minister, accordingly, must decide whether to hold an election on a Monday that is a federal or provincial holiday or to select another Monday.

The objections to Sunday voting do not have the same force with respect to advance polls because people can choose when to vote. Holding advance polls on Sunday would provide greater flexibility and improve access to the vote without forcing anyone to vote on a day to which they object.

Recommendation 2.3.2

We recommend that election day be a Monday.

VOTING HOURS

The polls are open on election day between 9 a.m. and 8 p.m., a total of 11 hours, in each time zone. The unofficial results start to become public as soon as the votes cast in regular polling stations have been counted, usually about one-half hour after voting has ended in each time zone.

Because Canada extends over six time zones, election results from eastern Canada can become known in the West well before the polls have closed there (see Table 3.3). The resulting perception that elections are decided before voters have even finished voting prompted several recommendations at our hearings.

Table 3.3
Voting hours, present situation

Province/region	Local time a.m. p.m.	Eastern time a.m. p.m.	Results available (eastern time)* p.m.
Newfoundland	9:00–8:00	7:30– 6:30	7:00
Maritimes	9:00–8:00	8:00– 7:00	7:30
Quebec	9:00–8:00	9:00– 8:00	8:30
Ontario	9:00–8:00	9:00– 8:00	8:30
Northwest Territories (Eastern Arctic)	9:00–8:00	9:00– 8:00	8:30
Manitoba	9:00–8:00	10:00– 9:00	9:30
Saskatchewan	9:00–8:00	10:00– 9:00	9:30
Alberta	9:00–8:00	11:00–10:00	10:30
Northwest Territories (Western Arctic)	9:00–8:00	11:00–10:00	10:30
British Columbia	9:00–8:00	12:00–11:00	11:30
Yukon	9:00–8:00	12:00–11:00	11:30

Source: Royal Commission Research Branch.

*Shaded area shows which results are available before voting ends in British Columbia and the Yukon.

As discussed in Volume 1, Chapter 2, our research suggests that the time zone effect is not a particularly important determinant of non-voting in western Canada. (Eagles 1991b RC) Notwithstanding this finding, western Canadian voters generally may feel that their vote counts for less if the election outcome has been determined before their votes are cast, and some may have decided not to vote for that reason. The 1980 general election provides a good example. By the time the results from Ontario were announced, the Liberals had won enough seats to form the government. Had the results been announced from west to east, Canadians would have had to wait for results from Prince Edward Island to learn who would form the government. Under those circumstances, the vote would likely have held a different meaning for western Canadian voters.

The *Canada Elections Act* makes it an offence to publish election results in any area before voting ends in that area. This provision, adopted at the time the telegraph was used to communicate election results, has been rendered obsolete by developments in broadcasting and telecommunications technology, which have made controlling the diffusion of election results more difficult. U.S. border stations can broadcast election results from eastern Canada before viewers or listeners in western Canada have finished voting. It is also impossible to stop results being relayed to the West via telephone or facsimile before the polls close and increasingly difficult to block eastern Canadian television stations carrying election news from being received in the West by satellite or cable.

Our research indicated that Canadians feel very strongly about premature release of election results and favour changes in voting hours to eliminate the problem. In a national survey (Environics 1990), 70 per cent of respondents said this was a problem and 41 per cent called it serious. This was echoed at our public hearings. Most interveners on the issue were from western Canada, but several witnesses from Atlantic Canada also underscored the importance of this issue.

Several recommendations were put forward at our hearings. They included delaying the count in eastern Canada until polls close in Alberta and British Columbia, extending the voting period to two days, or using different election hours in each time zone.

Our survey asked whether people approved of having all regions of the country vote at the same time so election results would be announced to everyone at once. More than half the respondents strongly approved, another 29 per cent approved, and only 11 per cent were opposed.

Changing voting hours also drew support in our consultations with returning officers and party officials, although not to the extent shown in the survey. Election officials were concerned about fatigue and security problems if poll officials had to work late into the evening.

Despite the support shown for uniform voting hours across Canada, we hesitate to recommend this for practical reasons. Voting would have to occur between 11:30 a.m. and 10:30 p.m. in Newfoundland, 11 a.m. and 10 p.m. in the other Atlantic provinces, 10 a.m. and 9 p.m. in Ontario and Quebec, 9 a.m. and 8 p.m. in Manitoba and Saskatchewan, 8 a.m. and 7 p.m. in Alberta and the Northwest Territories and 7 a.m. and 6 p.m. in British Columbia and the Yukon.

This would have disruptive effects at both ends of the country. In Atlantic Canada poll officials would have to work as late as midnight on election day, while in British Columbia and the Yukon the proposal would eliminate two hours when voting is traditionally heaviest, between 6 p.m. and 8 p.m. The change would not only be inconvenient; it could also discriminate against voters with jobs that make it more convenient to vote on their way home from work or after dinner. Closing the polls at 6 p.m. in British Columbia and the Yukon would also affect employers, who must give employees paid time off to vote. The impact on the political parties would probably also be unequal. These are the reasons why Bill C-113, a 1982 draft law that proposed staggered voting hours, proved unacceptable.

The challenge is therefore to devise a solution that responds to concerns in western Canada, is fair to different groups and regions, and is not too disruptive for voters or election workers. We believe this can be achieved if we recognize that the basic problem is ensuring that voters in western Canada do not know who will form the government before the polls close there. This means guarding against premature release of election results from Ontario and Quebec, whose 174 constituencies constitute more than half the seats in the House of Commons. We have concluded that the release of some election results before polls close in the West – specifically, results from the 32 seats in Atlantic Canada – would not constitute a major problem so long as other results from eastern Canada were not available until after the polls closed in the West.

The time difference between the eastern and Pacific time zones is three hours, and it takes about half an hour for poll workers to begin to report results once voting ends. Thus if voting ended at 9 p.m. in Ontario and Quebec, the first results would begin to be aired on radio and television at 9:30 p.m., or 6:30 p.m. local time in British Columbia and in the Yukon. If the count in Ontario and Quebec were delayed by a half-hour, and the polls in British Columbia and the Yukon closed an hour earlier, results would not be known until people in British Columbia and the Yukon had finished voting.

The difficulty with this scenario is that it requires delaying the counting of votes in Ontario and Quebec. After consulting returning officers we have concluded that a half-hour delay in counting the vote from ordinary polling stations would not be workable. Further, if staff had to stay for this additional time, it would appear logical to keep the polls open. Nor would delaying the transmission of election results to the returning officer's office be effective, because party scrutineers at the polls could spread results rapidly once the ballots had been counted.

We propose that polling stations be open from 9:30 a.m. to 9:30 p.m. local time everywhere from Newfoundland to the Ontario-Manitoba border; from 8:30 a.m. to 8:30 p.m. in Manitoba and Saskatchewan; from 8 a.m. to 8 p.m. in Alberta and the Northwest Territories; and from 7 a.m. to 7 p.m. in British Columbia and the Yukon. No polling station would be open later than 9:30 p.m. or close earlier than 7 p.m. While these new voting hours would delay the closing of the polls in certain parts of the country, similar closing hours can be found in other jurisdictions, such as England and several U.S. states. Table 3.4 shows that, based on the count taking half an hour, the only election results available to voters in the rest of Canada before their polls closed would be those from the 32 constituencies in Atlantic Canada; under the present arrangement, results from as many as 262 constituencies are available before the polls close in British Columbia.

Recommendation 2.3.3

We recommend that

(a) the voting day be extended from 11 hours to 12 hours; and
(b) local voting hours be from 9:30 a.m. to 9:30 p.m. in Newfoundland, Prince Edward Island, Quebec, New Brunswick, Nova Scotia and Ontario; 8:30 a.m. to 8:30 p.m. in Manitoba and Saskatchewan; 8 a.m. to 8 p.m. in Alberta and the Northwest Territories; and 7 a.m. to 7 p.m. in British Columbia and the Yukon.

Table 3.4
Proposed voting hours, 12-hour voting day

Province / region	Local time a.m. p.m.	Eastern time a.m. p.m.	Results available (eastern time)* p.m.
Newfoundland	9:30–9:30	8:00– 8:00	8:30
Maritimes	9:30–9:30	8:30– 8:30	9:00
Quebec	9:30–9:30	9:30– 9:30	10:00
Ontario	9:30–9:30	9:30– 9:30	10:00
Manitoba	8:30–8:30	9:30– 9:30	10:00
Saskatchewan	8:30–8:30	9:30– 9:30	10:00
Alberta	8:00–8:00	10:00–10:00	10:30
Northwest Territories	8:00–8:00	10:00–10:00	10:30
British Columbia	7:00–7:00	10:00–10:00	10:30
Yukon	7:00–7:00	10:00–10:00	10:30

Source: Royal Commission Research Branch.

*Shaded area shows which results would be available before voting ended in British Columbia and the Yukon.

DEATH OR WITHDRAWAL OF A CANDIDATE

Death of a Candidate

The *Canada Elections Act* requires that a constituency election be postponed if one of the candidates dies between the close of nominations (nomination day) and the close of the polls. Use of this provision has been relatively infrequent; just three candidates have died during an electoral period since 1945 (in 1957, 1962 and 1980). A new nomination date is set between 20 days and one month after the candidate's death, and the election date is set for

28 days after the new nomination day. Thus if a candidate dies after nomination day, the election in that constituency may be postponed by as much as 58 days. Further, there is no provision for the situation where a candidate who has filed nomination papers dies just before the official nomination date.

These arrangements need to be revisited. First, a delay of almost two months in filling the seat could create uncertainty should a minority government result from the general election. Second, a party that has lost its candidate through death just before nomination day could have difficulty recruiting a new candidate and fulfilling the nomination requirements by the statutory deadline.

The timeframe for a new election is also unnecessarily long and should be shortened (see Figure 3.1). In addition, the law should include a provision to cover the situation where a candidate who has filed nomination papers dies on or just before nomination day.

Figure 3.1
Death of candidate, present situation and recommended provisions

Present situation (writ period: 50 days)

Nomination day Day 28	Election day Day 0		Day 28	Day 58

*Each block of the first row represents a seven-day period.

Recommended provisions

Source: Royal Commission Research Branch.

*Each block of the first row represents a seven-day period.

Federal elections and by-elections are normally held on a Monday; this should also be used as the day for a special election held as a result of the death of a candidate. To give parties at least a week to find and nominate a new candidate, the new nomination date would be the second Monday after the death of the candidate. The new election day would be set 21 days after the new nomination date. These rules should also apply in the event that a candidate who has filed nomination papers dies in the week preceding nomination day. This will ensure that a party does not lose the right to have a candidate. These provisions would not apply in the case of the death of an independent candidate.

Recommendation 2.3.4

We recommend that

(a) **if a nominated candidate of a registered party dies during the last 21 days prior to the close of the polls on election day, the election in that constituency be postponed;**

(b) **a new nomination day for the postponed election be set for the second Monday after the death of the candidate, and that election day be 21 days after the new nomination day;**

(c) **in the case of a postponed election, the nominations of the remaining candidates stand;**

(d) **the revision period of the voters list be extended; and**

(e) **any special ballots received be destroyed and the returning officer be required to send a new special ballot to all voters who had applied for a special ballot, accompanied by a statement of when the postponed election will be held; further, if the candidate dies after the day of the advance poll, these ballots be destroyed.**

Withdrawal of a Candidate

The withdrawal of candidates after they have filed nomination papers is relatively common – about three or four candidates per election – but generally occurs within the time limit allowed by the *Canada Elections Act*. The Act does not allow candidates to withdraw a candidacy after the twenty-fifth day prior to election day, that is, two days after nomination day. If a candidate of a registered party withdraws after the close of nominations, the withdrawal is final; the party cannot nominate a replacement candidate. At the 1988 general election, one candidate withdrew two days after nomination day. Five days later, an individual who wanted to replace the withdrawn candidate applied to the Federal Court of Canada. The application was rejected. Subsequently, the candidate who had withdrawn sought to re-enter the contest but was refused on the grounds that the time limit for filing nomination papers could not be extended.

No public purpose is served by refusing to allow a candidate to withdraw during the last 25 days of a campaign. Ontario, Manitoba, Saskatchewan and Quebec have much more flexible provisions, allowing candidates to withdraw, in some cases, right up to the close of the polls. We suggest that candidates who wish to withdraw be able to do so until 6 p.m. on the day before election day. This would not provide sufficient time to change the printed ballots, but it would allow the news media to carry the announcement of the withdrawal and give the returning officer time to confirm the withdrawal to poll officials. Further, a candidate's withdrawal could be indicated prominently on the poster of candidates that we recommend be placed in every polling station. The Canada Elections Commission could issue additional instructions about how voters should be informed at the polling station.

No replacement candidate should be permitted, however, if the withdrawal occurs after the close of official nominations. This is to eliminate the possibility of a candidate being pressured to withdraw in favour of another candidate, for example, if a party's election prospects suddenly improved. The no-replacement rule is needed to protect the integrity of the electoral competition. This is in line with the practice in other jurisdictions.

Recommendation 2.3.5

We recommend that

(a) **candidates be allowed to withdraw up to 6 p.m. on the day before election day; and**
(b) **if a candidate withdraws after the close of nominations, the withdrawal be final and no replacement candidate be allowed.**

APPOINTMENT OF RETURNING OFFICERS

Many of our proposals involve new responsibilities for returning officers (ROs), who are the chief representatives of the Canada Elections Commission in each constituency and its only representatives between elections. The election period can be shortened only if the responsibilities of ROs are expanded.

The *Canada Elections Act* makes it almost impossible for returning officers to begin election preparations until a writ is issued. They cannot rent premises or recruit and appoint enumerators, and any preparatory work done before the election is called is unpaid. The consequence is a period of constant crisis in the returning officer's office after a writ is issued, with just 50 days in which to organize an office, hire and train nearly 1000 officials, and conduct the election. Moreover, the requirements of the Act must be met completely and with little room for error.

If the campaign were shortened to 40 days, as we recommend, returning officers would have to do as much preparation as possible before a writ is issued. Preparation should include locating polling places, consulting the parties, recruiting enumerators, and working with community groups to improve access to voting for people with special needs. Returning officers should be paid for this work on a part-time or retainer basis.

These added responsibilities for ROs underscore the need for qualified and competent people. We therefore propose modifications to the process for appointing them, as well as provisions for dismissal in cases of incompetence, incapacity, insubordination or lack of satisfactory performance.

Returning officers are appointed by the Governor in Council for an indeterminate period or, in practice, until their constituency is affected by boundaries readjustment. Governments have normally preferred to appoint new returning officers after boundaries readjustment instead of trying to keep experienced ROs who have performed well. There is no time limit for filling vacancies resulting from a change in the electoral map, and new appointments have frequently been delayed; as a consequence, each change in the electoral map brings a large number of inexperienced returning officers, many of them named too late to receive complete training. In the 1988 election, for example, which came just after a boundaries readjustment, 86 per cent of the returning officers were first-time appointments; in 1979, the proportion of new returning officers was 54 per cent.

The Act requires normal vacancies to be filled within 60 days, but this provision is often ignored. Moreover, the chief electoral officer has no control over RO appointments and no power to prevent the appointment of someone unsuitable or incompetent.

Chief electoral officers have urged in their reports to Parliament that the system for appointing returning officers be changed. Recommendations have included giving the chief electoral officer the authority to fill RO vacancies not filled by the government within 60 days and making appointments through a competitive application process, as is now the practice in Quebec.

Returning officer jobs were once considered patronage appointments. Our research showed that this view is changing, perhaps because the parties attach more importance to the need for well-run elections at the constituency level. Two-thirds of the constituency party presidents who responded to our survey favoured giving Elections Canada the power to appoint returning officers without requiring nominations by the local MP or the party in power; an almost equal number supported returning officers being paid to work part-time between elections.

We conclude that it would be preferable and more cost effective to build on the present appointment process rather than to change it completely. The current approach has proven to be effective in bringing to the position people with some experience and understanding of how federal elections work at the constituency level and with a commitment to the electoral process. It is now accepted that returning officers perform in an impartial manner after they have been appointed. There is no evidence to suggest that, on average, they perform less well than those appointed by a competitive process. At the same time, the Commission would not have to be involved in a process of appointing persons who in most cases have a partisan past. In maintaining the current approach, however, the capacity of the chief electoral officer and the Commission to ensure quality in election administration can be strengthened. As we recommend, this capacity should be strengthened by having the chief electoral officer and the Commission involved in evaluating the performance of returning officers after they have been appointed and have established a record in this position. This would be achieved by having returning officers be accountable to the Commission, by giving the Commission the power to recommend on their re-appointment and by enabling the Commission to retain those who perform well when minor changes are made to constituency boundaries. The chief electoral officer and the Commission would then be able to exercise authority and influence over returning officers after they have performed in this position. This is preferable to involving the Commission directly or indirectly in a process of appointment where most candidates for appointment would be expected to have a partisan past, given that such persons are likely to be those most interested and experienced.

The appointment procedure should be changed to require the government to fill vacancies in returning officer positions within 90 days and to give the Canada Elections Commission authority to make appointments after that time. ROs should be appointed for a term of seven years, renewable upon the recommendation of the Canada Elections Commission.

Changes resulting from boundaries readjustment are often relatively minor and should not result in returning officers being displaced. The chief electoral officer should be able to retain a returning officer after a boundaries readjustment if the boundaries are substantially the same as under the old electoral map and if the returning officer continues to live in the constituency. The chief electoral officer should decide which constituencies meet these criteria within 30 days of a boundaries readjustment becoming final; the government would then have 90 days to fill any vacancies. To ensure that ROs are responsive to the needs of voters, attention should also be given to more equitable representation in hiring returning officers, particularly in communities where there are significant numbers of voters whose ethnic origin is neither English nor French, including voters of Aboriginal descent.

Effective election management and supervision of returning officers require that ROs be accountable to the Canada Elections Commission. At present, the chief electoral officer has almost no power over returning officers except the ability to withhold payment for services. The Act does permit the Governor in Council to dismiss a returning officer for incompetence or incapacity, but this power has rarely been exercised. To ensure accountability, the new electoral law should transfer authority to dismiss returning officers from the Governor in Council to the Canada Elections Commission, acting on the advice of the chief electoral officer. Grounds for dismissal should include incompetence, incapacity, insubordination and lack of satisfactory performance.

The Act specifies that returning officers may be dismissed if they are "guilty of politically partisan conduct, whether or not in the course of the performance of [their] duties under this Act." This section appears to have been intended to rule out party activity by returning officers or any display of partisan bias in the course of their duties, but the new Act should make the partisan neutrality requirement for returning officers much clearer.

Elections Canada is currently reviewing the remuneration of returning officers. ROs should also be compensated for working part-time between elections on outreach activities and preparation for the next election.

Recommendation 2.3.6

We recommend that

(a) returning officers be appointed by the Governor in Council;

(b) if the Governor in Council does not nominate someone to fill a returning officer position within 90 days of the position becoming vacant, the Canada Elections Commission have the authority to make the appointment;

(c) returning officers be appointed for a term of seven years by the Governor in Council, renewable for seven years upon the recommendation of the Commission;

(d) the chief electoral officer be permitted to retain a returning officer whose constituency has been altered by boundaries readjustment if the boundaries remain substantially the same and the returning officer lives in the new constituency;

(e) the Canada Elections Commission have the power, on the advice of the chief electoral officer, to dismiss a returning officer for incompetence, incapacity, insubordination or lack of satisfactory performance;

(f) as a condition of office, returning officers be required to refrain from membership in a political party, from making a political contribution, from engaging in partisan political activity, and from demonstrating partisan bias in carrying out their duties;

(g) returning officers be engaged by the CEO between elections as necessary to prepare for the next election and to conduct outreach activities on behalf of the Canada Elections Commission; and

(h) greater attention be given to hiring returning officers capable of serving the needs of voters who do not speak French or English in constituencies where there is a significant community of such voters.

ELECTION-DAY OFFICIALS

Returning officers appoint a deputy returning officer for each polling station; the deputy returning officer then chooses a poll clerk. The Act does not provide for deputy returning officers to be nominated by a local candidate or candidates, as is the case with enumerators, but this practice is followed in a number of constituencies, with the nomination generally being made by the outgoing MP or the candidate of the party in government.

The Act provides that the poll clerk, who assists the deputy returning officer in administering and counting the vote on election day, be appointed by the deputy returning officer rather than by the returning officer. As a result, both may be from the same political party, potentially leading to an appearance of bias in the election process.

Some provinces avoid this problem by having deputy returning officers and poll clerks nominated by candidates from different parties. In Ontario and Prince Edward Island, the candidate of the party in government nominates deputy returning officers, while poll clerks are nominated by the opposition candidate whose party had the most votes in the constituency at the last election.

We recommend a somewhat similar approach for federal elections. Deputy returning officers and poll clerks should be appointed by the returning officer on the recommendation of the candidates whose parties stood first and second in the constituency at the previous election. However, the returning officer should appoint these officials if candidates have not submitted nominations by two weeks before election day or have not nominated enough qualified persons to fill the positions available. Local election-day officials must be eligible voters in the constituency.

If a deputy returning officer is ill or fails to report for duty, the poll clerk may not be able to serve as a substitute because poll clerks normally receive no training except from their deputy returning officer. In Quebec, poll clerks are trained alongside deputy returning officers so that they can take over the DRO's duties if required. This practice should be followed federally; it would eliminate the problem of replacing an absent deputy returning officer and would assist in the smooth operation of polling stations on election day.

The Act provides for the appointment of supervisory deputy returning officers in central polling places with five or more polling stations but does not make their appointment mandatory. The role of this official is to keep the returning officer informed and to maintain good order in the polling place.

Quebec provides for a supervisory deputy returning officer in every central polling place. This official, known as a PRIMO or *préposé à l'information et au maintien de l'ordre* ("officer in charge of information and order"), helps voters find their correct poll, helps sort out problems that may arise at a polling station, and reports the results of all polling stations to the returning officer's office after the vote is counted. The PRIMO also handles all communications with the returning officer's office during voting hours.

For federal elections, it should be mandatory to appoint a supervisory deputy returning officer in central polling places with five or more polls. In central polling places with fewer than five polls, the deputy returning officer from one of the polling divisions should also be assigned supervisory responsibilities.

The Act allows DROs to appoint a constable for a single poll and the RO to appoint constables for central polling places. The *Returning Officer's Manual*, published by Elections Canada, states that up to two constables are permitted for a central polling place with four or five polls, while four are permitted in a polling place with eight to ten polls. Special rules prohibit more than ten polls in one location except where this is accepted local practice and the chief electoral officer approves.

Some confusion surrounds the duties of constables. Although the term denotes some responsibility for maintaining order, constables spend most of their time on election day directing voters to polling stations and responding to simple enquiries – tasks for which they are often not trained. At the same time the Act permits all deputy returning officers to exercise the powers of a constable if these powers are needed to maintain order. If there is a disturbance of the peace or a case of election fraud, deputy returning officers and election constables are under instruction to call the local police for assistance.

The decision to hire constables should normally be made by the returning officer, even in the case of single polling stations. Returning officers should be able to hire people to fill these positions for very busy periods as well as for the full election day. Given their role in explaining the Act and assisting voters, constables should receive the same training as deputy returning officers.

Circumstances may still arise when a deputy returning officer needs assistance to maintain order in a polling station, but not to the extent of needing to call the police. In such cases the deputy returning officer should retain the power to engage a constable, but should consult with the returning officer before doing so if possible.

Recommendation 2.3.7

We recommend that

(a) deputy returning officers and poll clerks be appointed on the recommendation of the candidates whose parties stood first and second respectively in the constituency at the previous election;

(b) returning officers appoint deputy returning officers and poll clerks if candidates have not nominated enough qualified persons to fill the positions available by two weeks before election day;

(c) deputy returning officers, poll clerks and constables be required to be eligible voters in the constituency;

(d) poll clerks and constables be trained so that they can take over the responsibilities of the deputy returning officer in the event that a person appointed to that position is unavailable on election day or at an advance poll; and

(e) a supervisory deputy returning officer be appointed to all central polling places with five or more polling stations and a deputy returning officer be designated to take supervisory responsibility in all other central polling places.

OFFICIAL LANGUAGES

Elections Canada is governed by the *Official Languages Act* and meets its requirements in the sense that the public can communicate with its Ottawa office and receive its headquarters services in the two official languages. The *Official Languages Act* does not deal directly with the conduct of elections, however, and there is no reference to official languages in the *Canada Elections Act*. Elections Canada therefore has had to develop its own policy with respect to providing bilingual services at the constituency level. The language issue has at times generated controversy, for example, when a unilingual returning officer was appointed in the Moncton constituency in 1988.

The policy of Elections Canada has been to provide service in both official languages in constituencies designated bilingual by the chief electoral officer – a total of 98 constituencies at the 1988 general election (see Table 3.5). Constituencies are designated bilingual if 3 per cent of the population or more belongs to the official language minority group or if they are located in areas automatically designated bilingual for election purposes – the national capital region, metropolitan Montreal and the province of New Brunswick. In these constituencies election information from the returning officer must be bilingual; returning officers must have some bilingual staff at their offices; and deputy returning officers, rural enumerators, and 50 per cent of urban enumerators are expected to be bilingual.

In unilingual constituencies, callers who request service in the other official language are referred to Elections Canada for information or assistance if they cannot be served locally; Elections Canada maintains a toll-free number for this purpose. If there is a concentration of people from the minority official language group – for example, a pocket of one or two villages – the returning officer is to ensure that bilingual service is provided by deputy returning officers for the polls affected and that at least one enumerator for each poll speaks the minority language.

Some 100 official language complaints were filed in connection with the 1988 election. One-third of them concerned information provided for official language minority groups through Elections Canada advertising and on the Parliamentary Channel; the remainder related to a lack of bilingual services at enumeration or at the time of voting. There were no complaints about Elections Canada's services from its headquarters in Ottawa.

Table 3.5
Constituencies designated bilingual by Elections Canada

Province	Number of bilingual constituencies	Total number of constituencies
Newfoundland	0	7
Prince Edward Island	1	4
Nova Scotia	2	11
New Brunswick	10	10
Quebec	47	75
Ontario	25	99
Manitoba	6	14
Saskatchewan	4	14
Alberta	3	26
British Columbia	0	32

Source: Royal Commission Research Branch.

At our hearings the commissioner of official languages acknowledged that some problems with bilingual services are beyond the control of Elections Canada, because the chief electoral officer does not appoint returning officers and assistant returning officers and cannot require that they be bilingual, even if they are appointed in a bilingual area. The chief electoral officer also lacks powers to discipline or dismiss returning officers for failure to provide services in both official languages in bilingual constituencies, although a unilingual returning officer in a bilingual constituency can be denied the 7 per cent bilingual bonus.

In November 1990 the Treasury Board published draft regulations governing the provision of bilingual services by a number of federal agencies, including Elections Canada. The nature of Elections Canada activities, which rely on many temporary workers, was neither addressed nor resolved.

At the local level, returning officers cannot compel candidates and parties to nominate bilingual enumerators in constituencies where bilingualism is required. They can refuse to appoint an enumerator proposed by a candidate if that person is not bilingual, but this is difficult because of the limited time for enumeration and the difficulty of finding bilingual enumerators on short notice.

The *Canada Elections Act* should enshrine the principle of providing bilingual services, while the details should be left to the chief electoral officer and the Canada Elections Commission. The current practice of designating bilingual all constituencies in the national capital region should continue; all constituencies in a province should be bilingual if the province is officially bilingual according to its own legislation. No change is necessary in the present 3 per cent guideline for designating bilingual constituencies. The provision for serving official language minority pockets where the overall proportion from the minority is less than 3 per cent is adequate; there were no demands for change at our hearings.

Our proposals for increasing the authority of the chief electoral officer to supervise the work of returning officers should help to avoid problems in providing bilingual services at the local level in future elections. Our proposals would also give the chief electoral officer a greater say in the appointment of new returning officers. A clear policy of appointing bilingual returning officers in every bilingual constituency should be implemented. Where this is not possible, or where a unilingual returning officer is now in place, the assistant returning officer should be bilingual.

Failure to provide services in both official languages in a bilingual constituency should be grounds for dismissing a returning officer during or after an election. This would help to avoid the problem experienced in several bilingual constituencies, where returning officers simply refused to make bilingual services available and Elections Canada had no redress. Returning officers in bilingual constituencies should also have greater authority to recruit bilingual election personnel as required by Elections Canada's guidelines without having to depend on the parties. This would be easier to do if our recommendations for recruiting enumerators and election-day officials were adopted.

Elections Canada directives with respect to bilingual services and election officials are administrative in nature and do not have the force of law. These directives would be easier to enforce if the returning officer's responsibility for delivering services in both official languages were more explicit. The Act should specify that services in both official languages are to be available in bilingual constituencies during office hours and should include the requirement that the returning officer or assistant returning officer be bilingual. Canada Elections Commission policy should specify that bilingual enumerators and deputy returning officers are to be hired in these constituencies as a matter of course unless people with the minority language skill cannot be found or unless the minority language group is concentrated in one area of the constituency. If it is impossible to appoint a bilingual deputy returning officer, the poll clerk should be bilingual.

Recommendation 2.3.8

We recommend that

(a) the Canada Elections Commission designate bilingual for election purposes constituencies where 3 per cent or more of the population is from an official language minority and be required to provide bilingual services to voters in these constituencies;

(b) the present policy of providing bilingual services in other constituencies through a toll-free telephone service and the use of bilingual officials to serve small pockets of people from the official language minority be continued;

(c) all constituencies in any province officially bilingual according to its own legislation and in the national capital region be designated bilingual for election purposes;

(d) returning officers appointed to bilingual constituencies be bilingual or appoint a bilingual assistant returning officer; and

(e) specific standards for providing bilingual services in bilingual constituencies be established by the Canada Elections Commission.

PARTY REPRESENTATIVES

Candidates can have two representatives (or scrutineers) at any polling station to monitor the vote and assist their party's efforts to encourage its supporters to turn out to vote. The right to two scrutineers is rarely exercised, but it could result in an unreasonable number of scrutineers crowding a polling station and making it difficult to carry out the vote – particularly in urban constituencies where there may be ten candidates or more.

Most jurisdictions in Canada, including Ontario, Quebec, New Brunswick, Nova Scotia, Alberta, British Columbia and Newfoundland, as well as Great Britain and Australia, allow candidates to have only one scrutineer at each polling station when the vote is being taken or counted. This practice should also be followed in federal elections. However, the deputy returning officer should have discretion to allow another scrutineer to enter the poll for a short period, so long as this does not disrupt voting. This would permit candidates' runners to enter a polling station.

Recommendation 2.3.9

We recommend that

(a) candidates be allowed to have one representative at each regular, advance and mobile poll; and

(b) on election day candidates be allowed to designate a person for each place where polling stations are established and give the person power of attorney to collect a list of the persons who have already voted.

POLLING STATIONS

Under section 20 of the Act, polling divisions should normally be defined so they contain about 250 voters; this is a guideline, however, and is not mandatory. The 1988 election saw an average of 318 voters per polling division, and Elections Canada is now recommending a range of 350 to 400.

The use of central polling places containing two or more polling stations has increased in recent years, as has the number of voters in each polling division. The number of polling stations fell from 70 841 in the 1979 general election to 57 860 in 1988. This occurred partly to reduce costs and partly because of the difficulty of finding premises with level access.

We see this process continuing as election procedures become more efficient through the use of computers, but we are concerned about the potential effects of too much centralization. The average size of polling divisions should remain small enough to maintain relatively easy access by voters to their polling station.

The Act specifies that polling stations be located where possible in a school or other suitable public building but does not give returning officers the power to require that space be made available. This can create problems because of the need to provide level access at every central polling place and, wherever possible, at every polling station. Some polling stations have had to be located a substantial distance from the voters they are meant to serve because suitable space in public buildings was not available. School boards have on occasion refused to make space available or have even withdrawn space that had been committed, requiring polling places to be relocated a few days before the election. Needless to say, the risk of voters missing their chance to vote rises sharply when the location is changed at the last minute or when a returning officer is refused the use of otherwise suitable premises.

Ontario requires that space for a polling place be made available by a municipality, school board, or provincially funded institution, or by the landlord of a building containing 100 or more dwelling units if a returning officer determines it is needed. The *Canada Elections Act* should be amended to give returning officers a similar power to require that space for a polling place be made available in federal buildings and federally funded institutions and buildings with 100 dwelling units or more. Municipal governments and school boards should be encouraged to make their premises available, especially when they are accessible to persons with limited mobility and other premises are not available nearby. Obviously, as is now the practice, the Canada Elections Commission should pay for the use of that space.

Settling the location of polling places is one of the jobs returning officers could do if they had the authority to begin election preparations before a writ is issued. Returning officers could arrange locations for most polling stations, subject to quick confirmation once the election is called. Practical issues, such as barrier-free access and arrangements for telephones and furniture, could also be resolved in advance rather than during the busy first days of the campaign.

Many polling locations are in buildings where telephone service is not easily accessible. This can create difficulties in emergencies, if there is a need to consult the returning officer on election day, or in reporting results after the ballots have been counted. Changes in technology, particularly the widespread availability of cellular phones, have made it much easier to equip polling places with a telephone. In future, all polling places that do not already have an accessible telephone should be supplied with one on election day. This practice should also apply to advance polls.

Recommendation 2.3.10

We recommend that

(a) the number of voters per polling division be kept at a level that ensures that most voters live only a short distance from the polling station; and

(b) returning officers have the right to require that space for a polling place be made available in federal buildings, federally funded institutions and buildings containing 100 dwelling units or more.

PARTY PUBLICITY AT POLLING STATIONS

The Act prohibits the display of party emblems, signs, cards, or campaign literature of any kind in or on a polling station or by any person entering the polling station, but it does not restrict partisan demonstrations or signs a few feet from the polling station entrance. This anomaly should be corrected.

Apart from Ontario, all provinces have restrictions similar to those in the federal law, except that they generally extend the prohibition on party publicity for a distance of 15, 50 or even 100 metres from the polling station door. In Manitoba, the rule is applied within a 50-metre radius, but candidates' representatives are entitled to indicate their party allegiance by wearing a plain coloured ribbon or button. The restriction is in force inside and outside a polling place any day that voting takes place, including advance voting.

The current rule on party publicity should be clarified and should apply to all polling places at times when voting is taking place. It should also apply to the office of the returning officer, because its neutrality must be protected. Moreover, under our proposals, voters would be able to tender special ballots at this office.

Recommendation 2.3.11

We recommend that

(a) the display of emblems, signs or other partisan material be prohibited within a radius of 50 metres of any entrance to a polling place, as well as in or on the polling place, on election day or any day of advance voting; and

(b) these restrictions also apply to the returning officer's office.

RECORD KEEPING

The Act requires that the name and address of every voter be entered in a poll book at the polling station once it has been determined that the voter is qualified to vote. This is the most time-consuming part of the voting process because the poll clerk must write out in longhand each voter's name before the ballot can be handed out.

This procedure has been part of the Act since its inception in 1874; it is designed to protect the integrity of the vote by ensuring that an accurate record is kept of every person who votes. We are satisfied that the integrity of the vote can be protected by other means and that the poll book does not need to be maintained in its present form. The province of Ontario has already taken this step.

In future, the poll clerk should cross each voter's name off the list for the polling division as the voter arrives to vote. With computerization, the voters list for each polling division should be virtually complete on election day.

The poll book should continue to be used to record transactions that fall outside ordinary voting. These could include voting by a person who registered on election day, taking the ballot box outside the polling station to permit curbside voting, and allowing someone who had applied for a special ballot to vote in person. As at present, the poll book should continue to be used to record the names of voters whose identity or eligibility is challenged by a party scrutineer or an election official. The poll book for each polling division should be available for inspection at the Canada Elections Commission for a fixed period after every election.

These changes would allow poll clerks to spend less time with the poll book and more time helping the deputy returning officer to serve voters. This should result in fewer delays for voters at busy periods or in the event that a poll official has to help a voter needing assistance to vote.

The organization of the polling station should also recognize the role of candidates' workers in helping to mobilize the vote on election day. These workers need to know who has voted so they can encourage those who have not been to the polls to turn out. Each party naturally concentrates on voters they believe support its candidate, but the overall effect of this activity is to increase voter turnout.

To assist candidates and parties, poll clerks should have lists of voter numbers; when someone votes, the number can be recorded quickly by circling it or marking it off the list. If a new sheet is started every hour or two, candidates' workers would have easy access, without disturbing the voting process, to the record of who has voted during periods when they did not have a scrutineer present.

Recommendation 2.3.12

We recommend that

(a) the use of the poll book to record the names of voters voting at ordinary polling stations on election day be discontinued, but the poll book still be used to note extraordinary transactions, such as voting by voters registering on election day, challenges by scrutineers or election officials, and removal of the ballot box to permit a voter to vote outside the polling station;

(b) records continue to be kept in the poll book of the names of people voting at an advance poll; and

(c) poll clerks use a list of voter numbers to assist parties and candidates in keeping track of who has voted on election day.

IDENTIFICATION OF VOTERS

Voters can vote at an ordinary or advance poll simply by giving their name and address. They are not required to produce identification unless they are challenged by an election official or party scrutineer and do not wish to take an oath. Very few voters are challenged.

We agree with the present practice in general but recommend changes in the procedure involved if a voter is challenged. At present, a voter whose identity or eligibility is challenged may either swear an oath or provide satisfactory identification. We would require a voter whose name is on the voters list and who is challenged at an ordinary poll to produce satisfactory identification, with an oath or affirmation as the alternative if the voter cannot or will not produce satisfactory identification. The Canada Elections Commission should prescribe what constitutes satisfactory identification.

Some interveners at our hearings proposed that the Act be made more stringent, requiring voters to produce identification to be enumerated or to vote. This could discourage some people from voting, particularly new citizens from countries with no history of free elections. The Canadian system is based on trust and has worked well; no changes are required.

Recommendation 2.3.13

We recommend that

(a) the current procedure, allowing people to vote on election day by giving their name and address, be maintained;

(b) voters whose names are on the voters list and who are challenged at an ordinary poll be required to provide satisfactory identification or, if they cannot do so, to swear an oath or make an affirmation; and

(c) the Canada Elections Commission prescribe what constitutes satisfactory identification.

MARKING THE BALLOT

The Act directs that ballots be marked in the voting booth with a black lead
pencil, but it does not disallow a vote marked some other way, so long as
there is no 'identifying mark' on the ballot. Voters are meant to mark their
choice with an X, but this is not mandatory, provided they make only one
mark. A ballot marked with any kind of pen or pencil is acceptable, as is
one that is marked with a check, a line or a circle in the space provided to
the right of the name of the candidate for whom they intend to vote. However, a signature, initial, word or picture is considered an identifying mark
and makes the ballot invalid. These rules are workable and generally acceptable and should be retained in the Act.

Recommendation 2.3.14

**We recommend that the Act allow ballots marked with any
kind of pen or pencil to be accepted so long as they clearly signal the intention of the voter and do not contain any unusual
mark that could identify the voter.**

COUNTING THE VOTE

The Act directs how ballots are to be counted and how the vote is to be
reported after the polls close. The process begins with an accounting of the
used and unused ballot papers to make sure that the number of votes
received corresponds to the poll book record. Then the deputy returning
officer counts the votes while the poll clerk and the candidates' scrutineers
or other witnesses inspect the ballots and keep a tally.

The deputy returning officer then places the ballots for the various candidates in separate envelopes, prepares an official statement of the poll,
and places all election material in the ballot box to be returned to the returning officer's office. The preliminary results are phoned in to the returning
officer's office; these results are normally used to determine which candidate is the winner.

The process of counting ballots by hand is generally efficient and quick.
In most constituencies, results are reported rapidly enough that a winner
can usually be determined within 30 to 45 minutes of the close of voting.
Recounts normally determine that the initial count was accurate to within
a handful of votes.

The counting of the vote on election night was scarcely discussed during our hearings, a sign that the present process is widely accepted. An
archaic feature of the Act, however, is its requirement that all election records
for a polling division, except the statement of results, be sealed with the
ballot box and not be accessible except in the case of a recount or contested

election. Keeping these records is of questionable value if there is almost no way to consult them after the election is over. We would therefore recommend that the poll book and election records not be sealed but be returned separately from the ballots and ballot box and that these documents be available for inspection upon demand to the Canada Elections Commission by candidates' or parties' representatives for a period of one year after the election. They would thus be available throughout the period in which complaints about election irregularities or offences can be filed.

The Act provides that votes from advance polls be counted one hour after the close of polling on election day. This delay does not make sense and should be eliminated. The counting of advance votes should begin at the same time as the counting at ordinary polls. We also question the requirement that advance votes be counted in the location where the advance poll took place. This count should be allowed to take place at any polling station or in the returning officer's office, provided the returning officer has given notice to candidates and their representatives.

The procedure for handling special ballots would be as follows. Before it could be accepted as valid, each ballot would have to be checked to ensure that the voter had applied for it and was registered to vote before the deadline. This verification should be carried out at the returning officer's office on election day with scrutineers present. A second check would be needed after voting ends on election day to guard against double voting. This check, and the subsequent opening of the secrecy envelopes and count of special ballots, should be carried out by one or more teams, each consisting of a deputy returning officer and a poll clerk. Candidates should be permitted to have scrutineers present, as at a regular polling station.

Votes from Canadians on the register of non-resident voters and from prisoners in federal penitentiaries on the central list provided to the Canada Elections Commission by Correctional Service Canada should be counted at Commission headquarters or some other central place. Registered parties should be allowed to appoint scrutineers to monitor the process. The count should take place under secure conditions and should allow a potentially large number of special votes to be counted without unduly delaying the reporting of election results.

The results of these votes should be transmitted to the election office in each constituency a half-hour after counting begins in each time zone to ensure that they are recorded at about the same time that results are received from ordinary polling stations.

Recommendation 2.3.15

We recommend that

(a) votes from advance polls begin to be counted at the same time as votes from ordinary polls and counting of an advance

poll be permitted at any regular polling station or at the returning officer's office pursuant to an advance notice to the candidates;

(b) a team or teams consisting of a deputy returning officer and a poll clerk be appointed to verify and count special ballots on election day in the office of the returning officer in each constituency;

(c) candidates be invited to send representatives to the count of special ballots on the same basis as they have scrutineers at ordinary polling divisions;

(d) votes from Canadians on the register of non-resident voters and prisoners in federal penitentiaries on the list provided to the Canada Elections Commission by Correctional Service Canada be counted at Commission headquarters or some other central place and the results communicated to the returning officer's office in each constituency one-half hour after the count begins in ordinary polling stations in each time zone; and

(e) the poll book and election records for each polling division not be sealed but be deposited with the Canada Elections Commission at the time of the return of the writ or as soon as possible thereafter; and the Commission allow candidates' or registered parties' representatives to inspect them if it is satisfied as to the legitimacy of the request.

OFFICIAL COUNT

Following the election, the returning officer in each constituency must carry out the 'official addition' of the vote. Although often referred to as the 'official count', the process is actually an addition of the results reported in the official return of poll filed by each deputy returning officer; it does not involve an inspection or recount of the ballots. This is the basis for the certificate of the vote and the return of the election writ, in which the returning officer declares the winning candidate elected.

The Act does not specify a date for the official addition except to say that at a general election it should not be earlier than three days after the election. The date set for the official addition must be indicated in the proclamation at the start of the campaign. There is no deadline in the Act, but the addition normally occurs three or four days after election day.

If the ballot boxes containing the official returns from some polling stations are not available, the returning officer must postpone the official addition and recover the missing returns or determine the results by contacting the election officials concerned; these officials can be examined under oath if necessary. Up to two weeks beyond the date set for the official addition is allowed for this process.

The returning officer cannot certify the final result in a constituency until the official addition has been completed. Following the official addition, a defeated candidate has four days to seek a recount. Thus the time allowed for the official addition could affect how long it takes to determine the final result of an election, potentially causing some members to miss the first few days of the first session of a new parliament.

The official addition process could be shortened. The Act could require, for example, that the official addition be held as soon as possible after election day and, except in special circumstances, no later than seven days after election day. The returning officer should be permitted to certify a final result, even if written returns are missing from one or more polling stations. With modern technology this should not present problems.

As we recommend that recounts be the responsibility of the Canada Elections Commission rather than the courts, it should also be possible to shorten to three days the period allowed for this purpose. The returning officer should therefore be in a position to return the writ, thereby making the winning candidate's election official, on the fourth day following the official addition. All candidates should therefore be declared elected by the second Friday following election day. As a result, the new parliament could be called into session two weeks after the election instead of three as at present.

Recommendation 2.3.16

We recommend that

(a) **the period allowed for the official count be set at a maximum of seven days and the process be made simpler as described in this report;**

(b) **the returning officer be permitted to certify a final result even if some written returns are missing; and**

(c) **the period allowed to seek a recount be reduced to three days, allowing all candidates to be declared elected by the second Friday after election day except where a recount was allowed.**

RECOUNTS

Recounts are automatic if candidates are tied for first place or separated by fewer than 25 votes. This occurred in two constituencies in 1988, and none in 1984. A candidate or voter may initiate a recount if it appears that the results declared by the returning officer are in error or that a deputy returning officer has made an error in counting, administering, or reporting the vote. Applications must be made to a county court judge (or the equivalent) within four days of the official addition, and the judge must agree to the request for the recount to take place.

Recounts take place before a judge within four days of an application being granted. The judge has the discretion to base the recount on the deputy returning officer's returns or on a recount of the ballots and is entitled to accept or disallow any vote. If a judge fails to act on an application for a recount, another court may order that judge to proceed to a recount or may itself start a recount.

The present process is unwieldy, costly, and often long. There were six official recounts in 1988; results were confirmed in all cases except the constituency of York North, where it took 51 days to arrive at a final result. In that case, the recount eventually led to the election being contested and the result overturned because a number of ineligible voters had been allowed to vote.

Automatic recounts are paid for by Elections Canada. Otherwise, the candidate or voter who requested the recount must pay the legal costs of the winning candidate if the result is not changed. A $250 deposit is required to initiate a recount; if the result is not changed, this money goes toward costs.

All candidates in the constituency should have the right to ask for a recount. However, we see no reason to maintain the provision that a voter can call for a recount if the candidates involved do not ask for one.

Recounts would be carried out by a person designated by the Canada Elections Commission. A candidate requesting a recount should pay a $500 deposit to the Commission. If the candidate's request was unsuccessful, that is, if the winning margin was 35 votes or more, the money would remain with the Commission toward defraying its costs. If the winning margin was fewer than 35 votes, the deposit would be refunded. However, candidates could specify a partial recount and hence limit the costs. For example, a disputed result in two or three polls could be checked without the cost of a full recount. The Commission would be able to refuse to carry out a recount if it judged the evidence insufficient to suggest that the results of a recount would alter the outcome of the election. Any appeal from the result of a recount should be to the Commission.

We recommend giving returning officers the right to vote while eliminating their power to cast a deciding vote in the rare instances when an election is tied after a recount. If a tie occurred in a future election, the chief electoral officer would declare a new voting day for the constituency, to take place three weeks after the recount. This election would use the same voters list and involve the same candidates unless one of them withdrew; in the case of a withdrawal, however, no replacement candidate would be allowed.

Recommendation 2.3.17

We recommend that

(a) a recount be automatic if fewer than 35 votes separate the two leading candidates and no costs be charged to any of the candidates;

(b) only candidates in the constituency have the right to ask for a partial or total recount; the Canada Elections Commission have the right to refuse a recount if it judges that there is insufficient evidence to suggest that a recount may alter the outcome of the vote;

(c) the recount be carried out by a person appointed by the Canada Elections Commission;

(d) the candidate requesting the recount be allowed to specify a total or partial recount and forfeit the $500 deposit if the margin between the two leading candidates is 35 votes or more following the recount; and

(e) if an election is tied after a recount, the Canada Elections Commission declare a new voting day for the constituency to take place three weeks after the recount; in such cases the rules for delayed or postponed elections shall apply.

CONTESTED ELECTION RESULTS

If the results of an election are disputed because of fraud or irregularities, the challenge now goes before the courts under the *Controverted Elections Act*. Any candidate or voter may file a petition to contest a constituency election, making a deposit of $1000. The petition must be submitted within 28 days of the election result being published in *The Canada Gazette* or within 28 days of a candidate or agent being convicted of election fraud.

The election is annulled, or another candidate may be declared elected, if the court determines that there were more fraudulent or irregular votes than the winning candidate's majority. The decision can be appealed to the Supreme Court of Canada. The appeal must be launched within eight days of a lower court decision, and the Supreme Court has 12 days in which to make its decision.

The *Controverted Elections Act* is archaic, and its procedures can be costly and slow; the case of the 1988 York North election took more than four months to go through the courts. We see no point in retaining a separate law; provisions for contesting an election should be incorporated in the *Canada Elections Act*.

The decision to contest the results of an election can be based on almost any aspect of election law; the case can also call into question how the returning officer conducted the election. For these reasons, we believe that contested elections should continue to be handled by the courts, but before the Federal Court of Canada rather than a provincial court.

Complaints should be filed with the Federal Court of Canada within 30 days of the official announcement of the election result in *The Canada Gazette,* or 30 days after any person or party connected with the election in the constituency has been convicted of election fraud. This should allow sufficient time for a complainant to gather information about whether the fraud or irregularities were widespread enough to affect the election result;

this is the central issue in determining whether an election should be controverted or overturned. Under our proposals, complainants would also have access to poll books and other election records.

Any candidate or voter can file a petition to contest an election result; this provision should be continued. The *Controverted Elections Act* allows ten days for the defendant to respond to a petition contesting the election; this right to respond should also be retained.

The law requires a deposit of $1000 if an election is contested. This deposit should be made refundable if the complaint is successful. If not, the deposit would help defray the other party's costs. The Federal Court judge adjudicating a contested election should be empowered to dismiss a complaint that appears frivolous or unfounded before or during the course of a hearing. This decision should be appealable.

After a hearing the Court could dismiss the complaint, annul the election, or declare another candidate elected. This decision could also be appealed to the Federal Court of Appeal, provided the appeal is launched within seven days. The appeal court should hold its hearing within 14 days and should make its decision immediately after the hearing. Its decision should be final.

Recommendation 2.3.18

We recommend that the *Controverted Elections Act* be repealed and the following provisions added to the *Canada Elections Act*: (1) contested election results be adjudicated by the Federal Court of Canada; (2) the grounds for contesting election results continue to be that the result in a constituency was affected by irregularities in the vote or by election fraud; (3) complaints contesting election results and the grounds for the complaint be submitted to the Federal Court of Canada within 30 days after the election result for the constituency has been announced in *The Canada Gazette*, or 30 days after a conviction of election fraud involving that constituency; (4) any candidate or voter be permitted to file a complaint contesting a constituency election result; (5) a deposit of $1000 be required to file a complaint contesting an election result, and the deposit be refunded if the complaint was justified or the deposit go toward the costs of the other party, if the complaint was not justified; (6) the judge hearing the complaint be empowered to dismiss it prior to or during the hearing if the complaint appears frivolous or unfounded; (7) the judge adjudicating a contested election be empowered to reject the complaint, to annul the election, or to declare another candidate elected;

(8) a Federal Court decision on a contested election be subject to appeal within seven days of the judgement to the Federal Court of Appeal, whose decision shall be final; and
(9) the Federal Court of Appeal be required to hold an appeal hearing within 14 days of the appeal being made and to deliver its decision as soon as possible after the hearing.

RESTRICTIONS ON ALCOHOL SALES

Federal law prohibits any sale or offer of beer, wine or spirits in a store or in licensed premises during polling hours on election day. In by-elections, this prohibition applies within the boundaries of the constituency where the by-election is taking place.

This rule reflects the days when public attitudes about alcohol were more restrictive and alcohol played a more important role in elections than it does today. There are also anomalies in the rules. Sales of alcohol are banned on election day, but not on advance polling days. During a by-election, voters can easily procure alcohol on election day by leaving the constituency. In short, the law is inconsistent and potentially confusing. Most provinces allow the sale of alcoholic beverages on a provincial election day; there have been no reports of problems in jurisdictions that have dropped the restriction.

The law drew strong objections from representatives of the hospitality and beverage industries during our hearings; it was supported, however, by some community workers from downtown areas, who contended that having taverns open on election day could discourage some people from going to vote.

On balance, we believe the Act should conform with current attitudes and the practice in most provinces. The restriction on alcohol sales on election day should therefore be deleted from the Act. Individual provinces could still decide, however, whether to allow alcohol to be sold on the day of a federal election.

No polling place should be located in a tavern or bar; licensed premises, such as a hotel, should be used for a polling place only where there is clearly no alternative. In such cases, it would be up to the returning officer to ensure that an appropriate separation was maintained between the polling station and any lounge or bar on the premises.

The Act prohibits using drink as an inducement to vote. This provision is not designed to outlaw alcohol but to prevent it being used as a bribe. In Chapter 8 of this volume, we recommend that this be dropped as an offence but that the general prohibition on bribes and undue influence be maintained.

Recommendation 2.3.19

We recommend that the restriction on sales of alcohol be deleted from the *Canada Elections Act* and it be left to individual provinces to establish any rules with respect to the sale of alcohol on election day.

NOTE

1. Section 4(2) of the *Canadian Charter of Rights and Freedoms* provides for the following exception: "In time of real or apprehended war, invasion or insurrection, a House of Commons may be continued by Parliament and a legislative assembly may be continued by the legislature beyond five years if such continuation is not opposed by the votes of more than one-third of the members of the House of Commons or the legislative assembly, as the case may be." Prior to adoption of the Charter, the *British North America (No. 2) Act, 1949* included an identical provision in relation to the House of Commons, but not the provincial legislative assemblies; until 1982, a provincial legislature could thus "prolong its life as often and as long as it please[d]". (Forsey 1960, 604)

4

A Register of Voters

INTRODUCTION

O̲UR MANDATE REQUIRED us to report on "the compiling of voters' lists, including the advisability of the establishment of a permanent voters' list". This specific reference to a permanent voters list is not surprising. The current enumeration system, as we have outlined in Volume 2, Chapter 1, has been increasingly criticized. During our public hearings many interveners expressed interest in a permanent voters list. This list, or register of voters, is seen as a way to shorten election campaigns, address increasing difficulties in recruiting qualified federal enumerators and reduce duplication in voter registration – the result of separate enumeration by federal, provincial and municipal governments.* Among the more pronounced criticisms is that the current registration system is costly and time-consuming. Given these considerations, we have approached this part of our mandate guided by the following six principles.

First, registration should be primarily a state responsibility, as it currently is in Canada. This does not preclude that, in certain circumstances, registration be the responsibility of the voter. As a general rule, however, it is the foremost responsibility of democratic governments to ensure that all voters have the opportunity to vote. Second, voters should be able to register after the election writs are issued, including on election day. Third, a register of voters should be adopted only if it is nearly as efficient as an enumeration. A register must provide preliminary voters lists that are comparable to the coverage,[1] accuracy,[2] currency[3] and cost achieved by an enumeration. And the lists must be available when election officials and candidates need them for elections. Fourth, voters should have the right not to be registered and not to inform the state of their movements. Fifth, voters should have the right to have their names or addresses deleted from a voters register at any time. Finally, once the information has been entered into the voters register, it must be managed according to the strictest criteria for preserving privacy and confidentiality.

---

* In exploring the feasibility of a voter registration process that moves beyond the transitional and labour-intensive features of the current enumeration process, we favour the term 'register' rather than 'list'. Register more fully reflects the concept of permanence. A register is a system designed to manage the information needed to produce a specific voters list.

COMPARATIVE OVERVIEW: PERMANENT VOTERS LISTS IN OTHER COUNTRIES

Permanent voters lists are central to voter registration in most western democracies. They are used, for instance, in the United States, Great Britain, Australia, France and Germany. Among these nations, three major factors affect the coverage, accuracy, currency and cost of voter registration:

1. the degree to which registration is a voluntary act by citizens and the degree to which it is organized and administered by government authorities;
2. the role of national, state and local governments in maintaining and administering permanent voters lists, or, alternatively, the degree of centralization or decentralization; and
3. the degree that the lists are 'closed', that is, voters cannot register after a specific date before a general election and whether the registration process provides for revisions and election-day registration.

These three criteria will be used to assess the usefulness for Canada of the models of permanent voters lists in the United States, Great Britain, Australia, France and Germany.

United States

There is no national voter registration in the United States administered by the federal government. The administrative rules and procedures that govern registration for federal, state and municipal elections are established by each state and Congress. Although these rules and procedures differ considerably from state to state, all states except North Dakota use some form of a permanent voters register. (Courtney and Smith 1991 RC) As a general rule, registration is the responsibility of the individual citizen.

Several critical concerns have been raised about the registration process in the United States. First, almost all states impose a closing date for registration. How close this date is to election day is considered the key to how many voters register and how many actually cast ballots. In California the closing date is 29 days before voting day and in New York it is 30 days before voting day. The three American states that allow for election-day registration traditionally have turnout rates that are about 15 per cent higher than those of other states. Second, the accuracy of the information on the registration lists in many states is frequently questioned. The voter registration process is not designed to delete voters from the register who are no longer qualified to vote because of death or change in address. "Procedures for the timely removal of names from the lists vary among the different states and even on occasion among the counties of a single state. In many instances they have been found wanting." (Courtney and Smith 1991 RC) Third, because voter registration is voluntary, most states do not have in place a credible mechanism to ensure that their registers are continually updated.

For example, 45 states automatically delete names from their register if voters have not voted after a certain number of elections. This indiscriminate deletion of names effectively disqualifies many voters from casting ballots in subsequent elections, unless they re-register. (Mangum et al. 1991, 1) Proposed legislation at both the state and federal level would prohibit the purging of lists for failure to vote.

Consistently low voter turnout in U.S. municipal, state and federal elections has prompted several states to make voter registration more accessible, more flexible and more receptive to the needs of specific groups. In the mid-1980s, state-wide executive orders were issued to public agencies in Texas, Minnesota, Ohio, New York, New Mexico and West Virginia. The core of the executive orders strategy was to use state, municipal and county agencies, which regularly serve the public, as additional sites for voter registration. (Davidoff and Williams 1985) These offices include libraries, schools, unemployment offices, welfare offices and hunting and fishing licence bureaus. Most of the midwestern states have adopted one or several procedures, such as mail-in registration, election-day registration and extended registration deadlines, to facilitate registration. Minnesota has been particularly progressive in reforming its registration process.

From a technical perspective, only a few states have fully operational state-wide automated centralized voter registration systems. The first was implemented by Alaska in 1968, followed by Virginia and Kentucky in 1973 and Wyoming in 1976. Generally, these systems require local government units to send copies of registration affidavits to the central system for direct entry into the data base. The state is then responsible for updating and processing the information. Each local government is responsible for maintaining its local data base using information from the state's central data base. Hence, and as we will see is the case in other countries, the management of a comprehensive register of voters must rely extensively on a heavily decentralized information gathering system; local governments are best positioned to fulfil this role.

Linda Davidoff and Cynthia Williams reported in 1985 that "efforts to carry out ... broad, comprehensive reform are under study in Congress". (1985, 3) They still are. Congress recently considered legislation that would have established national registration standards; the legislation was passed by the House of Representatives, but it was narrowly defeated in the Senate. The legislation (H.R. 2190, *National Voter Registration Act of 1989*) provided for "motor voter" programs where persons are given the opportunity to be registered when they apply for or renew a driver's licence, or when they transact other business with the motor vehicle agency. It also authorized election officials to use the postal service's change of address program as an alternative to current purging procedures. A similar bill was introduced in the 1991 session of Congress. The recent efforts to reform the voter registration process in the United States reflect a growing sensitivity at the federal and state levels to the need for governments to make it easier for citizens to register.

Great Britain

Voter registration in Great Britain is administered through a permanent voters list that is updated annually. The updated list is published every 15 February. Once published, however, the list is effectively closed until the new list is published, even if a general election is called in the interim. Administrative procedures allow voters to have their name added to the list only if they demonstrate that they have been wrongly excluded. Consequently, only a few names can be added to the list after it has been closed. The list is used for local, national and European parliament elections.

Administering voter registration in Great Britain is the responsibility of local officials employed by district councils and boroughs in each of its 650 electoral districts. The act of registration, however, is very much based on the initiative of individual voters. If they are to be listed on the voters register, voters must complete a voter registration card and then mail it to local election officials.

The primary source of consistency in the registration process is the timetable established by national legislation on the compilation and publication of the annual voters register. There are, however, no standardized procedures for revision. For example, although door-to-door canvassing has been effective in updating the register, the quality and availability of canvasses vary considerably among constituencies. The percentage of households canvassed in the inner city constituencies is especially modest. Michael and Shelley Pinto-Duschinsky suggest that, although ethno-cultural groups tend to be more affected by under-registration compared with other groups of voters, this is more a reflection of the relatively high mobility and youth of ethno-cultural groups in Britain than of systemic barriers in the voter registration process. (1987, 18–21)

The accuracy of the permanent voters list in Great Britain has been questioned in recent years. Research suggests that the number of errors on the electoral registers for England and Wales doubled between 1966 and 1981. By 1981 the register contained more than five million inaccuracies. The inaccuracies were equally divided between those wrongly excluded or included. (Pinto-Duschinsky and Pinto-Duschinsky 1987, 3) Together, the inaccuracies accounted for approximately 14 per cent of the names on the list. The highly closed nature of the voter registration process in Great Britain provides voters with relatively few opportunities to seek revisions if their names are not on the list before it has been published.

Australia

Australia maintains a continuous voter register or roll. Voter registration has been mandatory in Australia since 1911. (Voting has been compulsory since 1924.) The register is maintained and updated by the Australian Electoral Commission through approximately 150 divisional offices, which, in turn, report to one of seven Australian electoral officers. A common register is shared by the national government, four of the six states and the northern territory. The remaining two states maintain separate voters registers, but they are based on data shared with the national government. The registers are used for general elections, referendums and elections held to resolve industrial disputes. They are continually updated, in part, through biennial door-to-door canvassing, known as the 'habitation review', conducted by the divisional offices. The Electoral Commission employs a large, permanent staff in its divisional offices to maintain and administer the voters list, and it manages the procedures and revision processes that keep the list accurate and current.

Australia's Constitution requires that no more than 10 days elapse between the dissolution of Parliament for a general election and the issue of the writs. In 1983 a problem arose because the writs for a general election were issued the day after Parliament had been dissolved. Once the writs are issued, the list is closed. Many voters were thus disfranchised in 1983 because they did not have sufficient time to ensure that they were registered. To rectify this problem, in 1984 the *Commonwealth Electoral Act* was amended to allow seven days between the issue of the writs and the close of the register. Even with this adjustment in the revision process, voters have limited opportunities to ensure their name is on the list after the writs are issued. (Courtney and Smith 1991 RC)

France

As in Great Britain, France maintains a permanent voters list that is updated and published at a fixed date each year. Maintenance of the list is a local responsibility. In contrast to Great Britain, however, there is greater flexibility in revising the list after the closing date. France also differs from Great Britain in the administration of the register: local electoral officials maintain the list in Great Britain; the list in France is maintained by a three-person local commission, which also provides the information to the National Institute of Statistics and Economic Studies. The Institute maintains a central register stored on computer, and it assists the local commissions in updating the list.

Nonetheless, it is very much the responsibility of individual French citizens, as is the case in the United States, to ensure they are on the list and their personal information is accurate and up to date. But unlike the United States, the national government in France takes an active role in the administration of the permanent voters list by issuing voter registration cards that are valid for three years and by informing commissions when made aware that a voter has moved from one area to another.

Germany[4]

Voter registration in Germany is part of a general, mandatory population registration process conducted by municipal governments. These population figures are used by the central and state governments to allocate financial aid to municipalities that qualify for it. The German voter registration process is among the most decentralized of those in the nations examined here, although the level of decentralization is comparable to other European nations such as the Netherlands and Belgium. Every registered citizen is issued a national identity card that is stamped by local authorities according to the location of the citizen's residence. Voters lists, in turn, are drawn up from the municipalities' general registers; they are closed 35 days before an election and publicly posted from the twentieth to the fifteenth day before an election. Voters who demonstrate that they were unable to register before closing day can do so no later than the date set by local officials (normally very close to election day). (Courtney and Smith 1991 RC)

Summary

Countries such as the United States and Great Britain that maintain voters lists based on voluntary registration and decentralized administration, but, without consistent standards for coverage, accuracy and currency, either produce lists that contain many inaccuracies or have a relatively high level of voter under-registration. The inaccuracies are exacerbated if there is little opportunity for revision once the lists have been published and closed. In those nations where registration is administered by the state, such as Germany and Australia, the permanent voters list tends to be more comprehensive and contain a more technically complex array of information. Voter registration in France is a blend of state involvement and voter responsibility because voter registration is voluntary, but there is close co-operation between local and national authorities in continually updating the list.

With the exception of Australia, the administration of permanent voters lists in these examples is highly decentralized. Primary responsibility for the registration process is assigned to local governments or to local election officials employed by the national government. The level of centralization or decentralization is unrelated to the completeness and accuracy of the permanent voters list.

The most critical factor in the coverage, accuracy and currency of the various lists is whether voter registration is mandatory or voluntary. In democratic nations where voter registration is mostly at the discretion of the individual, administrative complexities and inaccessible or inflexible registration procedures are deterrents. Further, when voluntary registration is coupled with voters lists that are closed well before election day and that also provide for minimal revisions, many citizens often do not register for reasons unrelated to the civic importance assigned to voting. In contrast, registration processes based on mandatory registration require a complex and elaborate administrative machinery to ensure citizens have frequent opportunities to exercise their franchise.

Most western countries that maintain permanent voters list use them for elections at different levels of government. Permanent voters lists in Great Britain, Germany and France are used for local, national and European parliamentary elections. In Australia, the electoral roll is used for national elections, for elections in four states, for referendum elections and for elections to resolve industrial disputes. The frequent use of the lists increases their cost-effectiveness and provides more opportunities to keep them current and accurate.

Comparative data on the cost-effectiveness of permanent voters lists are limited. Cost-effectiveness is conditioned by the degree to which the permanent lists are used for local, state, national and other elections. The more frequently lists are used, the more cost-effective is their maintenance and administration. The highly localized voter registration process in Great Britain, Germany, France and the United States results in considerable variation in costs. In Germany, the process is part of a general citizen registration system. In the United States, there is wide discrepancy among the 50 states in the level of resources and administrative support for voter registration. Consequently, it is difficult to obtain a general accounting of comparative costs between permanent voters lists and the federal enumeration process in Canada.

Australia, however, provides some basis for comparison because maintaining its permanent electoral roll in four states and two territories is the responsibility of the Australian Electoral Commission. The costs of voter registration per voter in Canada are comparable, even though the administration of the Australian electoral roll relies not only on an extensive permanent bureaucracy, but also on a biennial review that is similar to enumeration in Canada. The cost of enumeration and revision for the 1988 Canadian federal general election was $27 791 142. With a total electorate of 17 639 001 (excluding Special Voting Rules voters), the cost per voter was $1.58. For 1988–1989, which included a biennial 'habitation review', the total cost for voter registration in Australia was Can. $13 003 571 (or $14 367 000 Australian, based on 1991 currency exchange rates). The cost per voter for an electorate of 10 300 798 was Can. $1.26 ($1.39 Australian). (Courtney and Smith 1991 RC) It should be noted that the cost of enumeration in Canada for 1988 was for a single federal election; the Australian electoral roll, however, is used for state, national, referendum and industrial dispute elections. Because Australia uses the roll for a variety of electoral purposes, the voters list is kept current and the cost-effectiveness of the voter registration process is increased.

PERMANENT VOTERS LISTS IN CANADA AND THE PROVINCES

As we noted in Volume 2, Chapter 1, Canada is unique in compiling its voters lists after the issue of the election writs and in conducting an enumeration of its voters. Canada's only federal experiment with a register of voters in the early 1930s was considered a failure in large part because it was a 'closed' list. A former chief electoral officer examined this option again in 1968 and advised against it. (Canada, Representation Commissioner 1968) He suggested that the costs of maintaining a federal permanent voters list would have been prohibitive. More recently, a *White Paper on Election Law Reform* (Canada, Privy Council Office 1986) also advised against a permanent voters list for federal elections. The white paper argued that a permanent voters list created and maintained by the federal government would be far more costly than the current enumeration process. It was also suggested that Canadians would be unreceptive to providing regularly information needed to maintain an accurate and current list. Concern was expressed in the white paper that a permanent voters list would prompt political parties to use it "for other than political purposes". (Canada, Privy Council Office 1986, 43)

The only province in Canada to manage its voter registration process through a continually updated list of voters is British Columbia. A province-wide door-to-door enumeration is conducted the third year after a general election. Enumerators are given the names of voters currently listed on the voters list. Individual voters, however, are responsible for ensuring that the information contained on the list is accurate and current. Applications for registration are processed in 60 government access offices located across the province and then forwarded to six regional offices, which are responsible for ensuring that the list is updated. All qualified voters are mailed an identification card.

The cost of the continuous voter register in British Columbia for 1987–1990 was approximately $10 000 000, including $5.9 million for an enumeration in 1989, which also involved an extensive advertising campaign. Some of these costs, however, are recovered from municipalities that purchase the provincial lists rather than conduct separate door-to-door enumerations; taxpayers thus save money because municipalities are not required to conduct their own enumerations. (Courtney and Smith 1991 RC)

In May 1991, the minister responsible for electoral reform in Quebec expressed interest in establishing a permanent provincial register of voters. (*Le Soleil* 1991) Quebec initiated a permanent voters list in the early 1980s but stopped the project when the provincial government decided that the costs to implement the project and maintain the register were potentially too high. The government of Newfoundland is considering draft electoral legislation that would establish a permanent voters list. The list of voters compiled after the provincial enumeration in 1988 would be the basis for a continually updated register in Newfoundland. The list would be updated by voluntary participation and by using data bases from several government agencies. In the draft legislation, revisions would be conducted at the discretion of provincial returning officers. In Ontario, Revenue Ontario operates a continually updated data base that is used to produce voters lists for municipal and school board elections.

A REGISTER OF VOTERS: PROPOSALS AND CONCERNS

During our public hearings much time was devoted to the issue of a register of voters. There were criticisms of Canada's existing registration process based on enumeration, and concerns about the effects of a register of voters.

These criticisms and concerns echo those that have been raised in previous considerations of a register of voters. They are based, however, on assumptions that do not necessarily stand up to critical examination.

A Register of Voters vs. Enumeration

Those who question the feasibility of a register of voters do so based on the assumptions that an enumeration after the issue of the election writs constitutes the most effective and cost-efficient registration process and that an enumeration conducted properly will also register almost all voters.

These assumptions are questionable. The experiences of Newfoundland, Alberta and British Columbia demonstrate that an enumeration conducted during an election is not the only effective way to compile preliminary voters lists. These provinces, using different methods, compile preliminary lists outside the election period. The experience of the 1980 federal general election – for which the 1979 voters list was used – also proved that preliminary lists could be compiled from other than a post-writ enumeration, and at a much lower cost.

The current approach assumes that an enumeration must be as complete as possible if voter registration is to achieve full coverage. This ignores the fact that revision and election-day registration are integral components of a comprehensive process of registration. The Alberta and Newfoundland approaches, in contrast, are more realistic. They assume that an enumeration is but one part of a total process, however important it may be to register most voters in this manner. Revision and election-day registration acknowledge that, inevitably, there are voters who must be added to voters lists following any initial attempt to obtain the names and addresses of most voters. In the 1980 federal election, there was insufficient time for an enumeration because of the unexpected defeat of the Progressive Conservative government nine months after the 1979 federal election. The chief electoral officer, using his statutory power, decided to use the 1979 voters list as the preliminary list and conduct a registration drive to revise the list. This cost much less than another enumeration and resulted in fewer complaints than usual about the voter registration process. The 1980 experience demonstrated that a properly managed revision could produce a final list of high quality and that enumeration is not necessary when a reasonably complete list of voters already exists.

Another major assumption that underlies support for the current system is that an enumeration, conducted properly, counts almost all voters. This assumption ignores the fact that any 'census' of a large population is always to some degree incomplete and inaccurate. No large population is entirely static, even for short periods, and there are inevitably omissions in contacting voters and errors in the information supplied. The degree to which these limitations can be overcome depends on the capabilities of the enumerators, preparations, procedures and quality control mechanisms. But no census can overcome all these limitations.

Statistics Canada estimates, for example, that it undercounts the Canadian population at the decennial census by approximately 3 per cent. This error exists even though Statistics Canada is able to plan for its census and to give census takers far more in-depth training than Elections Canada and returning officers have the time and capacity to offer. Voter enumeration is subject to even further error, because not all residents of Canada are eligible to vote; some ineligible persons are bound to be enumerated.[5] Finally, unlike the census, the law does not require that citizens submit to enumeration.

The Responsibility of the State in the Voter Registration Process

Canadians do not favour any process that would reduce or eliminate the responsibility of the state to register voters. They regard any move in the direction of a register of voters as implying this consequence. This concern is based on comparing the record of the U.S. version of a permanent voters list, based on voluntary registration, with the Canadian state-driven enumeration process.

Any changes to Canada's registration process should have as a premise the continuation of the Canadian tradition of state-driven registration. Contrary to the perceptions of some Canadians, this does not automatically rule out a voters register. A voters register neither requires voluntary registration nor precludes state responsibility for registering voters. We cannot subscribe to the mandatory requirements for registration and the associated sanctions found in some countries. However, it must be emphasized that establishing and maintaining a register of voters does not presuppose that the process places the burden and primary responsibility for registration on voters. In fact, as we outline later in this chapter, a voters register enhances the capacity of the state to register those who are most likely to be missed by the current enumeration process.

Voter Turnout

Many Canadians are concerned that a voters register would diminish participation in Canada's electoral democracy. If a voters register were used for preliminary lists, voters already on these lists would not be visited by enumerators. Some have argued that these visits alert voters to the election. This is no doubt the case. Given the volume and reach of election campaign advertising and other information activities, however, few voters are unaware of the election by election day. Further, the administration of a register of voters would require mailing 'vote-at cards' to instruct voters on where to cast their ballots. The advantage of an enumeration over a voters register on this point is thus minimal.

If a voters register were used, enumerators would not be necessary. Some might argue that this would diminish interest in electoral participation, because enumerators are involved in the election, even if as employees of the state. This may have been the case in the past, when local political parties nominated persons for these positions as rewards for faithful service, as well as to ensure a supply of workers for subsequent canvassing and election-day activities. Recent experience demonstrates, however, that these benefits are decreasing.

Candidates now generally consider the requirement to nominate persons as enumerators as an unwanted chore at best and an impediment to their more pressing concerns at worst. In many constituencies candidates are simply incapable of providing enough names. What was once perhaps an advantage of the enumeration process has become one of its principal liabilities; the process is experiencing difficulties in securing enough competent persons to carry out its single function and this problem is getting worse. The advantage here goes to a voters register by default.

Length of Election Campaign

Almost everyone considers our federal election campaigns too long. The fact that Elections Canada must organize and conduct an enumeration after the writs are issued is considered the major reason for the length of the campaign period. Although there may be other ways to shorten the campaign (and we recommend several in Volume 2, Chapter 1), many advocate, as they did at our public hearings, establishing a federal voters register as a solution to this perceived problem.

The length of federal election campaigns in Canada averages 50 days, compared with as little as 21 days in Britain. In Australia, elections vary between 33 and 58 days; in two of Australia's three most recent elections, campaigns lasted 36 days. The election period is 29 days in British Columbia, the province most experienced in the use of a permanent list. A register of voters could reduce the length of the election by eliminating, at a minimum, the days required to conduct the enumeration.

Shorter federal election campaigns, however, do not necessarily depend on introducing a register of voters. As discussed in Volume 2, Chapter 1, a shorter election campaign is feasible even if the current enumeration process is retained. That said, it is improbable that the campaign could be shortened much beyond 40 days, the minimum period we recommend in Chapter 1 of Volume 2, given the time and resources needed for a competitive campaign that accommodates Canada's size and geography.

Candidates and political parties would clearly gain from the early availability of preliminary voters lists. With these lists, candidates and constituency associations could begin to organize their canvass of voters almost from the start of the election period; they would not have to wait for the enumeration to be completed. In this way, a shorter election period would not diminish the time available to conduct a campaign at the local level.

Revisions and a Register of Voters

Concern has been expressed that a voters register would restrict access to voting. The register could result in many voters being administratively disfranchised if adequate provisions for the continual updating of the list and for revisions were not in place. The permanent voters lists in most countries that use this system are 'closed' before an election or when the election is called, so that those who do not meet registration deadlines are denied the right to vote. Many thus assume, incorrectly, that closure is a fundamental and inherent prerequisite of this registration process. Although it may be convenient for election administrators, there are no sound technical reasons that require a closed list. A list can be 'open' after an election campaign begins; indeed, it can be open up to and including election day. Our tradition is to give voters the opportunity to be included on the voters list after enumeration and, for those who live in rural polling divisions, to be registered on election day. A voters register would not require rejecting this tradition. Indeed, as we recommend in Volume 2, Chapter 1, an improved revision process and election-day registration for all voters would extend and strengthen this Canadian tradition. Each of these features can and should be included in any use of a register of voters.

Protection of Privacy

In previous considerations of a voters register, objections to the use of certain information as well as the creation of huge data bases of personal information have raised major concerns. There are essentially three reasons for concern.

First, there are concerns about infringing on the right of privacy. These concerns assume that those who manage the register would require access to confidential personal information in government data bases, such as those maintained by Revenue Canada, Taxation, Statistics Canada Census Division, Health and Welfare Canada and provincial departments of health and social services. This need not and should not be the case. A high-quality voters register can be created and continually updated without using personal information from these sources. There is, therefore, no need to consider their use, and our conclusions on the feasibility of a register of voters did not contemplate, or factor in, their use. The information required by those who manage the register can be readily obtained from other sources of information. Such sources could include driver's licence offices and vital statistics.

Second, there is concern that a register of voters would be an unacceptable intrusion by the state into the lives of Canadians. The specific concerns here are that a register would require that citizens be registered, that they inform the state of their movements, and that their names, addresses and other electorally relevant personal information be continually updated and maintained in a central data base.

These concerns are misplaced. If accompanied by adequate revision and election-day registration, a register of voters need not require mandatory registration, constant monitoring of each citizen's movements or the inclusion of personal information on every voter. Voters can and should have the right to refuse registration (as they do now), the right not to inform election officials of their movements and the right to have their names removed from the list at any time. This would not remove their right to vote; it would merely require them to register for elections in which they want to vote.

Third, there are concerns that copies of the voters register could be obtained outside the election period and that the information could be used for other than legitimate political or electoral activities. By law, returning officers must make the preliminary and revised lists available to all official candidates for use by their agents and constituency associations. The lists must also be available in the office of the returning officer for public inspection. The same provisions apply to provincial, municipal and school board elections throughout Canada. If voters registers were not available except at elections, they would not constitute any departure from current practice. Further, administrative and technical safeguards could ensure the lists were used for electoral purposes only.

Administration of Electoral Law and Voters Registers

A voters register could make it easier to administer and enforce Canadian electoral law. (Carty 1990) Section 23 of the *Canada Elections Act*, for example, states that the nomination of a candidate cannot be considered complete unless he or she has the written support of 25 qualified voters. In Volume 1, Chapter 5, we recommend that only qualified voters participate in the candidate and leadership selection processes. As well, we recommend that political parties seeking to become registered between elections have the declared support of at least 5000 qualified voters who are party members in good standing. A register of voters would allow election officials to verify quickly whether individuals participating in these processes were qualified voters. As a result, public confidence in the administration of electoral law would be enhanced.

THE FEASIBILITY OF A VOTERS REGISTER

Many objections to a register of voters do not stand up to close scrutiny. The litmus test is whether a register would result in voter registration comparable with registration based on the current enumeration process. Any examination of the feasibility of a register of voters in Canada must proceed at three levels. First, we must assess whether a register of voters is a viable alternative to the current enumeration process, based on coverage, accuracy and currency. Second, we must determine if creating and maintaining a federal register of voters would be cost-effective and technically feasible. Third, we must determine whether federal authorities could use voters lists compiled provincially. These lists would have to be reasonably current and need only minimal adjustments to be used to establish preliminary lists for federal elections.

The Feasibility of a Federal Register of Voters

The creation of a voters register by the federal government would require an elaborate administrative structure to ensure the register obtained high coverage for each province and territory. A study carried out for our research program confirmed that the lists maintained by Revenue Canada, based on personal income tax returns, contained as many voters as the preliminary voters lists of Elections Canada. (Canada, Royal Commission and Revenue Canada, Taxation 1990) Lists prepared from the Income and Deduction data base of Revenue Canada would include an estimated 80 to 90 per cent of the Canadian electorate. The existence of this data base indicates that more than one government agency in Canada is able to compile lists comparable with those based on enumeration. Public sensitivities and the policy concerns with using information from income tax returns, however, complicate the use of these data for election purposes. It is not an approach we would recommend.

The cost of a register of voters maintained exclusively by the federal government without using confidential data bases would far exceed the cost of the current enumeration process, and it would not greatly increase accuracy or coverage. Maintaining a national voters register that meets the criteria of accuracy and coverage requires a mandatory registration of citizens. The experience of other countries conclusively demonstrates this. The level of state intervention in maintaining a centralized register would be incompatible with the traditional approach taken by the federal government in voter registration. The amount of information required for a centralized register is far greater than in the Canadian government's current registration process since the active management of the data base necessitates that voters have a unique identification number. Further, it is improbable that a federal register not used regularly at the provincial and municipal levels could be satisfactorily kept up to date without a comprehensive door-to-door canvass – in effect, a process similar to an enumeration would be required.

Our studies conclude that a national register would be much more expensive than federal enumerations at each general election. As noted, this was the conclusion reached by the federal *White Paper on Election Law Reform*. (Canada, Privy Council Office 1986)

A voters register maintained and used solely by the Canada Elections Commission and comparable in quality to enumeration (to produce preliminary lists of voters) would be more costly for two reasons. First, the continual additions to and deletions from the register would be expensive and a vast computerized data base would be required. In countries that use registers, 'purging' the lists can be the most controversial part of the process. Purging is commonly done to ensure the register is continually updated. Its effectiveness very much depends on the criteria used to initiate purging and the level of refinement that is achieved. It ensures that those ineligible to vote are excluded from the register, or it accommodates voters who move from one polling division to another by deleting them from the old polling division and adding them to the new one.

Second, the lists generated from this register would be used nationally only every three or four years for a federal general election. This would mean that the least costly way of updating the register, namely by adding the names and addresses of voters who are not already on the register but who registered at an election through revision or on election day, would occur infrequently. Instead, elaborate and expensive procedures would be needed to continually update the lists. These procedures could include obtaining data from revisions during the election period, from information held on existing data bases, from enumerations conducted in areas where data on the register are weak, and from registration-notification cards mailed to new voters. Such a strategy would have to accommodate a highly mobile population. Courtney and Smith estimate that an annual population mobility rate of 20.9 per cent would mean that 3 650 000 entries (based on the 1988 electorate of 17.6 million) would be required every year to keep a federal register of voters current. (1991 RC)

The cost of creating and maintaining a federal register of voters could be absorbed, in part, by selling preliminary lists to the provinces and territories. If the lists could be made technically compatible with provincial polling divisions, provinces could use them instead of conducting a separate enumeration. The provinces and territories using the lists would need to revise them, but the duplication of effort that has characterized voter registration in Canada could be reduced considerably. Such a scheme, however, would require a complex federal data base with information and individual voter profiles that satisfied the voter registration requirements of the provinces and territories.

The technical and administrative resources required to ensure the federal register was continually updated to accommodate these provincial and territorial requirements would be excessive. A federal register used to generate preliminary lists for individual provinces would need the birth dates of individual voters, because of provincial differences in the voting age. Since many provinces have minimum residency eligibility requirements, an individual's period of residency in a province would also have to be recorded. The technical complexities and costs would be further increased if the federal register was used to generate preliminary lists for municipal and school board elections. As noted in our feasibility study, "the addition of a third level of jurisdiction would require the maintenance of an additional file containing the municipal and school board boundaries. This would result in a significant amount of work to keep the register up-to-date." (Gauthier et al. 1991) For school board elections, the religious affiliation of voters would need to be recorded in several provinces. In Quebec, for example, religious affiliation determines if voters can cast ballots for Protestant or for Catholic school board elections. In contrast, a federal register designed exclusively for federal elections would need only minimal information on individual voters. The mandatory information would include address, age and sex. Such information could be readily obtained from provincial and territorial preliminary voters lists but the reverse is less straightforward.

The Feasibility of a Provincial System of Voters Registers

The exclusive creation and maintenance of a register of voters by the federal government would not necessarily meet the objectives of those who support this approach to registration. The limitations of a federal register, however, do not necessarily preclude the creation of provincially maintained voters registers, from which the Canada Elections Commission would purchase preliminary lists for federal polling divisions. In short, the inherent feasibility of a register of voters as an alternative to the current enumeration process does not depend on the federal government assuming exclusive responsibility for its implementation. A careful examination of several key policy and technical issues suggests that a system of provincial registers of voters represents a plausible alternative to the current federal enumeration process.

Duplication of Effort

Canadian voters are normally enumerated by two, even three, levels of government within two or three years. This raises the obvious concern of unnecessary duplication of effort and therefore unjustified additional costs to taxpayers. The duplication also confuses many voters – when have they been properly registered?

During the course of our research, several seminars were held with the federal and provincial chief electoral officers to consider a register of voters. The chief electoral officers supported a register, particularly if it was based on an address registry. They recognized duplication of effort in compiling preliminary lists. They recognized that federal and provincial enumerations have sometimes taken place within months of each other but these lists were not shared, despite the considerable savings that could have been realized.

In the 1988 federal general election, many voters did not use the revision process following enumeration because they believed recent enumerations by their province or municipality qualified them to vote in the federal election. (Courtney and Smith 1991 RC) In Alberta, for example, two enumerations were held within a month of each other. The *Calgary Herald* reported on 22 November 1988 that in Alberta "the principal reason for the confusion was September's provincial enumeration, which ended just days before the [October] 14 start of the federal enumeration. There were countless incidents of eligible federal voters ignoring the federal enumeration because they thought the earlier provincial enumeration covered the federal vote." Federal enumeration costs in Alberta for the 1988 election were approximately $2.4 million. A further $3.3 million was spent by the government of Alberta for the provincial enumeration. In each case, just over 1.5 million voters were enumerated for both the federal and provincial elections. The duplication or repetition of the process is neither cost-effective nor conducive to an efficient voter registration process. And it does not contribute to public confidence in the electoral process.

Opportunities exist for greater co-ordination and co-operation between federal and provincial governments to prepare accurate and current preliminary voters lists.

If different levels of government shared a continually updated register of voters, many voters would no longer be confused about whether they are properly registered. Federal and provincial governments, as well as many municipalities and school boards, have the authority to conduct their own enumerations, and may have different criteria to determine the eligibility of voters; yet in no respect does the preparation of preliminary lists of voters in these jurisdictions require a consideration of constitutional authority.

Preliminary Voters Lists: Comparing Provincial Data Bases and the Federal Enumeration Process

To determine if currently available provincial data bases could be used to create voters lists comparable with those established by Elections Canada through enumeration, we commissioned four comparative research projects.[6] (Gauthier et al. 1991)

The first project compared Elections Canada's enumeration lists for the 1990 federal by-election in the constituency of Oshawa, with lists for this district generated by the continually updated data base of Revenue Ontario. This data base was originally developed for municipal assessment. Since 1988 it has been used to generate voters lists for Ontario's municipal and school board elections.

In the study, Revenue Ontario's lists were based on information received by Elections Canada on boundary descriptions of 167 polls in the federal constituency of Oshawa. Based on a random sample of 65 polls, the probability of voters being correctly registered was approximately 85 per cent for both Elections Canada and Revenue Ontario.

The second study compared voters lists produced by Revenue Ontario and by Elections Ontario for the provincial constituencies of Scarborough–Ellesmere and Fort York during the September 1990 provincial general election. Using random samples of 48 polls for Scarborough–Ellesmere and 50 polls for Fort York, the probability of individuals being enumerated by Elections Ontario was 86 per cent in Scarborough–Ellesmere and 75 per cent in Fort York. The respective figures on the voters lists produced by Revenue Ontario were 88 per cent and 74 per cent.

In the provincial constituency of Scarborough–Ellesmere, the voters lists produced by Revenue Ontario and Elections Ontario were similar. The high mobility of the population in Fort York, however, impaired the coverage and accuracy of the lists produced by both Revenue Ontario and Elections Ontario.

The third study compared municipal voters lists in rural Ontario municipalities, prepared by Revenue Ontario for the 1988 municipal elections, with Elections Canada enumeration lists in the same areas for the 1988 federal election. The rural Ontario study was based on a random sample of 19 small towns, villages and townships identified from the 1990 Municipal Directory issued by the Ontario Ministry of Municipal Affairs. Fifteen of the 19 municipalities provided preliminary voters list prepared by Revenue Ontario. In turn, Elections Canada provided 58 corresponding preliminary lists from a random sample of 13 municipalities where comparable lists were available. The probability of being correctly enumerated by Elections Canada in this sample was between 92 and 94 per cent. The corresponding probability of being enumerated by Revenue Ontario's data base register was between 90 and 92 per cent.

The fourth study compared the lists from the continually updated data base of Elections British Columbia with lists from a special enumeration carried out by Elections Canada on behalf of the Commission's research program for a random sample of polling divisions in the province. Elections Canada's enumeration, it should be noted, had coverage comparable with its normal coverage in an election enumeration. To ensure valid comparisons with the provincial lists of Elections British Columbia, provincial poll definitions were used and the eligibility age was set at 19. Based on a random sample of 60 polls, the probability of being enumerated by Elections Canada in British Columbia was 84 to 88 per cent compared with 78 to 82 per cent for Elections British Columbia.

Table 4.1 summarizes the results of the four studies. We found that the continually updated data base of Revenue Ontario provided preliminary lists comparable with those produced by the enumerations of Elections Canada and Elections Ontario. The preliminary lists produced by Elections British Columbia were slightly less complete than the lists based on the enumeration carried out by Elections Canada.

Table 4.1
Voter registration: measuring coverage and accuracy
(per cent)

Study	Probability of being enumerated correctly	Probability of being listed correctly
Oshawa	84–85 (EC)	85 (RO)
Scarborough	86 (EO)	88 (RO)
Fort York	75 (EO)	74 (RO)
Rural Ontario areas	92–94 (EC)	90–92 (RO)
British Columbia	84–88 (EC)	78–82 (EBC)

Source: Adapted from Gauthier et al. 1991.

Note: EC: Elections Canada; EO: Elections Ontario; EBC: Elections British Columbia; RO: Revenue Ontario.

The differences between Revenue Ontario and Elections British Columbia are accounted for, in part, by three factors. First, the former is tied to municipal assessment and taxation, and thus it is likely to be more complete than lists used solely for electoral purposes. Second, voters in British Columbia know that they can be added to the lists by revision following the issue of the writs for a provincial election; until 1986, they could also register on election day. In the 1986 election, approximately 12 per cent of voters registered on election day. Third, Revenue Ontario lists are based on a register of addresses, and Elections British Columbia's lists are based on the names of voters. Because addresses are more stable than people, any continually updated lists based on addresses will be more complete and current than those based on names. The address register thus has a built-in quality control base reference. Further, our research shows that address registers exhibit a substantially lower deterioration in currency than do name-based registers. (Gauthier et al. 1991)

Establishing Voters Registers

Our research suggests that coverage, accuracy and especially currency would increase considerably if voters registers were based on address registers. They would have several internal quality control measurements. The address registers would need to be linked to individual voter profiles that have the information necessary to identify voters. This information would be obtained from data publicly available from other government agencies, and the process would adhere to the strictest standards of privacy and confidentiality.

An address register is a set of data containing all known 'qualifying dwellings' in Canada or in a province or territory. Once implemented, the register would contain the information needed to generate lists of voters' addresses. (Gauthier et al. 1991) An address register could be easily based on data available from public sources.

There are many ways to construct an address register and several exist or are being developed. Revenue Ontario's list, for instance, is an address register. The least costly way to construct such a register for election purposes is to use the final voters list from the previous election. All voters lists should contain the addresses of voters, as well as their names, because Canadian federal and provincial elections are based on geographically defined constituencies. After an election, lists of addresses could be easily entered on a master address file without being dependent on the definition of existing polling divisions and constituencies. The possibility of using information supplied by private sector companies has been investigated. The general conclusion of this survey is that no single source of information could be used to create an address register for electoral purposes. Telephone and electricity companies appear to be the best sources for an address register but they would be most useful as an ongoing source of information, once the address register was created.

The scope and feasibility of a provincial system of voters registers could be greatly enhanced by geographic information system (GIS) technology. GIS is a computer software technology used to generate maps of large and small geographic areas and to manage data bases. It has been used extensively by the Saskatchewan Central Survey and Mapping Agency to establish a province-wide geographical data base. The federal government has entered into a cost-sharing program with Saskatchewan to ensure the application of national standards and to avoid duplication.

GIS technology is also used extensively in the United States and Great Britain, and applications are being studied at Statistics Canada and Energy, Mines and Resources Canada. Changing electoral boundaries to reflect the number of voters, rather than census population – one of our recommendations – would clearly be easier with address registers and GIS technology. (Gauthier et al. 1991)

The provincial elections office in Saskatchewan has pioneered work on the use of GIS technology for election administration, and much can be gained from its experience. The Saskatchewan Electoral Office uses a software-based GIS technology that has the capacity to:

- maintain files of addresses and postal codes;
- generate reports of addresses and postal codes by poll number, constituency and city;
- list locations of polling place for each address;
- produce reports by poll-constituency-city and province or territory;
- redefine postal code lists where boundaries have been changed;
- define voter population by poll and constituency; and
- compute the number of voters in proposed new polls.

When fully operational, the Saskatchewan system will contribute to an enumeration process that is more complete, accurate and efficient. Fewer enumerators will be required and less time will be needed to train them. GIS technology can be used to produce 'vote-at cards'.

A test project was conducted for the Commission on the capacity of GIS technology to produce the maps and voters list required by Elections Canada. The project, carried out in a federal constituency in Saskatchewan, demonstrated that GIS technology could generate maps of polling divisions and assemble the necessary information to create voters lists and identify polling divisions. (Generation 5 Technology 1991)

TOWARD A CANADIAN SYSTEM OF VOTERS REGISTERS

The current voter registration process in Canada is characterized by separate processes at the provincial, territorial and federal levels. Consequently, 13 different governments either conduct separate enumerations or manage permanent voters lists to register what is effectively the same electorate. The cumulative result is a duplication of efforts, resources, personnel and

public bureaucracy. This duplication is not cost-effective and does not necessarily contribute to voter registration that has better coverage, accuracy
and currency than alternative approaches.

We conclude from our research studies that voters registers can provide voters lists that are comparable in coverage, accuracy and currency
to lists generated by an enumeration after the issue of the writs. Our cost
projections show that if the federal and provincial and territorial governments used a common register in each province and territory, the frequency
of its use would contribute considerably to maintaining its quality of coverage, accuracy and currency – and justify its cost. If municipalities and
school boards used it, its quality and cost-effectiveness would be enhanced
even further. It is at the municipal level that officials would be most informed
about population mobility and the changing demographics of local communities. The register could also be used to construct lists for referendums
outside of elections, as done in Australia.

There would need to be a transition period from the current enumeration process to a fully developed system of voters registers. The transition
would begin at the next federal election; there would then have to be agreements between the Canada Elections Commission and provinces that either
use a voters register or conduct enumerations within 10 to 12 months of a
federal election.

Obtaining Preliminary Voters Lists from British Columbia and Ontario for the Next Federal Election

For Ontario and British Columbia, the Canada Elections Commission should
prepare for the next federal election by entering into contractual agreements to produce preliminary lists using Revenue Ontario's and Elections
British Columbia's continually updated data bases.

In British Columbia there would be considerable cost savings if the
Canada Elections Commission were to acquire preliminary voters lists from
Elections British Columbia. To ensure technical compatibility, preliminary
voters lists could be generated for both provincial and federal elections in
British Columbia by Elections British Columbia's data base and – given
that the data base is not based on an address register – it would be preferable for the Canada Elections Commission to adopt British Columbia's
polling divisions as the basis for preliminary voters lists for the next federal
election.

There are currently 5705 federal polling divisions in British Columbia.
Elections Canada estimates that the average administrative cost for a polling
division on election day is approximately $390; the total cost for federal
polling divisions is therefore approximately $2.23 million. British Columbia
has 6345 provincial polling divisions; if these polling divisions were used
to produce preliminary voters lists for federal elections, the total cost would
be $2.48 million. In short, the cost of shifting from federal to provincial
polling divisions in British Columbia would be $250 000.

The cost of the federal enumeration in British Columbia in the 1988 election was just over $3 million. Our research into the feasibility of voters registers suggests that the total cost of registration and revision in the event the Canada Elections Commission acquired the preliminary voters lists from the Elections British Columbia register, even if enumeration-type revisions were required in one of five polling divisions, would be approximately half the cost of the current federal enumeration process in British Columbia. Generating preliminary voters lists from Elections British Columbia's register, based on provincial polling divisions, for the next federal election is feasible, as measured by coverage, accuracy and cost.

Revenue Ontario's data base could be used to generate preliminary voters lists for the next federal election. Creating preliminary lists that fit federal polling divisions could be readily achieved through existing computer software. For the next federal election, each federal constituency in Ontario would need a few trained operators to extract the preliminary voters list from computerized municipal lists generated by Revenue Ontario's data base. Because the Ontario data base is based on an address register, staff would be needed to identify the streets on the computerized list that constituted the appropriate federal polling division, and to select the corresponding entries to build an electronic file for that division. Based on eight-hour shifts, four two-person teams could prepare preliminary lists from the Revenue Ontario data base for the average Ontario federal constituency in approximately 43 hours. A nominal level of training would be necessary to ensure individuals were qualified to perform these tasks.[7]

There are 17 067 federal polling divisions in Ontario. For the 1988 federal general election, the average cost of enumeration per division, based on our recommendation in Volume 2, Chapter 1 that each division use one enumerator instead of two, but excluding printing and other administrative costs, would have been $356.56, for a total of $6 085 410. Our research shows that the average cost per polling division (labour and computer technology) to generate preliminary voters lists for federal polling divisions from Revenue Ontario's register would be $56.00. In addition, the total cost to the Canada Elections Commission for acquiring the voters lists from Revenue Ontario would be a maximum of $100 000 or $5.86 per polling division. The total average cost per polling division of producing preliminary lists for the next federal election from Revenue Ontario's register would be $61.86, for a total of $1 055 765. Even assuming an additional $1 million for incidental expenses and the costs of supervisory election officials, the total costs of purchasing lists from Revenue Ontario would be approximately $2 056 000. In contrast to the current enumeration process, then, the savings from buying the lists would be about $4 million.

Voters in Ontario and British Columbia constituted 47 per cent of the total number of voters enumerated for the 1988 federal general election. Agreements between the Canada Elections Commission and Ontario and British Columbia to acquire preliminary voters lists generated from existing provincial registers would reduce the costs of federal voter registration by some $5.5 million. Given the transitory nature of this arrangement, tests should be conducted to identify correctly the detailed procedures and the timeframe required to produce lists for all the polling divisions in the two provinces. With appropriate revisions, 'vote-at cards' and voting-day registration, the current accuracy and coverage in these provinces would be matched or exceeded. As noted, the federal elections of 1979 and 1980 demonstrated conclusively that accurate lists can be established through revisions, even if separate enumerations have not been conducted.

Newfoundland currently conducts an enumeration at the discretion of the provincial cabinet, and the province is considering a permanent register of voters. If Newfoundland establishes a register of voters in the interim, the Commission should enter into the necessary contractual arrangements.

Recommendation 2.4.1

We recommend that the Canada Elections Commission enter into agreements with the provinces of British Columbia and Ontario to acquire preliminary voters lists for the next federal election.

Obtaining Voters Lists from the Provinces and Territories

The procedures outlined above to secure voters lists for the next federal election in the provinces of British Columbia and Ontario are interim measures. In contrast, a long-term agreement should provide for the modification of current software systems to ensure the most current generations of technology are available and that there is compatibility with federal requirements. Moreover, the Canada Elections Commission should acquire as rapidly as possible computer technology and software that would allow it to translate voter registration information from provincial data bases into lists for federal polling divisions. Once the software is in place, information would be identified and assembled to produce lists for federal polling divisions without the need to train staff to directly input the information, as would be the case in Ontario for the next federal election. The computer technology would need the capacity to extract directly from provincial data bases the information necessary to generate preliminary lists. The system should be able to use data generated through an enumeration process, as well as those in a permanent register. This information would include the name, age, address and sex of voters.

Recommendation 2.4.2

We recommend that the Canada Elections Commission develop and use the computer technology and software that would allow federal voters lists to be produced from provincial and territorial data bases established as voters registers, as well as from provincial voters lists prepared through enumeration.

The Canada Elections Commission would have to verify the quality of the data bases from which lists would be generated. This could be done quickly and inexpensively; at one or more intervals between federal elections the Commission could survey random samples of polling divisions based on a random sampling of constituencies. Quality control procedures would be used on every occasion when the Commission considered it possible to procure its lists from a province or territory. If the necessary standards could not be met in specific constituencies or polling divisions in a province or territory, the Canada Elections Commission would conduct an enumeration. For example, enumeration would likely be required in polling divisions that had a high concentration of apartment blocks or high population mobility.

Our research into the registers of Elections British Columbia and Revenue Ontario shows that there is an 80 per cent probability that a voter will be registered either by a provincial enumeration or voters register; the coverage and accuracy is therefore sufficient for provincial lists to be used to generate preliminary federal voters lists. Combined with revisions and election-day registration, the coverage and accuracy of federal voter registration would match or exceed current levels at reduced costs. Registration cards could also be used by voters to voluntarily update the information on the register. The cards could be distributed through post offices, shopping malls and government agencies.

Contrary to what has been assumed in past considerations of a permanent voters list, voters registers would not require a comprehensive federal-provincial agreement that encompasses all provinces and territories. Such a comprehensive agreement is not even desirable. Rather, they would entail separate agreements between the Canada Elections Commission and each of the provincial and territorial governments. If one or more provinces or territories did not want to participate, the costs to the federal government and each province and territory that co-operated in a provincially or territorially based register would not be affected. In each case there would be savings. A voters register for a province or territory should be managed by the provincial election office rather than by the Canada Elections Commission. Although the Commission could decentralize its operations to each province or territory where a common voters register was agreed to, this would merely be a duplication of effort. Compared with the Canada Elections Commission, the provincial election office would have easier access to provincial and municipal government data bases (such as vital statistics, drivers' licences and property assessment records) that would be used to maintain address registers and the voters registers. Provincial or territorial officials would also possess more detailed and current knowledge of developments in the province or territory that might affect the maintenance of the address and voters registers. Provincial and territorial officials would also be more familiar with the information requirements of their own provincial or territorial electoral system, as well as those of their many municipalities and school boards. And they could use the voter and address registers for their own elections.

Maintaining and administering separate provincial data bases, therefore, would be far less onerous than if the federal government created a national data base to generate both federal and provincial preliminary voters lists. As noted, the amount of information required by the federal government is far less complex than the aggregated information needs of each province and territory. This analysis clearly demonstrates that the savings to Canadians from the adoption of a register of voters and the elimination of substantial duplication in the performance of enumeration can be achieved only if the ownership and responsibility for managing the register remain with the provinces. Moreover, the pursuit of a register based on national standards would accomplish little for such a costly diversion of resources.

For those provinces and territories where there was no register, the Canada Elections Commission would conduct an enumeration, unless there existed a recently compiled provincial voters list. In this case the Commission could procure this list as its preliminary list, assuming agreement from the provincial or territorial government. The computer technology and software we recommend the Commission acquire would be necessary to automatically rearrange the lists in accordance with the polling divisions in the federal constituencies. It is probable that a federal enumeration would be required in specific constituencies or polling divisions if the provincial lists had not been compiled within 10 to 12 months before they were required by the Canada Elections Commission. This is not to suggest, however, that portions of these lists would not meet federal standards for coverage and accuracy.

A clear incentive exists for the provinces to enter such contractual arrangements because costs to produce the lists would be shared by the Commission. The savings would be considerable, especially in the larger provinces. Public expenditures on producing the lists would likewise be reduced with each agreement. The Commission's share of the cost to produce the preliminary lists, however, should not exceed one-quarter of the cost of conducting a separate federal enumeration in the given province. Recourse to this approach would entail increased costs in other areas: postage costs for mailing the vote-at cards, greater revision costs, and greater advertising costs to inform voters how they should proceed to ensure their name is on the list.

Recommendation 2.4.3

We recommend that the Canada Elections Commission enter into an agreement with each province and territory to acquire from either provincial voters registers or provincial voters lists the information to generate preliminary voters lists for federal polling divisions.

NOTES

1. Coverage is the ratio of the number of voters' names on a voters list to the total number of eligible persons residing in a given constituency.

2. Accuracy is the ratio of the number of correctly registered names and addresses of voters on a voters list to the total number of names on the list.

3. Currency is a measure of the relative decay over time of the information following its publication.

4. The section on Germany is based on research completed before German unification. It deals with the registration process in the former Federal Republic of Germany.

5. In the November 1991 Ontario municipal elections, there were media reports of individuals being listed as qualified voters, even though they were not Canadian citizens. Although the registration of non-qualified voters is an inevitable facet of any system of voter registration, the number of cases involved is normally very small. Further, an extensive and longer revision process ensures that there are opportunities for non-qualified voters to be removed from the list prior to election day.

6. The development and implementation of these projects were made possible through the co-operation and assistance of Revenue Ontario, Elections Ontario and Elections British Columbia. The Royal Commission on Electoral Reform and Party Financing would like to thank these offices for their generous assistance and contributions to its research program. The participation of these offices allowed the Commission to acquire a comprehensive understanding of the feasibility of a register of voters and of the relative capacities of different systems to produce preliminary voters lists under a variety of circumstances. In particular, the co-operation between Elections British Columbia and Elections Canada in the production and comparison of preliminary voters lists based on a random sampling of polling divisions suggests that federal-provincial co-operation in the voter registration process can result in the production of preliminary lists based on a provincial voters register that match or exceed levels of coverage and accuracy achieved through federal enumeration.

7. A similar approach could be adopted in British Columbia.

5

Aboriginal Constituencies
Implementation

INTRODUCTION

Aboriginal seats should not be guaranteed. The reasons behind this conclusion are discussed in Volume 1, Chapter 4. However, Aboriginal constituencies could be created by a process that would be guaranteed in the *Canada Elections Act*. This process would provide for the creation of one or more Aboriginal constituencies in a province whenever sufficient numbers of Aboriginal voters choose to register on an Aboriginal voters list. This number of Aboriginal voters would not be less than 85 per cent of the provincial quotient to ensure that the minimum size of the electorate in an Aboriginal constituency is not less than the minimum size of other constituencies in the province. Once an Aboriginal constituency is created, the procedures to be followed would, in almost all respects, be the same as those in general constituencies and would respect the equality of the vote for all voters in a province.

Aboriginal constituencies would be the same as general constituencies in the following respects:

- provisions respecting candidates;
- the appointment and functions of election officials for the constituency;
- powers, duties and responsibilities of the returning officer;
- principles and procedures for the registration of voters – enumeration, revision and election-day registration;
- principles and procedures for advance and election-day voting;
- principles and procedures for regular and mobile polling stations;
- principles and procedures for special ballots; and
- the counting of ballots and the reporting of results.

All election laws governing offences under the *Canada Elections Act* and all provisions relating to election and party finances would also apply.

The following pages give particular attention to certain aspects of our proposal which differ from the general regime we recommend for general constituencies.

ELECTION ADMINISTRATION

Once an Aboriginal constituency has been created, a returning officer who is a voter in that constituency would be appointed. This returning officer would be assisted in the performance of his or her duties by officials, all of whom, with the possible exception of enumerators, would have to be voters from the constituency. As outlined in Volume 2, Chapter 1, a returning officer could appoint enumerators who are not voters.

Under our recommendations, the returning officer would be responsible for planning and preparing for the election before an election call. Nowhere would this be more appropriate and important than in an Aboriginal constituency, which would cover a large area and require the use of the complete range of measures available to returning officers.

The returning officer would consult with registered constituency associations, Indian bands and Aboriginal organizations to recruit assistant returning officers, deputy returning officers, poll clerks, constables, enumerators, supervisory enumerators, revising officers and revising agents. After appointing these officials, the returning officer, with the assistance of the Canada Elections Commission, would train them.

Polling divisions for the constituency would be established on the basis of the known concentrations of Aboriginal voters. The returning officer would work with Indian bands to determine where to place polling stations and advance polling stations on reserves. He or she would also work with Indian bands and Aboriginal organizations to identify other areas with sufficient numbers of Aboriginal voters to need polling stations and advance polling stations. The returning officer would secure premises for polling stations, which could be located in band offices, Métis locals or friendship centres, or other suitable locations.

The returning officer would arrange with appropriate Aboriginal media to publicize the election and to advise Aboriginal voters to call a toll-free number to obtain more information. As well, notices could be posted at the offices of Indian bands and Aboriginal organizations, or on community bulletin boards. In large urban areas, daily or weekly newspapers could be used; unfortunately, most Aboriginal newspapers do not publish that frequently.

The Canada Elections Commission would determine where services in Aboriginal languages should be provided. The Commission and the returning officer in each province, in consultation with Indian bands and Aboriginal organizations, would develop specific standards for providing Aboriginal language services. The Commission would be responsible for providing these services.

Recommendation 2.5.1

We recommend that the Canada Elections Commission, in consultation with Indian bands and Aboriginal organizations, develop standards for the provision of Aboriginal language services in Aboriginal constituencies.

VOTER REGISTRATION

An Aboriginal constituency is created in a province when a sufficient number of Aboriginal voters register for the purpose of creating an Aboriginal constituency before the province's constituency boundaries are redrawn. This procedure is discussed later in this chapter. Unless a general election was held less than a year after this special registration process, the information on the register of Aboriginal voters would be too dated for use as a preliminary voters list for the election. Moreover, because the register would not be used often enough to justify continual updating, we do not propose creating a permanent Aboriginal voters list in any province.

Given that Aboriginal voters would be dispersed across a province, the registration of voters, especially in the enumeration phase, would require the adoption of methods not normally used in general constituencies.

In addition to an enumeration of Aboriginal voters on all Indian reserves and in other areas where there are high concentrations of Aboriginal voters, the returning officer could also work with Indian bands and Aboriginal organizations to actively search for voters. Mail-in registration forms could be placed in newspapers so that Aboriginal voters could register themselves. These forms would be identical to the mail-in enumeration cards that would be left at residences by enumerators. In areas where there are high concentrations of Aboriginal and non-Aboriginal voters, the returning officer for the Aboriginal constituency and the returning officer for the general constituency would each assign one enumerator who would then work in pairs.

Voters absent from their residences during enumeration would be left a numbered mail-in enumeration card, as recommended in Chapter 1 of this volume. In provinces with an Aboriginal constituency, this card would have a box where an Aboriginal voter could indicate that he or she wished to be registered to vote in the Aboriginal constituency or in the general constituency. The card would be mailed to the returning officer for the general constituency, who would forward it to the returning officer for the Aboriginal constituency. If necessary, the returning officer for the Aboriginal constituency would contact the Aboriginal voters who had indicated they wished to be registered to vote in that constituency.

In areas where Aboriginal voters are concentrated and enumerators for the Aboriginal constituency are conducting their enumeration, the return address on the mail-in enumeration card would be that of the Aboriginal constituency's returning officer. Voters, including Aboriginal voters, who wish to register to vote in the general constituency in which they reside would mark the box accordingly. The Aboriginal constituency returning officer would then forward these cards to the returning officer for the general constituency.

Recommendation 2.5.2

We recommend that

(a) all Aboriginal voters in Aboriginal constituencies be enumerated in areas where there are concentrations of Aboriginal people;
(b) in co-operation with the returning officer for a general constituency, a joint enumeration be conducted in those polls with concentrations of both Aboriginal and non-Aboriginal voters; and
(c) eligible Aboriginal voters be permitted to register by mail using a registration form published in newspapers.

As elsewhere, when the enumeration process has been completed, Aboriginal voters missed during the enumeration period could still register with a revising officer for the Aboriginal constituency or in person at an office of the Aboriginal constituency returning officer. A revising officer could also send revising agents to the homes of Aboriginal voters when they know such voters have not been enumerated. In addition, the returning officer would have the power to undertake a new enumeration of one or more areas that were missed or poorly enumerated.

As in general constituencies, Aboriginal voters would be permitted to register on election day at an Aboriginal polling station if they presented the prescribed identification and swore an oath or made an affirmation about their identity.

Finally, Aboriginal voters could register and apply for a special ballot in person at the office or sub-offices of the Aboriginal constituency returning officer, at the office(s) of any returning officer in the province or, in remote areas, at designated government offices. In all these cases, the general provisions of the special ballot would apply. Aboriginal voters living abroad or away from their home constituency would also be able to avail themselves of the general provisions for the use of the special ballot.

The process for verifying voters lists would be the same as in general constituencies, except there could also be a challenge to a voter's right to vote in an Aboriginal constituency on the grounds that the voter did not self-identify as an Aboriginal person and did not have Aboriginal ancestry or was not accepted as Aboriginal by her or his community. Given these conditions of eligibility to vote in an Aboriginal constituency, the Canada Elections Commission would appoint one or more Aboriginal voter eligibility panels for each Aboriginal constituency. These panels would be composed of a revising officer and two other voters. This panel would rule on any objections. As in general constituencies, the burden of proof would rest with the person making the objection.

Recommendation 2.5.3

We recommend that a revising officer and two other voters, appointed by the Canada Elections Commission from a list of elders and other voters in consultation with Indian bands and Aboriginal organizations, constitute Aboriginal voter eligibility panels to decide on objections to the right of a voter to be registered on an Aboriginal voters list on the grounds of his or her Aboriginal status.

VOTING PROCESS

Our recommendations for mobile polls (Volume 2, Chapter 2), including advance mobile polls, would increase voter participation by making it much easier for Aboriginal voters to get to a polling station to vote. Because Aboriginal constituencies would cover a large area, they should be designated as remote constituencies, as defined in Volume 2, Chapter 2. This designation would allow even more flexibility in voting generally and in obtaining and returning a special ballot in particular. Taken together, these recommendations will help to remove the barriers to enumeration and voting identified by Aboriginal people in our public hearings and in the report of the Committee for Aboriginal Electoral Reform. (Canada, Royal Commission 1991, Vol. 4)

Recommendation 2.5.4

We recommend that the *Canada Elections Act* designate Aboriginal constituencies as remote constituencies.

CANDIDATE SPENDING LIMITS AND PUBLIC FUNDING

As the Committee for Aboriginal Electoral Reform noted in its report, the financing of elections in Aboriginal constituencies "raises the concerns of how to facilitate meaningful campaigns over vast areas by people largely of limited means". (Canada, Royal Commission 1991, Vol. 4) These concerns must be reflected in the spending limits for candidates in Aboriginal constituencies and the public funding for which the candidates might qualify.

The *Canada Elections Act* already allows additional spending in sparsely populated constituencies – that is, those where there are fewer than 10 voters per square kilometre. This provision allows candidates to incur additional 'election expenses', and hence acquire correspondingly larger reimbursements, in the geographically largest and most remote constituencies. In 1988, the average expense limit in 91 such constituencies was $48 501, compared with $46 167 in the more densely populated constituencies.

As part of our recommendations on spending limits, we propose that the additional allowable spending per square kilometre in the sparsely populated constituencies be raised to 30 cents (from the present 15 cents) and that the maximum amount by which the total 'election expenses' limit can be adjusted upward be 50 per cent (compared with the present 25 per cent). This represents an increase of 26.3 per cent over the average limit in those constituencies if an election were held before 1 April 1992.

None of the Aboriginal constituencies that might be created has a population density greater than one person per square kilometre. Based on our recommendations for general constituencies, all would be classified as sparsely populated constituencies. We therefore propose that the provisions for sparsely populated constituencies also apply to Aboriginal constituencies. The same definition of election expenses would apply, as would the exclusions from the spending limits we recommend. This would mean, for example, that 'personal expenses', including the cost of the candidate's travel, would not be counted against the spending limit.

Recommendation 2.5.5

We recommend that the limit for the election expenses of a candidate in an Aboriginal constituency be calculated based on the formula for sparsely populated general constituencies.

A second issue is the funding of the campaigns of candidates in Aboriginal constituencies. In its report, the Committee for Aboriginal Electoral Reform (Canada, Royal Commission 1991, Vol. 4) notes that candidates would face difficulties because of the smaller pool of resources within the Aboriginal community and because the political contribution tax credit provides little incentive to Indians living on reserves, since they are not subject to taxation. While it is to be hoped that political parties will provide assistance, not all Aboriginal candidates can be expected to run under a party banner. To parallel the provisions pertaining to spending limits, the post-election reimbursement to candidates should be the same as for candidates in sparsely populated constituencies.

Recommendation 2.5.6

We recommend that candidates in Aboriginal constituencies be reimbursed according to the same provisions that apply to candidates in sparsely populated general constituencies.

The principle behind reimbursements is that qualifying candidates receive a measure of public funding to help defray their campaign costs. However, some candidates, for example, women, may find it difficult to raise the funds to mount even a modest campaign. Similarly, some people in Aboriginal communities might not be able to afford to offer their alternative viewpoints as candidates, and the range of representation from within the Aboriginal population would be diminished. An additional measure of public funding during the campaign itself, rather than afterward, would encourage fuller debate and fairer competition within Aboriginal constituencies.

One approach would be to publish a booklet under the authority of the Aboriginal constituency returning officer. This booklet could include a statement from each Aboriginal candidate outlining his or her election platform. A number of U.S. jurisdictions distribute similar publications, sometimes called 'voters guides', which may also include basic information about voter registration and the location of polling places. An information booklet about the options presented to voters was distributed to residents of northern Quebec, who are mostly of Inuit origin, before the 1987 referendum on the options for drafting a constitution for their regional assembly.

If a booklet of this kind were made available in Aboriginal constituencies, candidates would submit the statements in the language of their choice and these would be reproduced 'as is'; it would be necessary, however, to develop minimum standards to follow in preparing the statements. (The New York City Campaign Finance Board (1990) has a set of regulations for candidates, and statements are reviewed to ensure they are not libellous.) A photograph of each candidate would also be useful. A copy of the booklet should be sent by the returning officer to each Aboriginal voter. Additional copies should be distributed to Indian bands and Aboriginal organizations and should be available in the office and sub-offices of the Aboriginal constituency returning officer. The Canada Elections Commission would cover the costs of producing and distributing the booklet. In this way, all candidates would have at least one opportunity to communicate with the entire Aboriginal electorate.

Recommendation 2.5.7

We recommend that

(a) during the period between the close of nominations and the seventh day before election day, the Aboriginal constituency returning officer mail to each person on the Aboriginal voters list a booklet with a statement from and a photograph of each candidate who wishes to participate;

(b) the returning officer distribute the booklet as widely as possible; and

(c) the Canada Elections Commission cover the costs of producing and distributing the booklet.

CREATING ABORIGINAL CONSTITUENCIES

As outlined in Volume 1, Chapter 4, one or more Aboriginal constituencies could be created in a province whenever sufficient numbers of Aboriginal voters choose to register as Aboriginal voters in that province. The number of Aboriginal constituencies that could be established would be determined before a province's electoral boundaries were redrawn, after a redistribution of seats or a general election.

If the process to create Aboriginal constituencies in the provinces where they don't yet exist were in place for the election immediately following the next adjustment of constituency boundaries, the following procedures would be followed. To determine the number of Aboriginal constituencies that could be established in a province, the estimated number of Aboriginal voters from the last census would be divided by the quotient for that province. Once this information was available, the Canada Elections Commission would publish the potential number of Aboriginal constituencies that could be established in each province. In provinces where one or more Aboriginal constituencies might be created, a special registration of Aboriginal voters in the provinces concerned would have to be completed as soon as possible.

The Registration of Aboriginal Voters

The first step in the process would be to determine the number of Aboriginal voters in a province who wished to vote in an Aboriginal constituency. The Canada Elections Commission would have to establish a registration office in each province where it was estimated that one or more Aboriginal constituencies could be created. This office would be headed by a registration officer appointed by the Commission. This official should be a voter who intends to register as an Aboriginal voter. In co-operation with Indian bands, Aboriginal organizations and the Aboriginal media, the Commission would undertake a special Aboriginal voter registration drive. A variety of communications techniques could be used, including videos and portable displays with information in Aboriginal languages. A community education program could deal with issues such as the purposes of Aboriginal constituencies, how they could be created and how voters could be registered on the register of Aboriginal voters.

Recommendation 2.5.8

We recommend that the Canada Elections Commission establish a voter registration office in each province where Aboriginal constituencies could be created to register eligible Aboriginal voters who wished to vote in an Aboriginal constituency.

Four approaches could be used to enable Aboriginal voters to register on the Aboriginal voters register. Although these approaches are similar to the ones used for registering voters before an election, they are modified so they can be used independently of an election.

First, enumerators appointed by the provincial registration officer could enumerate in areas where there are concentrations of Aboriginal persons. Second, newspaper advertisements could be published in Aboriginal and other print media with a mail-in registration form. Voters who used these forms to register would be required to provide their name and address so that a registration officer could verify the identity of voters if necessary. Third, the voter registration office could undertake an active search for Aboriginal voters and communicate with them. The provincial registration officer would work with Indian bands and Aboriginal organizations to complete this search. Fourth, the voter registration office could also organize a final 'registration-day' drive in co-operation with Indian bands and Aboriginal organizations, advertised through both Aboriginal and non-Aboriginal media, to encourage voters to register at various registration locations throughout the province. This last provision would be analogous to election-day registration during an election.

This process would be designed not only to enable Aboriginal people to register with the greatest possible ease, but also to identify and register Aboriginal voters who have not been inclined to register or vote in a general constituency but who might wish to register and vote in an Aboriginal constituency.

Recommendation 2.5.9

We recommend that for the purposes of registering Aboriginal voters to determine whether one or more Aboriginal constituencies would be created in a province:

(a) **an enumeration of voters be conducted in areas where there are concentrations of Aboriginal persons;**
(b) **eligible voters be permitted to register by mail;**
(c) **the voter registration office undertake an active search for eligible voters; and**
(d) **the Aboriginal voter registration office organize a final registration-day drive.**

At the conclusion of the registration process, the provincial registration officer would be required to prepare a register of Aboriginal voters with the name and address of each eligible voter. To respect a voter's right to privacy, the voter's address would not be published if a voter so requested. On completion, the register would be open for inspection by registered Aboriginal voters at the office of the registration officer.

Recommendation 2.5.10

We recommend that

(a) **a registered voter be permitted to give the address of an Indian band office, Métis local or friendship centre or the Aboriginal**

voter registration office in place of her or his actual place of
residence to ensure that individual's privacy; and

(b) the register of Aboriginal voters be open for inspection by registered Aboriginal voters at the provincial registration office.

After the registration of Aboriginal voters has been completed and the
register made available for inspection, any voter whose name appears on
the register should be permitted to object to the right of any other voter to
be included in the register. An objection must be made in writing to the
provincial registration officer within two weeks of the register being made
open for inspection. The objection must identify the person making the objection and give her or his address and phone number. The objection must state
the name of the person being objected to and grounds for the objection. The
objection must be dated and signed by the person making the objection.

Where it is determined by the registration officer, or an agent designated by her or him, that a prima facie case has been made against a registered voter, the voter being objected to must immediately be informed of the
objection. The Canada Elections Commission would then appoint a panel
or panels to hear and decide on objections. These panels would be chaired
by the registration officer, or her or his designate, and include two other
Aboriginal voters selected by the Canada Elections Commission from a list
drawn up in consultation with Indian bands and Aboriginal organizations
in the province. Voters appointed to a panel should come from the same
Aboriginal group as the voter being objected to; for example, an objection
to a voter who claims Métis identity would be heard by a panel whose two
appointed members were Métis voters. These panels would sit to hear
objections no later than one week after the deadline for the receipt of written objections. These panels would be required to hear presentations from
or on behalf of the person whose right to be registered as an Aboriginal
voter has been challenged. The person making the objection would have
the burden of proving that the person should be removed from the register
of Aboriginal voters. On application, a panel could grant intervener status
to other Aboriginal voters or to any Indian band or Aboriginal organization
having sufficient interest in the case. Following a hearing to hear objections,
a panel would have two days to render its decision.

Recommendation 2.5.11

We recommend that

(a) **Aboriginal voter eligibility panels, chaired by the provincial registration officer, or her or his designate, decide on
objections to a voter on the register of Aboriginal voters; and**

(b) **each panel include two registered Aboriginal voters
appointed by the Canada Elections Commission from a list
of elders and other qualified men and women drawn up in**

**consultation with Indian bands and Aboriginal organiza-
tions in the province.**

Any party to the proceedings should have a right to have a court of
law review the decision of an Aboriginal voter eligibility panel. We propose that the Federal Court of Canada be designated for this purpose. On
application, the Federal Court of Canada could grant intervener status to
other Aboriginal voters or to any Indian band or Aboriginal organization
having sufficient interest in the issue requiring adjudication.

Recommendation 2.5.12

**We recommend that a decision of an Aboriginal voter eligibility
panel be subject to review by the Federal Court of Canada.**

Each provincial boundaries commission should complete the register
of Aboriginal voters before drawing the electoral boundaries. This should
be completed within three months following the passage of the legislation
to establish a process for creating Aboriginal constituencies or the start of
a constituency boundaries adjustment in a province. A further one-month
period should be allowed to permit objections to be decided on. After this
period, the provincial Aboriginal registration officer would place a completed register before the electoral boundaries commission for the province
and the chief electoral officer. The latter would be responsible for determining the number of Aboriginal constituencies to be created. This would
be accomplished by dividing the number of voters whose names appear on
the register of Aboriginal voters in a province by the number equal to
85 per cent of the provincial quotient.

The foregoing procedures would be required only when no Aboriginal
constituencies exist in a province. Where they exist, no special registration
would take place because the determination of the number of Aboriginal
constituencies would be made on the basis of the number of voters registered on the final voters lists for Aboriginal constituencies for the previous
election, just as the electoral quotient and boundaries for each general constituency are established.

Drawing Aboriginal Constituency Boundaries

Under present legislation and our proposals, boundaries commissions for
each province are chaired by a judge appointed by the Chief Justice of that
province. The Speaker of the House of Commons chooses the other two
members. In a province where only one Aboriginal constituency would be
created, the boundaries of the province would serve as the boundaries of
that Aboriginal constituency.

Where the chief electoral officer has determined that more than one
Aboriginal constituency would be created, Aboriginal voters should be

represented on a commission for the determination of the boundaries of the Aboriginal constituencies. This could be done by having the Speaker of the House of Commons appoint two registered Aboriginal voters from the province to this commission. These two members, along with the chair of the boundaries commission, would be appointed to draw the boundaries of the Aboriginal constituencies only. The procedures to be followed for drawing the boundaries of Aboriginal constituencies would be the same as for general constituencies, namely, publishing proposed constituency boundaries, conducting public hearings, revising boundaries and submitting reports to the Canada Elections Commission for transmittal to the Speaker of the House of Commons. The report of the electoral boundaries commission on Aboriginal constituency boundaries would be an integral part of the commission's report for the entire province.

Aboriginal constituencies would be designed on the basis of comparable population and community of interest criteria. Depending on circumstances, Aboriginal constituencies could be created on a geographical basis or to reflect different communities within the Aboriginal population of a province. In the latter case, the territory of the Aboriginal constituencies may very well encompass the whole province and even overlap.

Recommendation 2.5.13

We recommend that where more than one Aboriginal constituency is to be created in a province, a special boundaries commission be created, composed of the chairperson of the boundaries commission for the province, who shall also act as chair for this special commission, plus two Aboriginal voters appointed by the Speaker of the House of Commons, with the mandate to determine the boundaries and names of the Aboriginal constituencies.

6

APPLYING THE REGULATORY FRAMEWORK FOR ELECTION EXPENSES AND THE REPORTING OF POLITICAL FINANCE

INTRODUCTION

CONSISTENT WITH OUR objectives of achieving greater fairness and strengthening the integrity of the electoral process, we recommend in Volume 1 reforms to the regulatory framework for party and election finance, including its extension to require registration of constituency associations and disclosure of their finances, spending limits for those seeking nomination as a candidate or the leadership of a registered political party, and disclosure of contributions to and spending during leadership and nomination campaigns.

The recommendations on party and election finance in Volume 1 are relatively specific, but they do not include the technical and procedural details needed to apply the regulatory framework we propose. In this chapter we provide recommendations on these matters, which in turn constitute the rationale for several sections of our draft legislative proposal in Volume 3.

This chapter contains several references to the *Report* of the Accounting Profession Working Group on Election/Party Finance Reporting at the Local Level. (Canada, Royal Commission 1991a) This Working Group included representatives from the major Canadian professional accounting organizations: the Canadian Institute of Chartered Accountants, the Certified General Accountants Association of Canada and the Society of Management Accountants of Canada. It was chaired by Denis Desautels, who was subsequently appointed Auditor General of Canada. We asked the Working Group to review the current legislation and procedures for reporting on candidates' expenses and contributions during federal elections, and to consider legislation and procedures that could apply to the ongoing activities of constituency associations.

The Working Group presented an initial proposal for discussion at our symposium on election and party financing at the constituency level in Winnipeg in November 1990. The participants at this symposium included official agents and other persons who have been active at the constituency level. Participants discussed the Working Group's proposal in detail and generally supported the approach that had been taken. The final report of the Working Group, submitted in February 1991, reflected comments from participants at the Winnipeg symposium and from others with experience in this area. The conclusions of the Working Group provided valuable guidance on a number of matters discussed in this chapter.

THE SCOPE OF THE SPENDING LIMITS

Definition of Election Expenses

To be effective in pursuing fairness in the electoral process, statutory election spending limits must be linked to a definition of 'election expenses'. The definition describes the scope of spending limits, that is, which aspects of campaign spending are to be controlled. Having a clear definition is critical. Vague or ambiguous language can lead to confusion about just what expenses are included in the limits; this could allow parties or candidates room to exempt certain items so their spending does not exceed the limit. If this happens, fairness in the electoral process will be undermined.

In addition, election campaigns involve thousands of Canadians who, as a rule, are genuinely concerned that the law be respected and that they not become personally involved in situations where their integrity would be questioned. Because the concept of 'election expenses' is such a key part of the spending limits framework, an ambiguous definition runs counter to the objective of promoting the active participation of Canadians in the electoral process. An unclear definition is also unfair to Canadians who work on election campaigns because it may put them at risk. This concern, voiced most strongly by official agents, is legitimate.

In Canada, approaches differ at the federal and provincial levels for defining election expenses. Under one approach, sometimes referred to as 'inclusive', an initial broad definition of election expenses is followed by a few specific exclusions and, in some cases, inclusions. Of the seven provinces that have statutory spending limits, five have adopted this inclusive approach (Quebec, Ontario, Nova Scotia, New Brunswick and Prince Edward Island). In contrast, the federal definition of election expenses entails an initial statement followed by a list of several items considered to be election expenses; the list, although not intended to be exhaustive, helps give meaning to the definition (see the appendix to this chapter).

Even the most carefully drafted definition may not be clear on all points, and changes in campaign practices may raise questions about whether the definition applies or not. It is thus not unusual to rely on guidelines or regulations to explain or clarify the definition of election expenses, particularly its exclusions or inclusions. Quebec's *Election Act* allows the chief electoral officer to issue regulations, and in Ontario the Commission on Election Expenses has the authority to issue guidelines. In contrast, the *Canada Elections Act* does not specifically provide for issuing either regulations or guidelines. However, guidelines were developed through an informal process and, in practice, have played a major role in determining the meaning of the definition of election expenses.

Not long after the *Election Expenses Act* came into effect, the chief electoral officer invited officials of the political parties represented in Parliament to a meeting to discuss implementation of the new Act. This led to the establishment of what came to be referred to as the Ad Hoc Committee. This Committee met regularly, and a number of its recommendations were incorporated in Bill C-5, enacted in 1977. The Committee also prepared, before the 1979 federal election, guidelines and procedures on election expenses. This document, intended for candidates and their official agents, explained certain aspects of the definition of election expenses. In this way, the work of the Ad Hoc Committee helped pave the way for the first election held under the new rules. Following discussions within the Ad Hoc Committee, the guidelines have been revised before each subsequent election. In 1984, a separate publication, *Guidelines Respecting Election Expenses of Registered Political Parties*, was issued; a revised version of this was prepared for the 1988 election. (Canada, Elections Canada 1988b)

In developing the guidelines, the wording of the definition of election expenses was significant. In particular, the definition includes what has been called a purpose test: election expenses are incurred "for the purpose of promoting or opposing, directly and during an election, a particular registered party, or … candidate".

Although the guidelines did not have the force of law, they reflected legal opinions and, in certain cases, jurisprudence. For example, the chief electoral officer concluded there was little advantage in giving a strict interpretation to the legislation if this would not stand in court, particularly since some judges have tended to give a broad interpretation to the election expenses provisions of the *Canada Elections Act*.[1]

The guidelines have also been relevant to enforcement: they specifically state that adherence to them will protect candidates and parties from legal action, as indicated in the 1988 *Guidelines and Procedures Respecting Election Expenses of Candidates*: "[These guidelines] represent a sort of insurance policy for the candidate and official agent. Compliance with these guidelines will ensure no prosecution will be initiated by the Commissioner [of Canada Elections]." (Canada, Elections Canada 1988a, 1) (The guidelines for registered parties included a similar statement.)

Based on the guidelines and specific provisions of the *Canada Elections Act*, the following items are not considered election expenses of *candidates*:

- any material that is not used and remains on hand at the end of the election;
- volunteer labour;
- the salary of those poll agents who are paid less than the commercial value of their services, as well as reimbursement of their expenses (for example, meals and transportation);
- the cost of printed material used to directly promote the election of a candidate before the issue of the writs;

- nomination expenses;
- the candidate's deposit;
- the cost of victory parties held after the polls close;
- auditors' fees;
- charges for legal services; and
- the costs of preparing returns required by the Act.

In addition, under the *Canada Elections Act*, a candidate's personal expenses are considered election expenses for the purposes of reimbursement, but they are not subject to the spending limit. A number of the above items are exempted from the definition of election expenses under the legislation in certain provinces and thus are not covered by the spending limits (see, for example, the Ontario and Quebec definitions found in the appendix to this chapter).

Under the present Act, federal candidates are nonetheless expected to report all election-related spending. There are three categories: (1) election expenses; (2) personal expenses; and (3) spending on goods and services that are excluded from the limits. This last category, which is not defined in the *Canada Elections Act* or explained in the guidelines, is referred to as campaign expenses or other expenses. In a 1989 publication, the chief electoral officer described campaign expenses as a "default concept which refers to anything not an election expense". (Canada, Elections Canada 1989, 1) Such spending is to be reported in a separate part of the candidate's post-election return. However, based on the Act's requirements for publishing in a newspaper after each election a summary of each candidate's election spending, the chief electoral officer has included only the election expenses and personal expenses.

Based on the guidelines, the definition of election expenses as it applies to *political parties* does not include the following main items:

- developing the party's policies or programs;
- developing the party's strategies;
- carrying out research and analyses relating to the [above two] activities;
- public opinion polling;
- training the party's candidates, official agents and workers;
- 50 per cent of the costs of fund-raising activities, including direct mail, that both solicit funds and promote and/or oppose a party;
- normal administrative costs of maintaining the party as an ongoing entity (the costs of staff and facilities as election expenses are to be allocated "reasonably"); and
- all other internal costs not incurred as an integral part of endeavours furthering the external exposure of the party. (Canada, Elections Canada 1988b, 2–9)

These federal exclusions for political parties differ much more from the legislation and practice in many provinces than do the federal exclusions for candidates. However, in large measure this reflects the wording of the federal definition of election expenses. Quebec's definition has a broader scope because spending to promote or oppose, directly *or indirectly*, the election of a candidate or candidates is considered an election expense under the Quebec *Election Act* (see the appendix to this chapter). Quebec's definition is considered one of the most comprehensive in Canada and has worked well (Quebec adopted spending limits in 1963).

While the purpose test in the federal definition is central to determining what is and is not an election expense for political parties, the guidelines provide additional interpretation based on the "primary objectives of a political party", namely:

(a) attracting adherents to [the party's] policies;
(b) soliciting others to join with them as members of the party; and
(c) attracting voters for candidates of the party in an election. (Canada, Elections Canada 1988b, 2)

The guidelines then state:

We consider all activities which directly promote these primary objectives during an election to give rise to election expenses of a political party. All other party activities, such as formation of policy and training of workers, are secondary to the primary objectives and are not election expenses. (Canada, Elections Canada 1988b, 3)

This rationale explains certain of these exclusions. In relation to polling, for example, the guidelines state: "The cost of collecting and analysing survey information is not an election expense as the activity does not result in the direct promotion of a party, its leader, candidates, members, programs or policies and therefore does not directly support the primary objectives of the party." (Canada, Elections Canada 1988b, 7) Needless to say, these Jesuitical rationalizations are not convincing!

The present definition of election expenses in the *Canada Elections Act* and the guidelines issued by Elections Canada raise a number of issues. First, the process used to develop these guidelines has been criticized, especially for the ways in which ambiguities about the definition have been resolved. The Ad Hoc Committee has always met in private, its minutes are confidential and it does not include political parties not represented in Parliament. Except when its recommendations have led to amendments to the Act, agreements reached by the Committee have not been subject to public or parliamentary debate. Yet, as noted above, the guidelines have had considerable authority in relation to enforcement.

Second, the definition of election expenses, particularly the words "for the purpose of promoting or opposing, directly", has allowed major items that would be covered by a more inclusive definition to be exempted from the spending limits. The legislation on spending limits in most provinces relies on a more inclusive definition. This is particularly the case for parties because the addition of the primary objectives test in the federal guidelines has narrowed the scope of the statutory spending limits even further.

Third, the division of candidates' election-related spending into three separate categories has not only caused complications for their official agents, but also has led some to question the effectiveness of the spending limits. The significant amounts sometimes reported as other expenses highlight this concern. The transparency of reporting procedures is also diminished by these categories because these 'other expenses' are not included in the chief electoral officer's post-election publications.

In considering the definition of election expenses, the Accounting Profession Working Group concluded that:

> The current definition of election expenses has proven confusing and difficult to enforce. The definition, as found in the current *Canada Elections Act* and interpreted by the current *Guidelines*, provides a lengthy list of what is meant by election expenses. The Working Group has rejected this approach. Instead, it favours a broadly worded inclusive definition that will include all expenses incurred by political entities. (Canada, Royal Commission 1991a, Part 1, 4–5)

A clear, straightforward and comprehensive definition of election expenses is essential. The definition must meet this standard because election campaigns, particularly at the constituency level, involve thousands of volunteers who need clear rules they can follow with relative ease. Such rules also help ensure that candidates and political parties fully respect the intent of the spending limits, and in so doing give Canadians reason to be confident that the limits are effective and apply to all contestants. As for the wording of the definition, we have given due consideration to relevant legislation at the provincial level and in other countries, and have reviewed a number of proposals, including that of the Working Group (see the appendix to this chapter). Accordingly, we recommend in Volume 1, Chapter 6 that election expenses be defined to include:

> the cost of any goods or services used during an election:
> 1. to promote or oppose, directly or indirectly, the election of a candidate;
> 2. to promote or oppose a registered party or the program or policies of a candidate or registered party; or
> 3. to approve or disapprove a course of action advocated or opposed by a candidate, registered party or leader of a registered party; and shall include an amount equal to any contribution of goods or services used during the election.

Subsections 1 to 3 would cover virtually all spending specifically relating to an election. The final part of the definition makes it clear that goods or services provided to a candidate or party and used during the election would have to be counted as election expenses because they are the equivalent of spending on behalf of the candidate or party. In its report, the Accounting Profession Working Group suggested that "for the purpose of calculating election expenses, the value of inventory consumed during the campaign period should be included". (Canada, Royal Commission 1991a, Part 1, 6) We agree with this approach, which means that the cost of materials and the depreciation of equipment owned by a constituency association and used by a candidate would be counted as election expenses of the candidate.

As noted above, at the federal level and in the seven provinces that have spending limits, electoral law stipulates a number of exclusions and/or inclusions in defining election expenses. In most cases, this determines which expenses are covered by the limits. The Accounting Profession Working Group recommended that *all* election-related spending be covered by the definition of election expenses and fully reported. Nonetheless, certain items, including personal expenses (as defined), would continue to be excluded from the spending limits. These would be reported separately from the expenses that would be subject to limits. This approach would provide full accountability and a high degree of transparency.

The final issue in considering the scope of the spending limits is what items should be specifically excluded from the limits. We have reviewed the relevant provincial legislation, guidelines and regulations, as well as the list proposed by the Accounting Profession Working Group.

Recommendation 2.6.1

We recommend that the *Canada Elections Act* provide for the following exclusions from the election spending limits:
(1) expenses incurred by or on behalf of a candidate in seeking nomination;
(2) a candidate's performance guarantee;
(3) expenses incurred in holding a fund-raising function, except if a deficit is incurred, in which case the deficit be counted against the limit;
(4) transfers of funds to a candidate, a registered party or a registered constituency association;
(5) expenses incurred exclusively for the ongoing administration of the registered party or registered constituency association;
(6) expenses incurred for post-election parties held and thank-you advertising published after the close of the polls;
(7) professional fees or labour required to help comply with the Act;
(8) the costs of communications addressed exclusively to members of the registered party or registered constituency association;

(9) interest accrued during the election on any loan lawfully granted to a candidate or official agent for election expenses; and

(10) the personal expenses of a candidate, meaning only the reasonable expenses incurred by or on behalf of the candidate during the election for

(i) the cost of care paid on behalf of a child or other family member for whom the candidate is normally directly responsible;

(ii) travelling costs to and within the constituency;

(iii) the cost of rental of the candidate's temporary residence necessary for the election;

(iv) the cost of lodging, meals and incidental charges while travelling to and within the constituency;

(v) expenses that result directly from a candidate's physical disability, including the services of a person required to assist a candidate to perform the functions necessary to seeking election; and

(vi) other expenses the Canada Elections Commission determines from time to time are personal expenses of a candidate.

Items 1 to 6 and item 10 in recommendation 2.6.1 are based on the proposal of the Accounting Profession Working Group. Items 1, 2 and 6 are currently exemptions at the federal level and in Ontario (nomination spending limits are discussed in Volume 1, Chapter 6). Item 3 is an exemption under the Ontario legislation. The costs of raising funds should not count against the candidate's limit, although the net amount raised should be reported as a contribution. To ensure this exemption is not abused, however, where a fund-raising function incurs a deficit, the amount of the deficit should be counted against the candidate's spending limit. In addition, transfers of funds within a party, item 4, should not be counted against the limit, although these transfers would have to be reported as contributions.

For item 5, the federal guidelines now exclude the "normal administrative costs of maintaining the party as an ongoing entity". Political parties and at least some constituency associations will continue to incur ongoing administrative costs during an election campaign. These should not be counted against the spending limit; however, any additional administrative costs incurred for election purposes should be counted against the spending limits. Item 7 has been included because costs of complying with the legislation should not be counted against the spending limit. Auditing and accounting fees are an exclusion under the Ontario Act, and the federal guidelines currently exclude auditors' fees and the costs of preparing returns required by the Act. In addition, the chief electoral officer previously ruled that lawyers' services related to complying with the Act should not be counted against the limits.

Although communications addressed to party members may have the effect of promoting a candidate or party, we propose in item 8 that the costs of such communications be exempted, if these communications are addressed *only to party members*. This means, for example, that the costs of a mailing that solicits funds would be excluded from the spending limit provided the letters were not addressed to anyone beyond the party membership. This is consistent with our proposal that communications with the members of interest groups and other non-registered participants not count against the spending limit for independent expenditures. However, if the communications were addressed to others who are not party members, as is often the case with direct mail campaigns, the entire cost would count against the spending limit. Print or electronic media advertisements would not fall under this exemption.

Quebec's *Election Act* exempts interest on loans from the beginning of the election period until 90 days after polling day. Although many candidates benefit from transfers from the constituency association or registered party, this is not always the case; independent candidates, for example, do not have access to such benefits. Candidates who are obliged to take out a loan for their campaign should not be put at a disadvantage in relation to candidates with greater access to financial resources. We therefore propose (item 9) that interest on loans be excluded from the spending limits. The list of personal expenses (item 10) follows the proposal of the Accounting Profession Working Group, with some modifications.

We recommend the above approach because it is essential to have full reporting of all election-related expenses. From experience at the federal and provincial levels, however, certain items should be excluded from the spending limits. These exclusions should be clearly stated and not so numerous or significant as to lead to what would be, in effect, a partial spending limit.

Recommendation 2.6.2

We recommend that candidates and registered parties be required to report all election expenses but that spending on items 1 to 10 listed in recommendation 2.6.1 be excluded from the relevant spending limit.

Other Definitions Related to Election Expenses
Effective application of the election expenses provisions requires that related matters be defined in the Act. Certain definitions found in the proposed legislation need to be explained. (Canada, Royal Commission 1991, Vol. 3)

Contribution of Goods or Services
Political parties and candidates receive contributions in the form of donations of goods or services and discounts on goods required for the election campaign. Contributions other than money must be counted as expenses

because they are, in fact, spending on behalf of the campaign that would otherwise have to pay for the goods or services. This matter is currently covered by the lengthy definition of election expenses in the *Canada Elections Act*. That definition includes as election expenses

(c)   the commercial value of goods and services donated or provided, other than volunteer labour, and

(d)   amounts that represent the differences between amounts paid and liabilities incurred for goods and services, other than volunteer labour, and the commercial value thereof where they are provided at less than their commercial value.

In essence, these parts of the current definition of election expenses define what is a contribution of goods or services; item (d) really defines what is normally called a discount. We recommend a more straightforward and inclusive approach to defining election expenses. This objective would be easier to achieve if separate definitions of related matters were provided. The Accounting Profession Working Group proposed the following separate and comprehensive definition of contribution of goods or services:

Contribution of goods or services includes,

(a)   a contribution by way of donation, advance, deposit, discount or otherwise of any tangible personal property, except money, or of services of any description, whether industrial, trade, professional or otherwise, but does not include

(b)   any goods produced or services performed for any political party, electoral district association or candidate by volunteer labour. (Canada, Royal Commission 1991a, Part 2, 2)

We find this proposed wording broadly acceptable. This definition exempts volunteer labour. A further issue is whether there should be an exemption for goods or services that have a commercial value below a certain threshold. The present definition of commercial value stipulates that if the aggregate commercial value of goods or services donated by someone is less than $100 the value is deemed to be nil; as a result, such a contribution of goods or services does not count as an election expense. This exemption means that the official agent does not have to assign a value to or count as an election expense smaller donations of goods or services – such as the case of someone who donates a few pounds of coffee to the campaign organization or offers to make a few hundred photocopies. The threshold for this exemption was set at $100 in 1974 and remains at the same level. This should be adjusted and we propose that, as with the threshold for disclosure of contributions, the exemption be raised to $250. It would also be preferable for this exemption to be part of the definition of contribution of goods or services rather than in a separate section of the *Canada Elections Act*.

The *Canada Elections Act* now stipulates that "the commercial value of any free broadcasting time ... [provided] to a ... political party ... shall not be taken into consideration in calculating its election expenses." We agree that free time should continue not to be counted as an election expense. Free broadcasting time should therefore be added as an item not considered a contribution of goods or services. Similarly, the value of any time provided on a regular or public affairs program or free advertising space or editorial content in a publication during the election should be excluded.

Recommendation 2.6.3

We recommend that the *Canada Elections Act* stipulate that a contribution of goods or services is:
(1) a contribution by way of donation, advance, deposit, discount or otherwise of any tangible personal property, except money, or of services of any description, whether industrial, trade, professional or otherwise; but not
(2) any goods produced or services performed by volunteer labour or goods or services that have a commercial value, in the aggregate and during any reporting period, of less than $250; the value of any broadcasting time provided on a regular or public affairs program; free advertising space in a newspaper, periodical or printed matter provided that it is made available on an equitable basis to all participants; editorials, news, interviews, columns, letters to the editor, commentaries or public affairs programs as part of a bona fide publication in a periodical or a broadcast by a radio or television station; or books produced, promoted and distributed at fair market value that were planned to be put on sale regardless of the election.

Volunteer Labour
Our proposed definition of contribution of goods or services excludes "any goods produced or services performed by ... volunteer labour". Volunteer labour must therefore be defined in the Act. Volunteer labour is now defined in the *Canada Elections Act* as:

> any service provided free of charge by a person outside of that person's working hours, but does not include a service provided by a person who is self-employed if the service is one that is normally sold or otherwise charged for by that person.

As a result of questions raised by parties and candidates, this definition had to be amplified by the *Guidelines and Procedures Respecting Election Expenses of Candidates* produced by Elections Canada. The guidelines (1988a, 19) provide examples of volunteer labour, among them the services of a secretary on "unpaid leave of absence working as a secretary in the campaign office;

a self-employed insurance [salesperson] working for the campaign free of charge doing door to door canvassing; and unemployed or retired persons working anytime". The guidelines indicate that donated labour must be reported as a contribution and as an election expense. An example of donated labour given in the guidelines is a secretary employed by an insurance agent who is paid her or his salary while working as a secretary for a campaign. (1988a, 20) The guidelines are relatively clear on these matters, but the Act should specify that volunteer labour does not include labour provided by a person whose services are made available by an employer or who is receiving remuneration for goods produced or services performed. This would mean, for example, that the services of a union organizer assigned to work on a campaign whose salary continues to be paid by the union would not be considered volunteer labour and therefore would constitute an 'election expense'. However, the services of someone who had taken an unpaid leave of absence to work on a campaign would be considered volunteer labour.

As for self-employed 'volunteers', the guidelines stipulate that "the services of a person who is self-employed are not volunteer labour if the service is one for which that person is normally remunerated". (1988a, 19) An example given is printing services provided free of charge by a self-employed printer. The issue of services provided by self-employed people was raised during our hearings. One witness made the following comment:

> The definition of volunteer labour discriminates between self-employed individuals and individuals employed by a corporation or other organization. For example, a sign painter employed by a corporation could paint signs for a campaign and not have his labour counted as an election expense provided he performed this service outside his normal working hours. On the other hand, a self-employed sign painter could not provide the identical service at any time without such service being counted as an election expense. (Harry Katz, Brief 1990, 13–14)

Although the witness raised a legitimate concern, the issue must be seen in a broader context. More and more Canadians are self-employed, and in a number of cases the work they do may be useful to campaign organizations. Many political consultants and pollsters, as well as writers and editors, are self-employed; they rely on contracts with their clients. A blanket exemption for services provided by self-employed people would create an inequity. Campaigns that could draw on a range of such people to produce the goods or perform the services they normally sell or charge for would have an advantage over campaigns that could not. Campaigns that do not have access to such contacts would be required to pay for such services or, if they were paid for by the person's employer, the service would be counted as a contribution and an election expense. We therefore propose that the Act continue to exclude from the definition of volunteer labour the goods or services provided by self-employed people who normally produce or sell such services. This would not, however, prevent self-employed people from participating in campaigns in other ways; and in such cases, their participation would be considered as volunteer labour.

This issue should also be seen in the context of our recommendation that professional fees required to help comply with the Act not be subject to the spending limits. This means, for example, that the cost or value of the services of an accountant or lawyer advising the official agent or candidate on the application of the election expenses provisions of the Act would not be counted against the limit; this would apply whether the accountant or lawyer was employed by a firm or self-employed. Because most campaigns rely on such services in one form or another, this should not lead to any considerable measure of inequity. For the definition of volunteer labour, we accept the proposal of the Accounting Profession Working Group.

Recommendation 2.6.4

We recommend that 'volunteer labour' be defined in the *Canada Elections Act* as any labour provided by an individual for which no remuneration or direct material benefit is received either during an election or otherwise, but does not include labour provided by:
(1) a person who is self-employed if the goods produced or services performed are normally sold or otherwise charged for by that person; or
(2) a person whose services are made available by an employer.

Commercial Value
Goods or services are frequently provided free of charge to election campaign organizations. At present, the *Canada Elections Act* requires that the value of these goods or services be recorded as election expenses if certain criteria are met. The Act defines the commercial value of goods or services donated or provided at less than their commercial value as meaning:

(a) where the person by whom the goods or services are so donated or provided is in the business of supplying those goods or services, the lowest amount charged by him for an equivalent amount of the same goods or services at or about the time they are so donated or provided, and

(b) where the person by whom the goods or services are so donated or provided is not in the business of supplying those goods or services, the lowest amount charged for an equivalent amount of the same goods or services at or about the time that the goods or services are so donated or provided by any other person providing those goods or services on a commercial basis in the market area in which the goods or services are so donated or provided if the amount charged is equal to or greater than one hundred dollars, and if the amount charged is less than one hundred dollars, a nil amount.

This lengthy definition makes a distinction between goods or services provided by someone who is in the business of supplying them and someone who is not. The Accounting Profession Working Group addressed this issue and concluded such a distinction is not necessary. The Working Group proposed that the commercial value of goods or services reflect the lowest price charged for such goods or services in the market area. We endorse this straightforward approach.

Recommendation 2.6.5

We recommend that the *Canada Elections Act* stipulate that commercial value in relation to goods or services means the lowest price charged for an equivalent amount of the same goods or services in the market area at the relevant time.

MAILINGS BY MEMBERS OF PARLIAMENT DURING THE ELECTION PERIOD

The *Canada Post Corporation Act* currently provides that Members of Parliament may send a 'householder' to their constituents, free of charge, up to 10 days *after* the writs are issued. Under the chief electoral officer's guidelines, if a householder "directly promotes or opposes a registered party or the election of a candidate", the cost of the mailing, as well as the preparation and printing costs, are to be considered election expenses. (Canada, Elections Canada 1988a, 11) Based on our proposals, the cost of such mailings would have to be claimed as an election expense because the householder would at least indirectly promote a candidate. Even so, this publicity for an outgoing Member of Parliament may be seen as providing incumbents with an advantage not available to other candidates. This potential advantage runs counter to the goal of fairness in the electoral process; such mailings should not be allowed once an election is called.

Recommendation 2.6.6

We recommend that

(a) **the *Canada Post Corporation Act* be amended to disallow outgoing Members of Parliament from mailing printed material free of charge to their constituents as of midnight the day Parliament is dissolved; and**
(b) **such material be defined as any printed matter without further address than 'householder', 'boxholder', 'occupant' or 'resident' (as in paragraph 35(3) of the *Canada Post Corporation Act*).**

THE ROLE OF AGENTS

The position of official agent has been part of Canada's federal electoral law since 1874, although the agent's responsibilities expanded considerably with adoption of the *Election Expenses Act*. The official agent is the linchpin of the regulatory framework for candidates' election spending and financing. The agent most often acts as treasurer or financial controller of the candidate's campaign, must authorize the payment of all expenses, is responsible for keeping spending within the limit, and, after the election, must report to the chief electoral officer (via the returning officer) on spending on behalf of the candidate as well as contributions received. The official agent must attest that the post-election return is accurate and is subject to penalties for contravening the law. As R.K. Carty noted, "this makes agents both an integral part of the local campaign apparatus and a key element in the state's enforcement mechanism." (1991b RC)

A candidate must appoint an agent as part of the nomination process. By definition, the task is of relatively short duration: once the election is over, the return is filed with the returning officer, the accounts are closed and the position disappears. As a result, official agents, like most of the thousands of others involved in constituency campaigns, are usually volunteers. Moreover, Carty's research indicates that only a small proportion of those acting as official agents in the 1988 general election had previously done so: 46 per cent of agents for Progressive Conservative candidates who responded to the questionnaire had previous experience, as did 24 per cent of Liberal and New Democratic Party agents. (1991b RC, Table 2.5) Our recommendation that professional fees or labour required to help comply with the Act not be counted against the candidate's spending limit is relevant here.

This exemption from the spending limit means that a candidate would not be penalized for choosing to have a professional accountant act as official agent. As a result, the number of official agents with relevant expertise could be expected to rise.

The *Canada Elections Act* refers to an official agent of a candidate as 'an individual', which could preclude a corporate body, such as a firm of accountants, from acting in that capacity. At the national level, both the Progressive Conservative and the Liberal parties rely on corporations to fulfil the function of chief agent. This approach could be useful to candidates and, in particular, to constituency associations, which under our recommendations would be obliged to report on their financial activities. At the same time, the requirement that the agent provide written consent before assuming the position should be retained. If a firm or corporation were to be appointed as agent, then a partner or officer of the firm would have to provide the consent to act.

Recommendation 2.6.7

We recommend that the *Canada Elections Act* permit an individual or a corporate body to act as the official agent of a political

party, candidate, constituency association, nomination contestant or leadership contestant.

Because the position of official agent is so central to election campaigns, it is important that the parties and those responsible for administering the law provide the necessary support to help official agents carry out their duties. As noted above, since the 1979 general election, the first held under the 1974 reforms, Elections Canada has provided *Guidelines and Procedures Respecting Election Expenses of Candidates* for candidates and agents (Canada, Elections Canada 1988a); guidelines for registered parties were also issued prior to the 1984 and 1988 elections. The guidelines have helped provide an understanding of how to apply the Act's election expenses and reporting provisions. We have reservations about the process through which they were developed, but the practice of issuing guidelines has helped clarify areas where the Act is not sufficiently detailed and allows flexibility as circumstances change from one election to another. After our proposed *Canada Elections Act* comes into force, new guidelines for candidates and registered parties will be required.

We recommend that all constituency associations of registered parties be required to register with the Canada Elections Commission. As a condition of registration, associations would have to appoint a constituency agent. This person's role would be analogous to that of the official agent, although the responsibilities would continue outside an election period. These responsibilities would include filing twice-yearly reports on all contributions totalling more than $250 from any source; submitting a full annual return on the association's income and spending, as well as a similar post-election return; and issuing tax receipts for contributions to the association and to nomination contestants. It is essential that guidelines be prepared and distributed to assist constituency agents and other officers of associations in adapting to these new requirements. It is important that the new procedure for registering constituency associations is carried out smoothly. We recommend many changes, however, in the regulatory framework for candidates and registered parties and the regulatory regime for nomination and leadership selection. The Canada Elections Commission should therefore hold hearings on draft guidelines to allow participants and interested Canadians to comment before the guidelines are finalized.

Recommendation 2.6.8

We recommend that the Canada Elections Commission

(a) develop new guidelines for official agents and candidates, constituency agents, nomination contestants and political parties; and

(b) hold public hearings on these guidelines before putting them into effect.

In Volume 1, Chapter 7, we recommend that the Canada Elections Commission have the power to issue policy statements and to respond to requests for advance rulings or interpretation bulletins. Advance rulings and interpretation bulletins should allow for timely resolution of difficulties not addressed by the guidelines or issues that apply to some but not all participants. Candidates, party officials and agents would benefit from this new procedure and revised guidelines, but it is important that those involved also receive the necessary training.

Since the period before the 1979 election, major parties and Elections Canada have sponsored training sessions for agents. Our research indicates there was considerable variation among the three largest parties: 71 per cent of agents for Progressive Conservative candidates who responded to Carty's survey indicated they had attended training sessions; the response for agents of the Liberal and New Democratic parties was 44 and 63 per cent respectively. At the same time, a much higher proportion, 45 per cent, of agents reported being trained by a party than by Elections Canada (24 per cent). (Carty 1991b RC, Table 2.6)

During our hearings, a number of interveners commented on the training for agents provided by auditors and accountants under contract with Elections Canada. One witness praised the quality of the presentation made to agents, but commented that the seminar he attended a month after the election was called would have been much more useful if it had been held earlier in the campaign. Carty found that more than 70 per cent of agents selected between January and June 1988 had attended an Elections Canada training session; for agents chosen after the election was called, the proportion was less than 40 per cent. He offered the following observation: "As long as candidates are being nominated in the midst of an election campaign it may be organizationally difficult for the staff of Elections Canada to provide training sessions for all those newly named agents, or for these individuals to arrange to attend a session while the campaign they are responsible for controlling is going on." (Carty 1991b RC)

The political parties have considered training one of their responsibilities, but their capacity to provide it may vary; moreover, they have no role in relation to independent candidates. The practice of Elections Canada has been to hold most training sessions during the election period, around the time of nomination day, to reach as many candidates as possible. This approach was understandable in the circumstances, particularly since a team of some 14 people was responsible for holding the training sessions across the entire country. It is essential, however, that official agents, constituency agents and the agents of nomination contestants have full access to adequate and timely training.

Recommendation 2.6.9

We recommend that the Canada Elections Commission provide an opportunity for official agents to attend a training session on the relevant aspects of the *Canada Elections Act* as soon as possible after an election is called; and that training sessions be provided for agents of constituency associations and nomination contestants.

SPONSOR IDENTIFICATION OF ADVERTISEMENTS

Print Advertisements

Identifying the sponsor of an election advertisement helps ensure accountability and assists in enforcing restrictions on election spending. Without such requirements, those wishing to sponsor advertisements to promote or oppose a party or candidate could hide behind the cloak of anonymity; it would be possible, for example, to supplement the efforts of a particular campaign without the costs being counted against the relevant spending limit.

An indirect form of sponsor identification was introduced in a 1908 amendment to the *Dominion Elections Act*. Under section 34, printed advertisements, including any "hand bill, placard, poster or dodger" were required to bear the name of the printer or publisher. At the time that the *Election Expenses Act* was adopted, section 72 of the *Canada Elections Act* read as follows:

> Every printed advertisement, handbill, placard, poster or dodger having reference to an election shall bear the name and address of its printer or publisher, and everyone printing, publishing, distributing or posting up, or causing to be printed, published, distributed or posted up, any such document unless it bears such name and address is guilty of an offence against this Act and, if he is a candidate or the official agent of a candidate, is also guilty of an illegal practice.

This section could serve to identify the sponsor of a printed advertisement only indirectly: someone who wanted to know who had paid for a particular advertisement could ask the printer or publisher whose name appeared on it. In the 1983 amendments to the *Canada Elections Act*, section 72 was revised to require any printed advertisement to bear the name of the registered agent of the party or official agent of the candidate who had authorized the advertisement. It subsequently read:

> (1) Every printed advertisement, handbill, placard or poster that promotes or opposes the election of a registered political party or candidate and that is displayed or distributed during an election by or on behalf of a registered party or a candidate shall indicate that it was authorized by the registered agent of the party or by the official agent

of the candidate, as the case may be, and bear the registered agent's or official agent's name.

(2) Every person who prints, publishes, distributes or posts up, or who causes to be printed, published, distributed or posted up, any document referred to in subsection (1) is, unless it bears the name and authorization required under that subsection, guilty of an offence.

Table 6.1
Print advertising requirements, provincial comparisons

Jurisdiction	Requirements/conditions
British Columbia	No provisions in provincial legislation.
Alberta	Section 133 (1)(2) Name and address of the sponsor (does not apply to a printed advertisement, handbill, placard or poster bearing only one or more of the following: the colours and logo of a registered political party, name of a registered political party or the name of a candidate).
Saskatchewan	Section 196 Name and address of the person who printed or produced it by any other process; name and address of the person who authorized it to be produced, published or distributed.
Manitoba	No provisions in provincial legislation.
Ontario	Section 23 (5) Name of the registered constituency association, registered political party, person, corporation or trade union authorizing the political advertising.
Quebec	Section 421 Name and address of printer or manufacturer and the name and title of the official agent or deputy who caused it to be produced. Newspapers or other publications in which an advertisement is published must indicate the name and title of the official agent or deputy who caused it to be published.
Nova Scotia	Section 160 (1)(2) Name and address of the printer and the person on whose behalf it was printed or published.
New Brunswick	Section 73 (2)(4) Name and address of the printer and the name of the registered political party or the candidate on whose behalf it was ordered. If not ordered by a chief agent or an official agent or person authorized by a chief or official agent, advertisement must bear the name of the person who ordered its publication.
Prince Edward Island	Section 7 (1)(2) Name and address of the printer and the person on whose behalf it was printed or published. Newspaper or other publication must mention name and address of person who has it published.
Newfoundland	Section 116 (1) Name and address of its printer and publisher and any person printing, publishing, distributing or posting up, or causing to be printed, published, distributed or posted up.

Source: Alberta *Election Act* (1980), Saskatchewan *The Elections Act* (1978), Ontario *Election Finances Act, 1986*, Quebec *Election Act* (1989), Nova Scotia *Elections Act* (1967), New Brunswick *Political Process Financing Act* (1978), Prince Edward Island *Election Expenses Act* (1983), Newfoundland *Election Act* (1970).

Subsection 2 was not intended to ban print advertising during an election if the advertising was sponsored by anyone other than registered parties or candidates. Indeed, this subsection was to be read with section 70.1(1), which provided that only registered parties and candidates could incur election expenses. Advertisements sponsored by others but that did not promote or oppose a registered party or candidate were not supposed to be affected. In addition, as indicated in Table 6.1, eight provinces have sponsor identification requirements for print advertising during an election. In 1984, however, section 72, along with section 70.1(1), was challenged in the Alberta Court of Queen's Bench by the National Citizens' Coalition. (*National Citizens' Coalition Inc*. 1984)

As a result of the decision in this case (known as the Medhurst decision), the current section 261 of the *Canada Elections Act* requiring identification of the agent who authorizes printed election advertisements on behalf of a registered party or candidate is no longer being applied. This situation could lead to abuse: freedom of expression does not mean that those who intervene in elections should be allowed to hide their identity. The three largest parties agreed to comply voluntarily with this section in the 1984 and 1988 elections, but the statutory gap must be corrected. This issue should also be seen in the context of our recommendations on independent expenditures. We propose that anyone who undertakes independent expenditures be subject to a spending limit of $1000; this could include printed advertisements. To enforce the $1000 spending limit for independent expenditures, it is essential that there be sponsor identification of any person who authorizes printed political advertisements during an election. In the case of registered parties, registered constituency associations and candidates, the financial or official agent would be identified as the sponsor; in other cases, the sponsor should be an individual or a legally constituted organization.

Recommendation 2.6.10

We recommend that every printed advertisement, handbill, placard or poster related to an election that is published, displayed or distributed during an election indicate the name of its sponsor, whether an agent of a registered political party or registered constituency association, the official agent of a candidate or any other person, and that it was authorized by the sponsor.

Broadcast Advertisements

Sponsors of partisan broadcast advertising during election and referendum campaigns have been required to identify themselves in the advertisements since 1936. The provision first appeared in the *Canadian Broadcasting Act* of 1936 in response to the "Mr. Sage" radio advertisements of the previous year.[2] However, section 19(2) of the 1968 *Broadcasting Act* was omitted in the 1991 revisions to that Act. The section read as follows:

> A licensee shall identify the sponsor and the political party, if any, on whose behalf a program, advertisement or announcement of a partisan character in relation to a referendum or an election of a member of the House of

Commons, the legislature of a province or the council of a municipal corporation is broadcast or received, as the case may be,

(a) both immediately preceding and immediately after the broadcast thereof where the program, advertisement or announcement is of more than two minutes duration; and

(b) either immediately preceding or immediately after the broadcast thereof where the program, advertisement or announcement is of two minutes or less duration.

Table 6.2
Broadcast advertising identification requirements: provincial comparisons

Jurisdiction	Requirements/conditions
British Columbia	No provisions in provincial legislation.*
Alberta	No provisions in provincial legislation.*
Saskatchewan	No provisions in provincial legislation.*
Manitoba	No provisions in provincial legislation.*
Ontario	Section 23 (5) Name of the registered constituency association, registered political party, person, corporation or trade union authorizing the political broadcast or telecast advertising.
Quebec	Section 421 Name and title of the official agent or deputy [official agent], as the case may be, at the beginning or at the end of any radio or television advertisement.
Nova Scotia	Section 160 (2) Name and address of the person who sponsors an advertisement at the beginning or at the end of any sponsored radio or television program.
New Brunswick	Section 73 (3)(4)(c) Name and address of the registered political party or the candidate on whose behalf it was ordered. If not ordered by a chief agent or an official agent or person authorized by a chief or official agent, an advertisement must indicate the name of the person who ordered the broadcast, at the beginning or at the end of any sponsored radio or television broadcast.
Prince Edward Island	Section 7 (2) Name and address of the sponsor of an advertisement at the beginning or at the end of any sponsored radio or television program.
Newfoundland	No provisions in provincial legislation.*

Source: Ontario *Election Finances Act, 1986*, Quebec *Election Act* (1989), Nova Scotia *Elections Act* (1967), New Brunswick *Political Process Financing Act* (1978), Prince Edward Island *Election Expenses Act* (1983).

*The former s. 19(2) of the *Broadcasting Act* (1968) applied in relation to provincial elections.

This sponsor identification provision was intended mainly as a "check on anonymous, scurrilous and untrue" advertisements and the provision helped election officials police the system to ensure compliance with spending limits and other aspects of the law. (Boyer 1983, 410) Five provinces have legislative requirements for sponsor identification of broadcast election advertising (see Table 6.2). In addition, the United States *Federal Election Campaign Act* requires that an advertisement on any broadcasting station clearly state the name of the candidate, authorized political committee or other person who "makes an expenditure for the purpose of financing communications expressly advocating the election or defeat of a clearly identified candidate, or solicits any contribution." In discussion of the issue at our symposium on the media and elections, party representatives suggested that anonymity on Canadian broadcast facilities could lead to the production of "scurrilous" advertisements. (Canada, Royal Commission 1991, Vol. 4)

As the new *Broadcasting Act* no longer obliges sponsor identification, the next election campaign could include anonymous political advertisements on television and radio, thereby weakening accountability and financial disclosure.

Recommendation 2.6.11

We recommend that the *Canada Elections Act* require sponsor identification of all broadcast political advertising during an election.

REPORTING OF SPENDING AND CONTRIBUTIONS

Categories of Contributors for Reporting Purposes

In Volume 1, Chapter 7 we recommend broadening disclosure requirements for political contributions and providing fuller and more timely information about contributions. A remaining question relates to the categories for reporting political contributions.

The Act now prescribes the following reporting categories: individuals, businesses, commercial organizations, governments, trade unions, corporations without share capital other than trade unions, and unincorporated organizations or associations other than trade unions. Based on the statutory power of the chief electoral officer to prescribe forms, that list was modified to require reporting according to the following five categories: individuals, business or commercial organizations, governments, trade unions and other organizations.

The Accounting Profession Working Group reviewed these reporting requirements and proposed certain adjustments. The Working Group recommended two separate categories for business contributions: (1) corporations; and (2) "unincorporated organizations or associations engaged in business or commercial activity". The current category, business or commercial organizations, is very broad, covering contributors ranging from large public corporations such as chartered banks to small owner-operated businesses. Separating contributions from corporations and unincorporated businesses would provide a more accurate picture of the funding basis of parties and candidates, as would our recommendation in Volume 1, Chapter 7 about contributions from numbered corporations.

The Working Group omitted governments from its list of categories. This category was included in the Act to provide for the reporting of in-kind contributions from a government to a party or candidate – for example, the value of the salary of a ministerial assistant working full- or part-time on an election campaign. To the degree that such practices may continue, contributions from governments should continue to be reported and a separate category for that purpose should therefore remain.

Recommendation 2.6.12

We recommend that contributions to registered parties, registered constituency associations, candidates, party leadership contestants and nomination contestants be reported according to the following categories:

- **individuals;**
- **corporations;**
- **unincorporated organizations or associations engaged in business or commercial activity;**
- **trade unions;**
- **not-for-profit organizations or associations;**
- **governments; and**
- **other contributors.**

Reporting by Registered Constituency Associations

Our recommendations would require that registered constituency associations, along with registered parties, file an unaudited report of contributions for the first six months of the fiscal year and a full audited return on their financial activities for the entire fiscal year. All reports and returns would have to be filed within three months of the end of the reporting period and be prepared in accordance with generally accepted accounting principles.

The requirements for submitting an annual audited return should be adjusted during an election year. A constituency association's financial activities may well be relevant to a candidate's campaign. Any election expenses incurred by an association would have to be reported as such by the candidate's official agent; but an association might also spend money on items that are not election expenses but that nevertheless assist the candidate, for example, sponsoring events to help raise the candidate's profile. In addition, an association may spend money before a writ is issued to promote a person selected as its candidate.

In such cases, disclosure of the constituency association's financial activities should occur sooner than in a non-election year. This is reflected in the Ontario legislation, which requires post-election reports from constituency associations; in Quebec, if the deadline for the annual report of a constituency association falls during an election, it is deferred, which means the report also includes election-related financial activity. We propose that, for an election year, associations be required to submit an audited return within three months of election day and that this return cover its financial activities from 1 January until election day; it should then submit a second return covering the period from the day after election day to 31 December. If election day falls between 1 November and the end of the year, the two returns should be combined; if an election is called in one calendar year (for example, in late November) and election day occurs in the next (for example, in mid-January), the return should cover the full year during which the election was called and the part of the election period that fell during the following year.

Recommendation 2.6.13

We recommend that the agent of a registered constituency association be required to submit audited returns of the association's financial activities for the following reporting periods:
(1) if no election is held within a year, for the year;
(2) if an election is held during a year, for the period from 1 January to election day and for the period from the day after election day until 31 December;
(3) if election day falls between 1 November and 31 December, the two returns referred to in (2) be combined; and
(4) if part of an election period falls in the year following the year when the writs for the election were issued, for the period from 1 January of the year the writs were issued to election day.

Under our proposals constituency associations will become registered entities, with responsibility for public accountability; the contents of their reports therefore deserve some comment. The Accounting Profession Working Group recommended that, in addition to reporting income, expenses and information on contributions, constituency associations should report their assets, liabilities and surplus as of the end of the reporting period. We agree with this recommendation. Reporting the three items in the last category is necessary to ensure full accountability. The cost of fixed assets acquired by a registered constituency association should be recorded; depreciation should be listed on fixed assets; and if an asset is sold or otherwise disposed of, the transaction should be recorded and the accounts adjusted accordingly. In certain cases, the constituency agent will need to attach notes to the statements regarding these items. Financial statements should be prepared according to generally accepted accounting principles. In addition, to allow flexibility, it should be possible for the Canada Elections Commission to require that the reports include other information. Finally, some registered constituency associations may have little financial activity in a reporting period; it would be reasonable, as recommended by the Accounting Profession Working Group, to allow an association to file a short-form return; we propose this be permitted where both its income and expenses are less than $5000. The Canada Elections Commission should have the authority, however, if circumstances warrant, to require an association to submit a full return.

Recommendation 2.6.14

We recommend that

(a) **reports on the financial activities of registered constituency associations include the following:**
- **the assets, liabilities and surplus as of the end of the reporting period;**
- **the income received and expenses incurred during the reporting period;**
- **all required information respecting contributions received during the reporting period;**
- **notes on the statements as necessary; and**
- **any other information prescribed by the Canada Elections Commission; and**

(b) **where the income and expenses of the registered constituency association are both less than $5000 during a reporting period, a short-form return, as prescribed by the Canada Elections Commission, may be filed, but the Commission have the power to request a full return.**

Candidates' Post-Election Returns

The *Canada Elections Act* requires that, within four months of the election, the official agent of a candidate submit to the returning officer a "return respecting election expenses", along with the auditor's report on the return. This practice will continue under our proposals, although, as with all other financial reports governed by the new legislation we propose, the deadline for submitting the report would be three months.

The reporting requirements for candidates should be similar to those for constituency associations. For example, the return should set out the assets, liabilities and surplus of the candidate's campaign as of the date the return is prepared. This is not required at present but is necessary to provide the full picture. There should also be provision for a short form to be filed by candidates whose campaigns have had only a small amount of financial activity.

Rules are also required to govern the benefit candidates may receive by using the fixed assets of their constituency association. A candidate who can use the association's computer or facsimile machine during the campaign has a financial advantage over other candidates who must rent or buy such equipment. As the Accounting Profession Working Group concluded, part of the value of any fixed assets of the constituency association used in a candidate's campaign should be charged to the candidate and shown as an election expense. For fixed assets other than real estate and fixtures, a charge of 10 per cent of the depreciated value would be reasonable. (The association's annual financial reports would reflect depreciation of fixed assets.) As for real estate and fixtures, the charge against the candidate's election expenses should be the fair market value of rental of premises equivalent to those owned by the constituency association.

Recommendation 2.6.15

We recommend that

(a) **the post-election returns of candidates submitted by the official agent include the following:**
   - **the assets, liabilities and surplus at the date the return was prepared;**
   - **all election expenses, including those not subject to limitation;**
   - **all information required to be disclosed on contributions received from the date a writ is issued to the date the return is prepared;**
   - **notes on these statements; and**
   - **any other information prescribed by the Canada Elections Commission;**

(b) **where a candidate's campaign organization uses the fixed assets of a registered constituency association, the following be considered election expenses of the candidate: for fixed assets except real estate and fixtures, 10 per cent of the depreciated value; for real estate and fixtures, the fair market value of premises equivalent to those owned by the constituency association; and**

(c) **where the income and expenses of the candidate are both less than $5000, a short-form return, as prescribed by the Canada Elections Commission, may be filed, but the Commission have the authority to request a full return.**

The Role of Auditors

As part of the 1977 amendments, the following definition of 'auditor' was added to the *Canada Elections Act*:

> a person who is a member in good standing of an association or institute of professional accountants of a province and who is recognized by that association or institute as qualified to carry out the duties of a public accountant or an auditor in that province, and includes a firm, every partner of which is such a person.

In 1983, the definition was amended to read as follows:

> a person who is a member in good standing of any corporation, associa-
> tion or institute of professional accountants, and includes a firm, every
> partner of which is such a person.

We received comments about the present definition during our hearings
and at the symposium on election and party financing at the constituency level.
The present definition was criticized because, unlike the version adopted
in 1977, it does not specify that those called on to audit financial reports
required by the *Canada Elections Act* should be experienced in the practice
of public accounting, including performing independent audits of financial
statements. Because registered parties and registered constituency associations would be required to submit audited financial statements, we agree
with the Accounting Profession Working Group that the definition should
include such a requirement.

A further issue is whether the Act should specify that an auditor must
be a member of an association or institute of accountants incorporated under
provincial legislation. Concerns have been raised that, in the absence of such
a requirement, auditors may be chosen from among accountants who have
insufficient experience in carrying out the type of auditing required. At the
federal level, the *Bank Act*, the *Trust Companies Act* and the *Loan Companies
Act* all require that an auditor be a member in good standing of an institute
or association of accountants incorporated by or under the authority of the
legislature of a province.[3] We agree with the Accounting Profession Working
Group that the *Canada Elections Act* should include a similar requirement
and accept the Working Group's proposed definition of auditor, which was
endorsed unanimously by the representatives of the three national professional accounting organizations on the Working Group.

Recommendation 2.6.16

**We recommend that, for the purposes of the *Canada Elections
Act*, 'auditor' be defined as "a professional member in good
standing of an institute, society or association of accountants
incorporated by or under an act of the legislature of a province, whose normal professional activities include the performance of independent audits of financial statements, and shall
include a firm of accountants that has such persons as partners
or shareholders."**

In Volume 1, Chapter 7 we recommend that candidates' post-election
returns, returns submitted by leadership contestants, as well as the returns
of registered parties and registered constituency associations (but not
the twice-yearly reports on contributions), be audited in accordance with

generally accepted auditing standards. Again, there may be examples of minimal financial activity; in these cases it would be reasonable to waive the audit requirement. To ensure effective enforcement, however, the law should allow the Canada Elections Commission to require that an audit be performed after it has reviewed an unaudited return.

Recommendation 2.6.17

We recommend that returns of the financial activities of registered parties, registered constituency associations and leadership contestants, and candidates' post-election returns be subject to audit unless the income and expenses during a reporting period are both less than $5000, but that the Canada Elections Commission, after reviewing any such report or return, may require that it be audited.

The position of auditor requires independence to ensure the credibility of auditors' reports. This independence might be compromised if the same person acted as both agent and auditor for a particular candidate, registered party, registered constituency association or leadership contestant, or if the same firm of accountants acted in both positions (even though the same person did not perform the two functions). The Act should therefore stipulate that the same person or firm cannot be appointed to both positions for any one of these registrants.

Recommendation 2.6.18

We recommend that no person or firm acting as the agent of a candidate, registered party, registered constituency association or leadership contestant be appointed as the auditor of the same candidate, registered party, registered constituency association or leadership contestant, as the case may be.

The *Canada Elections Act* provides for a payment from public funds to those who audit candidates' returns. The amount to be paid is the lesser of $750 and 3 per cent of the candidate's election expenses but cannot be less than $100. The principle behind these payments – which assist in enforcement of the Act – remains valid. However, the criteria for determining the amount of this payment require adjustment for inflation. In addition, we recommend that an audit of the financial returns of constituency associations be required if either the income or expenses of the association exceed $5000 during a reporting period. To assist in implementing our proposed framework for financial reporting, we propose that such payments also be made to auditors of registered parties, constituency associations and leadership contestants.

The Accounting Profession Working Group proposed that the payment to auditors of the returns of candidates and constituency associations be the lesser of $1000 and the amount the auditor charged. We agree with this straightforward approach.

Recommendation 2.6.19

We recommend that the auditor of the return of a candidate, registered constituency association, registered party or leadership contestant receive a payment from public funds equal to the lesser of $1000 and the amount of the auditor's fee.

PROVISIONS FOR BY-ELECTIONS AND POSTPONED ELECTIONS

At present, the election expenses of a candidate in a by-election must not exceed the amount allowed in that constituency during a general election. The registered party may spend an additional amount determined by multiplying the number of people on the preliminary voters lists in that constituency by the per-voter election expenses limit that applies in a general election. If more than one by-election is held on the same day, the party's permitted spending is based on the number of voters on the lists for all the constituencies.

In Quebec provincial elections, different rules apply: a candidate's election expenses limit in a by-election is double the limit for a general election, but any election spending by the candidate's party counts against the candidate's limit.

We evaluated these two approaches. The Quebec legislation has the advantage of providing clear accountability because all election expenses must be included in a single report. However, the federal approach gives parties greater flexibility if more than one by-election occurs on the same day. For example, a party might want to focus more of its resources on one of the by-election campaigns than on the others; it would be constrained in doing so by the Quebec law (although its total election expenses on behalf of the candidates cannot exceed the limit noted above). We therefore prefer to retain the current federal principles for limiting election expenses in by-elections.

As for reporting by-election spending, we see a need for improvement. At present, candidates must report on spending and contributions within four months, but any spending on the candidate's behalf by the party is reported in the party's annual return (which must now be submitted within six months of the end of a year). To improve accountability, each registered party with a candidate in a by-election should also be required to report on its election expenses on behalf of the candidate. When more than one by-election is held on the same day or the election periods for more than one by-election overlap, a reasonable course would be to have a party with candidates in more than one constituency submit a single return detailing its spending on behalf of all its candidates. The deadline for these post-election returns should be the same as the deadline we recommend for general elections, namely three months.

Recommendation 2.6.20

We recommend that

(a) **the limit for the election expenses of a candidate in a by-election be the same as for a general election;**

(b) **the limit for the election expenses of a registered party on behalf of a candidate in a by-election or on behalf of candidates in by-elections held on the same day be equal to the limit per voter that would apply in a general election times the number of voters on the final voters lists in the constituency or constituencies;**

(c) **within three months of a by-election, a registered party with a candidate in the by-election submit a return of its election expenses on the candidate's behalf;**

(d) **where more than one by-election is held on the same day, a registered party with candidates in more than one of the constituencies submit a single return on its election expenses on behalf of the candidates; and**

(e) **where the election periods for more than one by-election overlap, a registered party with candidates in more than one of the constituencies submit a single return of its election expenses on behalf of the candidates within three months of the last of the by-elections.**

Our recommendations provide for a postponed election if a nominated candidate dies during the last 28 days of a campaign or if there is a tied result in any constituency; the new election would take place 21 days after the new nomination day. The election period for a postponed election would be combined with the portion of the original election period that had elapsed. In the case of an election postponed because of the death of a candidate, bearing in mind that the extension of the election period would be about half the length of the election period for general and by-elections, it would be reasonable to increase the spending limit for the continuing candidates by 50 per cent of the spending limit that would otherwise apply. Any new candidate would face some of the costs any candidate must bear to launch a campaign – for example, publishing new communication materials – and should therefore be allowed to spend the same amount on election expenses as a candidate in a regular election.

If an election is postponed as a result of a tie, all the candidates must run an extended campaign and therefore should have a spending limit equal to

150 per cent of the limit that would otherwise apply. Reimbursements for candidates in postponed elections, where applicable, would reflect the same principles. The other provisions in the Act relating to election finance should apply without change to candidates in a postponed election.

Recommendation 2.6.21

We recommend that

(a) **if a postponed election is held because of the death of a candidate, the limit for the election expenses of any new candidate be equal to the limit that would otherwise apply and, if the candidate receives 1 per cent or more of the valid votes, he or she be reimbursed the same amount that would otherwise be reimbursed;**

(b) **if a postponed election is held because of the death of a candidate, the limit for the election expenses of the continuing candidates be equal to 150 per cent of the limit that would otherwise apply, and all such candidates who qualify be reimbursed 150 per cent of the amount that would otherwise be reimbursed; and**

(c) **if a postponed election is held because of a tied result, the limit for all candidates be equal to 150 per cent of the limit that would otherwise apply, and candidates in such an election who receive 1 per cent or more of the valid votes be reimbursed 150 per cent of the amount that would otherwise be reimbursed.**

DEREGISTRATION OF CONSTITUENCY ASSOCIATIONS, REGISTERED PARTIES AND PARTY FOUNDATIONS

A further issue relates to the financial situation of registered entities that are de-registered. In Volume 1, Chapter 5, we recommend that a constituency association be de-registered in specific circumstances: if the national party to which it belongs is de-registered; if the registered party requests de-registration of an association; or following any readjustment that changes the boundaries of the constituency in such a manner that the constituency association disappears or is merged with one or more other constituency associations. We also recommend that the Canada Elections Commission have the power to de-register an association if it violates the terms of its constitution (submitted as a condition of its registration) or fails to comply with the requirements of the Act.

On deregistration, an association should be required to file a closing statement detailing its assets, liabilities and surplus. (A similar statement is one of the requirements for registration of an association.) The disposition of the funds of a de-registered constituency association was addressed by the Accounting Profession Working Group. We agree with its proposal that these funds be held in trust by the registered party. However, when associations are de-registered as a result of their party being de-registered, the association funds should be held in trust by the Canada Elections Commission. If the association or a successor association of the same party becomes registered by the time the next general election is called (the party would have to be re-registered), the funds held in trust should be paid to the association; if a de-registered association is not re-registered before the next election, and the party remained registered or has re-registered, the funds should be paid to the party. If a party is no longer registered by the time the next general election is called, the funds of any association that was de-registered would revert to the Receiver General.

When associations are registered after a boundaries readjustment, the registered party should again act as trustee, and the relevant funds would be distributed to the new or reorganized constituency associations. Because there may be some ambiguities following a major boundaries readjustment, the registered party should have the power to determine the distribution of funds. In all these cases, the Canada Elections Commission should be responsible for determining the date when the deregistration of any constituency association is to take effect.

Recommendation 2.6.22

We recommend that

(a) when a constituency association is de-registered, all funds of the constituency association be paid over to the registered party and held in trust for the association;
(b) when a constituency association is de-registered as a result of the deregistration of a registered party, all funds of the association be paid over to the Canada Elections Commission and held in trust;
(c) funds held in trust under (a) or (b), together with any accumulated interest, be disposed of as follows:
(1) if the association or a successor association of the same registered party becomes registered by the time the writs for the next general election are issued, the funds be paid to the association;
(2) if the association or a successor association of the same registered party is not registered by the time the writs for the next general election are issued, and the party has remained registered or has re-registered, the funds be paid to the party;
(3) if the party that had endorsed the association is no longer registered by the time the writs for the next general election

are issued, the funds of any de-registered association revert
to the Receiver General for Canada;

(d) when an association of an independent Member of Parliament is de-registered, all funds be paid over to the Canada
Elections Commission and held in trust;

(e) with reference to (d), if the former independent Member
of Parliament is a candidate at the following general election or at a by-election during that period, the funds held
in trust be returned to the candidate; if not, the funds be
transferred to the Receiver General;

(f) when an association is de-registered following a boundaries readjustment, its assets be held in trust by the registered party and transferred to the appropriate successor
constituency associations following their registration;

(g) the registered party have the power to determine, if necessary,
how the funds of constituency associations de-registered
under (f) are to be distributed; and

(h) the Canada Elections Commission determine the date when
the deregistration of any constituency association is to take
effect.

Because they benefit from public funding, arrangements are also required
to cover the deregistration of political parties and party foundations. In the
case of registered parties, we propose that, on deregistration, all the funds of
a party be held in trust by the Canada Elections Commission. If the party
does not become registered by the time the next general election is called,
the funds should revert to the Receiver General. For party foundations, whose
registration status would depend on the party with which they are associated
remaining registered, a workable approach would be to adopt rules to the same
effect as those we propose for constituency associations, with one exception.
We recommend in Volume 1, Chapter 5 that registered party foundations be
obliged to comply with the requirements for charitable organizations under the
Income Tax Act. In cases when a foundation is de-registered, it would be reasonable to allow it to keep its funds, rather than have them paid over to the registered party or the Canada Elections Commission, provided it was in compliance with the *Income Tax Act* requirements.

Recommendation 2.6.23

We recommend that

(a) if a registered party is de-registered, all the funds of the
party be paid to the Canada Elections Commission and held
in trust;

(b) if the party becomes registered by the time the writs for the next general election are issued, the funds be returned to the party; and

(c) if the party does not become registered by the time the writs for the next general election are issued, the funds revert to the Receiver General for Canada.

Recommendation 2.6.24

We recommend that:

(a) when a party foundation is de-registered, all funds of the party foundation be paid over to the registered party and held in trust for the foundation;

(b) when a party foundation is de-registered as a result of the deregistration of the registered party with which it is associated, all funds of the foundation be paid over to the Canada Elections Commission and held in trust;

(c) funds held in trust under (a) or (b), together with any accumulated interest, be disposed of as follows:
(1) if the foundation becomes registered no later than six months after the next general election, the funds be paid to the foundation;
(2) if the foundation is not registered by six months after the next general election and the party has remained registered or has re-registered, the funds be paid to the party; and
(3) if the party is no longer registered by the time the writs for the next general election are issued, the funds of the foundation revert to the Receiver General for Canada; and

(d) when a party foundation is de-registered, it be allowed to keep all funds that would otherwise be paid over to the registered party or the Canada Elections Commission provided the foundation complies with the requirements for charitable organizations under the *Income Tax Act*.

NOTES

1. In two cases, it was alleged that the candidate had exceeded the permitted limit for election expenses in the 1984 general election. The judge in each case pointed to the difficulty of even the official agent being aware of the financial activities of all those involved in a campaign and to the need to prove the candidate was personally negligent. (*R*. v. *Roman* 1986; *Baillargeon* 1987)

2. During the 1935 general election, a series of anonymous dramatized broadcasts organized by the Conservative Party sparked a controversy. The first

two broadcasts, which did not identify the sponsor, featured a character known as Mr. Sage who, acting as a shrewd observer/village philosopher, made disparaging comments about Liberal leader Mackenzie King and converted lifelong Liberals to the Conservative Party. In response to criticism, the last four broadcasts had a weak form of sponsor identification: they merely gave the name R.L. Wright (an employee of the advertising agency) rather than that of the Conservative Party itself. (Peers 1969, 166)

3. The same requirement is found in the following proposed legislation, which was before Parliament in autumn 1991: Bill C-4 (*Trust and Loan Companies Act*), Bill C-19 (*Bank Act*) and Bill C-28 (*Insurance Companies Act*).

APPENDIX: DEFINITIONS OF ELECTION EXPENSES

Canada Elections Act

"Election expenses" means

(*a*) amounts paid,

(*b*) liabilities incurred,

(*c*) the commercial value of goods and services donated or provided, other than volunteer labour, and

(*d*) amounts that represent the differences between amounts paid and liabilities incurred for goods and services, other than volunteer labour, and the commercial value thereof where they are provided at less than their commercial value,

(all of which are in this definition referred to as "the cost") for the purpose of promoting or opposing, directly and during an election, a particular registered party, or the election of a particular candidate, and without limiting the generality of the foregoing, includes

(*e*) the cost of acquiring the right to the use of time on the facilities of any broadcasting undertaking, or of acquiring the right to the publication of an advertisement in any periodical publication,

(*f*) the cost of acquiring the services of any person, including remuneration and expenses paid to the person or on behalf of the person, as an official agent or registered agent or otherwise, except where the services are donated or provided at materially less than their commercial value,

(*g*) the cost of acquiring meeting space, of provision of light refreshment and of acquiring and distributing mailing objects, material or devices of a promotional nature, and

(*h*) the cost of goods or services provided by a government, crown corporation or any other public agency,

when such costs are incurred for a purpose set out in this definition.

Ontario Election Finances Act, 1986

"Campaign expense" means any expense incurred for goods or services in relation to an election by or on behalf of a political party, constituency association or candidate registered under this Act for use in whole or in part during the period commencing with the issue of a writ for an election and terminating on polling day, other than,

(a) expenses incurred by a candidate in seeking nomination in accordance with the *Election Act, 1984,*

(b) a candidate's deposit as required under the *Election Act, 1984,*

(c) auditor's and accounting fees,

(d) interest on loans authorized under section 36,

(e) expenses incurred in holding a fund-raising function referred to in section 24,

(f) expenses incurred for "victory parties" held and "thank you" advertising published after polling day,

(g) expenses incurred in relation to the administration of the political party or constituency association,

(h) transfers authorized under section 28,

(i) fees paid in respect of maintaining a credit card facility,

(j) expenses relating to a recount in respect of the election, and

(k) child care expenses of a candidate and other expenses not of partisan value that are set out in guidelines provided by the Commission under clause 4(1)(j),

but shall be deemed to include the value of any goods held in inventory or any fees or expenses for services for any candidate or political party, and any contribution of goods and services to the political party, constituency association or candidate registered under this Act, for use in whole or in part during the period commencing with the issue of the writ for an election and terminating on polling day.

Quebec *Election Act*

402. The cost of any goods or services used for the following purposes during an election period is an election expense:

(1) to promote or oppose, directly or indirectly, the election of a candidate or the candidates of a party;

(2) to propagate or oppose the program or policies of a candidate or party;

(3) to approve or disapprove courses of action advocated or opposed by a candidate or party; or

(4) to approve or disapprove any act done or proposed by a party, a candidate or their supporters.

403. In the case of goods or services used both during and before an election period, the part of the cost thereof which constitutes an election expense shall be established according to a method based on the frequency of use during the election period compared to the frequency of use before and during the election period.

404. The following are not election expenses:

(1) the cost of publishing articles, editorials, news, interviews, columns or letters to the editor in a newspaper, periodical or other publication, provided that they are published without payment, reward or promise of payment or reward, that the newspaper, periodical or other publication is not established for the purposes or in view of the election and that

the circulation and frequency of publication are as what obtains out-side the election period;

(2) the cost at fair market value of producing, promoting and distributing a book that was planned to be put on sale at the prevailing market price regardless of the election order;

(3) the cost of broadcasting by a radio or television station of a program of public affairs, news or commentary, provided that the program is broadcast without payment, reward or promise of payment or reward;

(4) the necessary costs of holding a meeting in an electoral division for the selection of a candidate, including the cost of renting a hall, of convening the delegates and of the publicity made at the meeting; the costs cannot exceed $3000 nor include any other form of publicity;

(5) the reasonable costs incurred by a candidate for attending a meeting to select a candidate in an electoral division; the costs cannot include any publicity except that made by the candidate at the meeting;

(6) the reasonable expenses incurred by a candidate or any other person, out of his own money, for meals and lodging while traveling for election purposes, if the expenses are not reimbursed to him;

(7) the transportation costs of a candidate, if not subject to reimbursement;

(8) the transportation costs of any person other than a candidate, paid out of his own money, if the costs are not reimbursed to him;

(9) the reasonable expenses incurred for the publication of explanatory commentaries on this Act and the regulations thereunder, provided the commentaries are strictly objective and contain no publicity of such a nature as to favour or oppose a candidate or a party;

(10) the reasonable ordinary expenses incurred for the day-to-day operations of not more than two permanent offices of the party the addresses of which are entered in the register of the chief electoral officer;

(11) interest accrued from the beginning of the election period to the day occurring ninety days after polling day, on any loan lawfully granted to an official representative for election expenses, unless the official agent has paid the interest and declared it as an election expense in his return of election expenses.

Accounting Profession Working Group
(Canada, Royal Commission 1991a, Part 2, 2)

"... Election expenses ... means any expense incurred by or on behalf of a registered party or registered electoral district association, or nominated candidate, for goods or services for use in whole or in part during the campaign period, and shall include,

(a) the value of inventory at the beginning of the campaign period after deducting the value of inventory at the end of the campaign period; and

(b) an amount equal to any contribution of goods or services for use during the campaign period...."

7

COMMUNICATION ISSUES

INTRODUCTION

Issues related to new communication technologies and special information needs must be addressed in any comprehensive electoral reform. First, the electoral system and regulatory framework must be adapted to technological innovations in communication. These changes have created new challenges and opportunities not only for parties and candidates, but also for election officials and the news media. They cannot be ignored. Second, much more careful attention must be paid to the needs of voters who have difficulty making use of conventional media and of voters in the North, where communication and transportation pose a particular challenge.

EXPANDING THE CHANNELS

Introduction

We are in a period of rapid change in communication technologies and practices. These changes seem likely to revolutionize campaign communication in the next few decades. (Abramson et al. 1988, chapter 1; Axworthy 1991 RC) New technologies – such as direct mail and videotaped messages – are opening new channels for parties and candidates and bringing changes to the media. As with the introduction of radio and television, each new technology can change the focus of campaigning by altering prevailing concepts of time and space or of public and private communication. The choices made in the next few years, by the parties, the media and the regulators, will influence campaign communication profoundly.

In considering new technologies, it is important to leave as much room as possible for innovation while trying to discourage less desirable developments. New channels to improve the information flow from parties and candidates to voters should be encouraged. A broader and more diversified flow of information might bring younger voters – who are less likely to vote than their elders – into the campaign discourse, along with others who lack confidence in or feel alienated from the electoral process.

Specialty Services

Campaign practices and regulations must be adapted to deal with the specialty cable services that have emerged in the past decade. These services are now available to more than 5 million English-speaking subscribers (TSN, MuchMusic, CBC Newsworld, and the Youth, Vision, and Weather networks) and 1.5 million French-speaking subscribers (Réseau des Sports, Musique Plus, Canal Famille, Météomédia). As these outlets fall under the definition of programming undertakings in the 1991 *Broadcasting Act*, there is no convincing reason not to treat them like any other broadcaster.

Recommendation 2.7.1

We recommend that

(a) specialty cable services be subject to the same rules regarding paid political party broadcast time that apply to other broadcasters (subject to their conditions of licence); and

(b) specialty cable services devoted primarily to news and public affairs programming, such as CBC Newsworld, that are available to a majority of cable subscribers whose primary language is the same as the language in which the service provides programming be required to provide free time on the same basis as licensed networks.

Although some 25 per cent of voters do not yet have access to these channels, they do reach segments of the electorate not usually reached through other channels. They therefore provide the prospect of more involvement in the process for some voters and a greater diversification of campaign communication channels for the parties.

Given an appropriate economic and regulatory environment, we can expect to see several new forms of broadcasting services before the end of the century. These will undoubtedly include new cable and satellite services. Although it has proved difficult to predict accurately the rate of diffusion and implications of new technologies, some trends are generally accepted: audience fragmentation and narrowcasting; possible loss of the economic base of major news organizations; more live coverage (i.e., on-location footage); and decline in public debate as electoral communication becomes more individualized. (SECOR 1990; Axworthy 1991 RC; Abramson et al. 1988) It is important that the regulatory framework adapt to these developments.

Indeed, several new broadcasting services are already emerging, such as pay-per-view and other interactive services and various satellite delivery systems. It is important that the Canadian Radio-television and Telecommunications Commission (CRTC) consider the implications of any new service for political broadcasting. The free-time and paid-time requirements and the limitations on advertising rates that apply to broadcasters should, for example, apply to all programming undertakings, regardless of how their signals are delivered. Almost all specialty cable services are available to most Canadian households – or at least to a majority of households whose primary language is the same as that of the programs typically transmitted –

and thus more closely approximate networks than individual broadcasting stations. It is clear that such television services should be subject to the same election broadcasting rules as network operators. Services that permit new forms of advertising should, where appropriate, be available to parties and candidates (for example, services that permit advertisements to be targeted to a single constituency or neighbourhood). It is impossible to predict the exact pattern of new technologies, but the CRTC and the Canada Elections Commission should be alert to the opportunities and difficulties they may bring. They should work together, including holding joint public hearings, to ensure that the regulatory framework meets the needs of the electoral process.

Parliamentary Channels

Among the new specialty cable services are the Parliamentary Channels. Since the late 1970s, the House of Commons broadcasting service has been transmitting to cable companies French and English coverage of House sittings and committee meetings for distribution on the Parliamentary Channels. The channels normally shut down during election campaigns, but Elections Canada used them experimentally in 1988 to communicate information about enumeration and voting; the experiment was judged a success. (Desbarats 1991 RC) The Parliamentary Channels provide an opportunity for an innovative campaign information service, incorporating information on the electoral process and perhaps selected campaign programming. Use of the channels by the Canada Elections Commission to provide information on registration and voting is an important service. The text-only broadcasts reached many voters in 1988; that approach should be continued and expanded, using a wider range of programming styles with broader audience appeal, including full-scale documentaries.

The Parliamentary Channels offer considerable scope for enhancing campaign information as well. (Desbarats 1991 RC) For example, round-table discussions involving party spokespeople on specific issues could be taped for broadcast. The round-table format, with a neutral moderator, would not compromise the non-partisan role of the Parliamentary Channels if all registered parties were invited to participate. It would meet the demonstrated preference of voters for information programming that permits comparison among parties and would also respond to voters' complaints that important issues are being overlooked in national campaigns. When voters are asked to identify issues important to them, a long list of specific issues invariably emerges, in addition to the general issues that are the focus of campaign advertising and news coverage. (Canadian National Election Study 1984, 1988) Individual round-table broadcasts might not draw large audiences, but if the issues were chosen carefully, they would meet the information needs of specific segments of the electorate.

Programming and formats might best be developed by a working group of party representatives and experienced broadcast journalists, perhaps under the sponsorship of a non-partisan body like the Canadian Journalism Foundation. We note that the League of Women Voters sponsors such discussions in the United States. (Green 1991)

In addition, the Parliamentary Channels should provide a second window for repeat broadcasts of campaign programming, such as leaders debates and free-time party broadcasts. To maintain the channels' impartiality, however, programming with any partisan content would have to adhere scrupulously to the canons of balanced and equitable treatment of all registered parties.

Although the Parliamentary Channels are carried by most cable systems (557 as of September 1990), carriage is optional and only about one-third present one of the Parliamentary Channels on the basic band, where it can be received without a converter. In addition, on some cable systems, the Parliamentary Channels share time with other specialty cable services, at the option of the cable operator. (CBC 1990b) In order to enhance the usefulness of these services as a source of election information, the Canada Elections Commission and the CRTC should consider mandatory carriage requirements during election periods to ensure that the information is available to as many voters as possible.

Recommendation 2.7.2

We recommend that

(a) the Parliamentary Channels be made available to the Canada Elections Commission for informational programming during election campaigns; and

(b) the Parliamentary Channels be given a mandate to repeat free-time political party broadcasts and leaders debates and be encouraged to broadcast other election debates.

In 1988, Elections Canada transmitted election information only in English on the English Parliamentary Channel and only in French on the French Channel. This led to complaints from members of official language minorities who were unable to receive information in their area in their own language. In future, the Canada Elections Commission should ensure that some of its election announcements on the two Parliamentary Channels are transmitted in the other official language, with the proportion depending on the region served.

Recommendation 2.7.3

We recommend that some of the voting information provided by the Canada Elections Commission on the English and French Parliamentary Channels be transmitted in the other official language.

CONSTITUENCY-LEVEL COMMUNICATION

The issue of the appropriate balance between national and local campaign information has been debated increasingly since the advent of election broadcasting, especially in parliamentary systems. It has often been suggested that there is an inherent tension between the nationalizing influence of the broadcast media, especially television, and the localized nature of representation in parliamentary systems. Despite parliamentary reforms providing increased influence for individual MPs and growing public sentiment in favour of a more visible representative role for them, there has been little research on political discourse during elections at the constituency level.

Interveners' concerns regarding campaign communication at the local level focused on the rules of access to local media. What rules should cable community channels and local broadcasters follow in providing free time to candidates? Should broadcasters be required to make time available to local candidates independent of party allocations? There were accusations of bias against minor parties on the part of the news media and, more generally, concerns about access to coverage. Some interveners noted with good reason that the poor fit between constituency boundaries and broadcasters' signal areas, especially in urban centres, made broadcast advertising too costly and inefficient for most candidates. As television stations, especially, expand their coverage areas, they incorporate too many constituencies for effective advertising by local candidates. News coverage is similarly affected.

In response to these concerns, we commissioned case studies of campaign communication in 10 constituencies and a specific study of media access for minor parties. (Fletcher and Bell 1991 RC; Hackett 1991 RC) Our researchers found that many of the local candidates, campaign managers and local journalists interviewed see the federal election as primarily a national event. "There are no local issues in federal elections," one campaign manager told our researchers. (Bell et al. 1991 RC) However, we noted considerable variation among constituencies regarding the importance of local candidates and some sentiment that local campaigns should at least communicate to voters the local and regional implications of national issues. (Bell et al. 1991 RC) In addition, the smaller parties were able to gain little coverage in the national media and, partly in consequence, the bulk of their campaign effort was focused at the constituency level, where in fact they received more equitable coverage. (Hackett 1991 RC)

For local campaigns, problems of cost and the poor fit between constituency boundaries and the areas covered by broadcast signals precluded extensive use of television, but radio was important in some constituencies, especially in rural areas. These campaigns also spent a great deal on the local print media. Although little work has been done on viewership for cable community channels and local campaigners have doubts about their effectiveness, use of these channels has been increasing. (Desbarats 1991 RC) An examination of campaign coverage and campaign materials revealed that the relevance of national issues to local interests is seldom explained. Yet communication theorists argue that the most effective communication makes more abstract concerns relevant to individual interests. (McQuail 1987, 274–78) Both campaigners and the media cited available resources – time and money – as a major constraint on their ability to perform their campaign functions effectively. (Bell et al. 1991 RC)

The significance of local campaigns and local candidates remains a contested issue. In election surveys, between one-fifth and one-fourth of voters say that the local candidate is the most important factor in their vote. (Clarke et al. 1991, 115) However, practitioners and voting researchers ascribe much lower importance to local candidates in a federal election. (Clarke et al. 1991, 113) Yet there are indications that, in some constituencies, the personal vote of the candidate can sway the outcome. (Ferejohn and Gaines 1991 RC)

The fact that many voters cite the local candidate as an important factor in their voting decision indicates a concern for the MP as constituency representative. Other data suggest that many voters seem also to feel a sense of frustration that they are not being effectively "represented," because of "excessive" party discipline. (Price and Mancuso 1991, 217) Richard Price and Maureen Mancuso conclude from their examination of survey data that "the Canadian people clearly believe a member's first responsibility is to his or her constituents". (1991, 210) These conclusions are supported by our attitudinal survey (Blais and Gidengil 1991 RC), which found that most voters believe that the primary function of MPs is to represent constituency interests. Yet the pattern of communication in the major media during election campaigns emphasizes party leaders and ignores local candidates and issues. (Frizzell and Westell 1989, 75–90)

While it is not our role to try to alter the focus of election campaigns, we have looked carefully at the opportunities available to local candidates to state their cases more effectively to the voters. We also considered options that might assist them in communicating with voters.

As Table 7.1 shows, constituency association executives were fairly satisfied with the news coverage for local campaigns. In their assessment of the effectiveness of campaign techniques, these local activists ranked the traditional means of persuading voters – canvassing, newspaper advertising and coverage, and literature drops – highest, but also considered direct mail and television important in 1988 (see Table 7.2). All-candidates meetings and radio were ranked lower, and cable television lower still. Nevertheless, radio remains important in certain areas and the cable community channel is becoming increasingly important and can be used innovatively.

The problem of fit between broadcast signal areas and constituency boundaries noted elsewhere does not apply to the same degree to cable community channels. The licence areas of these channels correspond much more closely to constituency boundaries. Their increasing importance in delivering information at the community and constituency level is primarily a result of the widening boundaries of other media. Cable systems can fill the gap. Indeed, new technologies allow many cable systems to send signals to particular communities.

Table 7.1
Satisfaction with media coverage of local campaign
(percentages)

How satisfied were you with the media coverage of the local campaign in 1988?

Very satisfied	8
Satisfied	32
Somewhat satisfied	29
Not very satisfied	31

Source: Carty 1991a RC.

Table 7.2
Ranking of importance of local campaign media to campaign
(percentages)

How would you rate the following methods of communication in terms of their importance to your local constituency association?

	Very important	Somewhat important
Canvassing	73	20
Literature drops	45	41
Direct mail	34	41
All-candidates meetings	28	39
Newspapers	57	34
Television	34	26
Cable television	9	29
Radio	25	41

Source: Carty 1991a RC.

The community channels were active in providing coverage and access to local candidates in 1988. (Desbarats 1991 RC) Although local campaign organizers are still uncertain about their effectiveness, community channels could become, with proper promotion by the candidates themselves, a significant factor in local campaign communication. As noted by the Canadian Cable Television Association (CCTA), the fact that community channels are localized makes them "probably the most important single source of information about local candidates, and their electoral platforms". (Brief 1990, 4) The potential of the community channels is made clear in Table 7.3.

There are "approximately 275 community programming studios across Canada ..., more than four times as many as conventional broadcast stations". (CCTA, Brief 1990, 1) The community channels present a variety of public affairs programs, including phone-in shows, all-candidates meetings, debates among candidates for nomination, round tables on issues (with interest group representatives as well as candidates), reports from incumbents outside election periods, interview shows on community issues, and others. We conclude that cable community channels should devote a minimum of one hour of prime time to local campaigns, plus some rebroadcast time. Many already meet this norm. (Desbarats 1991 RC)

Table 7.3
Why cable is a viable option

- 75 per cent of Canadian households have cable
- 87 per cent of cable licensees offered free time on the community channel to all candidates
- 46 per cent of cable systems initiated and produced an all-candidates debate in 1988
- 50 per cent covered locally such a debate
- many produced or covered two or more debates
- many repeated the debates (which averaged 95 minutes in length) two or three times (average repeat factor 2.66)

Source: Adapted from Desbarats 1991 RC, based on a survey by the Canadian Cable Television Association 1990; Ellis 1991, 46.

Recommendation 2.7.4

We recommend that

(a) **cable companies that operate community channels be required to provide a minimum of 60 minutes of free time per day during the election advertising period in prime time for coverage of or broadcasts by candidates, to be allocated among them equitably; and**
(b) **coverage of all-candidates debates – whether organized by the cable service or others – be counted toward fulfilling the time requirement.**

To broaden the potential audience of such electoral programming, these free-time political broadcasts should be aired more than once. As community channels do not rely on either ratings or commercial revenue, such repeat programming does not pose a burden to the cable television owners operating the community channels. Indeed, as the CCTA observed, the "program schedules [of the community channels] allow for programs to be repeated [thereby increasing] the opportunities for interested citizens to see election coverage at their convenience". (Brief 1990, 2)

Recommendation 2.7.5

We recommend that community channels be required to repeat these broadcasts at least once.

In considering the potential of community channels, we examined the fit between constituency boundaries and cable licence areas in one of the most difficult jurisdictions, Greater Toronto. As expected, we found that the fit was much better than for conventional broadcasters, though still far from perfect. The largest number of constituencies falling within a community channel licence area was 13; most community channels covered fewer constituencies, ranging from two to six.

In the longer term, community channels may well take advantage of the technical capacity to address signals to households in a particular constituency. Vidéotron, Quebec's largest cable operator, has been a pioneer in the development of this technology, called interactive capacity, but many cable systems do not have the necessary technology. While older cable technology can transmit the same signal to all, it is the newer technology, the hub system, that can transmit specific signals to separate neighbourhoods. Although this hub system can direct cable signals to constituents within specified regions, this new technology is still not widespread in Canada (owing, in part, to the current regulatory framework), but may become more common as pay-per-view or other interactive services are licensed. In the meantime, community channels can share coverage among the constituencies covered, allocating the required time equally among constituencies fully covered by the cable system and pro rata for those partially covered.

Recommendation 2.7.6

We recommend that

(a) **cable companies whose community channels serve more than one constituency must allocate time in 30-minute segments equally among the constituencies in which they serve a majority of voters; and**
(b) **where more than one cable company serves a constituency, each must provide time in proportion to the percentage of voters served.**

In 1988, most community channels divided time equally among candidates. Some 17 per cent, however, interpreted the CRTC requirement of equitable treatment to require application of the allocation formula in the *Canada Elections Act*. (Desbarats 1991 RC) It is our view that the allocation formula, based on the national standing and activities of the parties, is difficult to justify at the local level. We have suggested in our proposal for free time an allocation formula that gives a more meaningful and equitable voice to all registered parties. It is clear that any rule other than equality with respect to all-candidates debates and free time must consider local circumstances and the relative strength of the parties in the constituency.

In establishing these requirements, we do not intend to alter the public service nature of the community channel, but rather to enhance it. Therefore, we reject the request of a number of interveners that the community channels be permitted – or required – to sell paid time to candidates.

Recommendation 2.7.7

We recommend that no paid time be permitted on cable community channels as long as the current regulatory framework applies.

Notwithstanding the importance of broadcasting and cable in constituency communication, the print media remain important communication vehicles for local candidates and political parties in their attempts to persuade the electorate. The present *Canada Elections Act* prohibits the print media from charging a candidate or party a rate that exceeds the lowest rate charged others for an equal amount of equivalent advertising space in the same or other issue thereof made public during the electoral advertising period (section 321).[1] This provision should be retained in the new *Canada Elections Act* and will, along with the rate limit for broadcast advertising recommended in Volume 1, be fair to all candidates and parties, and help to control costs. The party paid-time rate that applies to broadcasters is justified by the obligation of broadcasters to serve the public interest in return for access to the public air waves and because the available time is, by necessity, limited. This rationale does not apply to the print media. However, some safeguards on advertising rates in the print media are required to ensure fairness among candidates and registered parties. Candidates, who rely more extensively than parties on print advertising, are not specifically eligible for discounted broadcast advertising (although a registered party might choose to allocate some of its broadcast time to a candidate or candidates). It is therefore essential that advertising rates be predictable and equitable for the competitors during campaigns. The rate limits for campaign advertising for broadcasting and for print ensure fairness both for parties and candidates and for the media.

Recommendation 2.7.8

We recommend that as now provided by the *Canada Elections Act*, during the period allowed for election advertising, the print media be prohibited from charging a candidate or political party a rate that exceeds the lowest rate charged for an equal amount of equivalent advertising space in the same or other issue thereof published or distributed during that period.

In addition to these recommendations, we have considered our research findings that journalists who covered local campaigns felt inadequately prepared for the task. Local community newspapers and some smaller dailies have a great deal of staff turnover. Reporters therefore felt a need for further background information on the electoral process and past elections in the constituencies they were covering.

Recommendation 2.7.9

We recommend that

(a) a private organization such as the Canadian Daily Newspaper Association or the Canadian Journalism Foundation establish election workshops for smaller media; and

(b) the Canada Elections Commission expand existing programs for the media to prepare and distribute information packages on the electoral process, with specific information for each constituency.

CBC NORTHERN SERVICE

Unique Characteristics of the North

The immense geographical breadth of Canada's North heightens the role of the media in electoral communication. Space in the Northwest Territories, Yukon and northern Quebec totals more than one-third of Canada's landmass and covers four time zones. Because of high transportation costs and the impossibility of travel in poor weather, northern residents depend on the media to provide the necessary linkages among community residents and between communities situated far apart. During federal election campaigns, candidates in northern constituencies are forced to rely on the media to inform voters because of the prohibitive cost of travel and the amount of time required to visit just one small community in a constituency. (Roth 1991 RC; Alia 1991 RC) Communication difficulties in the North reduce the amount of information that reaches voters. It was in this context that we travelled to Yellowknife, Whitehorse, Iqaluit and Kuujjuaq to hear the views of the public on communication and other difficulties in the region. To encourage greater participation, we organized in Iqaluit a televised phone-in show in Inuktitut, hosted by the Inuit Broadcasting Corporation, and answered calls from many small northern communities about our electoral system.

About 100 000 people live in Canada's North, nestled in communities that range from a total population of 83 (Burwash Landing) to larger urban centres such as Yellowknife, whose population exceeds 13 500. Although 47 per cent of Canada's total population is under 30 years old, the population of the North is still younger, with 60 per cent not yet 30 years old. Many live in small communities and a high proportion are residents who travel much of the year, be they government or industry employees, hunters or trappers. (Roth 1991 RC; Alia 1991 RC) Without the media, northern voters could easily miss an opportunity for involvement in the electoral process altogether.

Electoral communication in the North must take into account the region's social and linguistic make-up. The North has a unique social composition. While a majority of the 53 801 Northwest Territories residents are of Aboriginal origin, a majority of the 29 708 Yukon residents are not. The eastern part of the Northwest Territories has a substantial Inuit majority while the western part has a large Aboriginal minority consisting of Dene, Métis and Inuvialuktun (western Inuit). About 90 per cent of northern Quebec's population is Aboriginal. Linguistically, the region is complex, making electoral communication a challenge. Although Yukon residents speak English mostly, those living in the Yukon town of Old Crow speak Gwich'in. Three languages are spoken in northern Quebec: Inuktitut, Cree and Attikamek. The Northwest Territories are the most linguistically diverse, with nine official languages: Inuktitut, North and South Slavey, Chepewyan, Dogrib, Gwich'in, Inuvialuktun, English and French. (Canada, Statistics Canada 1987a, 1987b)

The region is usually considered to encompass five existing constituencies. The entire Yukon itself is a constituency (Yukon) while the Northwest Territories divides into the two constituencies of Western Arctic and Nunatsiaq. Nunatsiaq is Canada's largest constituency, encompassing 41 small communities and spanning a landmass of 2.6 million square kilometres. (Roth 1991 RC) Northern Quebec is divided into the two constituencies of Abitibi and Manicouagan. The unique nature and size of these constituencies prompted numerous submissions from the public and candidates on difficulties encountered in trying to run an election campaign.

In such constituencies, candidates need the media to "get the message" across to widely scattered and sometimes transient voters speaking several languages. In addition to the vital role of the CBC Northern Service, Canada's public broadcaster in the North, CANCOM serves 35 northern communities. Aboriginal communication organizations also play a potentially important role in electoral communication: Inuit Broadcasting Corporation, Northern Native Broadcasting (Yukon), Native Communications Society of the Western Northwest Territories, Inuvialuktun Native Communications Society, Taqramiut Nipingat Inc. (Quebec), James Bay Cree Native Communications Society (Mistinnini) and Société de Communications Attikamek Montagnais (SOCAM) (Huron Village). Subject to CRTC approval, in 1992 Television Northern Canada (TVNC) – a consortium of six Aboriginal communication societies, Yukon College and the Government of the Northwest Territories – will become a distribution network. Private broadcast undertakings exist in the western Arctic and the Yukon, along with Aboriginal community radio stations. Print media are also available. All these media complement the pivotal role played by the CBC Northern Service. The latter remains central, however, not only as the national public service, but also because it is the only medium available for some northern locations such as the Eastern Arctic. Further, the CBC Northern Service is the only existing institution capable of fully reflecting the linguistic diversity of northern regions. It is therefore in this context that the CBC Northern Service remains central to our recommendations.

Public Concerns

During our public hearings, we heard much about electoral communication difficulties in the area. Views ranged from the critical to the complimentary. For example, interveners discussed the inflexibility of the CBC Northern Service. The seven minutes provided to one particular candidate to communicate with the voters were not enough to deliver the campaign message adequately in four dialects. On the other hand, the Inuit Broadcasting Corporation and CBC North were praised for being a real benefit to the people in Baffin Island by broadcasting in Inuktitut, a language understood by residents there.

We heard calls for greater access by the candidates to the voters. More free broadcast time would allow political parties and candidates (who are currently not entitled to free time) to reach more voters more effectively. This is perceived as especially important in the North where other means of contact – for example, door-to-door canvassing – are often simply not feasible. As interveners noted, if the media were more directly accessible, the candidates would not need to spend excessive amounts of money to contact voters in remote areas. Indeed, given the distances, the uncertain weather and the costs involved, candidates typically cannot afford to visit the majority of communities in their constituency. As a result, with only limited news and current affairs coverage available, many voters have little opportunity to see and judge the candidates for themselves. Interveners also felt that journalists and management had too much control over the format of programming provided to candidates.

Other media-related issues concern the difficulty the media themselves have in covering the activities of candidates. Sometimes the media did not know in which of the many small communities to find the travelling candidate. Further, even if the media knew where to locate the candidate, it was often too expensive and time-consuming for journalists to travel there to see the candidate in action. Organizations such as Nunatsiaq News and the Inuit Broadcasting Corporation therefore called for more all-candidates meetings. Beyond stimulating debate about the issues, all-candidates meetings (in Iqaluit, Rankin and elsewhere) and live Panarctic phone-in shows featuring the candidates would address the budgetary and time constraints of both the media and the candidates.

In summation, the public hearings in the North and subsequent media-related research done on our behalf (Alia 1991 RC; Roth 1991 RC) point to five main complaints: (1) lack of access by candidates to free and paid broadcast time; (2) lack of appropriate coverage of election issues in Aboriginal languages; (3) lack of access by independent candidates to broadcast time and coverage (in the North's "non-partisan" political culture,

Roth 1991 RC); (4) the limited opportunities provided by the CBC Northern Service for candidates to communicate their positions to voters through appropriate news and public affairs programming; and (5) application to the North of political broadcasting rules, which are designed largely for southern Canadian broadcasting practices and access arrangements.

CBC Northern Service

The CBC plays a very important role in helping Canadians communicate with one another. In its submission to us, the network commented that "as Canada's national public broadcaster, the CBC arguably bears a special responsibility to respond, with sensitivity and alacrity, to the expectations of its 'shareholders', the people of Canada". (Brief 1990, 1) In the North, this special responsibility is particularly significant. The CBC Northern Service consists of the CBC Northern Service Television and Northern Service Radio. It primarily serves an area covering the Yukon, the Northwest Territories and the James Bay and Arctic (Nunavik) regions of Quebec. As the CBC itself notes, the Northern Service, headquartered in Ottawa, is the primary source of news, information and broadcasting services for "most northerners". (Brief 1990) Northern Service radio stations are in Whitehorse, Yellowknife, Inuvik, Rankin Inlet and Iqaluit and have assistance from the Kuujjuaq, Montreal and Ottawa bureaus. About 100 of the 200 weekly hours of Northern Service radio programming are produced in seven Aboriginal languages. "In the Eastern Arctic, the CBC is the only radio outlet and therefore has the ... responsibility of assuring accurate and focused coverage across a very large territory." (Roth 1991 RC) With its Yellowknife production centre and field production bureaus in Whitehorse and Iqaluit, CBC North produces about 50 hours of original television programming each year in English and various Aboriginal languages. The three weekly Aboriginal language television programs total 62 minutes. Much of what is broadcast over CBC North is repeat programming. Each hour of original programming is repeated at least once. (Roth 1991 RC)

CBC Northern Service 1988 Federal Election Coverage

In addition to the national free-time allocations given to political parties, it is CBC broadcasting policy to consider offering limited local free time to candidates during an election campaign if the candidates are part of a community not adequately served by other media. (CBC 1985) During the 1988 election, this option was considered by the CBC but rejected for four reasons: (1) with only three constituencies in the full Northern Service coverage area, local candidates and issues tend to consume a greater proportion of news and current affairs programming than in more southern constituencies; (2) the Service organizes all-candidates special election broadcasts, involving interviews and debates, and a format allowing the candidates to make the rough equivalent of free-time "statements" on identified issues in the Aboriginal language of their choice; (3) the candidates can take advantage of the "community access" capability of their local radio rebroadcast transmitters to make "statements" or participate in phone-in programs; and (4) paid time on radio and television at modest rates is available to political parties. (CBC 1990a)

We remain unpersuaded by these reasons. First, although the candidates may receive a greater share of news coverage during elections in the North, this access is mediated and does not respond to the need of the candidates and voters to give and hear more direct – that is, completely unmediated – communication. Second, for the all-candidates election specials, CBC television coverage consisted of a single half-hour election debate covering the three constituency races. The debate was not live but was taped in three different towns at different times. Key segments showing the response of each candidate to the same question in a highly controlled format were edited together for the program (Roth 1991 RC). Third, use of local rebroadcast transmitters is not an equivalent substitute for scheduled free time on CBC. Finally, as a result of poor internal party communication, most candidates did not know of the availability of paid time in the last election and, even if they did, the cost and logistical problems did not make it a practical option.

The CBC has, as a public broadcaster, special obligations in the North, and should provide additional services to candidates.

Recommendation 2.7.10

We recommend that with respect to the constituencies in its primary area of coverage, the CBC Northern Service:
(1) provide 60 minutes of free time for each candidate in each of these constituencies, with such allocations being in addition to those that the parties are entitled to on a national basis;
(2) make available up to 20 minutes of paid time to each candidate to be broadcast on a regional basis, with such paid-time allocations being in addition to those that the parties are entitled to on a national basis;
(3) inform the northern candidates of their right to free and paid time; and
(4) designate a representative to negotiate the times with the returning officer, the registered parties and the candidates for each of these constituencies.

In a difficult communication environment like the North, it is essential that the broadcasts reach voters as efficiently as possible. Therefore, the CBC Northern Service should cluster the free-time segments and announce when they will be broadcast.

We recognize and appreciate the efforts of the CBC Northern Service to date in providing election coverage that reflects the unique characteristics of the North. However, the CBC can do more.

Recommendation 2.7.11

We recommend that the CBC Northern Service

(a) provide more election campaign coverage in all of the languages used in the North, including English and French; and
(b) organize one televised all-candidates debate in each of the constituencies in the Service's primary area of coverage.

ELECTION INFORMATION PROGRAMS

Since 1972, Elections Canada has recognized an implicit obligation in its mandate to inform voters of their rights and to promote public confidence in the electoral process. This recognition led to a gradual expansion of its informational activities. The recognition of a constitutional right to vote and to be a candidate gave added impetus to this development. It was the view of Elections Canada that inherent in these rights is a right to receive full and timely information about them.

At present, Elections Canada does not have an explicit legal obligation to carry out these communication activities. Nevertheless, a number of interveners at our public hearings commented on the importance of non-partisan information in meeting the needs of voters. Many suggested new activities for Elections Canada that would help get its message to specific groups of voters, especially first-time voters and those facing communication difficulties. We commissioned two studies to look into the communications role of Elections Canada and have made recommendations regarding "hard-to-reach" voters. (Semple 1991; Green 1991 RC) The study that assessed the 1988 information program gave it high marks overall but noted weaknesses in reaching specific groups, such as the homeless, voters in the North and smaller ethno-cultural groups. (Semple 1991) The study recommends special programs for Aboriginal voters, persons with limited skills in the two official languages and the homeless. The Canada Elections Commission should consider increased use of radio in remote and rural areas, increased use of the ethno-cultural media, especially radio, in urban areas, and more direct communication through community groups. Special measures will be required to reach the homeless.

These measures would encourage participation and increase public confidence in the electoral process but the Canada Elections Commission also needs an explicit mandate for informational activities. The initiatives taken by Elections Canada in preparing information on the electoral process for journalists and others have been useful and should be expanded. Many journalists working for smaller news organizations expressed the need for additional information on the constituencies they were assigned to cover. (Bell et al. 1991 RC)

The new responsibilities of the Canada Elections Commission will require expanded information programs. The traditional responsibility of the chief electoral officer to ensure compliance with all provisions of the *Canada Elections Act* requires that all those involved – candidates, constituency and party officers, and voters – be fully informed of their rights and obligations. For example, party organizations would need to know the new rules for constituency association finances and for nomination contests to adjust their practices in these areas.

More than ever, ongoing information programs are required to promote the general acceptance and effective operation of the electoral system. Elections Canada research has found that Canadians, especially young Canadians, have a general lack of awareness of the electoral system. Many citizens were found to be unaware of such basic information as the enumeration process, their constituency and MP, and the voting age. Because of these findings, Elections Canada began to develop communication programs between elections, including a major travelling exhibition, election simulation packages for elementary and secondary schools, university visits, participation in citizenship ceremonies, and presentations to citizenship and adult literacy classes and community groups. These measures have been well received but are limited. There is a strong need to expand them, particularly to increase awareness within minority groups. In this regard, we agree with the recommendation of the Committee for Aboriginal Electoral Reform (Canada, Royal Commission 1991, Vol. 4) that a joint public education and awareness program be implemented by the Canada Elections Commission and Aboriginal organizations.

Our proposed shortened election period makes an ongoing information program even more imperative. The need for a continuing program is especially acute in the year before an election is expected. In the past, Elections Canada has experienced difficulty in reaching voters with important voter advisories during the election period because of competition for attention in the media. These difficulties are exacerbated when partisan advertising begins. A continuing program to promote awareness of the electoral process would offset these difficulties. In this context, working through established institutions and community groups will be particularly important. The network of returning officers could be used more effectively if a continuing program were established.

As new information technologies become available, especially interactive data bases, many new services will be possible. The Canada Elections Commission must remain abreast of these developments. Research is essential for the design and evaluation of information programs (Rice and Atkin 1989, 62–65) as well as for effective use of new technologies.

The *Commonwealth Electoral Act* of Australia provides a useful model for an information mandate and an ongoing communications program. Among the "functions and powers" of the Australian Commission are "to promote public awareness of electoral matters by means of the conduct of education and information programs and by other means" and "to publish materials on matters that relate to its functions". The Act also contains a provision permitting it to co-operate with the electoral authorities of a state or territory. We understand these provisions have worked well in Australia.

If the informational activities of Elections Canada are to be enhanced, it is essential that the Canada Elections Commission be given a legislative mandate for these vital activities.

Recommendation 2.7.12

We recommend that the *Canada Elections Act* give the following mandate to the Canada Elections Commission:
(1) to promote public awareness of the electoral process through information programs; and
(2) to co-operate with provincial and territorial electoral authorities in the conduct of joint education and information programs on the electoral process, particularly for segments of Canadian society with special needs.

In carrying out its mandate, the Canada Elections Commission would benefit greatly from financial contributions and the assistance of the private sector. Some businesses have indicated their interest in promoting public education about the election process, while lamenting the lack of an effective vehicle to play a role in such programs. Because of its credibility, the Canada Elections Commission would be well positioned to draw on their interest in being involved in this area. Accordingly, the Commission should be authorized to establish specific programs, to which individual Canadians, business and voluntary organizations could make financial contributions; they could also be involved in overseeing the development and management of these programs. Such contributions should benefit from the same federal tax credit as now applies to those who make gifts to the Crown (which include gifts of money and can be assigned to a designated department or agency or one of its activities).

Recommendation 2.7.13

We recommend that

(a) the Canada Elections Commission establish specific public educational programs about the electoral process to which those interested in supporting these activities may make financial contributions;
(b) contributions to this fund be eligible for the same tax credit as applies to gifts to the Crown; and
(c) those who provide financial support be involved in overseeing the development and management of these programs.

VOTERS WITH SPECIAL INFORMATION NEEDS

Background

The objective of ensuring that the democratic rights of all citizens as voters are secured and strengthened can be accomplished only to the extent that all citizens, including those with special information needs, have the ability to exercise an informed right to vote. Many voters in this country, such as those with hearing, visual or reading disabilities, currently have difficulty exercising their right to vote on a fully informed basis. For example, of the more than 970 000 Canadians classified as hearing impaired, more than 200 000 are profoundly deaf. Further, about "65 per cent of deaf Canadians may be classified as functionally illiterate". (Canadian Association of the Deaf, Brief 1990, 2) With respect to visual impairments, there are approximately 446 000 blind and visually impaired people in Canada; 54 per cent of these individuals are over the age of 65. (Canada, Statistics Canada 1990) Illiteracy is the third barrier to an informed right to vote. Illiteracy is a major problem in Canada with an estimated 16 per cent of our population being unable to meet the demands of everyday reading. An additional 22 per cent of Canadian adults "can only use reading materials to carry out simple reading tasks within familiar contexts with materials that are clearly laid out". (Canada, Statistics Canada 1989)

These facts point to the need for more electoral information in audio and visual form. (Green 1991 RC) New communication technologies can be harnessed to widen the distribution network to these potential voters. Indeed, Elections Canada and community groups have already undertaken initiatives to better serve underrepresented groups facing communication barriers to full electoral participation and information. The free-time broadcasts we propose should assist many voters but initiatives aimed at these groups specifically are also needed.

New technologies are emerging that hold considerable promise for giving many groups better access to the mass media. These include closed-caption decoders and other special add-ons to conventional receivers, as well as interactive data bases that can bring election-related information to many groups through microcomputers. Increasingly the information from these sources can be delivered orally as well as visually. It has proved difficult to predict how such innovations will develop or how they will be used but it is important that election authorities and parties be prepared to assess these new services as they emerge. Many of them should make it possible to expand effective electoral participation.

Public Concerns

Many interveners stressed that accessibility to the electoral process includes the right to information. It is not limited to physical access to polling booths and meeting areas but rather extends to the information that is needed to assist or inform an individual in exercising the right to vote.

On this issue, many interveners, such as the Canadian Human Rights Commission (Brief 1990), suggested that all materials, information, ballots and posters designed by Elections Canada and the various political parties be 'user friendly' from the perspective of persons with disabilities. Political parties were also called on to have campaign material available in Braille, on audio cassettes or in plainly written form. Similarly, groups such as the Greater Moncton Literacy Council (Brief 1990) recommended that election materials contain simpler language and larger print. The Canadian Ethnocultural Council (Brief 1990) pointed out that voters who mainly use languages other than English or French require election material in these other languages. The Canadian Association of the Deaf (Brief 1990) suggested that election materials be accessible to deaf and hard-of-hearing voters via sign language interpretation, closed captioning or open captioning. Ontario now has an arrangement to provide election information to people with impaired hearing through Telecommunication Devices for the Deaf or TDD and other telephone services. Other recommendations were for greater use of posters and public transit advertisements to reach homeless people and other segments of the population that use the media only infrequently.

To address the needs of deaf and hard-of-hearing Canadians, interveners suggested that sign language interpreters and personal FM systems should be provided at nomination meetings, all-candidates meetings and public meetings. The other main suggestions were for captioning all televised political advertisements. The Canadian Association of the Deaf recommended that televised leaders debates should be made accessible in as many forms as possible, including both visible sign language and captioning. The Association prefers open captioning to avoid restricting reception to people who can afford a closed-caption decoding machine. To address the needs of visually impaired voters, we heard submissions on greater use of formats such as Braille and audio cassettes. Political parties could make increased use of taped campaign messages by automated telephone dialling equipment.

In the hearings, interveners suggested that the captioning of political advertisements would be helpful. In the 1988 election, the Progressive Conservative Party captioned its three French-language advertisements but none of its advertisements broadcast in English. The NDP captioned six of its nine television spots. Although the Liberal Party did not close caption any of its English-language advertising, it did do so for all its French-language advertising. (Green 1991 RC) Captioning is not expensive. Organizations such as the National Captioning Centre charge about $375 per 30-second commercial and have quick turnaround times to meet the pressing needs of parties in the heat of a campaign. (Green 1991 RC) Open captioning was suggested by some interveners (owing to the expense of decoders) and opposed by the broadcasting industry; a change in U.S. law requiring television manufacturers to have built-in decoder circuitry after 1993 will help address this problem over the long term. (Green 1991 RC)

Literacy and language skills are an important factor in limiting the access of many voters to campaign information and their capacity to contribute to the public debate. Many Canadians, for example, have limited reading skills. Two-thirds of Canadians have no formal education beyond high school and more than 3.7 million adults have only a grade 8 education. (Southam News 1987) Much political information could be poorly understood by the electorate if the documents are written at a university level. For example, the reading level score for the federal government's free trade kit issued in 1987 was at the second year university level. In contrast, the Pro-Canada Network pamphlet had a reading level of grade 7 to 8. Elections Canada pamphlets on voting rights and procedures from the 1984 and 1988 elections were at the grade 13 level, as were several party campaign documents. (Bunch 1991) These assessments are based on style, not content. Careful preparation of documents can broaden their readership with no loss of substance.

Many minority language groups also have difficulty gaining access to campaign information, as well as to the debate itself. According to Eileen Saunders, minority language groups often lack media skills and organizational resources, as well as language skills. (Saunders 1991 RC) The Canada Elections Commission should expand its links with ethno-cultural groups and make greater use of the ethno-cultural media. Moreover, the Canada Elections Commission could prepare posters, pamphlets and cards with information about the electoral process in different languages in advance. A good starting point is the leaflet on voting that Elections Canada prepared in 17 languages for the 1988 election.

Among other special needs brought to our attention were those of the voters in the five northern constituencies. We have already recommended some measures to meet their needs through the CBC Northern Service. These measures cannot, however, fill all the information gaps noted by our researchers. (Alia 1991 RC; Roth 1991 RC) There is a particular need for information packages designed specifically for candidates and voters in these constituencies. In addition, it would be desirable to encourage associations and educational institutions in the North to sponsor seminars and conferences for potential candidates and journalists.

Information from the returning officer and from the Canada Elections Commission should be available in remote constituencies, such as, but not limited to, those in the North, through an 800 number for both telephone and facsimile communications. This would put voters in remote areas on an equal footing with people in urban constituencies, who can make a local telephone call to contact their returning officer.

To avoid what amounts to disfranchisement of segments of the Canadian population unable to see, hear or read election-related news, all participants in the electoral process, particularly the Canada Elections Commission, must work more closely with non-partisan groups already active in the community.

Recommendation 2.7.14

We recommend that

(a) the Canada Elections Commission provide voters with special needs essential election information in other formats, including Braille and audio cassette, and establish special telephone services to provide election information to people with impaired hearing and reading difficulties;

(b) closed captions be used on all broadcasts and advertising by the parties and by the Canada Elections Commission during an election period, including material broadcast on the Parliamentary Channels;

(c) sign language be used for information provided by the Canada Elections Commission and broadcast on the Parliamentary Channels during an election period;

(d) broadcasters be encouraged to use closed captions and sign language for televised leaders debates and other election programming; and

(e) an 800 number for both telephone and facsimile be available for voters who wish to communicate with the returning officer.

COLLECTION OF ELECTION RESULTS

Rapid and accurate reporting of voting results on election night is important to many Canadians. Audiences are large, and newspapers, networks and individual broadcasting outlets devote substantial resources to the collection and interpretation of the results. The official returns, which must be carefully validated, do not appear until much later and, except in cases of controversy, make little impression on the public. It is the media reporting of the results that attracts public attention and provides the basis for public understanding of the election. The election night broadcasts are, as Elly Alboim of the CBC noted at the workshop for media practitioners, "a form of national validation". (Canada, Royal Commission 1991, Vol. 4) They play an important role in promoting public confidence in the process.

Like other aspects of election coverage, the rapid and accurate collection of election results from almost 300 constituencies across the country on election night is costly. Based on discussions with major news organizations, our researchers estimate that the total cost to the major news organizations was between $700 000 and $1 million for the 1988 election.

In a brief to us, the Association canadienne de la radio et de la télévision de langue française (ACRTF) (1990) proposed creating a single system to collect and distribute election results. At present, each network and news service must place representatives across the country to report the results as they come in. This involves considerable duplication of effort. The ACRTF argued that the logical solution is a single system, with the costs shared among the networks and news services. The ACRTF proposal would make Elections Canada responsible for collecting and distributing election results to the media, but with the participating news organizations bearing the costs. The major benefit would be an improved quality of information for Canadians because the news media would be able to transfer resources from tallying the results to reporting and analysing them. The involvement of the Canada Elections Commission would be a logical extension of its mandate.

U.S. Experience

A system similar to that proposed by the ACRTF already exists in the United States, but is operated by a private organization. The News Election Service (NES) was founded in 1964 by the major television networks – ABC, CBS and NBC – and the two national news services, Associated Press (AP) and United Press (UP). The all-news television service, CNN, recently joined. The costs are shared equally by the six members. NES policies are set by a board with equal representation from the members.

The NES provides a running tally of voting results to its members for all major national and state elections. The complexity of voting procedures in the United States makes this task a substantial undertaking. The members have agreed on the form in which the tallies will be presented and receive both a hard copy and a computer feed of the results as they are compiled. The NES reporting system depends on the co-operation of local election officials, who provide the results from each polling place as they come in to representatives of the candidates and the media. (Smolka 1988; telephone interview with Robert Flaherty, Manager, NES, 6 September 1991)

Current Situation in Canada

The Canadian networks – the CBC, CTV and TVA – and the Canadian Press (CP) and its subsidiary, Broadcast News (BN), operate independent systems to collect the vote totals for their election night reports. Other large news organizations rely on CP/BN but may collect some voting data in their areas. The CBC has a single system for all of its networks, French and English, radio and television. The system will also serve Newsworld in future elections. These organizations compete for speed and accuracy, as well as for presentation and analysis.

Over the years, the news organizations have developed sophisticated systems for rapid reporting and verification, and they have considerable faith in these systems. To achieve the necessary speed and reliability, each major news organization must hire a reporter for every constituency and provide a communications infrastructure. This involves leasing telephones (installing lines or providing cellular phones) and sometimes other equipment for each reporter, as well as paying long distance charges. In addition, staff must be hired to ensure that the data are properly entered into the main computers.

The networks and CP/BN use a similar system for compiling the results of provincial elections. Newfoundland and Prince Edward Island are exceptions because their provincial election officials collect and compile the tallies from the constituency returning offices and make them available to the media at a central location. The news organizations appear to be satisfied with the service provided by the chief electoral officer in these provinces.

The most obvious benefit of a single system would be reduced costs to the individual news organizations. These savings could be substantial. The NES estimates that the cost of collecting and distributing the results of the 1988 presidential election results was about $5.2 million (Cdn.). Therefore, the cost to each of the five participants was a little more than $1 million. Given the fact that the United States has 185 000 polling stations and complex election procedures, the cost savings for each participant in the NES are significant. Each would have to spend five to six times its contribution to NES to obtain comparable results. While the Canadian and U.S. situations are not directly comparable, it is reasonable to conclude that the potential for savings in Canada is substantial. CTV officials estimate that the cost of collecting and compiling the vote is about $200 000 or 20 per cent of total election night expenditures. Actual savings would depend on the organizational and financial arrangements developed.

There are other possible benefits from the establishment of an equivalent to NES in Canada. First, because such an organization specializes in one function, it is able to work continually to improve the accuracy and completeness of its reporting. Second, because the system would provide the data to each network simultaneously, the focus of competition might shift from speed to presentation and analysis. Third, the system would provide a continuing repository of machine-readable data for journalists and other analysts. Even if smaller news organizations were not given simultaneous access to the tallies, they could realize some savings in gaining access to data for later analysis.

Requirements for a Single System
To create an effective equivalent to the NES in Canada, an attractive alternative to current arrangements is required, offering certain guarantees. First, the news organizations that currently maintain their own systems would have to be convinced that there would be appreciable cost savings. Second, there would have to be guaranteed simultaneous access to the results for all members. Third, it would have to be accurate, fast and efficient. Fourth, backup systems would need to be in place to avoid the possibility of computer failure. Fifth, agreement on a standard protocol for reporting the count and methods for accessing the data by the computers of the news organizations would be needed. Sixth, agreement would be required on the allocation of costs and the general policies and decision-making processes of the organization. Finally, the system would have to permit subscribing news organizations to make requests for additional

information from the returning officers. To meet these requirements, the agency would have to have some permanence. Attempts to establish co-operative ventures for specific elections have foundered on several occasions because negotiations did not begin soon enough.

Positions of the Networks

In discussions with us and our researchers, some networks expressed doubt that the necessary conditions could be met. They argue that there are important advantages to maintaining their own systems to collect and compile the tallies from the returning offices. First, having a representative in each constituency allows them to obtain information and anecdotes that go beyond the raw voting data and add colour to their reports. Second, the representatives can put questions to a returning officer if necessary. Third, the duplication guards against a system failure, as occurred with the NES central computer on one occasion.

Both CBC and CTV have confidence in their own systems and would be reluctant to enter into any co-operative arrangement without being certain of substantial benefits. For some organizations, the most important costs are not for collecting the results but for computer systems needed to compile and present them. If they had to maintain these systems to cover provincial (and perhaps municipal) elections, the cost savings would be smaller.

The CBC expressed the most serious reservations. Senior journalists trust their own system and believe a single system would provide only minimal savings for the CBC. With five networks, they expect to have to bear a high proportion of the cost of a new system. More important, however, CBC journalists argue that a single system would reduce the competitive advantage they have developed, which they are loath to contemplate in the current circumstances when much of their revenue must come from commercial sales. The CBC and CP/BN are the only news organizations that maintain a permanent election unit and cover all federal and provincial elections. CTV sells its services to its affiliates for some provincial elections.

In discussions with us, Tim Kotcheff, vice-president of news for CTV, expressed support in principle for the idea but doubted that such a system would emerge in the near future without the direct involvement of Elections Canada. Both the CBC and CTV stated that a private system would likely emerge only when the networks were unable to afford their own systems any longer.

One model suggested to us involved the creation of a publicly funded system that would provide high-quality information simultaneously to all media, rather than one developed by or in co-operation with the networks. Once the system had proved itself, the networks could well abandon their own systems. Election officials in Newfoundland and Prince Edward Island provide such a service.

An alternative model would involve one of the three national organizations serving as the primary compiler of the results and selling the tallies to other news organizations. As an independent organization serving all media, CP/BN believes that it is in the best position to fill this role. The CP/BN service is the only one in Canada that continues to collect results routinely until it has a complete count, as the NES does in the United States.

The most significant obstacle to agreement on a single agency is the desire among the major news organizations to maintain a competitive edge. Election night has been described as "the Olympics of political journalism" and the quality of election night coverage is viewed as critical in the competition among broadcast news organizations. The rivalry between the CBC and CTV is particularly acute, but CP/BN is also concerned about providing competitive information to its broadcast clients. The competition encompasses presentation and analysis, as well as speed and accuracy, but tends to focus on which news organizations can announce the winning party first.

Position of Elections Canada

Under the current Act, the chief electoral officer has no responsibility to communicate the results of an election to the public and does not release the official results until some weeks after the vote. By custom, Elections Canada, through the returning officers in each constituency, assists the news organizations by providing results to their representatives, as it does to the parties, but these results are unofficial. In addition, it is the policy of Elections Canada to require that every returning officer lease space that includes room for the media on election night, as well as electrical outlets for their equipment.

Elections Canada officials expressed concern that direct involvement in the compilation of unofficial returns would give the returns undue credibility, especially since the official returns are always marginally different.

However, news organizations do rely on returning officers for the tallies that they compile. At our workshop for media practitioners, it was noted that there is occasional inefficiency or lack of professionalism in the provision of information to the news media. Two examples were given: (1) information on nominated candidates has sometimes proved inaccurate; and (2) there were considerable delays in making voting results available at some returning offices. It was suggested that Elections Canada be given an explicit mandate to assist in meeting the needs of the news organizations.

Prospects for Change

The NES example indicates that a system to compile and distribute unofficial voting results on election night would have some important benefits. In addition to cost savings for the major news organizations, there is a reasonable expectation that the quality of information provided to citizens would improve. This conclusion assumes, however, that the news media would use the financial savings to improve reporting and analysis. This expectation would likely be met only if the agency had the support and co-operation of the news organizations that now operate their own systems. Not only would their expertise be needed to establish the new agency, but their involvement in the planning would be essential if the quality of information were to be improved.

Despite the reservations of the networks, noted above, the fact that the news budgets of most media organizations are being squeezed by increasing competition might lead to greater support for a co-operative arrangement in the future. The administrative difficulties they identified are by no means insurmountable. The prospects for more rapid communication through new computer technologies, the increasing professionalization of election admin- istration, and the changing nature of network television all suggest that the proposal has merit.[2] It is not, however, a matter that can be legislated.

Nevertheless, because communication of election results to the elec- torate is important for public confidence in the system, the Canada Elections Commission should hold regular meetings with representatives of major news organizations to help their work. In addition to assisting with elec- tion night coverage, it should explore other possible arrangements for pro- viding relevant information during elections, such as distributing to news organizations a regularly updated list of candidates nominated, with a final list on nomination night. We hope the news organizations that now com- pete in compiling these data will see the obvious benefits of a common agency and will collaborate with the Canada Elections Commission and provincial election officials to create such a system.

Recommendation 2.7.15

We recommend that

(a) **the Canada Elections Commission explore with the net- works and news services the possibility of creating a sys- tem for compiling and distributing, on a cost-recovery basis, unofficial voting results on election night; and**
(b) **the Canada Elections Commission meet annually with rep- resentatives of the networks and news services to discuss ways and means of facilitating the reporting of unofficial voting results on election night and other possible infor- mation services.**

NOTES

1. A similar provision exists for candidates in U.S. federal elections: *Federal Election Campaign Act*, s. 441d(b).

2. Elections Canada's Returning Office Automation Project will eventually make it possible for returning officers to forward the results to Elections Canada headquarters for compilation on a central computer. This could be done by direct data transfer. This would make it possible for the raw tallies to be 'accessed' by the news organizations as they come in and transferred to their own computers.

8

ELECTION LAW ENFORCEMENT

~

THE CURRENT APPROACH to election law enforcement treats all violations as criminal offences, even when they are administrative or regulatory in nature. The current approach is problematic for two reasons.

First, the designation 'criminal offences' should be reserved for violations of society's most fundamental values. An individual should be convicted of a crime and subjected to the corresponding stigma and punishment only where it can be demonstrated beyond a reasonable doubt that the prohibited conduct was carried out intentionally, knowingly or purposively. Most election violations do not fall under this rubric. Rather, they are primarily administrative or regulatory in nature. Thus, it is inappropriate for these violations to be investigated and prosecuted as crimes. The adherence to criminal standards of proof means that investigations of election violations are treated as criminal investigations by the RCMP or other investigators used by Elections Canada. This process is costly, time-consuming and inefficient. It also limits unnecessarily the enforcement of regulatory or administrative election violations because it is not suited to the nature of the great majority of infractions.

Second, to prove under the current law that an election violation has been committed, it must be demonstrated to the courts that a candidate, official agent or other person *intended* beyond a reasonable doubt to commit the violation. In other words, *mens rea* must be proved. It is not enough to prove that the violation has taken place. For example, if a candidate or official agent exceeded the statutory spending limit in a constituency, the *mens rea* standard would require the prosecutor to convince a court that the candidate or official agent intended to exceed the spending limit. This is usually extremely difficult to prove.

A NEW APPROACH TO ELECTION VIOLATIONS

An effective system of election law enforcement must have two dimensions. First, those accused of an election violation must have every opportunity to defend themselves against the allegation. Second, the system must act decisively and quickly to stop or to prosecute election violations that will either influence the outcome of an election or undermine public confidence in the integrity of the electoral process. Election law enforcement must not be centred on strict procedures and the imposition of severe penalties that are difficult to enforce. The investigation and prosecution of election violations should not be limited to criminal standards of proof or *mens rea*.

Electoral law should follow other areas of regulatory enforcement by adopting flexibility in standards of proof based on the seriousness of the violation. Canadian law has three categories of offences, which are explained below.

> In an **absolute liability** offence, the Crown must establish merely that the accused committed the physical act of the offence; it need not be concerned with the question of fault. Where, however, it is determined that liability is not absolute, but is based on some notion of fault, it is not always clear whether the offence is one of *mens rea* or strict liability. In a *mens rea* offence, the prosecution must prove that, in committing the offence, the accused had an "aware" state of mind, that is, that [the person] did the wrongful act with, for example, intent, knowledge, recklessness, or wilful blindness. In a **strict liability** offence, the standard is objective, not subjective as in the case of *mens rea*, and is based on the conduct of the reasonable person in similar circumstances. The accused may raise as a defence that [she or he] exercised reasonable care and, therefore, was not negligent. (Ontario Law Reform Commission 1990, 3, emphasis added)

We propose that all violations under the *Canada Elections Act* be defined as either infractions or offences. Infractions would be either procedural, administrative or regulatory and would involve less severe penalties. They would be adjudicated exclusively by the Canada Elections Commission, with the possibility of judicial review by the Federal Court of Canada. The second category of violations would be the more serious, involving some element of wilful misconduct. These violations could result in severe penalties, including higher fines, imprisonment or the loss of certain rights under the *Canada Elections Act*. Election offences would be prosecuted before the provincial courts as summary conviction offences.

We conclude that a new approach to election law enforcement is required, one that provides for the timely investigation, prosecution and adjudication of election violations, whether regulatory, administrative or criminal. As we have argued in Volume 1, Chapter 7, this objective can be achieved by having the Canada Elections Commission – acting as a tribunal – adjudicate most violations of the *Canada Elections Act*.

With respect to infractions, electoral law should be based on strict liability standards of proof. For instance, under our proposal, if a candidate or an official agent exceeded the spending limit, the director of enforcement would need only to convince the Canada Elections Commission tribunal that the facts indicated the candidate or official agent had exceeded the limit. Based on this standard of proof, the onus would shift to the candidate or official agent to show due diligence was exercised, that is, that reasonable care was exercised to ensure an election violation had not occurred. The due diligence defence for strict liability standards of proof was recently upheld by the Supreme Court of Canada in *R. v. Wholesale Travel Group Inc.* (1989).[1] The treatment of election violations as absolute liability offences is not a desirable alternative since those accused of such offences would not have the opportunity to present a defence.

The establishment of a strict liability offence procedure for administrative violations, however, does not mitigate the need for the investigation and prosecution of certain election violations based on the *mens rea* standard of proof. The possibility remains that a person may try to change the outcome of an election by deliberately violating the *Canada Elections Act*. Given the importance of maintaining the integrity of the electoral system, such behaviour should carry the risk of a severe penalty.

For election violations committed with intent, we propose to create a general offence category. Any person who wilfully contravenes any provisions under the Act with the intention of influencing the outcome of an election would be committing a general offence. The general offence category would be similar to the aiding and abetting and the conspiracy sections of the *Criminal Code* under which the accused is treated as if he or she committed another specified offence. This general offence would be prosecuted before the criminal courts and be punishable by up to two years' imprisonment or by loss of the right to sit in the House of Commons or to be a candidate at the next election. Prosecution of this general offence category would require proof of intent, as with conventional criminal offences, rather than being based on a strict liability standard of proof.

Recommendation 2.8.1

We recommend that

(a) **most violations of the *Canada Elections Act* be classified as strict liability infractions, which do not require proof of intent but are subject to a due diligence defence, and that these infractions be prosecuted before the Canada Elections Commission; and**

(b) **persons who wilfully violate the *Canada Elections Act* to influence or vary the outcome of an election or commit other election offences be liable to penalties that include imprisonment, loss of the right to sit in the House of Commons or loss of the right to be a candidate at the next election, and that these offences be prosecuted before the provincial courts.**

PROPOSED PENALTIES FOR ELECTION VIOLATIONS

There is little coherence in the list of violations and penalties contained in the current Act. Penalties vary from a maximum of $1000 or one year's imprisonment on summary conviction for most offences, to $5000 or five years' imprisonment on indictment. Many election fraud violations are now defined as 'illegal practices' and 'corrupt practices', and carry the additional penalty of loss of the right to vote. In addition, candidates or official agents can be denied the right to be a candidate for a period of five or seven years. These violations include voting illegally, undue influence, 'treating' voters (that is, trying to influence their vote by buying them food or drink), and, for candidates and official agents, wilfully exceeding the spending limit.

The provisions of the *Canada Elections Act* for penalties should reflect the gravity of the infractions or offences. The relationship between penalties and violations must consistently encourage compliance with the Act. To achieve this objective, the Commission and the courts must have a range of available penalties. These should include penalties that relate fines to the gravity of the violations. For example, failure to file a post-election return by the prescribed deadline could be punished by a fine of $100 a day for candidates and $1000 a day for parties, and fines for violation of election spending limits could be established as a percentage (100 per cent, 200 per cent) of the excess spending. When there are justifiable reasons, the deadline for filing could be extended, but only by application to the Commission. We propose that, as an example of an administrative penalty, the Commission be empowered to withdraw the right of a registered party to issue tax receipts for political contributions if it has not filed its return by a certain period after the deadline; for the most serious cases, the Commission would be able to de-register a party.

In Volume 3 of our report, we propose a new Canada Elections Act that would extend the election law enforcement process to many dimensions of the electoral process, including financial disclosure requirements for constituency agents, financial agents of leadership contestants, and individuals seeking to be candidates. Further, we have set out requirements for the filing of annual reports and financial statements for registered political parties, constituency associations and party foundations. The enforcement of election law would also apply to individuals and groups who exceed the spending limit of $1000 for independent expenditures, as outlined in Volume 1, Chapter 6. In Volume 3 of our report, we recommend a distinction between election infractions and election offences and establish a more precise relationship between the severity of an election violation and the possible range of penalties.

Imprisonment

When the courts adjudicate election offences, they should be able to impose higher fines, imprisonment and deprivation of the right to candidacy or to sit in the House of Commons. These penalties exist in the current Act but are rarely invoked. They should be retained to affirm that serious election violations will be treated with corresponding penalties. Keeping these penalties in the Act would deter those seeking to wilfully affect the outcome of an election. Levying fines that are 200 per cent of the amount by which a candidate or party exceeds spending limits would also encourage compliance. Similarly, when more serious matters are prosecuted before the courts, the available financial penalties should be substantially higher than the fines that can be levied by the Commission.

Generally, the punishment of imprisonment can be handed down only if the accused has all the protection associated with a conventional court trial. Therefore, offences that are punishable by imprisonment must be reserved for the courts.

Recommendation 2.8.2

We recommend that imprisonment be available as a penalty only for election offences that are prosecuted before the courts.

Loss of Fundamental Rights

The provisions for 'illegal practices' and 'corrupt practices' in the current Act are archaic and should be dropped, along with the automatic invoking of a loss of the right to vote or to be a candidate. Because these offences are narrowly defined, they expose candidates and official agents to greater penalties than other citizens who commit certain other election offences, without giving the courts any discretion to tailor penalties to suit particular circumstances. Although we would retain the penalty of loss of the right to candidacy for some offences, it is arbitrary to extend this penalty over five or seven years without considering the number of elections that may take place during that period. The loss of the right to candidacy as a result of an offence should be limited to the period up to and including the next general election only. This penalty should also be restricted to cases prosecuted before the courts. If a candidate is found guilty of an election offence, then the loss of the right to candidacy could be an appropriate penalty. The probability that this might occur would be an effective deterrent for most candidates.[2]

Losing the right to vote as a result of an election offence is no longer acceptable. In Volume 1, Chapter 2, we recommend that only prisoners convicted of an offence punishable by life imprisonment and sentenced to 10 years or more be denied the right to vote. However, denying the right to candidacy to those who wilfully attempt to influence or vary the outcome of an election represents a reasonable and demonstrable restriction in a free and democratic society, given that the penalty would apply to individuals who deliberately attempted to undermine the integrity of the electoral process.

Recommendation 2.8.3

We recommend that

(a) **the concepts of illegal acts and of corrupt practices, and the corresponding penalties, be removed from the *Canada Elections Act*;**

(b) the penalties of loss of candidacy and loss of the right to sit in the House of Commons be retained in the *Canada Elections Act*, but that these penalties apply only for one federal election and only for cases prosecuted before the courts; and

(c) no person lose the right to vote for having committed an election violation.

PROCEDURES FOR HANDLING INVESTIGATIONS

Time Limits for Complaints

At present, the *Canada Elections Act* requires that all complaints be received by Elections Canada within six months of the alleged violation being committed, and that prosecutions be initiated within 18 months of that date or of the date "on which the action ... might first have been brought or taken". This last clause is intended to cover situations where a violation does not come to light until some time after it is committed.

Since candidates are not required to file their election expense reports until four months after an election is held, the effect of the current law is that prosecutions arising from a particular election may be launched almost two years after that election, or half-way through a normal four-year election cycle. We consider the period allowed for complaints to be adequate; however, the period allowed for investigations is excessive and should be shortened to one year from the date of an initial complaint. This should not create any problems since the director of enforcement would have investigators on staff and could engage additional resources temporarily for investigation in the post-election period if necessary.

To instil public confidence in enforcement, it is also important that in each instance the complainant be notified whether the complaint will be prosecuted.

Recommendation 2.8.4

We recommend that

(a) the deadline for complaints of election violations remain at six months after the commission of the violation but the deadline for the commencement of prosecution of an election violation be shortened to one year after a complaint is filed or evidence of a violation becomes available; and

(b) the director of enforcement consider all complaints for activities regulated by the *Canada Elections Act*, decide whether to initiate an investigation, and if a complaint is not investigated, inform the complainant of the decision with reasons.

Investigations

We agree with the concerns expressed at our public hearings about the use of the RCMP to investigate election violations. The director of enforcement should have sufficient investigative powers so that she or he will need the assistance of law enforcement agencies only to investigate the most serious violations, which may require expertise not found at the Commission. One important investigative power is search and seizure. Police currently require a judge's warrant to use their power of search and seizure; in the case of the Canada Elections Commission investigations, the same requirements should apply.

Because of the adversarial nature of election campaigns, a number of unfounded allegations are often made against candidates or registered parties. To ensure credibility of the enforcement process, it is important that the director of enforcement not be required to act on anonymous complaints. At the same time, the director must have the discretion to investigate complaints based on reasonable information from staff and other sources.

The person against whom the complaint is filed may be notified before an investigation begins. However, the director of enforcement should have the discretion to begin an investigation without notifying that person if the director believes that notification would compromise or impede the investigation.

Once an investigation is complete, fairness demands that the director of enforcement notify the person being investigated of the investigation and its results before the matter proceeds further. A person accused of violating the Act must be given notice of all the information the director of enforcement intends to use before a prosecution is initiated before either the Commission or the courts.

Recommendation 2.8.5

We recommend that

(a) **the director of enforcement be granted full powers to investigate violations of the *Canada Elections Act*, and investigators of the Canada Elections Commission be given powers of search and seizure, subject to prior authorization from a judge;**

(b) **the director of enforcement request assistance from a law enforcement agency only in investigations involving the most serious violations, where the director of enforcement may lack particular experience or expertise;**

(c) **the director of enforcement not be required to act on anonymous complaints but be permitted to initiate investigations based on reasonable information from staff and other sources;**

(d) the subject of a complaint be notified before or during the investigation of the complaint, unless the director of enforcement believes that notification would compromise or impede the investigation; and

(e) a person or party who will be prosecuted before the Commission or the courts be notified of all information from the investigation that the director of enforcement intends to use before the matter proceeds before the Commission or the courts.

VOLUNTARY COMPLIANCE

We have argued that there is an alternative to having every election violation prosecuted in the traditional manner. Since most violations are essentially administrative, we propose that the primary jurisdiction for hearing these infractions be transferred from the courts to the Commission. To complement this, we propose that a mechanism for voluntary compliance be established.

In the United States, the Federal Election Commission (FEC) has developed a program of voluntary compliance for enforcing its rules for political finance disclosure. Many state election commissions have similar programs. When a violation occurs, FEC staff may negotiate an agreed settlement as an alternative to taking it to court, although any settlement must be approved by the Commission. These agreements are made public by the FEC both in Washington and in the area where the violation occurred, with details of the offender, the violation and the agreed penalty. Under the U.S. system, the FEC can only review proposed negotiated settlements; any cases where a settlement is not reached or approved by the Commission must be prosecuted before the courts. According to the FEC, less than 5 per cent of valid complaints reach the courts; 95 per cent of all valid complaints result in negotiated settlements.

Voluntary compliance gives the FEC two advantages: it provides greater certainty for resolving violations and it demands fewer resources for prosecuting offenders. It also allows a violation to be settled without going through lengthy adjudication processes. This procedure is not followed for criminal violations of U.S. election law because these are beyond the FEC's jurisdiction. We propose that the same rule apply in Canada.

At our public hearings, the former and current chief electoral officers both urged that enforcement procedures modelled on those of the *Canadian Human Rights Act* be used for election violations. In fact, the Canadian Human Rights Commission offers a good example of a voluntary compliance program at the federal level. As a normal part of its procedures, its investigators try to negotiate the settlement of most complaints before the Commission decides whether to send them to a human rights tribunal for adjudication. In 1989, of the complaints that were not dismissed, 60 per cent were resolved through this form of voluntary compliance.

A mechanism for voluntary compliance would permit the fair and efficient handling of election infractions as part of the enforcement process.

Once the director of enforcement was granted the authority to negotiate settlements of infractions under the *Canada Elections Act*, the process for voluntary compliance would work as follows:

1. The director of enforcement would notify anyone who is being investigated of the results of the investigation. When appropriate, the director of enforcement would indicate that it would be possible to enter into a voluntary compliance agreement. This agreement would set out the details of the investigation of the infraction and the penalty proposed by the director of enforcement, who would then seek to negotiate an agreement. Penalties in the voluntary compliance agreements could not exceed those available if the case was adjudicated by the Commission. Because of this limitation, this process would be restricted to election infractions.
2. If a settlement was reached, the agreement would be referred to a single commissioner, appointed by the chair. The commissioner would consider the agreement on a 'without prejudice' basis.
3. If the commissioner confirmed the agreement, it would be certified by the Commission. The name of the individual or party concerned, the nature of the infraction and the penalty would be published where applicable. This agreement would be enforced as if it were an order of the Commission.
4. If the commissioner rejected the agreement, the matter would proceed for determination before the Commission. The commissioner who considered the voluntary compliance agreement would not sit as a member of any panel considering the case.

Voluntary compliance agreements would eliminate the need to prosecute all violations and would make enforcement more efficient. At the same time, using these agreements would formally recognize that many election violations are administrative and result more from inexperience or carelessness than from an intention to break the law.

Recommendation 2.8.6

We recommend that

(a) **for election infractions, the director of enforcement have the authority to negotiate an agreement in the form of a voluntary compliance agreement, which would be subject to the approval of one commissioner of the Canada Elections Commission;**
(b) **the person accused of the infraction be notified of the voluntary compliance procedure;**
(c) **the chair appoint a commissioner to review the proposed negotiated settlement;**

(d) if the commissioner confirms the voluntary compliance agreement, the name of the individual and party concerned and the nature of the infraction and the penalty be published, where applicable; and the agreement be enforced as if it were an order of the Commission;

(e) if the commissioner rejects the agreement, it be referred to the Commission for adjudication; and

(f) any commissioner who assesses an agreement not be allowed to sit on any panel hearing the case.

PROSECUTION

As indicated in Volume 1, Chapter 7, the director of enforcement would have the authority to determine whether a complaint warranted further action either in the form of a voluntary compliance agreement or a prosecution before the Commission or the courts. The director of enforcement would determine that a matter should be prosecuted if a voluntary compliance agreement was not appropriate given the nature or gravity of the alleged violation or if an agreement could not be negotiated or confirmed. The director would then proceed with a prosecution before either the Commission or the courts, depending on whether the violation was being prosecuted as an infraction or as an offence. If it was prosecuted before the Commission, the chair of the Commission would appoint a panel. The panel would consist of at least one commissioner who would sit as a tribunal; if more than one commissioner were appointed, the chair of the tribunal would be appointed by the chair of the Canada Elections Commission.

Recommendation 2.8.7

We recommend that

(a) the director of enforcement have the authority to determine whether a complaint warrants further action, either in the form of a voluntary compliance agreement or prosecution before the Commission or the courts;

(b) when a voluntary compliance agreement cannot be reached or is not appropriate, the director of enforcement proceed with prosecution either before the Commission or the courts; and

(c) when the director of enforcement proceeds with prosecution before the Commission, the chair of the Commission appoint a panel of at least one commissioner to sit as a tribunal; and if more than one commissioner is appointed, the chair of the tribunal be appointed by the chair of the Canada Elections Commission.

CONFIDENTIALITY

The current policy of Elections Canada is to maintain strict confidentiality when it receives election-related complaints. This corresponds to the normal practice of police in dealing with suspected criminal cases: the identity of a suspect is normally not made public unless the person is charged. This policy should be continued for all election violations. Complaints and investigations should be kept confidential unless they have been referred to prosecution or resolved by an agreed penalty. There should be one exception: the director of enforcement should be required to disclose publicly information about a complaint when the person who was investigated requests a public statement that there was no substance to the complaint.

The policy of the U.S. Federal Election Commission is to put every complaint on the public record once it has been disposed of or adjudicated. The name of the complainant, the name of the person or party the complaint is filed against and the nature of the complaint are routinely made public at that time. Releasing the name of the complainant, in certain cases, could inhibit individuals from filing complaints about election violations. Publishing details of a complaint also runs contrary to the usual practice followed in legal investigations in Canada and for that reason should not be followed for election violations.

Recommendation 2.8.8

We recommend that complaints and investigations be kept confidential unless they have been brought before the Commission or courts for adjudication, resolved by a voluntary compliance agreement, or unless requested by the person or party that is the subject of the complaint.

NOTES

1. In 1978 the Supreme Court of Canada in *R. v. City of Sault Ste Marie* affirmed the distinction between regulatory and criminal offences; it also subdivided regulatory offences into categories of strict and absolute liability. More recently, in *R. v. Wholesale Travel Group Inc.* (1989) the Supreme Court stated that these categories did not violate the *Canadian Charter of Rights and Freedoms* and it reaffirmed the desirability of the distinctions among the offence and liability categories. Justice Cory of the Supreme Court of Canada stated:

    It follows that regulatory offences and crimes embody different concepts of fault. Since regulatory offences are directed primarily not to conduct itself but to the consequences of conduct, conviction of a regulatory offence may be thought to import a significantly lesser degree of culpability than conviction of a true crime. The concept of fault in regulatory offences is based upon a reasonable care standard and, as such, does not imply moral blameworthiness in the same manner as criminal fault. Conviction for breach of a regulatory offence suggests nothing more than that the defendant has failed to meet a prescribed standard of care. (1991, 14)

2.   We recommend in Volume 1, Chapter 3 that a voter lose his or her right to sit in the House of Commons if, after the deadline, the voter has failed to file an elections financial report with the Commission, and that a voter be ineligible as a candidate if, at the close of nominations for an election, the voter has not filed an elections financial report for a prior election.

9

DIRECT DEMOCRACY IN THE ELECTORAL PROCESS

INTRODUCTION

THE EMERGENCE OF new political parties and the heightened prominence of special-interest groups suggest many Canadians are critical of their existing political institutions. Many are concerned that these institutions are not sufficiently responsive to their views and interests. The recommendations in Volume 1 and Volume 2 reaffirm the role of the individual citizen in Canada's representative democracy. They directly address many concerns about the electoral process and the credibility of political parties as the primary political institutions. Strengthening representative government will ensure that individual citizens are provided with political institutions that reconcile conflicting views and interests.

The alternative to strengthening the institutions of representative government in Canada is increased support for the instruments of what has been traditionally described as 'direct democracy'. Support for direct democracy is based on the assumption that recall, referendums and citizen initiatives can increase the role individual citizens have in how they are governed. This support draws in part on so-called populist sentiments that are critical of several institutional mechanisms and traditions in Canada's system of parliamentary government, especially the practice of party discipline in which cohesive political parties operate within the House of Commons. Party discipline has contributed to popular perceptions that individual MPs are, in fact, prevented from adequately representing the interests of their constituents. Although the instruments of direct democracy may provide citizens with more opportunities to express their policy preferences or to pass judgement on their elected representatives outside of general elections, they are far less suited to accommodating and representing the many different interests of citizens. Effective reconciliation of these interests is crucial for any democratic government.

Not since the 1920s and 1930s have populist pressures in Canada been so strong. In that period, labour and agrarian movements recorded electoral successes federally and provincially based on anti-party platforms, on assailing established patterns of political and economic power, and on promises to make citizens key participants in the governing process. Promises of direct democracy were bandied about freely. And although the early populist movements led to the restructuring of the Canadian party system, their promises of a more direct approach to economic and political decision-making were not fulfilled. In the 1990s, populist sentiments have reappeared. Once again, the instruments of direct democracy are offered as antidotes to Canada's current form of representative government.

There are three instruments of direct democracy: recall, citizen initiative and referendum. The *recall* can be used by constituents to vote on the performance of elected officials before the end of a normal term of office. The *citizen initiative* or *citizen-initiated referendum*, also called the direct initiative, allows voters to propose legislation initiated through a citizen petition. If the required number of voters sign the petition, the proposed legislation is submitted directly to the voters for approval. The *referendum* can be one of two types: mandatory and advisory. In mandatory referendums, legislatures must submit legislation to voters for ratification. Presented with a specific question on a ballot, voters choose between two mutually exclusive propositions. Mandatory referendums are used in several jurisdictions to ratify constitutional amendments. Advisory referendums, or plebiscites, are used at the discretion of the legislature to measure popular opinion on controversial or extraordinary issues.

Although the practices of direct democracy provide citizens with opportunities to participate in the governing process, they do not necessarily involve electoral reform issues, which is our mandate. In this chapter, we focus on the use of the recall, as well as the practice of simultaneously holding referendums and general elections. The use of these instruments directly affects the electoral processes that underscore Canada's representative democracy.

THE HISTORY OF DIRECT DEMOCRACY IN CANADA

The instruments of direct democracy were first given serious attention in North America in the 1890s and early 1900s following the rise of the populist movement in the midwestern United States. The populists, led by agrarian and labour interests, were highly critical of state legislatures and legislators. American populists argued that the legislative process was dominated by big business and wealthy vested interests. Individual legislators were seen as beholden to monied interests and less concerned with representing their constituents. Populists promoted direct democracy as a way of giving individual citizens a greater role in how they were governed and as a way of correcting the perceived weaknesses of the legislative and representative processes. Specifically, the recall was seen as a device for removing corrupt politicians from office. Graft, corruption and bribery of elected officials in the midwestern states were widespread in this period, leading many citizens to question the integrity of representative government. (Cronin 1989) From 1890 to 1920, populist candidates won many seats in midwestern state legislatures. As a result of populist pressures, approximately half of the state legislatures passed legislation during that period approving the use of the recall, referendums and citizen initiatives.

The populist movement in the United States was received sympathet-
ically by Canadian farmers' organizations and groups in the three Prairie
provinces. In fact, the leadership of the farmers' organizations in western
Canada was influenced by immigrants from the United States. But unlike
the U.S. populists, Canadian populists initially channelled their reformist
energies through the traditional party system. As historian W.L. Morton
notes, the three provincial governments in the Prairie provinces "accepted
most of the farmers' programme which came within provincial jurisdiction over the years between 1911 and 1919, and soon these governments
were, in all but name and personnel, farmers' governments". (Morton 1967,
31) In Manitoba, the provincial Liberal party accepted, with very few exceptions, the programs of the farmers. "In Saskatchewan the grain growers
dominated the economy and politics of the province, and government had
the comparatively simple task of accommodating administration and legislation to the requirements of the organized farmers." (Morton 1967, 34–35)
Farmers' groups in Alberta were less willing to accept the traditional party
system and were more committed to independent political action.

In response to the populist pressures from the farmers' movements and
their critique of the practice of party government, each of the western provinces enacted 'direct legislation' laws. Between 1913 and 1919, the provincial legislatures of British Columbia, Alberta, Saskatchewan and Manitoba
passed legislation that allowed for referendums and citizen-initiated referendums. The direct legislation law of 1919 in British Columbia, however,
was never proclaimed by the provincial cabinet. Similar legislation in
Saskatchewan failed to win popular endorsement when it was submitted
to voters as a referendum question in 1913. The Manitoba direct legislation law was declared unconstitutional by the Judicial Committee of the
Privy Council in 1919. The Privy Council ruled that the law excluded the
Lieutenant-Governor from the legislative process, since legislation from
citizen-initiated referendums could be enacted without his consent. Section 92(1) of the *Constitution Act, 1867* (now s. 41 of the *Constitution Act,
1982*) prevents provincial legislatures from unilaterally changing the powers
of the office of Lieutenant-Governor. Finally, the direct legislation law in
Alberta was never used by voters. It was repealed by the Social Credit government of Premier E.C. Manning in 1958.

Despite their initial efforts, the traditional parties never fully adopted
the progressive and often radical changes sought by the farmers' groups.
The provincial Liberal and Conservative parties in the West were often
dominated by their federal counterparts who were less receptive to the
economic and political demands of farmers. Consequently, the Canadian
agrarian movement organized itself into political groups – provincially, the
United Farmers and, federally, the Progressive Party – to challenge the two
traditional parties. Between 1919 and 1921, these groups won elections in
Ontario and Alberta and formed the official opposition in several provinces.
The Progressive Party won 65 seats in the 1921 federal general election,
displacing the Conservatives as the second largest 'party' in Parliament.

Although these groups tapped into different populist strains, they shared a common dislike of political parties and the tradition of party discipline. (Laycock 1990) The populists argued that the Liberal and Conservative parties, and therefore the federal government, were controlled by large economic interests from eastern Canada and did not respond to the needs of farmers and workers.

Unlike American populists, the United Farmers and Progressives were less critical of representative democracy per se and far less committed to the traditional instruments of direct democracy. For them, the critical issue was how legislators represented their constituents. Canadian populists, in contrast to their American counterparts, favoured the concepts of 'group government' and 'delegate democracy'. They saw economic groups or classes, rather than political parties, as the basic political unit. Canadian populists argued that the party system could be replaced by political organizations of occupational or industrial groups. In turn, each group would nominate and elect its own representatives to the legislature. The occupational groups would meet in local communities to deliberate on public policy and then inform their elected representatives on what action to take. Members of the elected legislature would be directly responsible to their constituents, albeit through non-partisan community associations. The cabinet and party caucus would be secondary participants.

The United Farmers came to power in Alberta and Ontario in 1919. The United Farmers of Ontario were defeated in the following election; their counterparts in Alberta remained in power until 1935, when they were defeated by the Social Credit Party. The Social Credit Party, like the United Farmers of Alberta (UFA), came to power by campaigning on 'platforms' – as the parties' election promises were then called – against party and cabinet government.

Although populist movements appeared in Canada and the United States during the same period, the impact they had on their respective political processes was different. The U.S. populist movement appealed to the individualist values that have dominated U.S. political culture. American populists argued that individual citizens should be able to express their views directly on important public policy issues independent of the capacity of their governments to represent the public interest.

In contrast, Canadian populists adapted the theories and instruments of direct democracy to the more collectivist values that have been pre-eminent in Canada's political culture. Consequently, both the United Farmers and the Social Credit governments of Alberta remained committed to the essential characteristics of representative government. Their primary concern was whether political parties and cabinet government impeded the ability of legislators to represent directly their constituents. (Mac Donald 1991 RC)

Nonetheless, within two years of coming to power, the United Farmers and Social Credit governments each recognized that cabinet and party government provided them with the institutions they needed to implement their programs and policies. According to C.B. Macpherson, the UFA's elected representatives recognized their movement needed

> to prove its ability to govern and to finance the province.... In order to make a success of independent political action they had to support their government; in order to support the government they had to dispense with those principles of group government which conflicted with the cabinet system. Specifically, the primary responsibility of the member to his constituency association had to give way to his responsibility for maintaining the government, that is, to his responsibility to the cabinet. (Macpherson 1962, 80)

Even when political movements come to power based on platforms supporting the instruments of direct democracy, history shows that the responsibilities and exigencies of governance cannot be easily met through the use of the recall, the citizen initiative or the referendum.

REFERENDUMS IN CANADA

During our public hearings a few interveners supported the use of national referendums and nation-wide citizen initiatives. Although the issue of using referendums outside of elections does not fall within our mandate, some interveners proposed that referendums be held on election day. This matter indirectly relates to our mandate, and hence we have addressed it.

A total of 44 advisory referendums or plebiscites have been held in Canadian provinces, 31 in the four western provinces. No province has held a mandatory referendum. New Brunswick is the only province not to have held at least one referendum. Most of the referendum questions involved either prohibiting liquor sales or adopting daylight savings time. Of the 44 referendums, 31 were held before 1945.

A few referendums have been held in the last 10 years. A provincial referendum in Quebec on sovereignty-association was held on 20 May 1980. The legislation that governed the referendum requires that referendums are managed and administered by a Referendum Council composed of three provincial court judges. Referendum questions are proposed by the cabinet and approved by the National Assembly. Individuals or groups wanting to participate in a referendum debate must do so through 'yes' and 'no' umbrella organizations. "With the ... exception of Britain in 1975 during the Common Market referendum, no other democracy has conducted referendums under a statutory framework of umbrellas." (Boyer 1982, 206) Political parties and pressure groups in Quebec are not allowed to spend money or actively campaign independent of an umbrella organization. The laws regulating referendum expenses and campaigning parallel those in Quebec provincial elections.

A referendum was held in the Northwest Territories in 1982 on whether the territories should be divided into regions, with one having a majority of Aboriginal people. In 1987, residents of northern Quebec, who were mostly Inuit, were asked in a referendum what strategy should be used to draft a constitution for their regional assembly. The referendum campaign was organized by the chief electoral officer (CEO) of Quebec using the province's framework for referendums. In 1988, voters in Prince Edward Island voted on whether a fixed link between the Island and New Brunswick should be constructed.

Both British Columbia and Saskatchewan have recently enacted referendum acts. Referendums in the other provinces, except Prince Edward Island and Quebec, are held either under specific legislative statutes such as those relating to agriculture policy, or under the provincial electoral law. Most provinces have legislation that permits local and municipal level referendums and plebiscites.

Saskatchewan's *Referendum and Plebiscite Act* allows the provincial cabinet, at its discretion, to submit referendum and plebiscite questions to the electorate. If more than 60 per cent of voters vote 'yes' or 'no' on the specific referendum question, the results are binding on the government, as long as at least 50 per cent of those eligible to vote cast ballots. At least 15 per cent of registered voters in Saskatchewan's most recent general election can request, through a petition, that a particular policy question be put before the electorate in the form of a referendum question. Results from citizen-initiated referendums and plebiscites are not binding on the provincial cabinet. If a referendum or plebiscite campaign overlaps with a general election "all expenditures incurred by a registered political party or a candidate to promote or oppose a question put to electors ... are deemed to be election expenses". (Section 12, *Referendum and Plebiscite Act*)

In September 1991, the premier of Saskatchewan announced that three advisory plebiscite questions would be put on the ballot of the provincial election of 21 October 1991. The three questions were on balanced budget legislation, whether changes to the constitution should be approved by Saskatchewan voters through referendums, and whether the government of Saskatchewan should pay for abortions.[1]

Bill 55, the *Referendum Act*, was adopted by the British Columbia legislative assembly in July 1990. Referendum questions submitted to the electorate are determined by the provincial cabinet. If more than 50 per cent vote the same way on the referendum question, the results are 'binding' on the government that initiates the referendum, although the legislation merely requires that the provincial government take the necessary steps to ensure implementation "as soon as practicable". The *Referendum Act* allows the government to submit referendum questions to the electorate at any time; that is, referendums could be held simultaneously with a provincial general election. The legislation has no provisions for citizen-initiated referendums. In September 1991, the premier of British Columbia announced two referendum questions would be put before voters in the provincial election of 17 October 1991. The questions asked voters to consider the direct democracy instruments of the recall, and the citizen initiative; both were approved by a majority of voters.[2]

Canada has held two national referendums, although at the time the instruments were popularly known as plebiscites. The first was held in 1898 on the prohibition of liquor sales. The federal government took the unprecedented step of holding a national referendum on prohibition because previous efforts to resolve this volatile issue, including the use of a royal commission, had not worked. Although prohibition was endorsed by a small majority of Canadians, fewer than half of the registered voters voted in the referendum. Notwithstanding the results of the referendum, control over liquor laws became the responsibility of the provinces shortly after. The Mackenzie King government held a referendum in 1942 on imposing military conscription in Canada, although the wording of the question made no reference to conscription itself. Canadian voters were asked: "Are you in favour of releasing the government from any obligation arising out of any past commitments restricting the methods of raising men for military service?" The divisive outcome of the referendum has been well documented. (Boyer 1982; Lemieux 1985)

The issue of referendums in Canadian national politics, however, has not been limited to 1898 and 1942. For example, as leader of the Liberal opposition, Sir Wilfrid Laurier saw the referendum "as a possible way out of the pending collision between English-speaking Canada and Quebec over conscription for military service in World War I". (Boyer 1982, 52) In the mid-1960s, the use of the referendum was given cursory consideration during the negotiation of the Fulton-Favreau constitutional amending formula between the federal and provincial governments. Throughout the years, individual Members of Parliament have made periodic efforts to get a national referendum bill passed by introducing private member's bills, but they have not been successful. Most recently, in the fall of 1989, Patrick Boyer, MP, introduced a private member's bill on national referendums and plebiscites (Bill C-257). His draft bill prohibits holding referendums and federal elections at the same time.

The government of Prime Minister Pierre Elliott Trudeau introduced the *Canada Referendum Act* in 1978–79. When Parliament was dissolved for a general election in May 1979, Bill C-9 died on the order paper. The Trudeau government's initial 1980–81 constitutional reform package included provisions for the use of national referendums to ratify constitutional amendments. These measures were withdrawn as the result of opposition from several provincial governments.

Recent proposals have been made to use national referendums to ratify constitutional amendments. The Beaudoin–Edwards Special Joint Committee on the Process for Amending the Constitution of Canada argued, for example, that referendums should be used for such purposes. (Canada, Parliament 1991)

REFERENDUMS IN COMPARATIVE PERSPECTIVE

Advisory and mandatory referendums are not widely used as an instrument of decision-making by national governments. They are used frequently in many countries at the state and municipal levels. Nevertheless, almost all western democracies have used referendums at least once since the Second World War to receive direct citizen input on important public policy issues. Britain held its only national referendum in 1975 when voters were asked whether Britain should remain a member of the European Economic Community (EEC). Sixty-seven per cent of British voters endorsed continued membership in the EEC. As noted, the referendum campaign was conducted through two 'umbrella organizations' which had primary responsibility for co-ordinating the 'yes' and 'no' campaigns. Each organization received public funding assistance to mobilize British voters, although the pro-European Community forces were better organized and financed. Perhaps the "most remarkable special aspect of the referendum was the government's agreement to differ: 16 members of the Cabinet campaigned for EEC membership and seven against. The normal rules of collective responsibility, by which all ministers must support government policy or resign, were relaxed for three months with respect to this one question." (Butler 1978, 214) Cabinet solidarity was relaxed, in part, to prevent "the Labour party from tearing itself asunder", given the internal divisions within the party on continued membership in the EEC. (Butler 1978, 214)

The president of France can call advisory referendums on important issues of the state. Results of French referendums are a test of the president's personal credibility. For example, President Charles de Gaulle resigned in 1969 after his plans to change the French Senate and to strengthen the role of regional governments were rejected by voters in a national referendum. The referendum is banned by the German constitution, the Basic Law. Before the Second World War, the referendum had been abused by the Nazi regime to establish public support for controversial policies. Based on this experience, the drafters of the German constitution after the war saw the referendum as authoritarian and subject to abuse, rather than as an instrument of popular democratic control. (Chandler and Siaroff 1991 RC) The United States, the Netherlands and Israel are the only three western nations never to have held a national advisory or mandatory referendum.

A few national legislatures are constitutionally required to hold mandatory referendums. Constitutional amendments in Australia, Austria, Japan and Ireland must be ratified by voters. In Australia, constitutional amendments must be ratified by a double majority; that is, a national majority of voters and a majority of voters in four out of the six states must vote 'yes' for the proposed amendments. Since the early 1900s, approximately 40 constitutional amendments have been submitted to Australian voters for ratification; only eight have received the necessary double majorities.

Very few countries have provisions for citizen-initiated referendums. Most referendums, whether advisory or mandatory, are initiated by the central or national government. Switzerland and Italy are notable exceptions. In Switzerland, 100 000 electors (who sign a petition) can request that legislation enacted by the federal legislature be submitted for popular ratification, and the same procedure can be used to amend the national constitution. Constitutional amendments in Switzerland can vary from changes in the size of pensions to the scope of environmental protection laws. Italian voters can request that legislation passed by the national legislature be submitted for popular ratification before it comes into effect. Voters in Italy, however, seldom use the citizen initiative.

More referendums are held in U.S. states and Switzerland than in all other jurisdictions combined. In 49 U.S. states, constitutional amendments must be ratified by referendums. In 25 states, registered voters can petition their legislature to hold a referendum on a law that has been enacted. Filing of the required number of petition signatures suspends the legislation until the electorate determines whether it should be approved. Several states exempt financial appropriations and emergency measures from this referendum procedure. Citizen-initiated referendums can be used in 23 states to place proposed constitutional amendments before the electorate.

Although referendums and citizen-initiated referendums are used frequently in Arizona, California, Colorado, North Dakota, Oregon and Washington, they are used most in California. In California, "the institution [of the initiative] appears as firmly grounded in the political culture of the state as the legislature itself. Indeed, the initiative may be more widely employed and by more people in the state than in any other democratic society in the world." (Lee 1978, 88) In the November 1990 mid-term U.S. elections, there were 20 referendum questions on the California ballot. Each registered elector received a 144-page booklet to explain the various 'yes' and 'no' positions that came with each referendum question.

Switzerland conducts referendums at the national and canton (state) level. They are not held concurrently with elections. From 1848 to 1990 about 350 national referendums were held in Switzerland. Proposals submitted by the national parliament in mandatory referendums are normally accepted by voters. Legislation proposed by voters through a citizen initiative, which requires that 100 000 signatures be collected within 18 months for a referendum to be held, has usually been rejected by Swiss voters. Since 1891 when the federal initiative in Switzerland was introduced, only eight initiatives have been endorsed by Swiss voters. (Sigg 1987, 32; Aubert 1978)

Several salient features of the California and Swiss experiences with referendums and citizen-initiated referendums deserve attention. Voter turnout rates are very low in California, falling below 50 per cent in elections throughout the 1980s. In Switzerland, turnout rates for elections have declined to 47 per cent in recent years. (Sigg 1987, 28) Notwithstanding the widespread use of referendums, public attitude surveys have shown that non-voters in Switzerland have low levels of political efficacy. This widespread sense of "political helplessness" appears anomalous in a nation where the role of the individual citizen is the foremost concern of the governing process. (Sigg 1987, 25)

Political parties are weak in California and Switzerland. As a consequence, the referendum and initiative in California and Switzerland are dominated by highly organized interests committed to specific legislation and programs. Interest groups in California can spend as much money as they can raise. They play a key role in getting issues on the ballot, and with the help of paid professional organizers, they structure and manage the initiative campaigns. As Cronin (1989) has argued, the process of citizen-initiated referendums is "big business"; the so-called process of citizen-initiated referendums is dominated by public relations firms, media consultants, public opinion pollsters and direct mail specialists.

ADVANTAGES AND DISADVANTAGES OF REFERENDUMS

Referendums serve many purposes that can contribute to the effectiveness and credibility of representative democracy. As stated previously, governments can use referendums to allow citizens to directly express their views on important national issues. Governments may be seen to be more accountable if they receive the direct input of voters outside of a general election. One expert on the use of referendums has suggested that there is "considerable force in the case for referendum as a means of popular democratic control". (Johnson 1981, 26) The case for popular consultations, he says, "may also be reinforced by the growing complexity and remoteness of modern government, as a result of which many people feel alienated from their political institutions and suspicious of the decisions taken through them on their behalf". (Johnson 1981, 26)

Supporters of referendums also argue that legislation ratified by citizens directly enhances the legitimacy of public policies and, as a consequence, increases public confidence in the democratic process. Vincent Lemieux has argued that increased use of referendums in Canada would "promote a greater sense of attachment, on the part of Canadians, to the central institutions of the country, as well as a stronger feeling of participation in the decisions that concern us all". (Lemieux 1985, 138–39)

At the same time, however, referendums have disadvantages. First, the referendum can make governments reluctant decision makers. Rather than provide direction or leadership on controversial or volatile issues, governments may use the referendum to obfuscate or shun responsibility. Second, "the referendum is based on the unrealistic assumption there is a simple 'yes' or 'no' answer to complex questions, and sets up a confrontation between supporters and opponents of a proposition". (Zimmerman 1986, 57) Moreover, "there is no opportunity for continuing discussion of other alternatives, no way to search for the compromise that will draw the widest acceptance. Referendums by their very nature set up confrontations rather than encourage compromises. [Referendums] divide the populace into victors and vanquished." (Butler and Ranney 1978, 226) Third, in the absence of an appropriate framework, the referendum process can easily be dominated by wealthy special-interest groups.

REFERENDUMS AND FEDERAL GENERAL ELECTIONS IN CANADA

Notwithstanding the advantages and disadvantages, the use of referendums as an extension of the legislative and representative processes falls outside our terms of reference. The following discussion focuses only on the role of referendums as an issue of electoral reform.

Several interveners argued during our public hearings that holding national referendums on election day would be cost-effective. They noted that referendum campaigns would require large expenditures, similar to those incurred for general elections. Although reducing costs of referendum campaigns is a worthy objective, the savings from holding referendums and elections simultaneously should not be overstated. In previous chapters, we make recommendations that would reduce the administrative costs of a general election. Many of these reforms and changes could also extend to national referendums, even if they were held separately from elections. Accordingly, the costs incurred as a result of a national referendum would be less than envisaged by some, albeit they remain substantial.

Those who support simultaneous referendums and elections argue that joining the two processes would allow voters to register their approval or disapproval of specific policies and, consequently, that governments would be elected with explicit mandates. Individual citizens, they argue, could participate in the governing process in a more immediate and meaningful way. Several interveners suggested that the mandates governments receive from elections would be clearer if voters could also express their preferences on specific policy issues during election campaigns.

Much of the support for referendums on election day is based on the assumption that our political parties do not provide clear policy alternatives during elections. Referendums, it is argued, would formally indicate to parties the extent to which voters support or oppose specific policies. There is a further underlying assumption that if an important policy issue has not been put to a referendum vote, the government of the day does not have a mandate to take action. More specifically, many who support referendums on election day believe that our political parties do not give enough attention to the policy preferences expressed by most Canadians. In their submission to the Commission, the Reform Party of Canada (Brief 1990, 6) stated:

> The process of resolution of an issue is too often an accommodation to a particular region, pressure group or an attempt to gain the favour of a province. Referenda ensure that the resolution of an issue is public. The debate over issues is subject to the cleansing agent of public scrutiny. The doubts and concerns that many Canadians feel about the process of government would be allayed by a referendum or plebiscite.

The assumption that parties do not provide clear policy alternatives during election campaigns needs to be assessed in the context of the times.

The experience in recent elections, for instance, suggests that political parties have offered clear and precise policy choices to Canadians on many important policy issues. The distinctions among the Progressive Conservative, Liberal and New Democratic parties were most evident in the 1988 federal election on the implementation of a free trade agreement between Canada and the United States. Tom Kent (1989, 10) argues that "an election is not a referendum". He suggests:

> The 1988 election ... confirmed what has been apparent from many recent elections as well as public opinion surveys. A relatively educated public now has a firmer grasp of what an election is about than do many of our politicians. It is not to choose the politicians who will govern as they think best when in office. It is to choose the politicians whose declared policies and apparent capabilities best embody the direction of public policies as a whole that most Canadians favour for the next four years. (Kent 1989, 11)

The purpose of electoral competition in Canada's system of representative democracy is to provide political parties with periodic opportunities to demonstrate that they can present a broad package of policies and ideas that appeal to many voters in various regions throughout the country. Elections also allow voters to assess how well specific parties handle the complex and varied responsibilities of governance. During election campaigns political parties are required to address many diverse issues. A political party that restricts itself to supporting or opposing several referendum questions would not adequately indicate to voters the policies and ideas it would promote in government. In this respect, the presence of referendums at election time might contribute to confusing, rather than clarifying, the positions of political parties. Moreover, joining referendums and elections would actually undermine some of the benefits of referendums. There is an obvious tension between the argument that referendums on election day would require parties to stake out more precise positions on policy issues, and the suggestion that a party elected as the governing party should not take action on important issues unless it has received a mandate from a majority of voters as expressed through a referendum. (Mac Donald 1991 RC)

One of the benefits claimed for referendums is that they provide citizens with an unbiased, non-partisan instrument for input into government policies. This, however, is much less likely to occur when referendums and elections are held simultaneously. Recent experiences with referendums and elections held concurrently in Canada and in other nations suggest a paradox exists in the way referendum questions are treated by political parties and candidates. When referendum questions involve critical public issues and are extensively debated during election campaigns, voters are much more likely to vote on referendum questions based on partisan choice than they would in a period separate from the election. In Australia, party identification has been the most important determinant of voting choice when referendums are held on election day. When referendum questions involve minor public policies or are not an integral part of the election platforms of political parties or candidates, however, it appears that they are not extensively debated or discussed during election campaigns. For example, with the exception of the question on whether the government should pay for abortions, the referendum questions presented to voters in the 1991 Saskatchewan provincial election were not a prominent feature of the campaign. The referendum issues received moderate attention from the political parties and their candidates. Deficit reduction and economic stability in the agricultural sector were the important campaign issues. The experience in the 1991 British Columbia election was similar. The referendum questions on the recall and the citizen initiative were not widely debated or promoted by either the candidates or leaders of the major political parties. The state of the provincial economy and the record of the incumbent government were the dominant issues of the election campaign.

As outlined in Volume 1, Chapter 6 of this report, a fundamental principle of our electoral process is fairness. Fairness is achieved, in part, through the presence of election spending limits. Reasonable spending limits allow for vigorous electoral competition, while ensuring that the conduct of federal election campaigns is not based solely on the ability to spend money.

If referendums were held simultaneously with elections, a separate administrative regime would have to be set up to allow those groups or individuals with a valid stake in the results of a referendum question to participate in the campaign and to ensure, at the same time, the integrity of election spending limits. The separation of the two campaigns could be achieved by the creation of 'umbrella organizations'. All groups and participants who want to spend money promoting the 'yes' or 'no' side of a referendum question would be required to channel their expenditures through a single national organization. Given the partisan nature of election campaigns it is not obvious that competing parties would want to associate under the same umbrella or that it is in the long-term interest of the electorate that they do so. Such a scheme could help affirm the intent of spending limits, although the logistical and administrative complexities would be far less if referendums were held separately from general elections. At a minimum, then, holding referendums at election time under one set of rules, and then conducting the election proper under another set of rules would be administratively and organizationally complex.

In Canada's system of parliamentary government, elections are about mandates to govern. All evidence suggests that the Canadian electoral process allows voters to assess the performance of their governments. The high level of legislative turnover demonstrates Canadian voters do not hesitate to defeat elected representatives who make poor use of their mandate to govern. (Blake 1991 RC; Young 1991a RC) As noted in Volume 1, Chapter 5, Canada has more legislative turnover than do other countries, including the United States and Great Britain.

Referendums held on election day would strip elections of their meaning and value. Elections must be about voters who trust their own ability to pick governors who can judge, reflect, deliberate, compromise, lead and respond. And elections must be about accepting the need for governance. (Mac Donald 1991 RC)

More importantly, the comparative evidence indicates that, no matter when referendums are held, they are dominated by political parties, pressure groups or both. In jurisdictions where referendums and initiatives have been traditionally held in conjunction with elections, voter turnout tends to be lower, and those who do vote represent a small cross-section of the general population.[3] The benefits and strengths of referendums would be compromised rather than enhanced if they were held concurrently with federal general elections.

Recommendation 2.9.1

We recommend that referendums not be held simultaneously with federal general elections.

THE RECALL

From 1908 to 1926, 11 American states adopted provisions for the recall of state and local politicians. Those who advocated the recall did not see it as a substitute for representative government; they merely hoped to make their representatives more responsive and honest. (Cronin 1989, 131) Currently, 15 states, the District of Columbia, Guam and the Virgin Islands provide for the recall of state-wide politicians, and at least 36 states permit the recall of various local politicians. The recall procedure in the United States, however, has never extended to senators, members of the House of Representatives, members of the cabinet or the president. Recall provisions have been enacted by three cantons in Switzerland, but the recall itself has never been used.

There are three basic recall procedures in the United States. The most commonly used requires two elections: first, there is a vote on whether to remove the elected official. If a majority of voters vote for a recall, a second election is held to replace him or her. The second procedure requires citizens to vote simultaneously on removal and replacement; this approach is used in two states. A third procedure, used in two states, requires the elected official to seek re-election if a recall petition has been properly filed.

Each of the three recall procedures requires a petition signed by a large number of voters eligible to cast ballots in the constituency represented by the elected official. The proportion of voters' signatures required for a petition varies from 10 per cent for state-wide elected officials in Montana to 40 per cent in Kansas. In most states 25 per cent of eligible voters for the office in question during the most recent election must sign a petition before a recall can be initiated. In three states the recall is a quasi-judicial procedure, limited to malfeasance, misconduct, incompetence or failure to perform legal duties.

In the other states an elected official can be recalled for any reason that voters think appropriate. (McCormick 1991 RC)

Notwithstanding the many states with recall provisions, the instrument has not been widely used at the state level. The recall is used more extensively and more successfully at the municipal level. The only successful use of the recall to remove state-wide elected officials "occurred in North Dakota in 1921, when the governor, attorney general, and secretary of agriculture were recalled." (Maddox and Fuquay 1966, 333) Although the recall procedure has existed in the United States for approximately 90 years, only a few "state legislators have been recalled, including two in California in 1913, two in Idaho in 1971, two in Michigan in 1983, and one in Oregon in 1988". (Cronin 1989, 127) The increased use of the recall in the 1980s can be attributed, in part, to the rise of special-interest groups that are highly critical of politicians. Recall campaigns dominated by interest groups have been directed at those accused of imprudently managing state budgets. (Cronin 1989)

The strength of the populist movement in Canada after the First World War led to pressures for a recall procedure for Members of Parliament. Many Progressive MPs elected in 1921 were requested by their constituency associations to sign undated resignations so that their constituents could recall them by dating and publishing the document. (Ward 1963, 9) The request for undated resignations was prohibited when the *Dominion Elections Act* was amended immediately after the First World War to disqualify any member who signed an advance resignation. The provision can now be found in the *Canada Elections Act*, section 327. It states:

> It is an illegal practice and an offence for any candidate for election as a member to sign any written document presented to him by way of demand or claim made on him by any person, persons or associations of persons, between the date of the issue of the writ of election and the date of polling, if the document requires the candidate to follow any course of action that will prevent him from exercising freedom of action in Parliament, if elected, or to resign as a member if called on to do so by any person, persons or associations of persons.

Contrary to the American experience, the United Farmers of Alberta, when they came to power in 1919, explicitly rejected the recall as an instrument for constituents to hold their members in the provincial legislature accountable between elections. The leaders and members of the United Farmers movement concluded that, as a method for allowing constituents to hold their elected representative accountable, the recall procedure was not an adequate alternative to group government.

A statutory recall procedure was not adopted anywhere in Canada until the Social Credit Party defeated the United Farmers government in Alberta in 1935. The Alberta *Recall Act* was passed in 1936. Ironically, the first recall petition was initiated against Premier William Aberhart by his constituents in the same year. The recall petition was thwarted when the *Recall Act* was repealed by the Aberhart government in 1937. (McCormick 1991 RC)

ASSESSING THE RECALL

During our public hearings we heard from representatives of several political parties, such as the Reform Party, the Christian Heritage Party, the Green Party, the Communist Party and the Populist Party, who supported the use of the recall. We also heard from a handful of individuals who argued that constituents should have the right to recall MPs who do not vote on legislation in the House of Commons 'based on instructions' from their constituents. Some interveners supported the recall against MPs who do not implement their campaign promises. Recall was seen as a way of allowing citizens to remove from office representatives who had lost the confidence of their constituents. These interveners, however, provided very limited explanations as to how MPs would receive instructions from their constituents and how frequently, or how to determine precisely whether MPs had not acted on campaign promises.

The support for the recall has obviously struck a responsive chord. Many Canadians are concerned that MPs, because they belong to political parties, are unable to vote freely on legislation in the House of Commons. In a public attitudinal survey, respondents were asked whether MPs should vote on controversial issues in Parliament on the basis of what they believe to be in the public interest or what they deem to be the views of their constituents. Thirty-seven per cent of the respondents said MPs should follow their own interpretation of the public interest, and 63 per cent said MPs should follow the views of their constituents. (Blais and Gidengil 1991 RC)

The basic assumption underlying support for the recall is that it is a safety valve for citizens who no longer have confidence in their elected representatives. Proponents suggest that if voters had access to the recall, MPs would be more attentive to the concerns of their constituents. The presence of the recall, then, would deter MPs from neglecting their constituents' demands.

In Canada's system of parliamentary government, MPs are not elected as representatives who randomly come together in a national legislature simply to advance the views and interests of their constituents on matters of national policy. Rather, the House of Commons is a collective decision-making and representative institution that must weigh the competing interests of citizens against the national interest. The weakness in the argument that recall should be used against individual MPs who do not take direct instructions from their constituents is that MPs who isolate themselves from the collective deliberation of public policies will be less equipped to represent their constituents, not more so.

On occasion, MPs may be required to support policies that advance the national interest but that are not supported by their constituents. If MPs cannot support such policies, governments are unable to weigh the interests of minorities against the interests of majorities, nor can they decide what values and ideas to promote. Our system of parliamentary government brings together MPs in a national legislature that strives collectively to affirm the ideas and values that advance the national public interest.

The concern expressed by supporters of the recall – that Canadians have few opportunities to hold their MPs accountable – is dubious when assessed against Canada's recent electoral history. Since 1945 Canadians have gone to the polls in 15 general elections; the results have created nine majority and six minority governments. Only twice have governments been re-elected to two consecutive majorities. From 1945 to 1988, the average term of a Parliament was 3.1 years.

Compared with the United States, there is high legislative turnover in Canada. From 1974 to 1988, a period that saw four general elections, on average 24.9 per cent of MPs seeking re-election were defeated. The comparable figure for the United States House of Representatives was 6 per cent. Moreover, although the rate of defeat for members in the House of Representatives has been dropping, in Canada the rates of defeat in the last two elections (39.7 and 26.6 per cent, respectively) were much higher than in the 1979 and 1980 elections (20.3 and 15.9 per cent, respectively). (Adapted from Atkinson and Docherty 1991) The high turnover demonstrates Canadian voters are able to hold their MPs accountable for what they do and for what their parties do. The evidence suggests voters regularly act when dissatisfied with their MPs. Placed in this context, the argument that the recall should be used against MPs who do not act on their campaign promises seems misplaced.

Studies on voting behaviour, furthermore, demonstrate that Canadian voters use several criteria to elect Members of Parliament. Clarke et al. (1991) show that voters assess the qualities and experience of the individual candidate. From 1974 to 1988, 21 to 27 per cent of respondents in national election surveys ranked the individual candidate as the most important factor in their voting choice. Candidates are also seen as standard bearers for their parties, and for the values and policies their parties promote. From 1974 to 1988, 40 to 53 per cent of Canadians ranked parties as the most important determinant of their voting decision. In fact, the percentage of Canadians ranking parties as the most important factor increased in the 1984 and 1988 elections. Further, Canadians consider the party leader to be a critical determinant in their voting choice. The impact of the party leader as the most important factor in voting choice has ranged from 33 per cent in 1974 to 20 per cent in 1988. The evidence shows, then, that MPs are seldom elected *by voters* solely to represent local interests.

The presence of both a multi-party system and a single-member plurality electoral system in Canada can mean that many MPs are elected to the House of Commons even if they receive less than a majority of votes in the constituency. For example, in a competitive constituency campaign among three political parties, the successful candidate can be elected if he or she wins approximately one-third of the votes. The absence of an electoral majority, however, does not necessarily impair the ability of an MP to be a credible and effective representative of the constituency. The presence of the recall would be inconsistent with these primary characteristics of the electoral process in Canada. MPs subject to the recall would be required to sustain support from a majority of voters in the constituency, a requisite far beyond what the MP had to satisfy in a highly competitive general election. In short, the standards or criteria used to elect MPs at a general election or a by-election would not apply to MPs who have been recalled. The presence of both a recall and a single-member plurality system would lead to conflicting democratic principles in the electoral process, principles that could not be easily reconciled.

Our system of responsible government requires the prime minister and cabinet to have continuing support from a majority of MPs in the House of Commons. This ensures that the government's legislative program is only approved when there is majority support in the House of Commons. In this fashion, MPs can decide if the interests and values of their constituents are being addressed.

Under Canadian parliamentary government, the prime minister and almost all cabinet ministers seek election to the House of Commons as individual MPs from single-member constituencies. Even so, the prime minister and elected cabinet ministers have special responsibilities beyond those of their constituents. These responsibilities require them to consider the national interest when formulating public policies.

The prime minister and cabinet ministers would be particularly vulnerable to the use of the recall because vested interests or advocacy groups who are critical of a certain policy or decision could use it to serve their own ends. Although the recall petition could be signed only by constituents, and only constituents could vote in a recall election, both campaigns could be used by groups who were not constituents to exert an inordinate amount of pressure on the office holders. For example, pressure groups opposing abortion legislation could target the minister of justice, groups opposed to certain tax measures could seek to recall the minister of finance, and environmental activists could attempt to remove the minister of environment. In such circumstances, the value of the recall would be stripped away from constituents.

The recall is increasingly seen as a way to strengthen the ability of constituents to influence the actions of MPs. Although this is a laudable objective, the evidence from the United States indicates that the recall is not an effective instrument for this end. As a leading expert on the recall in the United States recently concluded, "the recall device ... has not significantly improved direct communication between leaders and led.... Neither has it produced better-qualified officeholders or noticeably enriched the quality of citizenship or democracy in those places permitting it. Whether it has strengthened representative government in any measurable way seems doubtful." (Cronin 1989, 155) In Canada, the particular vulnerability of the prime minister and cabinet ministers to the use and abuse of the recall would make this instrument of direct democracy especially detrimental to our system of representative democracy.

Recommendation 2.9.2

We recommend that the statutory recall of Members of Parliament not be adopted.

NOTES

1. In the October 1991 provincial election a large majority of Saskatchewan voters supported legislation for balanced budgets and the ratification of proposed constitutional changes through plebiscites (79.6 and 79.2 per cent of voters respectively said yes to these measures). On the third plebiscite question, 62.7 per cent of voters agreed that the provincial government should not pay for abortions.

2. In the October 1991 British Columbia provincial election, the implementation of a statutory recall device was supported by 81 per cent of voters casting ballots on this question, and 83 per cent of voters endorsed the use of citizen-initiated referendums. The number of voters casting ballots on the referendum questions was approximately the same as the number of voters casting ballots to elect candidates to the provincial legislature.

3. Voter turnout rates are determined by a number of factors, including specific systems of voter registration and the flexibility provided by the administration of the voting process. For example, those nations that employ a large number of administrative devices, such as voting-day registration and mail-in ballots, tend to have the highest turnout rates. The importance assigned to voting as an act of civic participation is also a critical determinant of voter turnout rates.

    The voter turnout rate for the 1991 Saskatchewan election was 83 per cent, a level consistent with the average turnout for provincial elections of 83.1 per cent in the 1980s. Voter turnout in British Columbia, however, dropped to 71.2 per cent, compared with the provincial average in the 1980s of 77.4 per cent. In each election, the incumbent government was defeated. Although the reasons for the variations in provincial turnout rates cannot be identified precisely, what is clear is that referendum questions on the election ballot did not result in higher electoral participation rates in these provinces than when such questions have not been placed on the ballot.

REFERENCES

Abramson, Jeffrey B., F. Christopher Arterton and Gary R. Orren. 1988. *The Electronic Commonwealth: The Impact of New Media Technologies on Democratic Politics*. New York: Basic Books.

Alexander, Herbert E. 1991 RC. "The Regulation of Election Finance in the United States and Proposals for Reform." In *Comparative Issues in Party and Election Finance*, ed. F. Leslie Seidle. Vol. 4 of the research studies of the Royal Commission on Electoral Reform and Party Financing. Ottawa: RCERPF.

Alia, Valerie. 1991 RC. "Aboriginal Peoples and Campaign Coverage in the North." In *Aboriginal Peoples and Electoral Reform in Canada*, ed. Robert A. Milen. Vol. 9 of the research studies of the Royal Commission on Electoral Reform and Party Financing. Ottawa: RCERPF.

Archer, Keith A. 1991a RC. "Leadership Selection in the New Democratic Party." In *Canadian Political Parties: Leaders, Candidates and Organization*, ed. Herman Bakvis. Vol. 13 of the research studies of the Royal Commission on Electoral Reform and Party Financing. Ottawa: RCERPF.

Archer, Keith A. 1991b RC. "The New Democrats, Organized Labour and the Prospects of Electoral Reform." In *Canadian Political Parties: Leaders, Candidates and Organization*, ed. Herman Bakvis. Vol. 13 of the research studies of the Royal Commission on Electoral Reform and Party Financing. Ottawa: RCERPF.

Atkinson, Michael, and David C. Docherty. 1991. "Moving Right Along: Roots of Amateurism in the Canadian House of Commons." Paper presented at the annual meeting of the Canadian Political Science Association, Kingston.

Aubert, Jean-François. 1978. "Switzerland." In *Referendums: A Comparative Study of Practice and Theory*, ed. David Butler and Austin Ranney. Washington, DC: American Enterprise Institute for Public Policy Research.

Axworthy, Thomas S. 1991 RC. "Capital-Intensive Politics: Money, Media and Mores in the United States and Canada." In *Issues in Party and Election Finance in Canada*, ed. F. Leslie Seidle. Vol. 5 of the research studies of the Royal Commission on Electoral Reform and Party Financing. Ottawa: RCERPF.

Baillargeon v. *Marin*, C.S.P. Qué. (district de Gaspé), no. 130-27-000058-865, 19 June 1987.

Barr, Cathy Widdis. 1991 RC. "The Importance and Potential of Leaders' Debates." In *Media and Voters in Canadian Election Campaigns*, ed. Frederick J. Fletcher. Vol. 18 of the research studies of the Royal Commission on Electoral Reform and Party Financing. Ottawa: RCERPF.

Barrie, Doreen P. 1991 RC. "Party Financing in Alberta: Low-Impact Legislation." In *Provincial Party and Election Finance in Canada*, ed. F. Leslie Seidle. Vol. 3 of the research studies of the Royal Commission on Electoral Reform and Party Financing. Ottawa: RCERPF.

Bashevkin, Sylvia. 1991 RC. "Women's Participation in Political Parties." In *Women in Canadian Politics: Towards Equity in Representation*, ed. Kathy Megyery. Vol. 6 of the research studies of the Royal Commission on Electoral Reform and Party Financing. Ottawa: RCERPF.

Beh, Andrew, and Roger Gibbins. 1991 RC. "The Campaign–Media Interface in Local Constituencies: Two Alberta Case Studies from the 1988 Federal Election Campaign." In *Reaching the Voter: Constituency Campaigning in Canada*, ed. Frederick J. Fletcher and David V.J. Bell. Vol. 20 of the research studies of the Royal Commission on Electoral Reform and Party Financing. Ottawa: RCERPF.

Bell, David V.J., and Catherine M. Bolan. 1991 RC. "The Mass Media and Federal Election Campaigning at the Local Level: A Case Study of Two Ontario Constituencies." In *Reaching the Voter: Constituency Campaigning in Canada*, ed. Frederick J. Fletcher and David V.J. Bell. Vol. 20 of the research studies of the Royal Commission on Electoral Reform and Party Financing. Ottawa: RCERPF.

Bell, David V.J., and Frederick J. Fletcher. 1991 RC. "Electoral Communication at the Constituency Level: A Framework for Analysis." In *Reaching the Voter: Constituency Campaigning in Canada*, ed. Frederick J. Fletcher and David V.J. Bell. Vol. 20 of the research studies of the Royal Commission on Electoral Reform and Party Financing. Ottawa: RCERPF.

Bell, David V.J., Frederick J. Fletcher and Catherine M. Bolan. 1991 RC. "Electoral Communication at the Constituency Level: Summary and Conclusion." In *Reaching the Voter: Constituency Campaigning in Canada*, ed. Frederick J. Fletcher and David V.J. Bell. Vol. 20 of the research studies of the Royal Commission on Electoral Reform and Party Financing. Ottawa: RCERPF.

Bernier, Luc. 1991 RC. "Local Campaigns and the Media: The 1988 Election in Outremont and Frontenac." In *Reaching the Voter: Constituency Campaigning in Canada*, ed. Frederick J. Fletcher and David V.J. Bell. Vol. 20 of the research studies of the Royal Commission on Electoral Reform and Party Financing. Ottawa: RCERPF.

Bernier, Robert, and Denis Monière. 1991 RC. "The Organization of Televised Leaders' Debates in the United States, Europe, Australia and Canada."

In *Media and Voters in Canadian Election Campaigns*, ed. Frederick J. Fletcher. Vol. 18 of the research studies of the Royal Commission on Electoral Reform and Party Financing. Ottawa: RCERPF.

Bertram, Eric. 1991 RC. "Independent Candidates in Federal General Elections." In *Issues in Party and Election Finance in Canada*, ed. F. Leslie Seidle. Vol. 5 of the research studies of the Royal Commission on Electoral Reform and Party Financing. Ottawa: RCERPF.

Black, Jerome H. 1991 RC. "Reforming the Context of the Voting Process in Canada: Lessons from Other Democracies." In *Voter Turnout in Canada*, ed. Herman Bakvis. Vol. 15 of the research studies of the Royal Commission on Electoral Reform and Party Financing. Ottawa: RCERPF.

Blais, André, and Elisabeth Gidengil. 1991 RC. *Representative Democracy: The Views of Canadians*. Vol. 17 of the research studies of the Royal Commission on Electoral Reform and Party Financing. Ottawa: RCERPF.

Blake, Donald E. 1991 RC. "Party Competition and Electoral Volatility: Canada in Comparative Perspective." In *Representation, Integration and Political Parties in Canada*, ed. Herman Bakvis. Vol. 14 of the research studies of the Royal Commission on Electoral Reform and Party Financing. Ottawa: RCERPF.

Boucher, Cécile. 1991 RC. "Administration and Enforcement of the Elections Act in Canada." In *Democratic Rights and Electoral Reform in Canada*, ed. Michael Cassidy. Vol. 10 of the research studies of the Royal Commission on Electoral Reform and Party Financing. Ottawa: RCERPF.

Boyer, J. Patrick. 1982. *Lawmaking by the People: Referendums and Plebiscites in Canada*. Toronto: Butterworths.

Boyer, J. Patrick. 1983. *Money and Message: The Law Governing Election Financing, Advertising, Broadcasting and Campaigning in Canada*. Toronto: Butterworths.

Brock, Kathy L. 1991 RC. "Fairness, Equity, and Rights." In *Political Ethics: A Canadian Perspective*, ed. Janet Hiebert. Vol. 12 of the research studies of the Royal Commission on Electoral Reform and Party Financing. Ottawa: RCERPF.

Brodie, Janine, with the assistance of Celia Chandler. 1991 RC. "Women and the Electoral Process in Canada." In *Women in Canadian Politics: Towards Equity in Representation*, ed. Kathy Megyery. Vol. 6 of the research studies of the Royal Commission on Electoral Reform and Party Financing. Ottawa: RCERPF.

Bunch, Gary. 1991. "Readability of Selected Election Campaign Documents." Report prepared for the Royal Commission on Electoral Reform and Party Financing. Ottawa.

Butler, David. 1978. "United Kingdom." In *Referendums: A Comparative Study of Practice and Theory*, ed. David Butler and Austin Ranney. Washington, DC: American Enterprise Institute for Public Policy Research.

Butler, David, and Austin Ranney. 1978. "Summing Up." In *Referendums: A Comparative Study of Practice and Theory*, ed. David Butler and Austin Ranney. Washington, DC: American Enterprise Institute for Public Policy Research.

Calgary Herald. 1988. "Forgotten Voters Angry." 22 November.

Canada. Chief Electoral Officer. 1989. *Report of the Chief Electoral Officer of Canada as per subsection 195(1) of the Canada Elections Act*. Ottawa: Minister of Supply and Services Canada.

Canada. Chief Electoral Officer. 1991. *Report of the Chief Electoral Officer of Canada as per subsection 195(1) of the Canada Elections Act*. Ottawa: Minister of Supply and Services Canada.

Canada. Elections Canada. 1988a. *Guidelines and Procedures Respecting Election Expenses of Candidates*. Ottawa: Elections Canada.

Canada. Elections Canada. 1988b. *Guidelines Respecting Election Expenses of Registered Political Parties*. Ottawa: Elections Canada.

Canada. Elections Canada. 1988c. *Returning Officer's Manual*. Ottawa: Elections Canada.

Canada. Elections Canada. 1989. "Electoral Campaign Finance, Lobbying, and Ethics/Conflict of Interest Legislation and Litigation in Canadian Federal, Provincial and Territorial Jurisdictions." Paper prepared for the December 1989 COGEL Conference. Ottawa: Elections Canada.

Canada. House of Commons. Special Committee on Elections and Franchise Acts. 1937. *Report*. Ottawa: King's Printer.

Canada. House of Commons. Special Committee on the Disabled and the Handicapped. 1982. *Obstacles*. 5th Report. Ottawa: Minister of Supply and Services Canada.

Canada. Parliament. Special Joint Committee of the Senate and the House of Commons on the Process for Amending the Constitution of Canada. 1991. *Report*. Ottawa: Queen's Printer.

Canada. Privy Council Office. 1986. *White Paper on Election Law Reform*. Ottawa: Queen's Printer.

Canada. Representation Commissioner. 1968. *Report of the Representation Commissioner on Methods of Registration of Electors and Absentee Voting*. Ottawa: Queen's Printer.

Canada. Royal Commission on Electoral Reform and Party Financing. 1991. *Final Report*. Ottawa.

Canada. Royal Commission on Electoral Reform and Party Financing. Accounting Profession Working Group on Election/Party Finance Reporting at the Local Level. 1991a. *Report*. Ottawa.

Canada. Royal Commission on Electoral Reform and Party Financing, with the assistance of Revenue Canada, Taxation. 1990. "Establishment of a Permanent Voters' List." Report of a study group. Ottawa.

Canada. Statistics Canada. 1987a. *Population and Dwelling Counts, Provinces and Territories. Northwest Territories*. 1986 Census. Cat. no. 92-120. Ottawa: Minister of Supply and Services Canada.

Canada. Statistics Canada. 1987b. *Population and Dwelling Counts, Provinces and Territories. Yukon*. 1986 Census. Cat. no. 92-119. Ottawa: Minister of Supply and Services Canada.

Canada. Statistics Canada. 1989. *Survey of Literacy Skills Used in Daily Activities*. Survey conducted on behalf of the National Literacy Secretariat of the Department of the Secretary of State. Ottawa: Statistics Canada.

Canada. Statistics Canada. 1990. *Highlights: Disabled Persons in Canada*. Health and Activity Limitation Survey. Ottawa: Minister of Supply and Services Canada.

Canada. Treasury Board of Canada. 1989. "Access to Information and Privacy." Implementation Report No. 20. Ottawa: Treasury Board.

Canadian Broadcasting Corporation (CBC). 1985. *CBC Regulations Governing Party Political Broadcasts*. Ottawa: CBC.

Canadian Broadcasting Corporation (CBC). 1990a. Letter to Mr. Pierre Lortie, Chairman, Royal Commission on Electoral Reform and Party Financing, 1 August. Ottawa: CBC.

Canadian Broadcasting Corporation (CBC). 1990b. "Parliamentary Channels of the CBC National Satellite Network: An Update of Availability, Programming and Audience to September 1990." Ottawa: CBC Research.

Canadian Cable Television Association. 1990. "Community Channel Survey Results." Ottawa: CCTA.

Canadian National Election Study. 1984. Institute for Social Research, York University. Principal investigators: Steven Brown, Ronald Lambert, James Curtis, Barry Kay and John Wilson. Funded by the Social Sciences and Humanities Research Council.

Canadian National Election Study. 1988. Institute for Social Research, York University. Principal investigators: Richard Johnston, André Blais, Henry E. Brady and Jean Crête. Funded by the Social Sciences and Humanities Research Council.

Carty, R. Kenneth. 1990. "Does Canada Need a Permanent Voters' List?" Issue paper prepared for the Royal Commission on Electoral Reform and Party Financing. Ottawa.

Carty, R. Kenneth. 1991a RC. *Canadian Political Parties in the Constituencies: A Local Perspective*. Vol. 23 of the research studies of the Royal Commission on Electoral Reform and Party Financing. Ottawa: RCERPF.

Carty, R. Kenneth. 1991b RC. "Official Agents in Canadian Elections: The Case of the 1988 General Election." In *Issues in Party and Election Finance in Canada*, ed. F. Leslie Seidle. Vol. 5 of the research studies of the Royal Commission on Electoral Reform and Party Financing. Ottawa: RCERPF.

Carty, R. Kenneth, and Lynda Erickson. 1991 RC. "Candidate Nomination in Canada's National Political Parties." In *Canadian Political Parties: Leaders, Candidates and Organization*, ed. Herman Bakvis. Vol. 13 of the research studies of the Royal Commission on Electoral Reform and Party Financing. Ottawa: RCERPF.

Chandler, William M., and Alan Siaroff. 1991 RC. "Parties and Party Government in Advanced Democracies." In *Canadian Political Parties: Leaders, Candidates and Organization*, ed. Herman Bakvis. Vol. 13 of the research studies of the Royal Commission on Electoral Reform and Party Financing. Ottawa: RCERPF.

Charron, Jean. 1991 RC. "Relations between Political Parties and the Media in Quebec Election Campaigns." In *Reporting the Campaign: Election Coverage in Canada*, ed. Frederick J. Fletcher. Vol. 22 of the research studies of the Royal Commission on Electoral Reform and Party Financing. Ottawa: RCERPF.

Citizens' Commission on Civil Rights. 1988. *Barriers to Registration and Voting: An Agenda for Reform*. Washington, DC: National Center for Policy Alternatives.

Clarke, Harold D., Lawrence LeDuc, Jane Jenson and Jon H. Pammett. 1991. *Absent Mandate: Interpreting Change in Canadian Elections*. 2d ed. Toronto: Gage.

Constantinou, Peter P. 1991 RC. "Public Funding of Political Parties, Candidates and Elections in Canada." In *Issues in Party and Election Finance in Canada*, ed. F. Leslie Seidle. Vol. 5 of the research studies of the Royal Commission on Electoral Reform and Party Financing. Ottawa: RCERPF.

Courtney, John C., and David E. Smith. 1991 RC. "Registering Voters: Canada in a Comparative Context." In *Democratic Rights and Electoral Reform in Canada*, ed. Michael Cassidy. Vol. 10 of the research studies of the Royal Commission on Electoral Reform and Party Financing. Ottawa: RCERPF.

Covell, Maureen. 1991 RC. "Parties as Institutions of National Governance." In *Representation, Integration and Political Parties in Canada*, ed. Herman Bakvis. Vol. 14 of the research studies of the Royal Commission on Electoral Reform and Party Financing. Ottawa: RCERPF.

Crête, Jean. 1991 RC. "Television, Advertising and Canadian Elections." In *Media and Voters in Canadian Election Campaigns*, ed. Frederick J. Fletcher. Vol. 18 of the research studies of the Royal Commission on Electoral Reform and Party Financing. Ottawa: RCERPF.

Cronin, Thomas E. 1989. *Direct Democracy: The Politics of Initiative, Referendum, and Recall*. Cambridge: Harvard University Press.

Davidoff, Linda, and Cynthia Williams. 1985. *Executive Orders: A New Strategy to Use Public Agencies to Increase Voter Registration*. Conference on Alternative State and Local Policies. New York: Human Serve Fund.

Denoncourt, Yves. 1991 RC. "Reflections Concerning Criteria for the Vote for Persons with Mental Disorders." In *Democratic Rights and Electoral Reform in Canada*, ed. Michael Cassidy. Vol. 10 of the research studies of the Royal Commission on Electoral Reform and Party Financing. Ottawa: RCERPF.

Desbarats, Peter. 1991 RC. "Cable Television and Federal Election Campaigns in Canada." In *Election Broadcasting in Canada*, ed. Frederick J. Fletcher. Vol. 21 of the research studies of the Royal Commission on Electoral Reform and Party Financing. Ottawa: RCERPF.

Dornan, Christopher. 1991 RC. "Free to Be Responsible: The Accountability of the Print Media." In *Reporting the Campaign: Election Coverage in Canada*, ed. Frederick J. Fletcher. Vol. 22 of the research studies of the Royal Commission on Electoral Reform and Party Financing. Ottawa: RCERPF.

Dyck, Rand. 1991 RC. "Links between Federal and Provincial Parties and Party Systems." In *Representation, Integration and Political Parties in Canada*, ed. Herman Bakvis. Vol. 14 of the research studies of the Royal Commission on Electoral Reform and Party Financing. Ottawa: RCERPF.

Eagles, Munroe. 1991a RC. "Enhancing Relative Vote Equality in Canada: The Role of Electors in Boundary Adjustment." In *Drawing the Map: Equality and Efficacy of the Vote in Canadian Electoral Boundary Reform*, ed. David Small. Vol. 11 of the research studies of the Royal Commission on Electoral Reform and Party Financing. Ottawa: RCERPF.

Eagles, Munroe. 1991b RC. "Voting and Nonvoting in Canadian Federal Elections: An Ecological Analysis." In *Voter Turnout in Canada*, ed. Herman Bakvis. Vol. 15 of the research studies of the Royal Commission on Electoral Reform and Party Financing. Ottawa: RCERPF.

Elkins, David J. 1991 RC. "Parties as National Institutions: A Comparative Study." In *Representation, Integration and Political Parties in Canada*, ed. Herman Bakvis. Vol. 14 of the research studies of the Royal Commission on Electoral Reform and Party Financing. Ottawa: RCERPF.

Ellis, David. 1991. *Networking*. Toronto: Friends of Canadian Broadcasting.

Environics Research Group Ltd. 1990. *Youth Attitudes Towards Voting.* Poll prepared for the Royal Commission on Electoral Reform and Party Financing between 28 May and 12 July 1990. Ottawa.

Erickson, Lynda. 1991 RC. "Women and Candidacies for the House of Commons." In *Women in Canadian Politics: Towards Equity in Representation,* ed. Kathy Megyery. Vol. 6 of the research studies of the Royal Commission on Electoral Reform and Party Financing. Ottawa: RCERPF.

Ferejohn, John, and Brian Gaines. 1991 RC. "The Personal Vote in Canada." In *Representation, Integration and Political Parties in Canada,* ed. Herman Bakvis. Vol. 14 of the research studies of the Royal Commission on Electoral Reform and Party Financing. Ottawa: RCERPF.

Fleras, Augie. 1991 RC. "Aboriginal Electoral Districts for Canada: Lessons from New Zealand." In *Aboriginal Peoples and Electoral Reform in Canada,* ed. Robert A. Milen. Vol. 9 of the research studies of the Royal Commission on Electoral Reform and Party Financing. Ottawa: RCERPF.

Fletcher, Frederick J., and David V.J. Bell, eds. 1991 RC. *Reaching the Voter: Constituency Campaigning in Canada.* Vol. 20 of the research studies of the Royal Commission on Electoral Reform and Party Financing. Ottawa: RCERPF.

Fletcher, Frederick J., and Robert Everett. 1991 RC. "Mass Media and Elections in Canada." In *Media, Elections and Democracy,* ed. Frederick J. Fletcher. Vol. 19 of the research studies of the Royal Commission on Electoral Reform and Party Financing. Ottawa: RCERPF.

Forsey, Eugene. 1960. "Extension of the Life of Legislatures." *Canadian Journal of Economics and Political Science* 26: 604–16.

Fortin, Pierre. 1991 RC. "Ethical Issues in the Debate on Reform of the *Canada Elections Act*: An Ethicological Analysis." In *Political Ethics: A Canadian Perspective,* ed. Janet Hiebert. Vol. 12 of the research studies of the Royal Commission on Electoral Reform and Party Financing. Ottawa: RCERPF.

Frizzell, Alan. 1991. "Report." Carleton University Survey Centre telephone survey conducted for the Royal Commission on Electoral Reform and Party Financing. Ottawa.

Frizzell, Alan. 1991 RC. "In the Public Service: Representation in Modern Canada." In *Drawing the Map: Equality and Efficacy of the Vote in Canadian Electoral Boundary Reform,* ed. David Small. Vol. 11 of the research studies of the Royal Commission on Electoral Reform and Party Financing. Ottawa: RCERPF.

Frizzell, Alan, and Anthony Westell. 1989. "The Media and the Campaign." In Alan Frizzell, Jon H. Pammett and Anthony Westell, *The Canadian General Election of 1988.* Ottawa: Carleton University Press.

Gallup Report. 1989. "Poll on Confidence in Political Parties." 9 February. Toronto: Canadian Institute of Public Opinion.

Garant, Patrice. 1991a RC. "Political Rights of Public Servants in the Political Process." In *Democratic Rights and Electoral Reform in Canada*, ed. Michael Cassidy. Vol. 10 of the research studies of the Royal Commission on Electoral Reform and Party Financing. Ottawa: RCERPF.

Garant, Patrice. 1991b RC. "The Possibilities of Reopening the Voting Age Issue under the Charter of Rights and Freedoms." In *Youth in Canadian Politics: Participation and Involvement*, ed. Kathy Megyery. Vol. 8 of the research studies of the Royal Commission on Electoral Reform and Party Financing. Ottawa: RCERPF.

Gauthier, A., J.-P. Laperrière and S. Delisle. 1991. "A Permanent Register of Electors: Feasibility Study." Working paper prepared for the Royal Commission on Electoral Reform and Party Financing. Ottawa.

Generation 5 Technology Ltd. 1990. *A Rural Simulation Project.* Joint project of Canada Post Corporation and the Royal Commission on Electoral Reform and Party Financing. Ottawa.

Gerstlé, Jacques. 1991 RC. "Election Communication in France." In *Media, Elections and Democracy*, ed. Frederick J. Fletcher. Vol. 19 of the research studies of the Royal Commission on Electoral Reform and Party Financing. Ottawa: RCERPF.

Gibbins, Roger. 1991 RC. "Electoral Reform and Canada's Aboriginal Population: An Assessment of Aboriginal Electoral Districts." In *Aboriginal Peoples and Electoral Reform in Canada*, ed. Robert A. Milen. Vol. 9 of the research studies of the Royal Commission on Electoral Reform and Party Financing. Ottawa: RCERPF.

Gilsdorf, William O., and Robert Bernier. 1991 RC. "Journalistic Practice in Covering Federal Election Campaigns in Canada." In *Reporting the Campaign: Election Coverage in Canada*, ed. Frederick J. Fletcher. Vol. 22 of the research studies of the Royal Commission on Electoral Reform and Party Financing. Ottawa: RCERPF.

Graber, Doris A. 1991 RC. "The Mass Media and Election Campaigns in the United States of America." In *Media, Elections and Democracy*, ed. Frederick J. Fletcher. Vol. 19 of the research studies of the Royal Commission on Electoral Reform and Party Financing. Ottawa: RCERPF.

Green, Joseph. 1991. "Free Time Television Broadcasts." Paper prepared for the Royal Commission on Electoral Reform and Party Financing. Ottawa.

Green, Lyndsay. 1991 RC. "An Exploration of Alternative Methods for Improving Voter Information." In *Media and Voters in Canadian Election Campaigns*, ed. Frederick J. Fletcher. Vol. 18 of the research studies of the Royal Commission on Electoral Reform and Party Financing. Ottawa: RCERPF.

Greene, Ian. 1991 RC. "Allegations of Undue Influence in Canadian Politics." In *Political Ethics: A Canadian Perspective*, ed. Janet Hiebert. Vol. 12 of the research studies of the Royal Commission on Electoral Reform and Party Financing. Ottawa: RCERPF.

Hackett, Robert A. 1991 RC. "Smaller Voices: Minor Parties, Campaign Communication and the News Media." In *Reporting the Campaign: Election Coverage in Canada*, ed. Frederick J. Fletcher. Vol. 22 of the research studies of the Royal Commission on Electoral Reform and Party Financing. Ottawa: RCERPF.

Heintzman, Keith. 1991 RC. "Electoral Competition, Campaign Expenditure and Incumbency Advantage." In *Issues in Party and Election Finance in Canada*, ed. F. Leslie Seidle. Vol. 5 of the research studies of the Royal Commission on Electoral Reform and Party Financing. Ottawa: RCERPF.

Hiebert, Janet. 1991a RC. "A Code of Ethics for Political Parties." In *Political Ethics: A Canadian Perspective*, ed. Janet Hiebert. Vol. 12 of the research studies of the Royal Commission on Electoral Reform and Party Financing. Ottawa: RCERPF.

Hiebert, Janet. 1991b RC. "Interest Groups and Canadian Federal Elections." In *Interest Groups and Elections in Canada*, ed. F. Leslie Seidle. Vol. 2 of the research studies of the Royal Commission on Electoral Reform and Party Financing. Ottawa: RCERPF.

Hogarth, David, and Bill Gilsdorf. 1991 RC. "The Impact of All-News Services on Elections and Election Coverage." In *Election Broadcasting in Canada*, ed. Frederick J. Fletcher. Vol. 21 of the research studies of the Royal Commission on Electoral Reform and Party Financing. Ottawa: RCERPF.

Hudon, Raymond, Bernard Fournier and Louis Métivier, with the assistance of Benoît-Paul Hébert. 1991 RC. "To What Extent Are Today's Young People Interested in Politics? An Inquiry among 16- to 24-Year-Olds." In *Youth in Canadian Politics: Participation and Involvement*, ed. Kathy Megyery. Vol. 8 of the research studies of the Royal Commission on Electoral Reform and Party Financing. Ottawa: RCERPF.

Inter-Parliamentary Union. 1986. *Parliaments of the World: A Comparative Reference Compendium*. 2d ed. New York: Facts on File Publications.

Jenson, Jane. 1991a RC. "Citizenship and Equity: Variations across Time and in Space." In *Political Ethics: A Canadian Perspective*, ed. Janet Hiebert. Vol. 12 of the research studies of the Royal Commission on Electoral Reform and Party Financing. Ottawa: RCERPF.

Jenson, Jane. 1991b RC. "Innovation and Equity: The Impact of Public Funding." In *Comparative Issues in Party and Election Finance*, ed. F. Leslie Seidle. Vol. 4 of the research studies of the Royal Commission on Electoral Reform and Party Financing. Ottawa: RCERPF.

Johnson, David. 1991 RC. "The Ontario Party and Campaign Finance System: Initiative and Challenge." In *Provincial Party and Election Finance in Canada*, ed. F. Leslie Seidle. Vol. 3 of the research studies of the Royal Commission on Electoral Reform and Party Financing. Ottawa: RCERPF.

Johnson, Nevil. 1981. "Types of Referendum." In *The Referendum Device*, ed. Austin Ranney. Washington, DC: American Enterprise Institute for Public Policy Research.

Kent, Tom. 1989. *Getting Ready for 1999: Ideas for Canada's Politics and Government*. Halifax: Institute for Research on Public Policy.

Kernaghan, Kenneth. 1991 RC. "The Political Rights of Canada's Federal Public Servants." In *Democratic Rights and Electoral Reform in Canada*, ed. Michael Cassidy. Vol. 10 of the research studies of the Royal Commission on Electoral Reform and Party Financing. Ottawa: RCERPF.

Kline, Stephen, Rovin Deodat, Arlene Shwetz and William Leiss. 1991 RC. "Political Broadcast Advertising in Canada." In *Election Broadcasting in Canada*, ed. Frederick J. Fletcher. Vol. 21 of the research studies of the Royal Commission on Electoral Reform and Party Financing. Ottawa: RCERPF.

Krashinsky, Michael, and William J. Milne. 1991 RC. "Some Evidence on the Effects of Incumbency in the 1988 Canadian Federal Election." In *Issues in Party and Election Finance in Canada*, ed. F. Leslie Seidle. Vol. 5 of the research studies of the Royal Commission on Electoral Reform and Party Financing. Ottawa: RCERPF.

Lachapelle, Guy. 1991 RC. *Polls and the Media in Canadian Elections: Taking the Pulse*. Vol. 16 of the research studies of the Royal Commission on Electoral Reform and Party Financing. Ottawa: RCERPF.

Landreville, Pierre, and Lucie Lemonde. 1991 RC. "Voting Rights for Inmates." In *Democratic Rights and Electoral Reform in Canada*, ed. Michael Cassidy. Vol. 10 of the research studies of the Royal Commission on Electoral Reform and Party Financing. Ottawa: RCERPF.

Landry, Réjean. 1991 RC. "Inducements Created by the Institution of Representative Democracy: Their Effect on Voters, Political Parties and Public Policy." In *Representation, Integration and Political Parties in Canada*, ed. Herman Bakvis. Vol. 14 of the research studies of the Royal Commission on Electoral Reform and Party Financing. Ottawa: RCERPF.

Laycock, David. 1990. *Populism and Democratic Thought in the Canadian Prairies, 1910 to 1945*. Toronto: University of Toronto Press.

Lee, Eugene C. 1978. "California." In *Referendums: A Comparative Study of Practice and Theory*, ed. David Butler and Austin Ranney. Washington, DC: American Enterprise Institute for Public Policy Research.

Lemieux, Vincent. 1985. "The Referendum and Canadian Democracy." In *Institutional Reforms for Representative Government*, ed. Peter Aucoin.

Vol. 38 of the research studies of the Royal Commission on the Economic Union and Development Prospects for Canada. Toronto: University of Toronto Press.

Lemieux, Vincent. 1991 RC. "Public Sector Ethics." In *Political Ethics: A Canadian Perspective*, ed. Janet Hiebert. Vol. 12 of the research studies of the Royal Commission on Electoral Reform and Party Financing. Ottawa: RCERPF.

McCormick, Peter. 1991 RC. "Provision for the Recall of Elected Officials: Parameters and Prospects." In *Democratic Rights and Electoral Reform in Canada*, ed. Michael Cassidy. Vol. 10 of the research studies of the Royal Commission on Electoral Reform and Party Financing. Ottawa: RCERPF.

MacDermid, Robert. 1991 RC. "Media Usage and Political Behaviour." In *Media and Voters in Canadian Election Campaigns*, ed. Frederick J. Fletcher. Vol. 18 of the research studies of the Royal Commission on Electoral Reform and Party Financing. Ottawa: RCERPF.

Mac Donald, David. 1991 RC. "Referendums and Federal General Elections." In *Democratic Rights and Electoral Reform in Canada*, ed. Michael Cassidy. Vol. 10 of the research studies of the Royal Commission on Electoral Reform and Party Financing. Ottawa: RCERPF.

Macdonald, Doug. 1991 RC. "Ecological Communities and Constituency Districting." In *Drawing the Map: Equality and Efficacy of the Vote in Canadian Electoral Boundary Reform*, ed. David Small. Vol. 11 of the research studies of the Royal Commission on Electoral Reform and Party Financing. Ottawa: RCERPF.

Macpherson, C.B. 1962. *Democracy in Alberta: Social Credit and the Party System*. 2d ed. Toronto: University of Toronto Press.

McQuail, Denis. 1987. *Mass Communication Theory: An Introduction*. 2d ed. Newbury Park: Sage Publications.

Maddox, Russell W., and Robert F. Fuquay. 1966. *State and Local Government*. 2d ed. Princeton: Van Nostrand.

Mangum, Kim, Jamie Cooper and Robert Stumberg. 1991. *Voter Purging: The Perils and the Promise*. Washington, DC: Center for Policy Alternatives.

Massicotte, Louis. 1991 RC. "Party Financing in Quebec: An Analysis of the Financial Reports of Political Parties 1977–1989." In *Provincial Party and Election Finance in Canada*, ed. F. Leslie Seidle. Vol. 3 of the research studies of the Royal Commission on Electoral Reform and Party Financing. Ottawa: RCERPF.

Mellon, H. 1991 RC. "The Evolution of Political Financing Regulation in New Brunswick." In *Provincial Party and Election Finance in Canada*, ed. F. Leslie Seidle. Vol. 3 of the research studies of the Royal Commission on Electoral Reform and Party Financing. Ottawa: RCERPF.

Michaud, Pascale, and Pierre Laferrière. 1991 RC. "Economic Analysis of the Funding of Political Parties in Canada." In *Issues in Party and Election Finance in Canada*, ed. F. Leslie Seidle. Vol. 5 of the research studies of the Royal Commission on Electoral Reform and Party Financing. Ottawa: RCERPF.

Milen, Robert A. 1991 RC. "Aboriginal Constitutional and Electoral Reform." In *Aboriginal Peoples and Electoral Reform in Canada*, ed. Robert A. Milen. Vol. 9 of the research studies of the Royal Commission on Electoral Reform and Party Financing. Ottawa: RCERPF.

Morley, Terry. 1991 RC. "Paying for the Politics of British Columbia." In *Provincial Party and Election Finance in Canada*, ed. F. Leslie Seidle. Vol. 3 of the research studies of the Royal Commission on Electoral Reform and Party Financing. Ottawa: RCERPF.

Morton, W.L. 1967. *The Progressive Party in Canada*. Toronto: University of Toronto Press.

Mutch, Robert E. 1991 RC. "The Evolution of Campaign Finance Regulation in the United States and Canada." In *Comparative Issues in Party and Election Finance*, ed. F. Leslie Seidle. Vol. 4 of the research studies of the Royal Commission on Electoral Reform and Party Financing. Ottawa: RCERPF.

National Citizens' Coalition Inc. / Coalition nationale des citoyens inc. v. *Canada (Attorney General)* (1984), 32 Alta L.R. (2d) 249 (Q.B.).

Nevitte, Neil. 1991 RC. "New Politics, the Charter and Political Participation." In *Representation, Integration and Political Parties in Canada*, ed. Herman Bakvis. Vol. 14 of the research studies of the Royal Commission on Electoral Reform and Party Financing. Ottawa: RCERPF.

New York City Campaign Finance Board. 1990. *Dollars and Disclosure: Campaign Finance Reform in New York City*. New York: NYCCFB.

Ontario Law Reform Commission. 1990. *On the Basis of Liability for Provincial Offences*. Toronto: Ontario Government, Publications Services.

Padget, Donald. 1991 RC. "Large Contributions to Candidates in the 1988 Federal Election and the Issue of Undue Influence." In *Issues in Party and Election Finance in Canada*, ed. F. Leslie Seidle. Vol. 5 of the research studies of the Royal Commission on Electoral Reform and Party Financing. Ottawa: RCERPF.

Pammett, Jon H. 1991 RC. "Voting Turnout in Canada." In *Voter Turnout in Canada*, ed. Herman Bakvis. Vol. 15 of the research studies of the Royal Commission on Electoral Reform and Party Financing. Ottawa: RCERPF.

Pammett, Jon H., and John Myles. 1991 RC. "Lowering the Voting Age." In *Youth in Canadian Politics: Participation and Involvement*, ed. Kathy Megyery. Vol. 8 of the research studies of the Royal Commission on Electoral Reform and Party Financing. Ottawa: RCERPF.

Peers, Frank. 1969. *The Politics of Canadian Broadcasting, 1920–1921*. Toronto: University of Toronto Press.

Pelletier, Alain. 1991 RC. "Politics and Ethnicity: Representation of Ethnic and Visible-Minority Groups in the House of Commons." In *Ethno-Cultural Groups and Visible Minorities in Canadian Politics: The Question of Access*, ed. Kathy Megyery. Vol. 7 of the research studies of the Royal Commission on Electoral Reform and Party Financing. Ottawa: RCERPF.

Pelletier, Réjean. 1991 RC. "The Structures of Canadian Political Parties: How They Operate." In *Canadian Political Parties: Leaders, Candidates and Organization*, ed. Herman Bakvis. Vol. 13 of the research studies of the Royal Commission on Electoral Reform and Party Financing. Ottawa: RCERPF.

Perlin, George. 1991 RC. "Attitudes of Liberal Convention Delegates Towards Proposals for Reform of the Process of Leadership Selection." In *Canadian Political Parties: Leaders, Candidates and Organization*, ed. Herman Bakvis. Vol. 13 of the research studies of the Royal Commission on Electoral Reform and Party Financing. Ottawa: RCERPF.

Pinto-Duschinsky, Michael. 1991 RC. "The Party Foundations and Political Finance in Germany." In *Comparative Issues in Party and Election Finance*, ed. F. Leslie Seidle. Vol. 4 of the research studies of the Royal Commission on Electoral Reform and Party Financing. Ottawa: RCERPF.

Pinto-Duschinsky, Michael, and Shelley Pinto-Duschinsky. 1987. *Voter Registration in England and Wales: Problems and Solutions*. London: Constitutional Reform Centre.

Preyra, Leonard. 1991 RC. "Riding the Waves: Parties, the Media and the 1988 Federal Election in Nova Scotia." In *Reaching the Voter: Constituency Campaigning in Canada*, ed. Frederick J. Fletcher and David V.J. Bell. Vol. 20 of the research studies of the Royal Commission on Electoral Reform and Party Financing. Ottawa: RCERPF.

Price, Richard G., and Maureen Mancuso. 1991. "Ties that Bind: Parliamentary Members and Their Constituencies." In *Introductory Readings in Canadian Government and Politics*, ed. Robert M. Krause and R.H. Wagenberg. Toronto: Copp Clark Pittman.

R. v. Roman and Donkin, Ont. Prov. Ct., Zimmerman J., 19 June 1986.

R. v. Sault Ste Marie (City), [1978] 2 S.C.R. 1299.

R. v. Wholesale Travel Group Inc. (1989), 70 O.R. (2d) 545 (C.A.); affirmed S.C.C., Nos. 21779, 21786, 24 October 1991.

Rice, Ronald E., and Charles K. Atkin. 1989. *Public Communication Campaigns*. 2d ed. Newbury Park: Sage Publications.

Roach, Kent. 1991 RC. "One Person, One Vote? Canadian Constitutional Standards for Electoral Distribution and Districting." In *Drawing the Map:*

Equality and Efficacy of the Vote in Canadian Electoral Boundary Reform, ed. David Small. Vol. 11 of the research studies of the Royal Commission on Electoral Reform and Party Financing. Ottawa: RCERPF.

Robinson, Gertrude J., and Armande Saint-Jean, with the assistance of Christine Rioux. 1991 RC. "Women Politicians and Their Media Coverage: A Generational Analysis." In *Women in Canadian Politics: Towards Equity in Representation*, ed. Kathy Megyery. Vol. 6 of the research studies of the Royal Commission on Electoral Reform and Party Financing. Ottawa: RCERPF.

Romanow, Walter I., Walter C. Soderlund and Richard G. Price. 1991 RC. "Negative Political Advertising: An Analysis of Research Findings in Light of Canadian Practice." In *Political Ethics: A Canadian Perspective*, ed. Janet Hiebert. Vol. 12 of the research studies of the Royal Commission on Electoral Reform and Party Financing. Ottawa: RCERPF.

Roth, Lorna. 1991 RC. "CBC Northern Services and the Federal Electoral Process: Problems and Strategies for Improvement." In *Election Broadcasting in Canada*, ed. Frederick J. Fletcher. Vol. 21 of the research studies of the Royal Commission on Electoral Reform and Party Financing. Ottawa: RCERPF.

Saunders, Eileen. 1991 RC. "Mass Media and the Reproduction of Marginalization." In *Reporting the Campaign: Election Coverage in Canada*, ed. Frederick J. Fletcher. Vol. 22 of the research studies of the Royal Commission on Electoral Reform and Party Financing. Ottawa: RCERPF.

Sayers, Anthony M. 1991 RC. "Local Issue Space at National Elections: Kootenay West–Revelstoke and Vancouver Centre." In *Reaching the Voter: Constituency Campaigning in Canada*, ed. Frederick J. Fletcher and David V.J. Bell. Vol. 20 of the research studies of the Royal Commission on Electoral Reform and Party Financing. Ottawa: RCERPF.

Scarrow, Howard A. 1991 RC. "Apportionment, Districting, and Representation in the United States." In *Drawing the Map: Equality and Efficacy of the Vote in Canadian Electoral Boundary Reform*, ed. David Small. Vol. 11 of the research studies of the Royal Commission on Electoral Reform and Party Financing. Ottawa: RCERPF.

Schoenbach, Klaus. 1991 RC. "Mass Media and Election Campaigns in Germany." In *Media, Elections and Democracy*, ed. Frederick J. Fletcher. Vol. 19 of the research studies of the Royal Commission on Electoral Reform and Party Financing. Ottawa: RCERPF.

SECOR Group. 1990. "The Impact of New Technologies on the Electoral Process and Party Management in Canada." Report prepared for the Royal Commission on Electoral Reform and Party Financing. Ottawa.

Semetko, Holli A. 1991 RC. "Broadcasting and Election Communication in Britain." In *Media, Elections and Democracy*, ed. Frederick J. Fletcher.

Vol. 19 of the research studies of the Royal Commission on Electoral Reform and Party Financing. Ottawa: RCERPF.

Semple, George. 1991. "The Broadcasting Media and Public Opinion Aspects of the Royal Commission on Electoral Reform and Party Financing." Paper prepared for the Royal Commission on Electoral Reform and Party Financing. Ottawa.

Sigg, Oswald. 1987. *Switzerland's Political Institutions.* 2d rev. ed. Zurich: Pro Helvetia Division Documentation-Information-Press.

Simard, Carolle. 1991 RC. "Visible Minorities and the Canadian Political System." In *Ethno-Cultural Groups and Visible Minorities in Canadian Politics: The Question of Access,* ed. Kathy Megyery. Vol. 7 of the research studies of the Royal Commission on Electoral Reform and Party Financing. Ottawa: RCERPF.

Siune, Karen. 1991 RC. "Campaign Communication in Scandinavia." In *Media, Elections and Democracy,* ed. Frederick J. Fletcher. Vol. 19 of the research studies of the Royal Commission on Electoral Reform and Party Financing. Ottawa: RCERPF.

Small, David. 1991 RC. "Enhancing Aboriginal Representation within the Existing System of Redistricting." In *Drawing the Map: Equality and Efficacy of the Vote in Canadian Electoral Boundary Reform,* ed. David Small. Vol. 11 of the research studies of the Royal Commission on Electoral Reform and Party Financing. Ottawa: RCERPF.

Smith, Jennifer. 1991 RC. "The Franchise and Theories of Representative Government." In *Democratic Rights and Electoral Reform in Canada,* ed. Michael Cassidy. Vol. 10 of the research studies of the Royal Commission on Electoral Reform and Party Financing. Ottawa: RCERPF.

Smolka, Richard G. 1988. "How Election Results Are Reported in the U.S." Backgrounder 88–83. Ottawa: United States Embassy.

Le Soleil. 1991. "M.-Y. Côté opterait pour la liste électorale permanente." 18 May.

Southam News. 1987. "Literacy in Canada: A Research Report." Report prepared for Southam News by The Creative Research Group. Toronto.

Spencer, David Ralph, with the assistance of Catherine M. Bolan. 1991 RC. "Election Broadcasting in Canada: A Brief History." In *Election Broadcasting in Canada,* ed. Frederick J. Fletcher. Vol. 21 of the research studies of the Royal Commission on Electoral Reform and Party Financing. Ottawa: RCERPF.

Stanbury, W.T. 1991 RC. *Money in Politics: Financing Federal Parties and Candidates in Canada.* Vol. 1 of the research studies of the Royal Commission on Electoral Reform and Party Financing. Ottawa: RCERPF.

Stasiulis, Daiva K., and Yasmeen Abu-Laban. 1991 RC. "The House the Parties Built: (Re)constructing Ethnic Representation in Canadian Politics." In *Ethno-Cultural Groups and Visible Minorities in Canadian Politics: The Question of Access*, ed. Kathy Megyery. Vol. 7 of the research studies of the Royal Commission on Electoral Reform and Party Financing. Ottawa: RCERPF.

Stewart, Alan. 1991 RC. "Community of Interest in Redistricting." In *Drawing the Map: Equality and Efficacy of the Vote in Canadian Electoral Boundary Reform*, ed. David Small. Vol. 11 of the research studies of the Royal Commission on Electoral Reform and Party Financing. Ottawa: RCERPF.

Sutherland, S.L. 1991 RC. "The Consequences of Electoral Volatility: Inexperienced Ministers 1949–1990." In *Representation, Integration and Political Parties in Canada*, ed. Herman Bakvis. Vol. 14 of the research studies of the Royal Commission on Electoral Reform and Party Financing. Ottawa: RCERPF.

Tanguay, A. Brian, and Barry J. Kay. 1991 RC. "Political Activity of Local Interest Groups." In *Interest Groups and Elections in Canada*, ed. F. Leslie Seidle. Vol. 2 of the research studies of the Royal Commission on Electoral Reform and Party Financing. Ottawa: RCERPF.

Thomas, Paul G. 1991 RC. "Parties and Regional Representation." In *Representation, Integration and Political Parties in Canada*, ed. Herman Bakvis. Vol. 14 of the research studies of the Royal Commission on Electoral Reform and Party Financing. Ottawa: RCERPF.

Trudel, Pierre, and France Abran. 1991 RC. "The Legal and Constitutional Framework for the Regulation of Election Campaign Broadcasting." In *Election Broadcasting in Canada*, ed. Frederick J. Fletcher. Vol. 21 of the research studies of the Royal Commission on Electoral Reform and Party Financing. Ottawa: RCERPF.

Ward, Norman. 1963. *The Canadian House of Commons: Representation*. 2d ed. Toronto: University of Toronto Press.

Warhurst, John. 1991 RC. "Campaign Communication in Australian Elections." In *Media, Elections and Democracy*, ed. Frederick J. Fletcher. Vol. 19 of the research studies of the Royal Commission on Electoral Reform and Party Financing. Ottawa: RCERPF.

Young, Lisa. 1991a RC. "Legislative Turnover and the Election of Women to the Canadian House of Commons." In *Women in Canadian Politics: Towards Equity in Representation*, ed. Kathy Megyery. Vol. 6 of the research studies of the Royal Commission on Electoral Reform and Party Financing. Ottawa: RCERPF.

Young, Lisa. 1991b RC. "Toward Transparency: An Evaluation of Disclosure Arrangements in Canadian Political Finance." In *Issues in Party and Election*

Finance in Canada, ed. F. Leslie Seidle. Vol. 5 of the research studies of the Royal Commission on Electoral Reform and Party Financing. Ottawa: RCERPF.

Zimmerman, Joseph F. 1986. *Participatory Democracy: Populism Revived*. New York: Praeger.

LIST OF RECOMMENDATIONS

Following are the Commission's recommendations as they appear in volumes 1 and 2 of the Final Report.

VOLUME 1

Chapter 2

Recommendation 1.2.1
We recommend that the *Canada Elections Act* state that the right to vote entails the right to a secret ballot.

Recommendation 1.2.2
We recommend that all members and officers of the Canada Elections Commission, including the chief electoral officer, be qualified to vote.

Recommendation 1.2.3
We recommend that returning officers be qualified to vote.

Recommendation 1.2.4
We recommend that, in the event that an election remains tied after a recount, a special second election involving all candidates be conducted within three weeks of the recount.

Recommendation 1.2.5
We recommend that judges be qualified to vote.

Recommendation 1.2.6
We recommend that the following persons not be qualified to vote in federal elections:
(1) a person subject to a regime established to protect the person or the person's property, pursuant to the law of a province or territory, because the person is totally incapable of understanding the nature and consequences of his or her acts; and
(2) a person confined to a psychiatric or other institution as a result of being acquitted of an offence under the *Criminal Code* by reason of insanity.

Recommendation 1.2.7
We recommend that persons convicted of an offence punishable by a maximum of life imprisonment and sentenced for 10 years or more be disqualified from voting during the time they are in prison.

Recommendation 1.2.8
We recommend that eligible voters not resident in Canada be qualified to vote in federal elections, provided they certify that they have not voted in a foreign national election since becoming a non-resident.

Recommendation 1.2.9
We recommend that the voting age be set at 18 years of age.

Recommendation 1.2.10
We recommend that the right to vote extend only to Canadian citizens.

Recommendation 1.2.11
We recommend that

(a) every employee who is a qualified voter have four consecutive hours to vote on election day;
(b) employers be required to provide whatever time off is necessary to provide for these four consecutive hours at the convenience of the employer;
(c) employers be required to provide regular pay for time off for voting to a maximum of two hours; and
(d) this provision not extend to persons working as election officials on election day, Canada Elections Commission employees, or employees who, by reason of their employment, are too far from their polling station to be able to vote on election day during the hours the polling station is open.

Chapter 3

Recommendation 1.3.1
We recommend that only qualified voters be eligible to be candidates.

Recommendation 1.3.2
We recommend that senators be disqualified as candidates for election to the House of Commons while they hold office.

Recommendation 1.3.3
We recommend that judges, including federal, provincial and territorial judges, other than citizenship judges be disqualified as candidates for election to the House of Commons while they hold office.

Recommendation 1.3.4
We recommend that election officers, members of the Canada Elections Commission and the Commission's managerial and professional staff be disqualified as candidates for election to the House of Commons while they hold office.

Recommendation 1.3.5
We recommend that

(a) members of provincial legislatures and territorial councils be qualified as candidates for election to the House of Commons but be required to resign their seat in a provincial legislature or on a territorial council if elected; and
(b) the *Parliament of Canada Act* be amended accordingly.

Recommendation 1.3.6
We recommend that

(a) federal public service employees and members of the boards and staff of commissions, agencies and Crown corporations have the right to a leave of absence, following the issue of the writ, to seek a nomination and to be a candidate in a federal election;
(b) if the individual is not nominated, this leave of absence expire seven days after the nomination date; if the individual is a candidate, it expire seven days after a candidate has been declared elected;
(c) public servants on such a leave of absence continue to receive the non-salary benefits to which they are regularly entitled; and
(d) this not preclude any agreement between the above-noted employees and their employer about a leave of absence before or after the writ period.

Recommendation 1.3.7
We recommend that the disqualification from being candidates of voters holding contracts with the government be removed.

Recommendation 1.3.8
We recommend that voters who have been legally deprived of the right to manage their property be ineligible to be candidates.

Recommendation 1.3.9
We recommend that any voter not a resident of Canada on the date on which her or his nomination is filed be ineligible to be a candidate, unless a member of the Canadian forces on active service as a consequence of war.

Recommendation 1.3.10
We recommend that any prisoner who is serving a sentence that includes the period from nomination day to election day be ineligible to be a candidate.

Recommendation 1.3.11
We recommend that the *Parliament of Canada Act* be amended to require that any sitting member sentenced to prison for six months or more resign his or her seat.

Recommendation 1.3.12
We recommend that the penalties for conviction of serious election offences include the provision that a judge can disqualify a person from being a candidate at the next election.

Recommendation 1.3.13
We recommend that

(a) the *Canada Elections Act* prohibit a person from being a candidate for election in more than one constituency at the same time; and
(b) the *Parliament of Canada Act* be amended accordingly.

Recommendation 1.3.14
We recommend that

(a) in the case of candidates of registered constituency associations, the signatures of a member of the executive and the official agent of the constituency association be required, certifying that the nomination has been made in accordance with the constitution of the association;
(b) in all other cases, the number of signatures required for nomination be 250 voters in that constituency, except in remote constituencies, where the number required be 100; and
(c) the returning officer be permitted to accept, as an original document, nomination papers received via facsimile.

Recommendation 1.3.15
We recommend that candidates be required to provide a performance guarantee of $1000, the guarantee to be cancelled or fully refundable to candidates who meet their obligations to file reporting documents in accordance with the requirements of the *Canada Elections Act*.

Recommendation 1.3.16
We recommend that

(a) the requirement in the *Canada Elections Act* to submit the required reporting documents or lose the right to sit or vote in the House of Commons until the conditions are fulfilled be retained; and
(b) candidates who have not complied with the *Canada Elections Act* reporting requirements for a previous election by the deadline for filing nominations in a subsequent election be ineligible to be candidates at that election.

Recommendation 1.3.17

We recommend that

(a) every employer, on receiving written notice, grant a leave of absence following the issue of an election writ to an employee seeking nomination and candidacy in a federal election;

(b) if the individual is not nominated, this leave of absence expire seven days after the nomination date; if the individual is a candidate, it expire seven days after a candidate has been declared elected;

(c) employees on such a leave of absence continue to receive the non-salary benefits to which they are regularly entitled; and

(d) this not preclude any agreement between employees and employers about a leave of absence before or after the writ period.

Recommendation 1.3.18

We recommend that

(a) the provision pertaining to the issue of a writ for a by-election be deleted from the *Parliament of Canada Act*;

(b) the *Canada Elections Act* require that a by-election be called and held within 180 days of the day the Speaker of the House of Commons is informed of the vacancy;

(c) the recommended election period of 40 to 47 days apply to by-elections;

(d) if a vacancy occurs within six months of the expiration of the time limit for the duration of the House of Commons, the provisions pertaining to the issue of the writ for the by-election not apply; and

(e) if a writ has been issued ordering a by-election to be held on a date after the dissolution of Parliament, the writ be deemed to have been superseded and withdrawn.

Recommendation 1.3.19

We recommend that limits be set on spending by all persons seeking the nomination of a registered constituency association during the nomination period.

Recommendation 1.3.20

We recommend that contributors to the campaigns of those seeking the nomination of a registered constituency association be eligible for tax receipts issued by an authorized officer of the association.

Recommendation 1.3.21

We recommend that the *Income Tax Act* be amended to include, in the list of activities for which such expenses are tax deductible, child care expenses incurred by the primary caregiver when she or he is seeking the nomination of a registered constituency association during the nomination period or election as a candidate during the writ period.

Recommendation 1.3.22
We recommend that

(a) the *Income Tax Act* be amended to broaden the definition of attendant care to include the services of a person required to assist a disabled person to perform the functions necessary to seek the nomination of a registered constituency association during the nomination period or to be a candidate during the writ period; and
(b) candidates who have obtained at least 1 per cent of the vote be reimbursed 75 per cent of their expenses incurred during the election period for assistive devices related to their specific needs in conducting an election campaign, for expenses totalling a maximum of 30 per cent of their overall spending limit.

Recommendation 1.3.23
We recommend that the by-laws and constitutions of registered political parties require the establishment of formal search committees and commit the parties to processes that demonstrably promote the identification and nomination of broadly representative candidates.

Chapter 4

Recommendation 1.4.1
We recommend that section 51 of the *Constitution Act, 1867* be amended to embody the following principles:
(1) Quebec be assigned 75 seats, and other provinces be assigned seats on the basis of the ratio of their population to the population of Quebec; and
(2) if necessary, additional seats be assigned to provinces to ensure that
(i) the senatorial floor guarantee is respected;
(ii) no province loses more than one seat relative to the previous redistribution; and
(iii) no province has fewer seats than a province with a smaller population.

Recommendation 1.4.2
We recommend that the use of independent electoral boundaries commissions for each province and the Northwest Territories, as well as the composition and manner of their appointment, be maintained.

Recommendation 1.4.3
We recommend that the boundaries commission for each province establish the boundaries of the constituencies in its province according to the principles that the vote of each voter is of equal weight and that each constituency reflects communities of interest.

Recommendation 1.4.4

We recommend that

(a) electoral boundaries commissions be permitted to deviate from their provincial electoral quotient by no more than 15 per cent; and
(b) the rules for dividing the two constituencies of the Northwest Territories remain different with respect to the population criterion.

Recommendation 1.4.5

We recommend that the provision be removed whereby boundaries commissions may exceed the permitted variation from their provincial electoral quotient under circumstances they deem extraordinary.

Recommendation 1.4.6

We recommend that

(a) electoral boundaries be drawn to represent communities of interest formed on the basis of demographic, sociological and geographic considerations, taking into account the accessibility, shape and ecology of a region, the boundaries of local government and administrative units, as well as treaty areas; and
(b) electoral boundaries commissions justify their proposals and final decisions with reference to these community of interest considerations and contextual factors.

Recommendation 1.4.7

We recommend that

(a) electoral boundaries be redrawn in all provinces after each redistribution on the basis of the number of voters registered for the most recent federal election;
(b) after each general election the Canada Elections Commission determine the electoral quotient for each province and recommend whether adjustments to boundaries should be undertaken;
(c) electoral boundaries be redrawn after each general election in any province where 25 per cent or more of the constituencies contain a number of voters deviating from the provincial quotient by more than 15 per cent;
(d) no boundaries commission be established according to (a) for any province if there was no change to the number of members of the House of Commons assigned to the province and a boundaries commission had been established for the province after the most recent general election according to (b) and (c); and
(e) no boundaries commission be established for any province after a general election according to (c) during the period commencing on the first day of the year before the year of a decennial census and ending on

the day the final report is completed by the boundaries commission established after the census.

Recommendation 1.4.8
We recommend that

(a) electoral boundaries commissions be established and appointed by the end of September in the year that a decennial census is conducted or within 60 days of the Canada Elections Commission determining that a boundaries adjustment is required in one or more provinces following a general election; and

(b) electoral boundaries commissions report to the Canada Elections Commission within eight months after they have received from the Canada Elections Commission the official census data or within eight months after the date of establishment of an electoral boundaries commission in a province following a general election, unless a second round of hearings is held, in which case the reporting date shall be extended a further four months.

Recommendation 1.4.9
We recommend that

(a) the representation order issued after a redistribution of seats following a decennial census be effective on the first dissolution of Parliament that occurs at least six months after the day on which the order was issued; and

(b) a representation order be issued for each province, when following a boundaries readjustment as required after a general election, to be effective on the first dissolution of Parliament that occurs at least six months after the day on which the order was issued.

Recommendation 1.4.10
We recommend that

(a) the present procedure for parliamentary committee hearings on electoral boundaries be discontinued; and

(b) where revisions to the preliminary report of an electoral boundaries commission are made, the commission invite submissions and hold public hearings on these changes; and that where, in the aggregate, revisions involve the addition to or removal from a constituency of 25 per cent or more of the number of voters in any constituency, the commission invite submissions on these revisions and hold public hearings to consider the submissions.

Recommendation 1.4.11

We recommend that

(a) electoral boundaries commissions be encouraged to use other than geographic names to designate constituencies, particularly where this would avoid the use of multiple hyphenation;

(b) the legislation specify that the name of a constituency not be changed other than during the boundaries readjustment process; and

(c) the commissions ask the Canadian Permanent Committee on Geographical Names to suggest names for constituencies where changes are required or contemplated and that the designations of these constituencies and the rationale for the choice be presented in the commissions' preliminary reports.

Recommendation 1.4.12

We recommend that

(a) the *Canadian Elections Act* provide for the creation of Aboriginal constituencies by electoral boundaries commissions in any province where the number of self-identified Aboriginal voters enrolled on an Aboriginal voters register warrants the establishment of one or more such constituencies in relation to a province's electoral quotient;

(b) where two or more such constituencies are to be established within a province, the distinct Aboriginal representational needs within that province be the primary basis for drawing the boundaries of these Aboriginal constituencies, on either a province-wide or geographical basis, provided that the province's electoral quotient is respected; and

(c) the name of Aboriginal constituencies be in an Aboriginal language, reflect the historical link of the community to the land or a historic Aboriginal name or event, and be determined in consultation with the Aboriginal people concerned.

Recommendation 1.4.13

We recommend that the number of Aboriginal constituencies in a province be equal to such integer as is obtained by dividing the number of voters on the Aboriginal voters register by a number equal to 85 per cent of the electoral quotient for the province.

Recommendation 1.4.14

We recommend that section 51 of the *Constitution Act, 1867* provide that any province, where the redistribution of seats in the House of Commons calls for the reduction of one seat and the boundaries readjustment for the creation of an Aboriginal constituency, be assigned this additional seat for as long as the province has one or more Aboriginal constituencies.

Recommendation 1.4.15

We recommend that the *Canada Elections Act* state that the creation of Aboriginal constituencies not be construed so as to abrogate or derogate from any Aboriginal, treaty or other rights or freedoms that pertain to Aboriginal peoples.

Recommendation 1.4.16

We recommend that

(a) Aboriginal voters have the right to enrol on the Aboriginal voters register in their province; and
(b) an Aboriginal voter be defined as a voter who self-identifies as an Aboriginal person, but if an objection is raised, he or she may be required to provide evidence of Aboriginal ancestry or community acceptance, although the burden of proof should rest with those making the challenge.

Recommendation 1.4.17

We recommend that

(a) the registration of Aboriginal voters in each province to determine whether the number of Aboriginal voters warrants the creation of one or more Aboriginal constituencies be undertaken under the general supervision of the Canada Elections Commission;
(b) the registration process be administered by persons qualified to be registered as Aboriginal voters; and
(c) the Commission be required to seek the co-operation of Aboriginal organizations and media in conducting Aboriginal voter registration drives.

Chapter 5

Recommendation 1.5.1

We recommend that registered political parties, as the primary political organizations formed on the basis of a shared set of ideas and principles for the purposes of:
> nominating candidates for election to Parliament; mobilizing electoral support for their candidates; engaging their members in discussion of democratic governance; providing forums for the development of alternative policies and programs; preparing their elected members for their parliamentary responsibilities; and organizing the processes of representative and responsible government,

have constitutions that promote democratic values and practices in their internal affairs and that are consistent with the spirit and intent of the *Canadian Charter of Rights and Freedoms*.

Recommendation 1.5.2

We recommend that

(a) the democratic constitution of a party and of its registered constituency associations be submitted as part of the registration application to the Canada Elections Commission, and contain the following:
(1) provisions that those members who nominate a candidate for election to the House of Commons, select delegates to a leadership convention, or elect the party leader, be voters;
(2) clear and consistent rules applying to all aspects of the selection process for candidates, leaders, delegates and party officers, as well as membership requirements;
(3) rules and procedures for meetings and proceedings;
(4) a rule that a person may vote only once at a meeting and may vote only at one meeting to select a constituency candidate, delegates for a leadership convention, or a leader or to conduct the affairs of a constituency association;
(5) provisions for remedies and processes to fairly resolve disputes between party members and the constituent parts of the party; and
(6) specific sanctions that would be applied in cases of violation of its constitutions and rules; and
(b) nothing in the above requirements be construed to imply that a registered political party cannot have provincial associations that may exercise all or part of the responsibilities of the national party; and in such cases, the powers of the provincial associations be delineated in the constitution and by-laws of the party, and the constitution and the by-laws of the provincial associations be consistent with the requirements of the *Canada Elections Act* and filed with the Canada Elections Commission.

Recommendation 1.5.3

We recommend that

(a) all registered parties, as a condition of registration provide:
(1) the full name of the party;
(2) the party name or the abbreviated identification and logo, if any, of the party to be shown in any election documents, and that these be distinct from any other party currently or formerly registered or that was represented in the House of Commons;
(3) the address of the office where party records are maintained and to which communications may be addressed;
(4) the names and addresses of financial institutions where the party's accounts are kept;
(5) the name and address of the party leader or designated head, who must be a voter;

(6) the names and addresses of the officers of the party, who must be voters;

(7) the name and address of the person who has been appointed auditor of the party;

(8) the name and address of the chief agent of the party;

(9) a statement in writing signed by the persons who are identified as the chief agent and auditor of the party stating that each has accepted the appointment; and

(10) a recent audited financial statement;

(b) a political party be allowed to register at any time before the issue of the writs by:

(1) satisfying the administrative requirements for registration;

(2) submitting its constitution and by-laws, which must be in accordance with the requirements of the *Canada Elections Act* and duly adopted by a general meeting of members;

(3) undertaking to nominate candidates in at least 50 constituencies for the subsequent federal election; and

(4) submitting the declared support of 5000 voters who are members in good standing of the party;

(c) a political party that has nominated candidates in at least 50 constituencies in the most recent federal election or that is recognized as a parliamentary party under the *Parliament of Canada Act*, qualify automatically as a registered party by:

(1) filing for registration;

(2) satisfying the above administrative requirements for registration; and

(3) submitting its constitution and by-laws which must be in accordance with the requirements of the *Canada Elections Act* and duly adopted by a general meeting of members; and

(d) the Canada Elections Commission not accept the application for registration nor register a political party during the period from the close of nominations to election day.

Recommendation 1.5.4

We recommend that

(a) the Canada Elections Commission have the power to suspend the registration of a political party for any period;

(b) a registered party be subject to suspension when it is determined that it has violated conditions of its registration;

(c) a registered party be subject to deregistration if the Commission deems the party has violated terms of its constitution or failed to comply with the requirements of the Act;

(d) a registered party be automatically suspended if it nominates candidates in fewer than 50 constituencies; and

(e) a registered party, including a parliamentary party recognized under the *Parliament of Canada Act*, be allowed to have its party name placed on the ballot if the party fails to nominate candidates in at least 50 constituencies, but nominates candidates in at least 15 constituencies.

Recommendation 1.5.5

We recommend that

(a) all constituency associations of registered parties be required to register with the Canada Elections Commission;

(b) the Commission register only constituency associations of registered parties;

(c) constituency associations be allowed to issue income tax receipts as long as their registration remains valid and they are in compliance with the requirements of the Act; and

(d) the Canada Elections Commission register only one association of a registered party in each constituency.

Recommendation 1.5.6

We recommend that

(a) the application for registration of a constituency association include the following information:

(1) the name of the constituency association and the written endorsement of the registered party;

(2) the constitution of the constituency association, which must be in accordance with the requirements of the Act and have been adopted by a general meeting of members;

(3) the name and address of the president of the constituency association;

(4) the name and address of the constituency agent and the auditor of the association;

(5) the address where the association's accounting records are kept;

(6) the name and address of financial institutions where the association's accounts are kept;

(7) a written statement from the constituency agent and auditor stating that each agrees to act; and

(8) a statement of the assets, liabilities and any surplus of the constituency association;

(b) if an application is satisfactory, the information be entered in a registry of constituency associations maintained by the Canada Elections Commission, and both the association and endorsing party be informed that it has been registered; and

(c) constituency associations be obliged to notify the Canada Elections Commission promptly of any changes to their registration information.

Recommendation 1.5.7

We recommend that a constituency association be de-registered when:
(1) the national party is de-registered;
(2) the registered party asks for an association to be de-registered;
(3) the boundaries of the constituency are adjusted so that the association disappears or is merged with one or more other constituency associations; or
(4) the constituency association violates the terms of its constitution or fails to comply with the requirements of the *Canada Elections Act*.

Recommendation 1.5.8

We recommend that a political party be entitled to be identified on a ballot beside the name of its candidates in a general election and any election that follows until the next general election if:
(1) it satisfies the administrative requirements identified in recommendation 1.5.3;
(2) the leader of the party is a voter;
(3) the name of the political party is distinct from any other party currently or formerly registered or represented in the House of Commons; and
(4) it endorses candidates in at least 15 constituencies in the general election by the close of nominations.

Recommendation 1.5.9

We recommend that the candidate nominated by a registered constituency association be selected by an open convention of members held for this express purpose.

Recommendation 1.5.10

We recommend that candidates of a registered political party or of a party that has qualified for ballot identification who want to use the party name, logo or abbreviated identification on election documents have the written endorsement of either the party leader, his or her designate or a person designated by the governing body of the party.

Recommendation 1.5.11

We recommend that should the overall percentage of women in the House of Commons be below 20 per cent following either of the next two elections, then:
(1) at the two elections following the next election, the reimbursement of each registered political party with at least 20 per cent female MPs be increased by an amount equivalent to the percentage of its women MPs up to a maximum of 150 per cent;
(2) this measure be automatically eliminated once the overall percentage of women in the House of Commons has attained 40 per cent; and
(3) following the third election, if this measure is still in place, the Canada Elections Commission review it and recommend to Parliament whether it should be retained or adjusted.

Recommendation 1.5.12

We recommend that, as a condition of registration, the constitution of a party be filed with the Canada Elections Commission and include the following provisions:

(1) only members residing in the constituency who are in good standing for 30 days before the date set for a meeting to select delegates for a leadership convention be able to vote for delegates;

(2) for members who reside outside a constituency that is selecting delegates for a leadership convention, only members who are in good standing at least six months before the date set for the meeting be able to vote for the election of delegates;

(3) only members who are in good standing at least 30 days before the date set for the election of the leader through universal suffrage of party members be able to vote for the election of the party leader; and

(4) immediately on determination that the process for the selection of a leader will be initiated, specific rules to govern the process be adopted by the relevant party authorities, including

(i) obligations for leadership contestants to provide full disclosure of financial activities, including size and source of financial contributions of $250 or more in the aggregate;

(ii) spending limits, which may be less than the 15 per cent of the election expenses permitted the party under the *Canada Elections Act* for the most recent federal general election; and

(iii) requirements for a preliminary report by leadership contestants on their expenses and revenues on the day preceding the election of the leader.

Recommendation 1.5.13

We recommend that the *Canada Elections Act* be amended to include the following provisions:

(1) leadership contestants be required to file a report on expenses and revenues to the Canada Elections Commission within three months of the day the vote is held to select the leader;

(2) spending by individual leadership contestants of registered parties not exceed 15 per cent of the election expenses permitted the party under the *Canada Elections Act* for the most recent federal general election;

(3) each contestant for the leadership of the party be required to appoint an agent with responsibilities similar to those of the official agent of a candidate;

(4) the spending limits for leadership campaigns take effect from the time the party sets and announces a date for the election of its leader, and apply to the date when the party leader is elected;

(5) bona fide contestants for a registered party's leadership, as determined by the party, be eligible to use the tax credit system in fund-raising activities, through a mechanism established by the registered party;

(6) tax credits for leadership campaigns be issued only by the party, and the total amount of contributions to a leadership contestant for which tax

credits are attributed not exceed the total spending limit established by the party for each leadership contestant; and

(7) any portion of financial surpluses accumulated by leadership contestants that would have qualified for tax credits revert, at the discretion of the leadership contestant, to the registered political party, to the party's registered party foundation or to one of the party's registered constituency associations.

Recommendation 1.5.14

We recommend that

(a) each registered party adopt a code of ethics; and
(b) each party set up an ethics committee to help ensure adherence to and promotion of the code.

Recommendation 1.5.15

We recommend that

(a) registered parties be encouraged to create party foundations;
(b) the purpose of the party foundations be:
(1) to provide registered parties with a permanent institutional base for the development and promotion of policy alternatives;
(2) to bring together party members to participate in seminars and conferences on public policy issues;
(3) to maintain a publication program to promote the education of party members;
(4) to serve as a source of policy and research advice to registered parties in their roles as opposition and government parties; and
(5) to assist registered parties during transitions from opposition to government, and from government to opposition; and
(c) to be eligible for direct and/or indirect funding, party foundations be required:
(1) to meet the requirements for a non-profit organization established under the *Canada Corporations Act*;
(2) to have a constitution separate from their party's, explicitly stating the mission and goals of the organization, outlining procedures for selecting board members and the director, and providing a reasonable degree of autonomy to allow for and encourage the free flow of ideas and debate on important issues;
(3) to have a board of directors that represents the constituent parts of the party including, if the party so decides, the party leader or any party officer;
(4) to have specific provisions prohibiting the director and other full-time personnel from participating directly in the preparation of election-related material or in the conduct of election campaigns, unless they take unpaid leave from their positions;

(5) to present annual reports to the Canada Elections Commission on their activities and programs, including full disclosure of all revenues, expenditures and contributions, consistent with the financial disclosure requirements for political parties; and

(6) to prohibit any transfers of funds from the foundation to the political party other than for specific administrative services provided by the party.

Recommendation 1.5.16

We recommend that

(a) public funding be provided for registered party foundations, subject to the threshold of a registered party having at least 5 per cent of the national vote in the preceding election, in the form of an annual grant of $0.25 for each vote received by the registered party in the preceding election;

(b) the application for the creation of a party foundation be presented to the Canada Elections Commission by the registered party;

(c) a registered party that has not set up a foundation be ineligible for the annual grants;

(d) if the foundation is set up in any calendar year following a general election, the foundation be entitled to the total annual grant for that year;

(e) the *Income Tax Act* be amended to provide that contributions to registered party foundations be eligible for a tax credit on the same scale as the credit that now applies to donations to charitable organizations;

(f) foundations be obliged to comply with the requirements for charitable organizations under the *Income Tax Act*; and

(g) the composition of the board of directors for the foundations be consistent with the requirements for charitable organizations registered under the *Income Tax Act*.

Recommendation 1.5.17

We recommend that

(a) a registered party that has established a foundation but does not receive 5 per cent of the national vote in the following election be permitted to continue to have its foundation accredited by the Canada Elections Commission;

(b) any registered party that has been de-registered have its foundation de-registered by the Canada Elections Commission; and

(c) public funding provisions for party foundations be reviewed after seven years by the Canada Elections Commission and that the Commission report to Parliament on the results of its review.

Recommendation 1.5.18
We recommend that the scale of the federal political contribution tax credit not be changed.

Recommendation 1.5.19
We recommend that the *Income Tax Act* be amended to specify that receipts allowing taxpayers to claim the political contribution tax credit be issued only for contributions intended to support the activities of a federally registered party, including its registered constituency associations, a candidate during a federal election or a person seeking the nomination as the candidate of a federally registered constituency association or the leadership of a federally registered party.

Chapter 6

Recommendation 1.6.1
We recommend that 'election expenses' be defined to include "the cost of any goods or services used during an election:
(1) to promote or oppose, directly or indirectly, the election of a candidate;
(2) to promote or oppose a registered party or the program or policies of a candidate or registered party; or
(3) to approve or disapprove a course of action advocated or opposed by a candidate, registered party or leader of a registered party;
and include an amount equal to any contribution of goods or services used during the election."

Recommendation 1.6.2
We recommend that a candidate's 'election expenses' not exceed the aggregate of:
- $2.00 for each of the first 20 000 registered voters for the constituency;
- $1.00 for each registered voter between 20 001 and 30 000; and
- $0.50 for each additional registered voter.

Recommendation 1.6.3
We recommend that

(a) for calculating a candidate's election expenses limit, any constituency where the number of voters is less than 30 000 be deemed to have 30 000 voters; and
(b) candidates in constituencies with, on average, fewer than 10 voters per square kilometre be allowed to incur additional election expenses of $0.30 for each square kilometre, but that the additional permitted spending not exceed 50 per cent of the election expenses limit that would otherwise apply.

Recommendation 1.6.4

We recommend that a registered party's election expenses not exceed the aggregate of $0.70 for each registered voter in constituencies where the party has candidates.

Recommendation 1.6.5

We recommend that there be no statutory restrictions on the ability of groups, associations, unions and employers to communicate directly and exclusively with their bona fide members, employees or shareholders on election issues.

Recommendation 1.6.6

We recommend that

(a) election expenses incurred by any group or individual independently from registered parties and candidates not exceed $1000;
(b) the sponsor be identified on all advertising or distributed promotional material; and
(c) there be no pooling of funds.

Recommendation 1.6.7

We recommend that the blackout period for election advertising at the end of the election period include advertising by groups and individuals.

Recommendation 1.6.8

We recommend that

(a) the Canada Elections Commission annually determine adjustments to the spending limits for candidates, registered parties, individuals and groups;
(b) the adjustments reflect changes in the costs of major goods and services used in election campaigns; and
(c) the adjustments be in effect from 1 May each year and apply to any election for which the writ was issued during the following 12 months.

Recommendation 1.6.9

We recommend that

(a) spending by those seeking the nomination of a registered constituency association not exceed 10 per cent of the limit for a candidate's election expenses in that constituency in effect at the time of the nomination meeting, except if the rules of the registered party provide for a lower limit;
(b) this limit apply during a nomination period of a maximum of 30 days; and

(c) during an election period, the expenses incurred by the constituency association or registered party for the nomination of a candidate not exceed 10 per cent of a candidate's allowable election expenses in that constituency.

Recommendation 1.6.10

We recommend that

(a) those seeking the nomination of a registered constituency association be required to notify the constituency association agent of their intention to do so, in accordance with the rules in the constitution of the registered party or association;

(b) each nomination contestant be required to appoint an agent, with responsibilities similar to those of the official agent of a candidate;

(c) contributions to a nomination contestant's campaign be eligible for income tax receipts issued by the constituency agent, but that once the value of contributions to any contestant for which receipts are issued reaches the amount of the nomination spending limit, no further receipts be issued with respect to this nomination contestant;

(d) as a condition of registration, a party or constituency association submit to the Canada Elections Commission its by-laws or rules concerning the financial activities of nomination contestants, including an obligation to disclose contributions, spending limits and a requirement that, no later than the day of the nomination meeting, each nomination contestant submit to the association a preliminary report on his or her nomination expenses and contributions;

(e) no later than a month after the nomination meeting, nomination contestants be required to submit to the Canada Elections Commission a report on their spending and contributions during the nomination period, except if the nomination takes place during the election period, in which case the contestant nominated as the candidate be required to submit the report no later than the date for submission of his or her post-election return; and

(f) after the first election to which nomination spending limits apply, the Canada Elections Commission report to Parliament on the initial experience with the limits.

Recommendation 1.6.11

We recommend that

(a) registered political parties that receive at least 1 per cent of all the valid votes cast be reimbursed $0.60 for each vote received but that no party be reimbursed an amount greater than 50 per cent of its election expenses;

(b) candidates who receive 1 per cent of the valid votes in a constituency be reimbursed $1.00 for each vote received, except that

(1) candidates in constituencies with, on average, fewer than 10 voters per square kilometre be reimbursed $1.25 for each vote received;

(2) candidates in 'remote' constituencies be reimbursed $1.50 for each vote received; and

(3) candidates in constituencies with fewer than 30 000 voters be reimbursed the amount obtained by multiplying their share of the vote by 30 000 times the amount per vote that would otherwise apply;

but that no candidate be reimbursed an amount greater than 50 per cent of his or her election expenses;

(c) after each election, the Canada Elections Commission review the scale of the reimbursements; and

(d) any adjustments to the scale of the reimbursements be made through a regulation of the Commission.

Recommendation 1.6.12

We recommend that

(a) following an election, the surplus of any candidate other than those nominated by a registered constituency association be held in trust by the Canada Elections Commission; and

(b) if she or he is a candidate in the subsequent general election or a by-election during the intervening period, the funds be transferred to the financial agent of the candidate; if a constituency association is registered in her or his constituency, the funds be transferred to that constituency association upon the request of the former candidate; and, if not, the funds be transferred to the Receiver General for Canada.

Recommendation 1.6.13

We recommend that

(a) constituency associations of independent Members of Parliament be eligible to register as local associations and be authorized to issue income tax receipts for political contributions;

(b) any such association be de-registered as soon as the Member of Parliament retires, indicates she or he will not stand for re-election or is defeated, and its funds be held in trust by the Canada Elections Commission; and

(c) if the former independent Member of Parliament is a candidate at the following general election or at a by-election during that period, the funds held in trust be transferred to the financial agent of the candidate and, if not, the funds be transferred to the Receiver General for Canada.

Recommendation 1.6.14

We recommend that

(a) an advertising period be designated to begin 11 days after the day the writs are issued and to end at midnight on the second day before election day;
(b) the registered parties and broadcasters seek agreement on the scheduling of paid campaign advertising time by the end of the tenth day after the writs are issued; and
(c) failing agreement, the Canada Elections Commission establish a schedule.

Recommendation 1.6.15

We recommend that only registered parties be eligible to purchase the paid time broadcasters are obliged to make available under the *Canada Elections Act*.

Recommendation 1.6.16

We recommend that each broadcaster be required to make 360 minutes available in prime time (or such other time as mutually agreed on) for purchase by registered parties during the advertising period, subject to a maximum of 100 minutes for purchase by any registered party from any broadcaster.

Recommendation 1.6.17

We recommend retaining the prohibition in the *Canada Elections Act* against the purchase of time from broadcasting stations outside Canada during an election.

Recommendation 1.6.18

We recommend that

(a) each broadcaster be required to provide time to registered parties at 50 per cent of the most favoured rate at which comparable time is sold to other advertisers;
(b) notwithstanding any provision in the *Broadcasting Act*, CRTC regulations or conditions of licence, each broadcaster be permitted to classify one-half of the paid political advertising sold during the advertising period as program time, not to be counted against its maximum permitted advertising time; and
(c) each broadcaster that makes available paid time to individual candidates must do so on an equitable basis and at a rate that does not exceed the lowest rate charged for an equal amount of time on the same facilities to any person at any time in the same period.

Recommendation 1.6.19

We recommend that

(a) the Canada Elections Commission issue directives and guidelines regarding the booking and cancellation of paid time and its fair distribution among parties; these should reflect normal commercial practices, with due regard for the urgent needs of election campaigns and the need to make every effort to accommodate the scheduling requests of parties; and

(b) the Commission assume the functions currently performed by the broadcasting arbitrator.

Recommendation 1.6.20

We recommend that any community broadcaster or provincially operated educational broadcaster that sells advertising time to any registered party or candidate during the election period be automatically subject to the requirements of the *Canada Elections Act*.

Recommendation 1.6.21

We recommend that

(a) broadcasters be explicitly protected from liability for the bumping of commercial advertisements by party advertisements if such occurrence arises from the requirements of the *Canada Elections Act;* and

(b) broadcasters not be required to accept advertisements from parties in languages other than the language in which they normally broadcast.

Recommendation 1.6.22

We recommend that

(a) the current provision on the free-time political broadcasting system set out in the *Canada Elections Act* be abolished; and

(b) a free-time broadcasting regime be established, with programs to begin on a date after the writs to be set by the Canada Elections Commission and to end on the second day before election day, with the following characteristics:

(1) television and radio network operators, as well as specialty broadcast undertakings presenting primarily general news and public affairs programs, be required to provide to the Canada Elections Commission ten 30-minute free-time broadcasts in prime time (at least 24 minutes of which would be available to parties);

(2) networks broadcasting in French whose primary audience is in Quebec and those networks reaching a majority of Canadians outside Quebec whose primary language is French be required to provide to the Canada Elections Commission five 30-minute free-time broadcasts in

prime time (at least 24 minutes of which would be available to parties); and

(3) the specific days and times of these broadcasts be mutually agreed upon by the networks and registered parties, and in the event there is no agreement by the first day of the free-time broadcasting period established by the Canada Elections Commission, the Commission be mandated to establish forthwith the specific days and times for the programs.

Recommendation 1.6.23

We recommend that

(a) participants in the broadcasts include all registered parties;
(b) the broadcasts be a magazine show format made up of party segments of approximately four minutes each; and
(c) the Parliamentary Channels be required to repeat each of the French and English broadcasts a minimum of three times, and broadcasters have the option of repeating these broadcasts except during the blackout period at the end of the election period.

Recommendation 1.6.24

We recommend that

(a) broadcast time on the free-time programs be allocated as follows:
   (1) one program segment to all registered parties;
   (2) one additional segment to all parties registered by the issue of the writs that were registered at the previous general election but received less than 5 per cent of the vote;
   (3) one additional segment to all registered parties with candidates nominated in more than half the constituencies;
   (4) one additional segment to any registered party represented in the House of Commons (that is, at least one Member of Parliament) when the writs are issued, if the party was not registered or did not receive more than 5 per cent of the vote in the previous general election; and
   (5) the remaining segments to be allocated among those registered parties that received more than 5 per cent of the vote in the previous general election, in proportion to the votes each received;
(b) if the total time allocated to those parties that did not reach the 5 per cent threshold in the previous election exceeds 40 per cent of the total time made available, individual party allocations be reduced proportionately to remain within that cap; and
(c) for the French networks, the time be allocated to each registered party on a similar basis as for other networks, with due consideration for fairness and the number of candidates endorsed by each party in the area these networks are licensed to serve.

Recommendation 1.6.25
We recommend that

(a) to ensure high production values for free-time broadcasts, the Canada Elections Commission appoint a producer for each official language, after consulting with the registered parties; and
(b) the producers oversee the programs and assist the parties on request.

Recommendation 1.6.26
We recommend that

(a) the schedule of broadcast for party segments in the free-time broadcasts be decided by negotiation among those parties participating and the producers; and
(b) if there is no agreement, the schedule be decided forthwith by the Canada Elections Commission.

Recommendation 1.6.27
We recommend that

(a) televised leaders debates not be required by law;
(b) all matters of organization continue to be negotiated among the networks and the parties, subject to the appropriate CRTC regulations and guidelines;
(c) parties participating in the debates and networks select a chairperson by the fifth day following the issue of the writs; and
(d) televised leaders debates be closed-captioned, and sign language also be provided.

Recommendation 1.6.28
We recommend that all federal government advertising during the election period be governed by the following rules:

(a) no department of the government of Canada and no Crown agency or corporation shall during an election period publish or advertise in any manner in the area where the election is held any information concerning the programs or activities of the department or Crown agency or corporation except
(1) in continuation of earlier publications or advertisements concerning ongoing programs; or
(2) to solicit applications for employment or to solicit tenders for goods and services; or
(3) where the publication or advertisement is required by law; or
(4) where the publication or advertisement is deemed necessary by the Canada Elections Commission for the administration of an election; and

(b) on receipt of a complaint, the Canada Elections Commission shall consider the alleged violation of these prohibitions, investigate the matter if it is deemed necessary, and, if it so judges, issue a cease-and-desist order.

Chapter 7

Recommendation 1.7.1

We recommend that registered parties and registered constituency associations file an unaudited report of contributions for the first six months of the year and a full audited return on their financial activities for the entire year.

Recommendation 1.7.2

We recommend that

(a) no later than three months after the end of the reporting period or the election, all financial reports filed by registered political parties, candidates and registered constituency associations be submitted to the Canada Elections Commission;

(b) no later than a month after the nomination meeting, nomination contestants be required to submit to the Canada Elections Commission a report on their spending and contributions during the nomination period, except if the nomination takes place during the election period, or if the reporting deadline falls during the election period, in which case the candidate be required to submit the report no later than the date for submission of his or her post-election report; and

(c) no later than three months after the day of the vote to select the leader of a registered party, leadership contestants be required to submit to the Canada Elections Commission a final return on their spending and revenue.

Recommendation 1.7.3

We recommend that

(a) for contributions that must be reported:
(1) the contributor's full address (including street address, city/town/municipality, province and postal code) and the date of the contribution be required;
(2) numbered corporations be required to disclose one of the following: the name under which the corporation is registered provincially, the name that appears on the corporation's letterhead, or the names of the directors of the corporation as registered with Consumer and Corporate Affairs Canada; and
(3) registered parties, registered constituency associations, candidates, nomination contestants and leadership contestants be required to make their best effort to collect this information;

(b) use of disclosed information for non-election purposes be illegal; and

(c) to enforce this provision, 'dummy' entries on lists of contributors be permitted.

Recommendation 1.7.4

We recommend that

(a) registered parties and registered constituency associations report all contributions from any one source totalling $250 or more in any year;

(b) candidates, nomination contestants and leadership contestants report all contributions from any one source totalling $250 or more in the reporting period; and

(c) the Canada Elections Commission review this threshold every five years and adjust it accordingly.

Recommendation 1.7.5

We recommend that as part of any returns they are required to file under the *Canada Elections Act*, registered political parties, registered constituency associations, candidates and leadership contestants submit financial statements prepared according to generally accepted accounting principles and audited according to generally accepted auditing standards.

Recommendation 1.7.6

We recommend that

(a) contribution information be available in computerized format and accessible in machine-readable form, and in its printed form be arranged alphabetically by category of contributor and by province; and

(b) the Canada Elections Commission implement procedures for computerized filing of financial returns.

Recommendation 1.7.7

We recommend that the Canada Elections Commission develop and publish, annually and after every general election, an analysis and summary of party and election finance information and include contextual information in publications to enhance their utility to users.

Recommendation 1.7.8

We recommend that the *Parliament of Canada Act* be amended to require Members of Parliament to disclose any contribution received in a manner and format that conforms to the requirements in the *Canada Elections Act* for contributions to registered parties and registered constituency associations.

Recommendation 1.7.9
We recommend that

(a) in training sessions and guides or manuals for candidates, agents and executive officers, political parties explain sections 119 and 121 (and successor sections) of the *Criminal Code* relating to bribery and fraudulent payments, as well as the relevant penalties for offenders; and
(b) sections 119 and 121 of the *Criminal Code* be included in the code of ethics of each political party.

Recommendation 1.7.10
We recommend that the *Canada Elections Act* not impose limits on the size of contributions to registered political parties, registered constituency associations, candidates, nomination contestants and leadership contestants.

Recommendation 1.7.11
We recommend that the *Canada Elections Act* not impose a ban on political contributions from business, trade unions or other organizations, except as noted in recommendation 1.7.12.

Recommendation 1.7.12
We recommend that

(a) political contributions from foreign sources be banned and that foreign sources be defined as:
(1) any individual who is not a Canadian citizen, permanent resident or landed immigrant;
(2) any corporation that is foreign controlled, and that a corporation be considered foreign controlled if a majority of its voting shares are held by residents of foreign countries or by corporations that are foreign controlled;
(3) any trade union that does not hold bargaining rights for employees in Canada; and
(4) any foreign political party or government;
(b) the law provide that recipients of a contribution must show due diligence in seeking to ensure that a contribution is not from a foreign source; and
(c) if it is determined that a contribution was from a foreign source, the recipient be required to return it; if this is not possible, the contribution be remitted to the Receiver General for Canada.

Recommendation 1.7.13
We recommend that

(a) individual taxpayers be allowed to make a political contribution not exceeding $100 to a registered political party when filing their federal income tax returns and to claim the tax credit for that fiscal year; and

(b) the Receiver General forward to each registered political party an amount equal to the political contributions made under this procedure without revealing the names of the individual contributors.

Recommendation 1.7.14
We recommend that the publication or announcement of opinion polls be prohibited from midnight the day preceding election day until the close of all polls on election day.

Recommendation 1.7.15
We recommend that any news organization that sponsors, purchases or acquires any opinion poll and is the first to publish or announce its results in Canada during an election campaign be required to include in that report technical information on the methodology of the poll, including
- the name of the polling organization,
- the sponsor who paid for the poll,
- dates of the interviewing period,
- the method of collection (for example, telephone, in person, mail questionnaire),
- the population from which the sample was drawn,
- number of respondents (completed interviews),
- the refusal rate (%),
- margin of error,
- the exact wording of each question for which data are reported, and
- the size, description and margin of error for any sub-samples used in the report.

Recommendation 1.7.16
We recommend that any news organization that is the first to publish or announce in Canada any opinion poll that it has sponsored, purchased or acquired during a campaign be required to make available to any person, for the cost of duplication and within 24 hours of publication, a full report on the results of questions published, including the results on which the publication or announcement is based and the following technical information:
- the name and address of the polling organization,
- the sponsor who paid for the poll,
- dates and times of interviewing,
- the method of collection (for example, telephone, in person, mail questionnaire),
- the population from which the sample was drawn,
- the sampling method,
- the size of the initial sample,
- the number of ineligible respondents,
- number of respondents (completed interviews),
- the refusal rate (%),
- the response rate (%),

- the margin of error,
- weighting factors/normalization procedures (if any),
- the exact wording of each question for which data are reported,
- the size, description and margin of error for any sub-samples used in the report, and
- the method used to recalculate percentages when those with no opinion or who did not answer a question are left out.

Recommendation 1.7.17
We recommend that reports in the news media of polls done privately or by other news organizations, when presented for the first time in Canada in a manner similar to formal reports of media polls, be subject to the same disclosure rules as noted in recommendation 1.7.15.

Recommendation 1.7.18
We recommend that

(a) polling organizations engaged in election campaign polling for publication develop a professional code of conduct and an association to promote adherence to it; and
(b) polling organizations work with the media to improve the standards of poll reporting.

Recommendation 1.7.19
We recommend that the current end-of-campaign blackout provisions in the *Canada Elections Act* remain.

Recommendation 1.7.20
We recommend that the Canadian Advertising Foundation establish a working group with the registered political parties and the media to develop standards and compliance procedures for campaign advertising.

Recommendation 1.7.21
We recommend that broadcasters retain legal liability for the content of partisan advertising.

Recommendation 1.7.22
We recommend that the *Canada Elections Act* not be construed as requiring broadcasters to place partisan advertising sponsored by registered parties in news and public affairs programs.

Recommendation 1.7.23
We recommend that

(a) press and broadcast councils develop standards for campaign coverage and procedures for dealing with complaints about it;

(b) organizations such as the Canadian Association of Journalists and the Fédération professionnelle des journalistes du Québec continue to hold post-election evaluations of coverage and that other industry organizations institute them; and

(c) organizations such as the Canadian Daily Newspapers Association or the new Canadian Journalism Foundation set up regular seminars on campaign coverage.

Recommendation 1.7.24

We recommend that

(a) a commission be established to be known as the Canada Elections Commission consisting of seven members appointed by a two-thirds vote of the House of Commons;

(b) the House of Commons designate a member of the Commission to be the chief electoral officer who will chair the Commission and be its chief executive officer;

(c) the House of Commons designate two members of the Commission to be vice-chairs;

(d) the chief electoral officer/chair of the Commission be appointed for a seven-year term or until a successor is appointed;

(e) other members of the Commission be appointed for a five-year term or until a successor is appointed;

(f) when the Commission is established, three of its first six members be appointed for seven years to ensure continuity;

(g) the terms of the chief electoral officer and commissioners be renewable;

(h) (1) a majority of commissioners be permitted to request the Canadian Judicial Council to inquire into whether a commissioner should be removed from office for any of the reasons set out in paragraph 65 (2) (a) to (d) of the *Judges Act*;

(2) the Council's recommendation be made to the Speaker of the House of Commons; and

(3) commissioners be removed only on a two-thirds majority address of the House of Commons;

(i) during their terms in office, the chief electoral officer and commissioners not hold office in or be employed in any capacity by a political party, not be members of a political party and not make political contributions or contributions to a party foundation; and

(j) the chief electoral officer/chair of the Commission be paid a salary equal to that of the Chief Justice of the Federal Court of Canada; the two vice-chairs be paid a salary equal to that of the justices of that court; and the remuneration of the other members of the Commission be fixed by the Governor in Council.

Recommendation 1.7.25

We further recommend that the powers of the Canada Elections Commission include the following:

(1) to formulate policy and direct the chief electoral officer on policy implementation;

(2) to issue policy statements to registered political parties, candidates, agents and other interested individuals or groups;

(3) to review decisions by election officials when requests have been filed by citizens, candidates, parties and their agents;

(4) to conduct public hearings on regulations, policies and guidelines;

(5) to respond to requests for advance rulings or interpretation bulletins from registered political parties, candidates or agents;

(6) to recommend changes to legislation;

(7) to make regulations that are submitted directly to the Speaker of the House of Commons and deemed approved if not referred for debate or to a committee within 15 sitting days after being tabled;

(8) to exercise the functions of the current broadcasting arbitrator;

(9) to submit its annual operating budget to the Treasury Board;

(10) to submit an annual report to Parliament on elections administration and enforcement; and

(11) to maintain a register of political parties, constituency associations and party foundations.

Recommendation 1.7.26

We recommend that

(a) when a case is referred to the Commission for adjudication, the chair, or in her or his absence a vice-chair, designate the panel to hear the case;

(b) a panel consist of any number of commissioners; and

(c) the quorum for meetings of the Commission be two members.

Recommendation 1.7.27

We recommend that

(a) a deputy chief electoral officer be appointed by the Canada Elections Commission;

(b) the deputy chief electoral officer be deemed to be employed in the federal public service; and

(c) a vice-chair be designated to act as chair in the absence of the chair.

Recommendation 1.7.28

We recommend that election violations be brought before the Commission or prosecuted before provincial criminal courts, depending on the nature and gravity of the alleged violation.

Recommendation 1.7.29

We recommend that

(a) the Canada Elections Commission be constituted as an administrative tribunal to adjudicate infractions under the *Canada Elections Act* with the powers, rights and privileges vested in a superior court of record, but that the Commission not participate in decisions related to investigation and prosecution, which would be the responsibility of the director of enforcement;

(b) the Commission be empowered to issue mandatory injunctions and cease-and-desist orders when required to protect the integrity of the electoral process, provided that the person or party affected by such an order has the right to appear before the Commission before the order is handed down, except in cases deemed to be emergencies;

(c) the Commission provide written reasons for its decisions;

(d) the Commission be empowered to rescind or vary any decision or order it has made at its own initiative or pursuant to a request made before it; and

(e) any person or party have the right to seek review of a decision of the Commission to the Federal Court of Canada within 30 days of the decision upon any question involving the jurisdiction of the Commission.

Recommendation 1.7.30

We recommend that

(a) the Governor in Council appoint a director of enforcement who will hold office for a five-year term during which she or he may be removed only for cause and with the unanimous approval of the Commission, and the mandate of the director of enforcement be renewable;

(b) the office of the director of enforcement be an independent office responsible for investigation and prosecution of offences before the Commission and the courts; and

(c) the director of enforcement have exclusive authority over the investigative and prosecutorial staff of her or his office.

Recommendation 1.7.31

We recommend that

(a) where regulations are provided for under the *Canada Elections Act*, they be made by the Canada Elections Commission and submitted directly to the Speaker of the House of Commons, who must table them forthwith;

(b) regulations be deemed to be approved if not referred for debate or to a committee within 15 sitting days after they have been submitted to the House;

(c) if a regulation made by the Commission has been referred for debate or to a committee of the House of Commons, it require approval by the House of Commons to take effect; and

(d) the initial set of regulations required to implement the new *Canada Elections Act* take effect immediately and remain in force for six months, then be approved or rejected by the House of Commons.

Recommendation 1.7.32

We recommend that

(a) the Commission be empowered to issue policy statements; and

(b) the chief electoral officer be empowered to issue interpretation bulletins as a guide to the law and be required to respond within a reasonable time to requests for advance rulings on its interpretation of election law and regulations.

Recommendation 1.7.33

We recommend that the Canada Elections Commission be responsible for all matters relating to broadcasting as found in the *Canada Elections Act*.

Recommendation 1.7.34

We recommend that the Commission's non-statutory budget estimates, as submitted by the Commission, continue to be subject to Treasury Board approval prior to their submission to Parliament.

Recommendation 1.7.35

We recommend that

(a) the Canada Elections Commission report annually to the House of Commons on its activities and on recommended changes in legislation and election practice; and

(b) the Committee responsible for election matters respond to the Commission's annual report and meet with the chief electoral officer and members of the Commission at least once a year.

Recommendation 1.7.36

We recommend that during their terms of office, returning officers, assistant returning officers and the management and professional staff of the Canada Elections Commission not hold office in or be employed in any capacity by a political party and not be members of a political party or contributors to a political party or candidate.

Recommendation 1.7.37

We recommend that the *Public Service Staff Relations Act* be amended to allow for the designation of all staff of the Canada Elections Commission as excluded from the right to strike.

Recommendation 1.7.38

We recommend that

(a) the Canada Elections Commission be given a mandate to provide materiel and professional and technical assistance to other countries, provided that all such requests be approved by a House of Commons committee; and
(b) the expenditures required be allocated from the non-allocated consolidated fund or assumed by the sponsoring department or agency.

VOLUME 2

Chapter 1

Recommendation 2.1.1

We recommend that

(a) returning officers be required to
(1) request names of enumerators from all registered constituency associations;
(2) appoint enumerators as soon as possible after the writ is issued with due regard to the standings in the previous election of the candidates of registered constituency associations that have submitted names;
(3) consult with community organizations and shelters to recruit potential enumerators; and
(b) measures be taken to provide voters from ethno-cultural communities with information and assistance on the enumeration and voter registration process.

Recommendation 2.1.2

We recommend that every person appointed enumerator be a Canadian citizen and at least 16 years of age.

Recommendation 2.1.3

We recommend that one enumerator be appointed for each polling division, except where it is deemed prudent or advisable to appoint two.

Recommendation 2.1.4

We recommend that returning officers be authorized by the chief electoral officer to appoint supervisory enumerators to assist in managing the enumeration process.

Recommendation 2.1.5

We recommend that

(a) enumerators submit completed enumeration forms with the names and addresses of voters to the office of the returning officer as directed by the supervisory enumerator or returning officer for entry on the voters lists; and

(b) one copy of the preliminary list for each polling division in each constituency be made available in machine-readable form or printed format to the candidates in each constituency two days after the enumeration ends.

Recommendation 2.1.6

We recommend that, on request, the address of the office of the returning officer be given as a voter's address for all lists made available to candidates.

Recommendation 2.1.7

We recommend that returning officers determine the methods and hours of enumeration to be used by enumerators in their constituencies.

Recommendation 2.1.8

We recommend that every enumerator, upon producing proper identification and during reasonable hours, be given free access to the entrance door to each dwelling unit in any multiple residence building in order to conduct an enumeration of voters.

Recommendation 2.1.9

We recommend that homeless voters be permitted to give the address of a shelter, soup kitchen, Indian band office or Métis friendship centre as their place of residence.

Recommendation 2.1.10

We recommend that

(a) voters not contacted by enumerators be left a numbered mail-in enumeration card, containing the phone number of the returning officer and the Canada Elections Commission's logo, with which they can register by listing the name and address of all qualified voters at their residence, certifying that the information on the card is correct, and returning the card by mail or in person to the returning officer's office or sub-office, provided that the card is received by 6 p.m. on the fifth day before election day; and

(b) in provinces with Aboriginal constituencies, mail-in enumeration cards

(1) contain information pertaining to the right of Aboriginal voters to register to vote in an Aboriginal constituency or a general constituency;

(2) provide a place for voters to mark that it be forwarded to the returning officer for the Aboriginal constituency, if applicable, when dropped
off in an area predominantly populated by non-Aboriginal people; and
(3) provide a place for voters to mark that it be forwarded to the returning officer for the general constituency, if applicable, when dropped
off in an area predominantly populated by Aboriginal people.

Recommendation 2.1.11
We recommend that enumerators be paid according to a fee structure based
on the number of visits made, as indicated by the number of names of
voters collected, addresses without voters, and addresses at which mail-in
enumeration cards were left.

Recommendation 2.1.12
We recommend that

(a) the length of the enumeration period for each province and territory be
designated by the Canada Elections Commission immediately following
the issue of writs;
(b) the length of the enumeration period be designated the same for all
constituencies in a province or territory;
(c) the chief electoral officer be authorized to extend the enumeration
period for one or more constituencies or one or more polling divisions
as deemed necessary; and
(d) where the chief electoral officer deems it necessary to extend the period
of enumeration in one or more constituencies or one or more polling
divisions, the candidates and voters in these constituencies be informed.

Recommendation 2.1.13
We recommend that

(a) returning officers appoint revising officers in revision divisions approved
by the chief electoral officer and revising agents for the constituency;
(b) revising officers (or returning officers and assistant returning officers)
enter the names of voters on the voters lists as requested by voters at
the office(s) of the returning officer or revising officer, at the residence
of voters, or after receiving mail-in enumeration cards;
(c) revising officers direct revising agents, who shall work in pairs and not
represent the same political interest, to visit residences that were not
visited by the enumerators;
(d) revising officers, when so directed by the returning officer, conduct an
enumeration, in lieu of revision, in any area where the returning officer deems this to be necessary; and
(e) revising officers make corrections to the voters list when requested by
a voter to revise the names or addresses of a voter or voters; and delete

the name of a voter when requested to do so by the voter in question or by a member of the immediate family in the case of a deceased voter.

Recommendation 2.1.14
We recommend that voters be able to register, with identification, or to register voters of their immediate family or those living at the same residence provided that they present identification for these voters, at their returning officer's office (or sub-office) up to 6 p.m., the fifth day before election day.

Recommendation 2.1.15
We recommend that

(a) any voter be permitted to object to the inclusion of a person on a preliminary voters list on the ground that the person does not have the right to vote in the polling division for which he or she is registered;
(b) a voter who objects to a person on a preliminary voters list be required to send a written objection to the returning officer no later than the seventeenth day before election day;
(c) the written objection state the name, address and phone number of the person making the objection, the name of the person being objected to, and the grounds for the objection, and be dated and signed by the person making the objection;
(d) any person objecting to the inclusion of a person on a preliminary voters list have the burden of proving that the person should be removed from the list;
(e) the returning officer, on receipt of an objection, be required to inform the person being objected to and each candidate in the constituency of the receipt of the objection, their right to attend a hearing and make presentations, and the place and time of the hearing; and
(f) each revising officer conduct a hearing on the twelfth day before election day to hear presentations, and decide on any objections.

Recommendation 2.1.16
We recommend that

(a) following the close of registration on the fifth day before election day, the returning officer prepare a list of all voters added to the certified preliminary voters list and, on the fourth day before election day, make this list available to any candidate who requests it; and
(b) each revising officer, before noon constituency time on the fourth day before election day, meet with candidates or candidates' representatives to review this list of voters and, where an objection cannot be resolved, make a reasonable effort to inform those objected to that they may be challenged at their polling station when they appear to vote.

Recommendation 2.1.17

We recommend that

(a) voters be permitted to register on election day provided they present prescribed identification, including confirmation of their address, and swear an oath or make an affirmation that they are a qualified voter and reside in the polling division;

(b) the provision whereby a voter may be vouched for by another registered voter from the same polling division be removed from the *Canada Elections Act*; and

(c) returning officers appoint revising officers at central polling locations to provide for an efficient election-day registration that does not hamper the conduct of the vote.

Recommendation 2.1.18

We recommend that

(a) Voter Information cards be given to those enumerated, given to those registered by revising officers or at the office(s) of the returning officer and mailed to voters registered by means other than visits to residences; and

(b) Voter Information cards provide information on the location of the voter's regular polling station and the availability of barrier-free access (using the international symbol for such access), the location of the voter's advance polling station, the hours of the voter's mobile polling station where appropriate, and the phone number and location of the office and sub-office(s), if any, of the constituency returning officer.

Recommendation 2.1.19

We recommend that a voter's home constituency be one of the following as selected by the voter: the constituency that includes the voter's ordinary place of residence, the voter's last place of residence before assuming a residence elsewhere, or the residence of a voter's spouse, dependant or next of kin.

Recommendation 2.1.20

We recommend that

(a) the Canada Elections Commission maintain a voter register of Canadian voters living abroad;

(b) voters living abroad register by mail by sending a completed registration form to the Commission;

(c) Canadian forces voters abroad be on the list of voters abroad maintained by the Department of National Defence on behalf of the Commission and be provided to the Commission at the time the writ is issued;

(d) applications contain a signature, Social Insurance Number, identification as prescribed by the Commission, the last address in Canada or the Canadian address of the spouse, dependant or next of kin, and the voter's current address;

(e) each registered voter be assigned a unique voter registration number;

(f) the *Canada Elections Act* authorize the use of Social Insurance Numbers to provide voter registration numbers;

(g) this registration be for three years and renewable, provided that the voter remains qualified by not voting in a foreign national election since taking up residence abroad; and

(h) following the issue of the writ, the Commission make available to candidates the list of voters (name and address only) from their constituency on the register.

Recommendation 2.1.21

We recommend that

(a) voters away from their home constituency be permitted to register and apply for a special ballot at any office, including any temporary office, of any returning officer in Canada, at designated Canadian government offices in Canada or abroad;

(b) all such voters apply in person, provide a signature, present identification as prescribed by the Commission, provide their address in their home constituency and sign a declaration that they will vote only once in the election;

(c) the election official or agent who registers every such voter certify on the application form for registration and the special ballot that the prescribed identification was presented and that a special ballot was given to the voter, and record the number of the certificate envelope;

(d) the completed application be forwarded forthwith by mail or facsimile by the official or agent who registers the voter to the returning officer in the home constituency of the voter;

(e) on receipt of a completed and certified application, the returning officer enter the name of the voter on the voters list for the appropriate polling division, note that the voter has received a special ballot and the number of the certificate envelope; and

(f) registration be accepted only if received by the office of the returning officer in the home constituency of the voter by 6 p.m. eastern time on the fifth day before election day.

Recommendation 2.1.22

We recommend that returning officers in whose constituency are located major clusters of voters who must vote by special ballot, including inmates in provincial and local prisons, full-time students at post-secondary institutions, workers at temporary worksites and Canadian forces personnel on training, make provisions, as the chief electoral officer deems appropriate, for registration and the provision of special ballots.

Recommendation 2.1.23
We recommend that

(a) Correctional Service Canada provide the Canada Elections Commission with a list of all qualified voters who are inmates in federal institutions at the time of the issue of the writs;
(b) this list contain the names of the home constituencies of each such voter; and
(c) the Canada Elections Commission designate an election agent in each federal institution to register and accept applications for special ballots for any inmates in these institutions who are qualified voters and who were not on the list provided to the Canada Elections Commission.

Recommendation 2.1.24
We recommend that voters in hospital on election day be permitted to register and vote by special ballot in their hospital.

Chapter 2

Recommendation 2.2.1
We recommend that

(a) the basic process of ordinary voting on election day be retained, with the improvements recommended in this report; and
(b) voting on election day continue to take place at polling stations serving a defined group of voters in a limited geographic area.

Recommendation 2.2.2
We recommend that each voter be allowed to deposit his or her own ballot in the ballot box after the deputy returning officer has checked the initials and serial number.

Recommendation 2.2.3
We recommend that

(a) mobile polls be established where they will make voting more accessible for groups of voters who would have difficulty going to an ordinary polling station;
(b) with the exception of the hours of voting, voting procedures and the right of candidates to be represented at mobile polls be the same as at ordinary polls;

(c) mobile polls not be required to remain open for the same period as ordinary polling stations on election day, provided that voting at any mobile poll end no later than voting at ordinary polling stations in the constituency;

(d) mobile polls be permitted to move to several locations on election day, provided that the schedule of opening hours and locations be made available in advance to candidates and voters in that mobile poll;

(e) voting in mobile polls be organized in co-operation with the appropriate authorities of any institution, such as hospitals, shelters, soup kitchens or Aboriginal community centres, where a mobile poll is located;

(f) when a residence or institution has been designated to be served by a mobile poll, the people living there be registered for the mobile poll and not for the ordinary polling division where the institution is located;

(g) ballots from mobile polls be counted at the same time as the ordinary polls are counted; and

(h) the count take place at the returning officer's office or at another location approved by the returning officer, with prior notification to candidates.

Recommendation 2.2.4

We recommend that

(a) every voter who would find it more convenient to vote at an advance poll than at an ordinary polling station be eligible to do so;

(b) there be two days of advance polling in areas of more than 5000 voters; in areas with fewer than 5000 voters, the returning officer have the flexibility to determine whether an advance poll is warranted;

(c) a mobile advance poll be provided during the nine days preceding election day to serve any community of fewer than 5000 voters where they would not otherwise have reasonable access to an advance poll;

(d) the days set aside for advance polling be the Sunday of the second weekend before election day and the Saturday immediately before election day;

(e) the hours for advance polling be noon to 8 p.m. on Sunday and 9 a.m. to 6 p.m. on Saturday; and

(f) the plan for advance polling in each constituency be made available to the candidates and registered parties and subject to review by the chief electoral officer on the request of any candidate or registered party.

Recommendation 2.2.5

We recommend that

(a) every voter who would find it more convenient to vote by special ballot be eligible to do so;

(b) three separate envelopes be issued with each special ballot: the first to preserve the secrecy of the ballot, the second to allow election officials to identify the voter and verify the voter's eligibility, and the third to allow delivery of the special ballot;

(c) special ballots take the form of blank ballots on which voters mark the name of a candidate or party;

(d) the Special Voting Rules be deleted from the Act; and

(e) the proxy vote be abolished.

Recommendation 2.2.6
We recommend that

(a) voters be required to apply in person for a special ballot at any returning officer's office or at other designated government offices in Canada or abroad;

(b) if a voter is unable to go to an election office because of illness or disability, the returning officer be allowed to accept a signed application from the voter with suitable identification delivered by a member of the immediate family or to send an election official to the voter's home to allow the voter to apply for and tender a special ballot;

(c) where a voter is unable to provide a signature and indicate his or her voting choice on the special ballot, a witnessed mark constitute an acceptable signature, the witness be allowed to complete the special ballot on the voter's instruction and the witness be sworn to secrecy;

(d) to qualify for a special ballot, voters be required to provide satisfactory identification, as determined by the Canada Elections Commission, and a signature, and attest that they will not vote more than once; in addition, Canadians abroad be required to certify that they have not voted in a foreign national election since taking residence abroad;

(e) any election official or agent designated by the returning officer or the Canada Elections Commission be authorized to receive and process applications for special ballots and thereafter issue special ballots;

(f) special ballots be available as soon as the returning officer's offices open at the beginning of an election campaign;

(g) voters be allowed to apply for a special ballot at any office of the returning officer in their own constituency or designated government offices in remote areas up to 6 p.m. on the fifth day before election day;

(h) voters away from their home constituency be allowed to apply for a special ballot at an office of any returning officer or at embassies or other Canadian government offices abroad provided that their application is received at the office of the returning officer in their home constituency by 6 p.m. eastern time on the fifth day before election day;

(i) the role of parties and candidates be limited to providing information about the special ballot; and

(j) the exercise of undue influence or violation of the secrecy of the vote be an offence under the *Canada Elections Act*.

Recommendation 2.2.7

We recommend that

(a) voters who receive special ballots be responsible for ensuring that the ballot is delivered to the appropriate election office by the closing of the polls on election day for a special ballot sent directly to the voter's constituency and 6 p.m. eastern time for a special ballot sent to the Canada Elections Commission;

(b) voters who apply for a special ballot in their home constituency be able to tender a special ballot at any office of the returning officer in that constituency by delivering it in person; and

(c) any special ballot received after the deadline on election day not be opened, counted or considered valid, regardless of why it was not received on time.

Recommendation 2.2.8

We recommend that

(a) a special ballot be invalid if the voter does not register by the deadline for the special ballot in the constituency in which the vote is cast, if the signature on the certificate envelope does not match the signature on the voter's application, or if the special ballot is not received by the deadline;

(b) a person who seeks to vote on election day and whose name is on the list as having applied for a special ballot be allowed to vote upon production of satisfactory identification as prescribed by the Canada Elections Commission and upon signing a declaration promising not to vote more than once; in the absence of satisfactory identification, the voter be required to swear an oath or make an affirmation as to his or her identity and sign a declaration promising not to vote more than once; the DRO be required to notify the RO of that voter's name and the special ballot issued in that name be invalidated;

(c) certificate envelopes containing special ballots not be opened until 30 minutes after the close of polls on election day, so that any special ballots that duplicate votes cast in person on election day can be invalidated;

(d) if more than one special ballot is cast in the name of a voter, all these special ballots be ruled invalid;

(e) candidates be permitted to have scrutineers present on election day to validate special ballot envelopes and ensure that the count of special ballots is carried out fairly and accurately;

(f) votes by special ballot be recorded separately from ordinary votes in the returns for each constituency; and

(g) it be an offence to exercise undue pressure on someone casting a vote by special ballot or to violate the secrecy of a vote by special ballot.

Recommendation 2.2.9

We recommend that the use of special ballots replace the present procedures for voting in the returning officer's office.

Recommendation 2.2.10

We recommend that

(a) voters living abroad vote in their home constituency using the special ballot;

(b) special ballots be mailed to voters on the Commission's register of non-resident voters shortly after the writ is issued;

(c) ballots be returned to the Commission, verified and counted centrally and the results transmitted to home constituency returning officers;

(d) the chief electoral officer invite each registered party to appoint scrutineers for the count of special ballots;

(e) counting of special ballots begin on a date to be fixed by the chief electoral officer, at the earliest on the fifth day before election day; and

(f) special ballot envelopes sent from abroad be verified by comparing the unique voter number on the certificate envelope against the number on the voter's registration; and that, in cases where the voter's signature is missing or the envelope is received after 6 p.m. on election day, the certificate envelope be put aside unopened.

Recommendation 2.2.11

We recommend that

(a) votes cast by Canadians who are away from their home constituency, whether in Canada or abroad, be returned to the returning officer's office in their home constituency and be counted along with the other special ballots cast in that constituency, except for votes cast by inmates registered on the list provided to the Canada Elections Commission by Correctional Service Canada;

(b) voters away from their home constituency be responsible for delivering the ballot back to the home constituency by the close of the polls on election day; and

(c) ballots cast by inmates in federal prisons who are registered on the central list provided to the Commission by Correctional Service Canada be returned to the Canada Elections Commission by 6 p.m. on election day and be counted centrally by the Commission and the results reported to each constituency along with the votes of Canadians registered with the Commission as non-resident voters.

Recommendation 2.2.12

We recommend that

(a) the training of returning officers and election officials include training on how to serve voters with special needs; and
(b) enumerators be instructed to report whether there are voters with special needs who have asked to use specific voting provisions.

Recommendation 2.2.13

We recommend that

(a) the Canada Elections Commission be responsible, along with local returning officers, for ensuring access to the vote for voters with physical disabilities;
(b) barrier-free access be available at all ordinary polling stations and their polling booths except where no suitable premises exist and ramps cannot be built; and that barrier-free access be available to the returning officer's office and sub-offices and all advance polling stations and their polling booths;
(c) if barrier-free access is not provided at a polling station, the returning officer be required to justify his or her decision to locate the poll at that place;
(d) the voter information card given to voters indicate whether their ordinary polling station has barrier-free access and provide the telephone number of the returning officer, in both cases using international symbols;
(e) if barrier-free access is not provided at a polling station, voters be able to transfer their names to the voters list for a polling station that is accessible, through a simple request to the enumerator or to the returning officer;
(f) the system of transfer certificates be abolished; and
(g) election officials be permitted to take the ballot box to a voter outside the polling station if barrier-free access is not available.

Recommendation 2.2.14

We recommend that

(a) the Canada Elections Commission publicize its logo and use it prominently during election periods to assist people in identifying election offices and polling stations;
(b) the ballot include a party's initials or logo next to the name of each candidate representing a party that is registered or allowed to be identified on the ballot;
(c) parties' initials or logos used on ballots be in a standard form for each party and subject to approval by the Commission;
(d) logos not appear beside the names of independent candidates;
(e) a poster in the form of a ballot be displayed at every polling station, advance poll, and returning officer's office showing the name and

photograph of candidates in the constituency and the name and logo (or initials) of their parties (if authorized to be identified on the ballot); and

(f) candidates who wish their photograph to be used on the poster be required to submit it upon filing their nomination documents.

Recommendation 2.2.15

We recommend that where polling divisions have a concentration of voters from a language group other than English or French, the returning officer assign to the polling stations election-day officials able to speak that language, or when that is not possible, interpreters be used.

Recommendation 2.2.16

We recommend that

(a) voters not be required to swear an oath to obtain assistance to vote;

(b) a friend or relative who assists a voter be required to sign a declaration, in the form established by the Commission, to keep the ballot secret and not to coerce the voter and have her or his name recorded in the poll book;

(c) no person assist more than one voter at an election, except for an election official or a person assisting members of his or her immediate family; and

(d) a voter be entitled to have the assistance of a deputy returning officer in the presence of the poll clerk only.

Recommendation 2.2.17

We recommend that

(a) returning officers ensure that voting procedures are accessible in any hospital or institution where people may have difficulty getting out to vote at an ordinary polling station;

(b) mobile polling stations be used in hospitals and similar institutions and be open long enough that everyone in the institution who wishes to vote can do so;

(c) bedside voting continue to be permitted in any institution served by a regular or mobile poll;

(d) arrangements for voting in hospitals and institutions be worked out in advance between the returning officer for the area and the institution's administration;

(e) voters in a hospital not in their constituency on election day be permitted to register and vote by special ballot on election day;

(f) returning officers establish adequate polling facilities for each hospital in their constituency for registering and providing special ballots to voters;

(g) persons voting in this manner tender their ballots to the deputy returning officer in charge of the polling station; and

(h) the vote be counted at this polling station at the close of the poll and the results be transmitted to the Canada Elections Commission, which will communicate them to the constituency.

Recommendation 2.2.18

We recommend that the Act provide for the use of a template at every polling station for voting by persons with visual impairments.

Recommendation 2.2.19

We recommend that returning officers work with groups representing deaf and hearing-impaired persons in their constituency to establish whether and how sign-language interpreters should be provided to help with voting or to provide other assistance that may be required by voters with hearing impairments where warranted.

Recommendation 2.2.20

We recommend that remote constituencies where special provisions for voting apply be designated in an appendix to the *Canada Elections Act* but be subject to change by regulation.

Recommendation 2.2.21

We recommend that

(a) voters in remote constituencies and in other remote areas designated by the Canada Elections Commission be able to obtain a special ballot through local election officials or through a designated government office in their area;

(b) if it would be difficult to deliver a special ballot to the election office by election day, voters in remote constituencies be permitted to tender ballots to the deputy returning officer so that they can be counted with the votes for that poll on election day; and

(c) a returning officer be able to take a voter's vote or authorize the deputy returning officer to do so by telephone, radio or facsimile and to register it as a special ballot if there are no other means of taking the vote and if the returning officer is satisfied as to the voter's identity; and that a record of such a vote be entered in the poll book.

Recommendation 2.2.22

We recommend that

(a) returning officers in remote areas be allowed to distribute election documents by facsimile where this is required to serve polling stations in isolated areas; and

(b) returning officers be allowed to designate polling stations in isolated areas as mobile polls and to vary the hours of voting at these polls, provided that voters and candidates are told in advance.

Recommendation 2.2.23

We recommend that the *Canada Elections Act* authorize the Canada Elections Commission to introduce new means of communicating election documents as these means become available and that such changes be introduced through regulation.

Chapter 3

Recommendation 2.3.1

We recommend that

(a) the minimum election period be 40 days and the maximum 47 days; and
(b) the deadline for official nominations be 21 days before election day.

Recommendation 2.3.2

We recommend that election day be a Monday.

Recommendation 2.3.3

We recommend that

(a) the voting day be extended from 11 hours to 12 hours; and
(b) local voting hours be from 9:30 a.m. to 9:30 p.m. in Newfoundland, Prince Edward Island, Quebec, New Brunswick, Nova Scotia and Ontario; 8:30 a.m. to 8:30 p.m. in Manitoba and Saskatchewan; 8 a.m. to 8 p.m. in Alberta and the Northwest Territories; and 7 a.m. to 7 p.m. in British Columbia and the Yukon.

Recommendation 2.3.4

We recommend that

(a) if a nominated candidate of a registered party dies during the last 21 days prior to the close of the polls on election day, the election in that constituency be postponed;
(b) a new nomination day for the postponed election be set for the second Monday after the death of the candidate, and that election day be 21 days after the new nomination day;
(c) in the case of a postponed election, the nominations of the remaining candidates stand;
(d) the revision period of the voters list be extended; and

(e) any special ballots received be destroyed and the returning officer be required to send a new special ballot to all voters who had applied for a special ballot, accompanied by a statement of when the postponed election will be held; further, if the candidate dies after the day of the advance poll, these ballots be destroyed.

Recommendation 2.3.5

We recommend that

(a) candidates be allowed to withdraw up to 6 p.m. on the day before election day; and
(b) if a candidate withdraws after the close of nominations, the withdrawal be final and no replacement candidate be allowed.

Recommendation 2.3.6

We recommend that

(a) returning officers be appointed by the Governor in Council;
(b) if the Governor in Council does not nominate someone to fill a returning officer position within 90 days of the position becoming vacant, the Canada Elections Commission have the authority to make the appointment;
(c) returning officers be appointed for a term of seven years by the Governor in Council, renewable for seven years upon the recommendation of the Commission;
(d) the chief electoral officer be permitted to retain a returning officer whose constituency has been altered by boundaries readjustment if the boundaries remain substantially the same and the returning officer lives in the new constituency;
(e) the Canada Elections Commission have the power, on the advice of the chief electoral officer, to dismiss a returning officer for incompetence, incapacity, insubordination or lack of satisfactory performance;
(f) as a condition of office, returning officers be required to refrain from membership in a political party, from making a political contribution, from engaging in partisan political activity, and from demonstrating partisan bias in carrying out their duties;
(g) returning officers be engaged by the CEO between elections as necessary to prepare for the next election and to conduct outreach activities on behalf of the Canada Elections Commission; and
(h) greater attention be given to hiring returning officers capable of serving the needs of voters who do not speak French or English in constituencies where there is a significant community of such voters.

Recommendation 2.3.7

We recommend that

(a) deputy returning officers and poll clerks be appointed on the recommendation of the candidates whose parties stood first and second respectively in the constituency at the previous election;

(b) returning officers appoint deputy returning officers and poll clerks if candidates have not nominated enough qualified persons to fill the positions available by two weeks before election day;

(c) deputy returning officers, poll clerks and constables be required to be eligible voters in the constituency;

(d) poll clerks and constables be trained so that they can take over the responsibilities of the deputy returning officer in the event that a person appointed to that position is unavailable on election day or at an advance poll; and

(e) a supervisory deputy returning officer be appointed to all central polling places with five or more polling stations and a deputy returning officer be designated to take supervisory responsibility in all other central polling places.

Recommendation 2.3.8

We recommend that

(a) the Canada Elections Commission designate bilingual for election purposes constituencies where 3 per cent or more of the population is from an official language minority and be required to provide bilingual services to voters in these constituencies;

(b) the present policy of providing bilingual services in other constituencies through a toll-free telephone service and the use of bilingual officials to serve small pockets of people from the official language minority be continued;

(c) all constituencies in any province officially bilingual according to its own legislation and in the national capital region be designated bilingual for election purposes;

(d) returning officers appointed to bilingual constituencies be bilingual or appoint a bilingual assistant returning officer; and

(e) specific standards for providing bilingual services in bilingual constituencies be established by the Canada Elections Commission.

Recommendation 2.3.9

We recommend that

(a) candidates be allowed to have one representative at each regular, advance and mobile poll; and

(b) on election day candidates be allowed to designate a person for each place where polling stations are established and give the person power of attorney to collect a list of the persons who have already voted.

Recommendation 2.3.10
We recommend that

(a) the number of voters per polling division be kept at a level that ensures that most voters live only a short distance from the polling station; and
(b) returning officers have the right to require that space for a polling place be made available in federal buildings, federally funded institutions and buildings containing 100 dwelling units or more.

Recommendation 2.3.11
We recommend that

(a) the display of emblems, signs or other partisan material be prohibited within a radius of 50 metres of any entrance to a polling place, as well as in or on the polling place, on election day or any day of advance voting; and
(b) these restrictions also apply to the returning officer's office.

Recommendation 2.3.12
We recommend that

(a) the use of the poll book to record the names of voters voting at ordinary polling stations on election day be discontinued, but the poll book still be used to note extraordinary transactions, such as voting by voters registering on election day, challenges by scrutineers or election officials, and removal of the ballot box to permit a voter to vote outside the polling station;
(b) records continue to be kept in the poll book of the names of people voting at an advance poll; and
(c) poll clerks use a list of voter numbers to assist parties and candidates in keeping track of who has voted on election day.

Recommendation 2.3.13
We recommend that

(a) the current procedure, allowing people to vote on election day by giving their name and address, be maintained;
(b) voters whose names are on the voters list and who are challenged at an ordinary poll be required to provide satisfactory identification or, if they cannot do so, to swear an oath or make an affirmation; and

(c) the Canada Elections Commission prescribe what constitutes satisfactory identification.

Recommendation 2.3.14
We recommend that the Act allow ballots marked with any kind of pen or pencil to be accepted so long as they clearly signal the intention of the voter and do not contain any unusual mark that could identify the voter.

Recommendation 2.3.15
We recommend that

(a) votes from advance polls begin to be counted at the same time as votes from ordinary polls and counting of an advance poll be permitted at any regular polling station or at the returning officer's office pursuant to an advance notice to the candidates;
(b) a team or teams consisting of a deputy returning officer and a poll clerk be appointed to verify and count special ballots on election day in the office of the returning officer in each constituency;
(c) candidates be invited to send representatives to the count of special ballots on the same basis as they have scrutineers at ordinary polling divisions;
(d) votes from Canadians on the register of non-resident voters and prisoners in federal penitentiaries on the list provided to the Canada Elections Commission by Correctional Service Canada be counted at Commission headquarters or some other central place and the results communicated to the returning officer's office in each constituency one-half hour after the count begins in ordinary polling stations in each time zone; and
(e) the poll book and election records for each polling division not be sealed but be deposited with the Canada Elections Commission at the time of the return of the writ or as soon as possible thereafter; and the Commission allow candidates' or registered parties' representatives to inspect them if it is satisfied as to the legitimacy of the request.

Recommendation 2.3.16
We recommend that

(a) the period allowed for the official count be set at a maximum of seven days and the process be made simpler as described in this report;
(b) the returning officer be permitted to certify a final result even if some written returns are missing; and
(c) the period allowed to seek a recount be reduced to three days, allowing all candidates to be declared elected by the second Friday after election day except where a recount was allowed.

Recommendation 2.3.17

We recommend that

(a) a recount be automatic if fewer than 35 votes separate the two leading candidates and no costs be charged to any of the candidates;
(b) only candidates in the constituency have the right to ask for a partial or total recount; the Canada Elections Commission have the right to refuse a recount if it judges that there is insufficient evidence to suggest that a recount may alter the outcome of the vote;
(c) the recount be carried out by a person appointed by the Canada Elections Commission;
(d) the candidate requesting the recount be allowed to specify a total or partial recount and forfeit the $500 deposit if the margin between the two leading candidates is 35 votes or more following the recount; and
(e) if an election is tied after a recount, the Canada Elections Commission declare a new voting day for the constituency to take place three weeks after the recount; in such cases the rules for delayed or postponed elections shall apply.

Recommendation 2.3.18

We recommend that the *Controverted Elections Act* be repealed and the following provisions added to the *Canada Elections Act*:
(1) contested election results be adjudicated by the Federal Court of Canada;
(2) the grounds for contesting election results continue to be that the result in a constituency was affected by irregularities in the vote or by election fraud;
(3) complaints contesting election results and the grounds for the complaint be submitted to the Federal Court of Canada within 30 days after the election result for the constituency has been announced in *The Canada Gazette*, or 30 days after a conviction of election fraud involving that constituency;
(4) any candidate or voter be permitted to file a complaint contesting a constituency election result;
(5) a deposit of $1000 be required to file a complaint contesting an election result, and the deposit be refunded if the complaint was justified or the deposit go toward the costs of the other party, if the complaint was not justified;
(6) the judge hearing the complaint be empowered to dismiss it prior to or during the hearing if the complaint appears frivolous or unfounded;
(7) the judge adjudicating a contested election be empowered to reject the complaint, to annul the election, or to declare another candidate elected;
(8) a Federal Court decision on a contested election be subject to appeal within seven days of the judgement to the Federal Court of Appeal, whose decision shall be final; and
(9) the Federal Court of Appeal be required to hold an appeal hearing within 14 days of the appeal being made and to deliver its decision as soon as possible after the hearing.

Recommendation 2.3.19
We recommend that the restriction on sales of alcohol be deleted from the *Canada Elections Act* and it be left to individual provinces to establish any rules with respect to the sale of alcohol on election day.

Chapter 4

Recommendation 2.4.1
We recommend that the Canada Elections Commission enter into agreements with the provinces of British Columbia and Ontario to acquire preliminary voters lists for the next federal election.

Recommendation 2.4.2
We recommend that the Canada Elections Commission develop and use the computer technology and software that would allow federal voters lists to be produced from provincial and territorial data bases established as voters registers, as well as from provincial voters lists prepared through enumeration.

Recommendation 2.4.3
We recommend that the Canada Elections Commission enter into an agreement with each province and territory to acquire from either provincial voters registers or provincial voters lists the information to generate preliminary voters lists for federal polling divisions.

Chapter 5

Recommendation 2.5.1
We recommend that the Canada Elections Commission, in consultation with Indian bands and Aboriginal organizations, develop standards for the provision of Aboriginal language services in Aboriginal constituencies.

Recommendation 2.5.2
We recommend that

(a) all Aboriginal voters in Aboriginal constituencies be enumerated in areas where there are concentrations of Aboriginal people;
(b) in co-operation with the returning officer for a general constituency, a joint enumeration be conducted in those polls with concentrations of both Aboriginal and non-Aboriginal voters; and
(c) eligible Aboriginal voters be permitted to register by mail using a registration form published in newspapers.

Recommendation 2.5.3
We recommend that a revising officer and two other voters, appointed by the Canada Elections Commission from a list of elders and other voters in

consultation with Indian bands and Aboriginal organizations, constitute Aboriginal voter eligibility panels to decide on objections to the right of a voter to be registered on an Aboriginal voters list on the grounds of his or her Aboriginal status.

Recommendation 2.5.4
We recommend that the *Canada Elections Act* designate Aboriginal constituencies as remote constituencies.

Recommendation 2.5.5
We recommend that the limit for the election expenses of a candidate in an Aboriginal constituency be calculated based on the formula for sparsely populated general constituencies.

Recommendation 2.5.6
We recommend that candidates in Aboriginal constituencies be reimbursed according to the same provisions that apply to candidates in sparsely populated general constituencies.

Recommendation 2.5.7
We recommend that

(a) during the period between the close of nominations and the seventh day before election day, the Aboriginal constituency returning officer mail to each person on the Aboriginal voters list a booklet with a statement from and a photograph of each candidate who wishes to participate;
(b) the returning officer distribute the booklet as widely as possible; and
(c) the Canada Elections Commission cover the costs of producing and distributing the booklet.

Recommendation 2.5.8
We recommend that the Canada Elections Commission establish a voter registration office in each province where Aboriginal constituencies could be created to register eligible Aboriginal voters who wished to vote in an Aboriginal constituency.

Recommendation 2.5.9
We recommend that for the purposes of registering Aboriginal voters to determine whether one or more Aboriginal constituencies would be created in a province:

(a) an enumeration of voters be conducted in areas where there are concentrations of Aboriginal persons;
(b) eligible voters be permitted to register by mail;

(c) the voter registration office undertake an active search for eligible voters; and

(d) the Aboriginal voter registration office organize a final registration-day drive.

Recommendation 2.5.10

We recommend that

(a) a registered voter be permitted to give the address of an Indian band office, Métis local or friendship centre or the Aboriginal voter registration office in place of her or his actual place of residence to ensure that individual's privacy; and

(b) the register of Aboriginal voters be open for inspection by registered Aboriginal voters at the provincial registration office.

Recommendation 2.5.11

We recommend that

(a) Aboriginal voter eligibility panels, chaired by the provincial registration officer, or her or his designate, decide on objections to a voter on the register of Aboriginal voters; and

(b) each panel include two registered Aboriginal voters appointed by the Canada Elections Commission from a list of elders and other qualified men and women drawn up in consultation with Indian bands and Aboriginal organizations in the province.

Recommendation 2.5.12

We recommend that a decision of an Aboriginal voter eligibility panel be subject to review by the Federal Court of Canada.

Recommendation 2.5.13

We recommend that where more than one Aboriginal constituency is to be created in a province, a special boundaries commission be created, composed of the chairperson of the boundaries commission for the province, who shall also act as chair for this special commission, plus two Aboriginal voters appointed by the Speaker of the House of Commons, with the mandate to determine the boundaries and names of the Aboriginal constituencies.

Chapter 6

Recommendation 2.6.1

We recommend that the *Canada Elections Act* provide for the following exclusions from the election spending limits:

(1) expenses incurred by or on behalf of a candidate in seeking nomination;

(2) a candidate's performance guarantee;

(3) expenses incurred in holding a fund-raising function, except if a deficit is incurred, in which case the deficit be counted against the limit;

(4) transfers of funds to a candidate, a registered party or a registered constituency association;

(5) expenses incurred exclusively for the ongoing administration of the registered party or registered constituency association;

(6) expenses incurred for post-election parties held and thank-you advertising published after the close of the polls;

(7) professional fees or labour required to help comply with the Act;

(8) the costs of communications addressed exclusively to members of the registered party or registered constituency association;

(9) interest accrued during the election on any loan lawfully granted to a candidate or official agent for election expenses; and

(10) the personal expenses of a candidate, meaning only the reasonable expenses incurred by or on behalf of the candidate during the election for

(i) the cost of care paid on behalf of a child or other family member for whom the candidate is normally directly responsible;

(ii) travelling costs to and within the constituency;

(iii) the cost of rental of the candidate's temporary residence necessary for the election;

(iv) the cost of lodging, meals and incidental charges while travelling to and within the constituency;

(v) expenses that result directly from a candidate's physical disability, including the services of a person required to assist a candidate to perform the functions necessary to seeking election; and

(vi) other expenses the Canada Elections Commission determines from time to time are personal expenses of a candidate.

Recommendation 2.6.2
We recommend that candidates and registered parties be required to report all election expenses but that spending on items 1 to 10 listed in recommendation 2.6.1 be excluded from the relevant spending limit.

Recommendation 2.6.3
We recommend that the *Canada Elections Act* stipulate that a contribution of goods or services is:

(1) a contribution by way of donation, advance, deposit, discount or otherwise of any tangible personal property, except money, or of services of any description, whether industrial, trade, professional or otherwise; but not

(2) any goods produced or services performed by volunteer labour or goods or services that have a commercial value, in the aggregate and during any reporting period, of less than $250; the value of any broadcasting time provided on a regular or public affairs program; free advertising space in a newspaper, periodical or printed matter provided that it is made available on an equitable basis to all participants; editorials, news, interviews, columns,

letters to the editor, commentaries or public affairs programs as part of a bona fide publication in a periodical or a broadcast by a radio or television station; or books produced, promoted and distributed at fair market value that were planned to be put on sale regardless of the election.

Recommendation 2.6.4

We recommend that 'volunteer labour' be defined in the *Canada Elections Act* as any labour provided by an individual for which no remuneration or direct material benefit is received either during an election or otherwise, but does not include labour provided by:
(1) a person who is self-employed if the goods produced or services performed are normally sold or otherwise charged for by that person; or
(2) a person whose services are made available by an employer.

Recommendation 2.6.5

We recommend that the *Canada Elections Act* stipulate that commercial value in relation to goods or services means the lowest price charged for an equivalent amount of the same goods or services in the market area at the relevant time.

Recommendation 2.6.6

We recommend that

(a) the *Canada Post Corporation Act* be amended to disallow outgoing Members of Parliament from mailing printed material free of charge to their constituents as of midnight the day Parliament is dissolved; and
(b) such material be defined as any printed matter without further address than 'householder', 'boxholder', 'occupant' or 'resident' (as in paragraph 35(3) of the *Canada Post Corporation Act*).

Recommendation 2.6.7

We recommend that the *Canada Elections Act* permit an individual or a corporate body to act as the official agent of a political party, candidate, constituency association, nomination contestant or leadership contestant.

Recommendation 2.6.8

We recommend that the Canada Elections Commission

(a) develop new guidelines for official agents and candidates, constituency agents, nomination contestants and political parties; and
(b) hold public hearings on these guidelines before putting them into effect.

Recommendation 2.6.9

We recommend that the Canada Elections Commission provide an opportunity for official agents to attend a training session on the relevant aspects of the *Canada Elections Act* as soon as possible after an election is called; and that training sessions be provided for agents of constituency associations and nomination contestants.

Recommendation 2.6.10

We recommend that every printed advertisement, handbill, placard or poster related to an election that is published, displayed or distributed during an election indicate the name of its sponsor, whether an agent of a registered political party or registered constituency association, the official agent of a candidate or any other person, and that it was authorized by the sponsor.

Recommendation 2.6.11

We recommend that the *Canada Elections Act* require sponsor identification of all broadcast political advertising during an election.

Recommendation 2.6.12

We recommend that contributions to registered parties, registered constituency associations, candidates, party leadership contestants and nomination contestants be reported according to the following categories:
- individuals;
- corporations;
- unincorporated organizations or associations engaged in business or commercial activity;
- trade unions;
- not-for-profit organizations or associations;
- governments; and
- other contributors.

Recommendation 2.6.13

We recommend that the agent of a registered constituency association be required to submit audited returns of the association's financial activities for the following reporting periods:
(1) if no election is held within a year, for the year;
(2) if an election is held during a year, for the period from 1 January to election day and for the period from the day after election day until 31 December;
(3) if election day falls between 1 November and 31 December, the two returns referred to in (2) be combined; and
(4) if part of an election period falls in the year following the year when the writs for the election were issued, for the period from 1 January of the year the writs were issued to election day.

Recommendation 2.6.14

We recommend that

(a) reports on the financial activities of registered constituency associations include the following:

- the assets, liabilities and surplus as of the end of the reporting period;
- the income received and expenses incurred during the reporting period;
- all required information respecting contributions received during the reporting period;
- notes on the statements as necessary; and
- any other information prescribed by the Canada Elections Commission; and

(b) where the income and expenses of the registered constituency association are both less than $5000 during a reporting period, a short-form return, as prescribed by the Canada Elections Commission, may be filed, but the Commission have the power to request a full return.

Recommendation 2.6.15

We recommend that

(a) the post-election returns of candidates submitted by the official agent include the following:
- the assets, liabilities and surplus at the date the return was prepared;
- all election expenses, including those not subject to limitation;
- all information required to be disclosed on contributions received from the date a writ is issued to the date the return is prepared;
- notes on these statements; and
- any other information prescribed by the Canada Elections Commission;

(b) where a candidate's campaign organization uses the fixed assets of a registered constituency association, the following be considered election expenses of the candidate: for fixed assets except real estate and fixtures, 10 per cent of the depreciated value; for real estate and fixtures, the fair market value of premises equivalent to those owned by the constituency association; and

(c) where the income and expenses of the candidate are both less than $5000, a short-form return, as prescribed by the Canada Elections Commission, may be filed, but the Commission have the authority to request a full return.

Recommendation 2.6.16

We recommend that, for the purposes of the *Canada Elections Act*, 'auditor' be defined as "a professional member in good standing of an institute, society or association of accountants incorporated by or under an act of the legislature of a province, whose normal professional activities include the performance of independent audits of financial statements, and shall include a firm of accountants that has such persons as partners or shareholders."

Recommendation 2.6.17

We recommend that returns of the financial activities of registered parties, registered constituency associations and leadership contestants, and candidates' post-election returns be subject to audit unless the income and expenses during a reporting period are both less than $5000, but that the Canada Elections Commission, after reviewing any such report or return, may require that it be audited.

Recommendation 2.6.18

We recommend that no person or firm acting as the agent of a candidate, registered party, registered constituency association or leadership contestant be appointed as the auditor of the same candidate, registered party, registered constituency association or leadership contestant, as the case may be.

Recommendation 2.6.19

We recommend that the auditor of the return of a candidate, registered constituency association, registered party or leadership contestant receive a payment from public funds equal to the lesser of $1000 and the amount of the auditor's fee.

Recommendation 2.6.20

We recommend that

(a) the limit for the election expenses of a candidate in a by-election be the same as for a general election;

(b) the limit for the election expenses of a registered party on behalf of a candidate in a by-election or on behalf of candidates in by-elections held on the same day be equal to the limit per voter that would apply in a general election times the number of voters on the final voters lists in the constituency or constituencies;

(c) within three months of a by-election, a registered party with a candidate in the by-election submit a return of its election expenses on the candidate's behalf;

(d) where more than one by-election is held on the same day, a registered party with candidates in more than one of the constituencies submit a single return on its election expenses on behalf of the candidates; and

(e) where the election periods for more than one by-election overlap, a registered party with candidates in more than one of the constituencies submit a single return of its election expenses on behalf of the candidates within three months of the last of the by-elections.

Recommendation 2.6.21
We recommend that

(a) if a postponed election is held because of the death of a candidate, the limit for the election expenses of any new candidate be equal to the limit that would otherwise apply and, if the candidate receives 1 per cent or more of the valid votes, he or she be reimbursed the same amount that would otherwise be reimbursed;

(b) if a postponed election is held because of the death of a candidate, the limit for the election expenses of the continuing candidates be equal to 150 per cent of the limit that would otherwise apply, and all such candidates who qualify be reimbursed 150 per cent of the amount that would otherwise be reimbursed; and

(c) if a postponed election is held because of a tied result, the limit for all candidates be equal to 150 per cent of the limit that would otherwise apply, and candidates in such an election who receive 1 per cent or more of the valid votes be reimbursed 150 per cent of the amount that would otherwise be reimbursed.

Recommendation 2.6.22
We recommend that

(a) when a constituency association is de-registered, all funds of the constituency association be paid over to the registered party and held in trust for the association;

(b) when a constituency association is de-registered as a result of the deregistration of a registered party, all funds of the association be paid over to the Canada Elections Commission and held in trust;

(c) funds held in trust under (a) or (b), together with any accumulated interest, be disposed of as follows:
(1) if the association or a successor association of the same registered party becomes registered by the time the writs for the next general election are issued, the funds be paid to the association;
(2) if the association or a successor association of the same registered party is not registered by the time the writs for the next general election are issued, and the party has remained registered or has re-registered, the funds be paid to the party;
(3) if the party that had endorsed the association is no longer registered by the time the writs for the next general election are issued, the funds of any de-registered association revert to the Receiver General for Canada;

(d) when an association of an independent Member of Parliament is de-registered, all funds be paid over to the Canada Elections Commission and held in trust;

(e) with reference to (d), if the former independent Member of Parliament is a candidate at the following general election or at a by-election during that period, the funds held in trust be returned to the candidate; if not, the funds be transferred to the Receiver General;

(f) when an association is de-registered following a boundaries readjustment, its assets be held in trust by the registered party and transferred to the appropriate successor constituency associations following their registration;

(g) the registered party have the power to determine, if necessary, how the funds of constituency associations de-registered under (f) are to be distributed; and

(h) the Canada Elections Commission determine the date when the deregistration of any constituency association is to take effect.

Recommendation 2.6.23

We recommend that

(a) if a registered party is de-registered, all the funds of the party be paid to the Canada Elections Commission and held in trust;

(b) if the party becomes registered by the time the writs for the next general election are issued, the funds be returned to the party; and

(c) if the party does not become registered by the time the writs for the next general election are issued, the funds revert to the Receiver General for Canada.

Recommendation 2.6.24

We recommend that:

(a) when a party foundation is de-registered, all funds of the party foundation be paid over to the registered party and held in trust for the foundation;

(b) when a party foundation is de-registered as a result of the deregistration of the registered party with which it is associated, all funds of the foundation be paid over to the Canada Elections Commission and held in trust;

(c) funds held in trust under (a) or (b), together with any accumulated interest, be disposed of as follows:

(1) if the foundation becomes registered no later than six months after the next general election, the funds be paid to the foundation;

(2) if the foundation is not registered by six months after the next general election and the party has remained registered or has re-registered, the funds be paid to the party; and

(3) if the party is no longer registered by the time the writs for the next general election are issued, the funds of the foundation revert to the Receiver General for Canada; and

(d) when a party foundation is de-registered, it be allowed to keep all funds that would otherwise be paid over to the registered party or the Canada Elections Commission provided the foundation complies with the requirements for charitable organizations under the *Income Tax Act*.

Chapter 7

Recommendation 2.7.1

We recommend that

(a) specialty cable services be subject to the same rules regarding paid political party broadcast time that apply to other broadcasters (subject to their conditions of licence); and
(b) specialty cable services devoted primarily to news and public affairs programming, such as CBC Newsworld, that are available to a majority of cable subscribers whose primary language is the same as the language in which the service provides programming be required to provide free time on the same basis as licensed networks.

Recommendation 2.7.2

We recommend that

(a) the Parliamentary Channels be made available to the Canada Elections Commission for informational programming during election campaigns; and
(b) the Parliamentary Channels be given a mandate to repeat free-time political party broadcasts and leaders debates and be encouraged to broadcast other election debates.

Recommendation 2.7.3

We recommend that some of the voting information provided by the Canada Elections Commission on the English and French Parliamentary Channels be transmitted in the other official language.

Recommendation 2.7.4

We recommend that

(a) cable companies that operate community channels be required to provide a minimum of 60 minutes of free time per day during the election advertising period in prime time for coverage of or broadcasts by candidates, to be allocated among them equitably; and
(b) coverage of all-candidates debates – whether organized by the cable service or others – be counted toward fulfilling the time requirement.

Recommendation 2.7.5

We recommend that community channels be required to repeat these broadcasts at least once.

Recommendation 2.7.6
We recommend that

(a) cable companies whose community channels serve more than one constituency must allocate time in 30-minute segments equally among the
constituencies in which they serve a majority of voters; and
(b) where more than one cable company serves a constituency, each must
provide time in proportion to the percentage of voters served.

Recommendation 2.7.7
We recommend that no paid time be permitted on cable community
channels as long as the current regulatory framework applies.

Recommendation 2.7.8
We recommend that as now provided by the *Canada Elections Act*, during
the period allowed for election advertising, the print media be prohibited
from charging a candidate or political party a rate that exceeds the lowest
rate charged for an equal amount of equivalent advertising space in the
same or other issue thereof published or distributed during that period.

Recommendation 2.7.9
We recommend that

(a) a private organization such as the Canadian Daily Newspaper Association or the Canadian Journalism Foundation establish election workshops
for smaller media; and
(b) the Canada Elections Commission expand existing programs for the
media to prepare and distribute information packages on the electoral
process, with specific information for each constituency.

Recommendation 2.7.10
We recommend that with respect to the constituencies in its primary area
of coverage, the CBC Northern Service:
(1) provide 60 minutes of free time for each candidate in each of these constituencies, with such allocations being in addition to those that the parties
are entitled to on a national basis;
(2) make available up to 20 minutes of paid time to each candidate to be
broadcast on a regional basis, with such paid-time allocations being in addition to those that the parties are entitled to on a national basis;
(3) inform the northern candidates of their right to free and paid time; and
(4) designate a representative to negotiate the times with the returning officer, the registered parties and the candidates for each of these constituencies.

Recommendation 2.7.11

We recommend that the CBC Northern Service

(a) provide more election campaign coverage in all of the languages used in the North, including English and French; and
(b) organize one televised all-candidates debate in each of the constituencies in the Service's primary area of coverage.

Recommendation 2.7.12

We recommend that the *Canada Elections Act* give the following mandate to the Canada Elections Commission:

(1) to promote public awareness of the electoral process through information programs; and

(2) to co-operate with provincial and territorial electoral authorities in the conduct of joint education and information programs on the electoral process, particularly for segments of Canadian society with special needs.

Recommendation 2.7.13

We recommend that

(a) the Canada Elections Commission establish specific public educational programs about the electoral process to which those interested in supporting these activities may make financial contributions;
(b) contributions to this fund be eligible for the same tax credit as applies to gifts to the Crown; and
(c) those who provide financial support be involved in overseeing the development and management of these programs.

Recommendation 2.7.14

We recommend that

(a) the Canada Elections Commission provide voters with special needs essential election information in other formats, including Braille and audio cassette, and establish special telephone services to provide election information to people with impaired hearing and reading difficulties;
(b) closed captions be used on all broadcasts and advertising by the parties and by the Canada Elections Commission during an election period, including material broadcast on the Parliamentary Channels;
(c) sign language be used for information provided by the Canada Elections Commission and broadcast on the Parliamentary Channels during an election period;
(d) broadcasters be encouraged to use closed captions and sign language for televised leaders debates and other election programming; and
(e) an 800 number for both telephone and facsimile be available for voters who wish to communicate with the returning officer.

Recommendation 2.7.15

We recommend that

(a) the Canada Elections Commission explore with the networks and news services the possibility of creating a system for compiling and distributing, on a cost-recovery basis, unofficial voting results on election night; and

(b) the Canada Elections Commission meet annually with representatives of the networks and news services to discuss ways and means of facilitating the reporting of unofficial voting results on election night and other possible information services.

Chapter 8

Recommendation 2.8.1

We recommend that

(a) most violations of the *Canada Elections Act* be classified as strict liability infractions, which do not require proof of intent but are subject to a due diligence defence, and that these infractions be prosecuted before the Canada Elections Commission; and

(b) persons who wilfully violate the *Canada Elections Act* to influence or vary the outcome of an election or commit other election offences be liable to penalties that include imprisonment, loss of the right to sit in the House of Commons or loss of the right to be a candidate at the next election, and that these offences be prosecuted before the provincial courts.

Recommendation 2.8.2

We recommend that imprisonment be available as a penalty only for election offences that are prosecuted before the courts.

Recommendation 2.8.3

We recommend that

(a) the concepts of illegal acts and of corrupt practices, and the corresponding penalties, be removed from the *Canada Elections Act*;

(b) the penalties of loss of candidacy and loss of the right to sit in the House of Commons be retained in the *Canada Elections Act*, but that these penalties apply only for one federal election and only for cases prosecuted before the courts; and

(c) no person lose the right to vote for having committed an election violation.

Recommendation 2.8.4
We recommend that

(a) the deadline for complaints of election violations remain at six months after the commission of the violation but the deadline for the commencement of prosecution of an election violation be shortened to one year after a complaint is filed or evidence of a violation becomes available; and

(b) the director of enforcement consider all complaints for activities regulated by the *Canada Elections Act*, decide whether to initiate an investigation, and if a complaint is not investigated, inform the complainant of the decision with reasons.

Recommendation 2.8.5
We recommend that

(a) the director of enforcement be granted full powers to investigate violations of the *Canada Elections Act*, and investigators of the Canada Elections Commission be given powers of search and seizure, subject to prior authorization from a judge;

(b) the director of enforcement request assistance from a law enforcement agency only in investigations involving the most serious violations, where the director of enforcement may lack particular experience or expertise;

(c) the director of enforcement not be required to act on anonymous complaints but be permitted to initiate investigations based on reasonable information from staff and other sources;

(d) the subject of a complaint be notified before or during the investigation of the complaint, unless the director of enforcement believes that notification would compromise or impede the investigation; and

(e) a person or party who will be prosecuted before the Commission or the courts be notified of all information from the investigation that the director of enforcement intends to use before the matter proceeds before the Commission or the courts.

Recommendation 2.8.6
We recommend that

(a) for election infractions, the director of enforcement have the authority to negotiate an agreement in the form of a voluntary compliance agreement, which would be subject to the approval of one commissioner of the Canada Elections Commission;

(b) the person accused of the infraction be notified of the voluntary compliance procedure;

(c) the chair appoint a commissioner to review the proposed negotiated settlement;

(d) if the commissioner confirms the voluntary compliance agreement, the name of the individual and party concerned and the nature of the infraction and the penalty be published, where applicable; and the agreement be enforced as if it were an order of the Commission;

(e) if the commissioner rejects the agreement, it be referred to the Commission for adjudication; and

(f) any commissioner who assesses an agreement not be allowed to sit on any panel hearing the case.

Recommendation 2.8.7
We recommend that

(a) the director of enforcement have the authority to determine whether a complaint warrants further action, either in the form of a voluntary compliance agreement or prosecution before the Commission or the courts;

(b) when a voluntary compliance agreement cannot be reached or is not appropriate, the director of enforcement proceed with prosecution either before the Commission or the courts; and

(c) when the director of enforcement proceeds with prosecution before the Commission, the chair of the Commission appoint a panel of at least one commissioner to sit as a tribunal; and if more than one commissioner is appointed, the chair of the tribunal be appointed by the chair of the Canada Elections Commission.

Recommendation 2.8.8
We recommend that complaints and investigations be kept confidential unless they have been brought before the Commission or courts for adjudication, resolved by a voluntary compliance agreement, or unless requested by the person or party that is the subject of the complaint.

Chapter 9

Recommendation 2.9.1
We recommend that referendums not be held simultaneously with federal general elections.

Recommendation 2.9.2
We recommend that the statutory recall of Members of Parliament not be adopted.